ADVANCES IN SUPPLY CHAIN ANALYSIS IN AGRI-FOOD SYSTEMS

ADVANCES IN SUPPLY CHAIN ANALYSIS IN AGRI-FOOD SYSTEMS

University of São Paulo and University of Wageningen:
18 years of academic cooperation

Edited by

Decio Zylbersztajn and Onno Omta

USP

WAGENINGEN UNIVERSITEIT
WAGENINGEN UR

PENSA

Rabobank

unica
SUGAR CANE INDUSTRY ASSOCIATION
ETHANOL · SUGAR · ENERGY BRAZIL

EDITORA SINGULAR

2009

A244 Advances in supply chain analysis in agri-food systems. University of São Paulo and University of Wageningen: 15 years of academic cooperation. / Editado por Decio Zylbersztajn e Onno Omta. São Paulo: Singular, 2009.
366 p.

Textos de: Cláudio A.P. Machado Filho, Danny P. Claro, Decio Zylbersztajn, Eduardo Eugênio Spers, Emiel F.M. Wubben, Fabio Matuoka Mizumoto, Frances T.J.M. Fortuin, Gert Jan Hofstede, H.J. (Harry) Bremmers, Jacques Trienekens, Jan Omvlee, Jos Bijman, Marcos Fava Neves, Maria de Graaf, Maria Sylvia Macchione Saes, Michael L. Cook, Miranda P.M. Meuwissen, Molly J. Burress, Monique C.M. Mourits, Paul van Beek, Peter J.P. Zuurbier, Ruud B.M. Huirne, S.W.F. (Onno) Omta, Samuel Ribeiro Giordano, Wijnand van Plaggenhoef

ISBN: 978.85.86626-52-4

1. Alimento, abastecimento. 2. Segurança alimentar. 3. Alimento, produção. 4. Produção Agrícola. 5. Produto agrícola, segurança, Brasil. 6. Etanol Brasil. I. Zylbersztajn, Decio. II. Omta, S.W.F. (Onno). III. Machado Filho, Cláudio A.P. IV. Claro, Danny P. V. Spers, Eduardo E. VI. Wubben, Emiel F.M. VII. Mizumoto, Fabio M. VIII. Fortuin, Frances T.J.M. IX. Hofstede, Gert Jan. X. Bremmers, H.J. XI. Trienekens, Jacques. XII. Omvlee, Jan. XIII. Bijman, Jos. XIV. Neves, Marcos F. XV. Graaf, Maria de. XVI. Saes, Maria Sylvia Macchione. XVII. Cook, Michael L. XVIII. Meuwissen, Miranda P.M. XIX. Burress, Molly J. XX. Mourits, Monique C.M. XXI. Van Beek, P. XXII. Zuurbier, Peter. XXIII. Huirne, Ruud B.M. XXIV. Giordano, Samuel Ribeiro. XXV. Van Plaggenhoef, Wijnand. XXVI. Título.

CDU: 351.778.2(81) CDD: 338.1981

Revisão: Paola Morsello
Diagramação: Microart
Capa: Aeroestúdio

Publicado pela Editora Singular
Telefone: 11 3862-1242
Internet: www.editorasingular.com.br
E-mail: singular@singular.com.br

Summary

Part 6
Innovation and Entrepreneurship

Contributors

Cláudio A.P. Machado Filho: Assistant Professor of Administration. School of Economics, Business and Accounting. University of São Paulo. PENSA

Danny P. Claro: Assistant Professor. INSPER: Institute of Research and Business Education. São Paulo, Brazil.

Decio Zylbersztajn: Professor of Economics and Organizations. School of Economics, Business and Accounting at the University of São Paulo.

Eduardo Eugênio Spers: Assistant Professor. Department of Agricultural Economics. School of Agriculture Luiz de Queiros. University of São Paulo.

Emiel F.M. Wubben: Associate professor at the Department of Business Administration – Wageningen University

Fabio Matuoka Mizumoto: School of Economics and Business. University of São Paulo. PENSA.

Frances T.J.M. Fortuin: Senior Project Manager Expertise Centre for Innovation – Food Valley. Researcher at the Department of Business Administration

Gert Jan Hofstede: Associate Professor at the Department of Logistic Decision and Information Sciences – Wageningen University

H.J. (Harry) Bremmers: Associate Professor at the Department of Business Administration – Wageningen University

Jacques Trienekens: Associate professor at the Department of Business Administration – Wageningen University

Jan Omvlee: Director Export Rijk Zwaan Seeds and Services

Jos Bijman: Assistant Professor at the Department of Business Administration – Wageningen University

Marcos Fava Neves: Professor of Marketing and Strategy. School of Economics, Business and Accounting (Ribeirão Preto) – University of São Paulo. PENSA.

Maria de Graaf: Department of Business Economics – Wageningen University

Maria Sylvia Macchione Saes: Associate Professor of Economics and Organizations. School of Economics, Business and Accounting. University of São Paulo. PENSA.

Michael L. Cook: Robert Partridge Professor Applied Social Sciences. University of Missouri- Columbia. USA.

Miranda P.M. Meuwissen: Assistant Professor at the Department of Business Economics – Wageningen University

Molly J. Burress: University of Missouri-Columbia.USA.

Monique C.M. Mourits: Assistant Professor at the Department of Business Economics – Wageningen University

Onno Omta: Professor at the Department of Business Administration – Wageningen University

Paul van Beek: Professor at the Department of Business Administration – Wageningen University

Peter J.P. Zuurbier: Director of the Latin America Office – Wageningen University and Research Centre. Professor at at the University of São Paulo/ ESALQ and at the Department of Business Administration – Wageningen University.

Ruud B.M. Huirne: Director of Social Sciences – Wageningen University. Professor at the Department of Business Economics – Wageningen University

Samuel Ribeiro Giordano: Sustainability Specialist. Continuous Education Program. PENSA.

Wijnand van Plaggenhoef: Senior Consultant at Significant Consultancy

Acknowledgements

This book is the result of 18 years of scientific cooperation between the Agribusiness Program of the University of São Paulo – PENSA and the Mansagement Studies Group of the University of Wageningen. The origin of this initiative was due to the positive intervention of Dr. Teunis (Tony) de Boon from Rabobank.

Back in 1991, the Agribusiness Studies Group at the University of São Paulo has been organized, aiming to stablish relations with important international knowledge centers. The relevance of Wageningen University for the global agribusiness and the good quality sectorial studies published by Rabobank, reflected the importance of agribusiness in The Netherlands. Dr. Tony de Boon, that had just started Rabobank operations in Brazil was the connection between PENSA-USP and the Management Studies Gruoup.

The bank's office in São Paulo was contacted and the person who answered the phone was Tony himself. He was responsible to start the operations of what turned out to be one of the most important offices of Rabobank in the world. Tony received us very warmly and offered to bridge the contact with the University of Wageningen. He then introduced us to Prof. Muellenberg, that was then the head of the group of Marketing Studies at the Management Department. I did a first visit to Wageningen sponsored by Rabobank and then the first academic work was published. Since then a continuous and productive collaboration was carried. Many Brazilian faculty and students went to Wageningen and likewise faculty and students from Wageningen visited the University of São Paulo.We own the existence of the collaborative research program on chains and networks studies in agribusiness to the vision, inspiration and incentive offered by Tony. That is why this book is dedicated to him.

Decio Zylbersztajn
and Onno Omta

Introduction

Producers, processors, traders and retailers of agricultural and food products operate in an increasingly globalized world. Agri-food supply chains and networks are swiftly moving toward globally interconnected systems with a large variety of complex relationships. This is changing the way food is brought to the market. Currently, even fresh produce can be shipped from halfway around the world at competitive prices. Unfortunately, accompanying diseases and pollution can spread equally rapidly. This requires constant monitoring and immediate responsiveness. This means that integrated production, logistics, information- and innovation systems are needed. To achieve these integrated global supply chains, strategic and cultural alignment, trust and compliance to national and international regulations have become key issues. In recent years the tracking and tracing of products has become vital in international agribusiness and food chains to provide information to society at large, governmental agencies and, ultimately, consumers. Societal concerns regarding animal welfare and environmental issues have to be met in this very competitive, increasingly global environment. The growing concern of consumers regarding quality, traceability and environmental friendliness of products and processes, call for fundamentally new ways of developing, producing and marketing products. New ways of organizing food chains, with new network ties between firms and even between formerly separate sectors are needed to cope with these new demands. This book brings together a rich collection of material on management and organization in agri-food chains and networks. It presents theoretical and practical insights from many different parts of the world. Topics covered include classical supply chain management issues like logistics, information exchange (e.g. tracking and tracing), quality control, safety assurance, and chain performance. Other issues are joint innovation, and shared responsibility for sustainability in agri-food supply chains. Special attention is given to issues of governance and organization of chains and networks, for example, by focusing on the role of producer organizations (such as farmer cooperatives) in their effort to combine horizontal and vertical collaboration in international supply chains. This book is therefore very relevant for academics and managers interested in the latest advances in research on management and organization of international agri-food chains and networks.

This book reflects the research programs carried at the Wageningen University and The University of São Paulo in cooperation with organization scientists from other important knowledge centers. Our research objectives are the same. To focus on the relevant questions and challenges that are faced by the globan food-fiber-energy chains and networks.

The University of Wageningen and The University of São Paulo organize traditional conferences on Chain and Networks in The Netherlands and in Brazil. This book reflects the research initiatives of both Universities and introduces the relevant topics that are part of the contemporaneous debate in food-fiber and energy chains and networks. The book is organized in six parts, reflectig recent topics that are part of our research programs.The first part discusses trust and culture, and presents two papers focused on the role of trust to explain the observed cooperation arrangements in food production and marketing systems. The contributions are authored by Danny Claro, Peter Zuurbier and Decio Zylbersztajn. Part 2 discusses collaboration and vertical coordinatin in food chains and in research and contains contributions from Jos Bijman and Peter Zuurbier . Part 3 introduces the topic of food quality and safety, very relevant in modern global food systems with contributions from Wijnard van Plaggenhoef, Jack Trienekens, Onno Omta, M Meuwissen, Miranda Mouritz, Maria de Graaf, Ruud Huirne, Eduardo Spers and Decio Zylbersztajn. The topics of sustainability and governance are presented in part 4 with contributions from Pinheiro Machado, Harry Bremmers, Samuel Gioordano, Mike Cook and Molly Burress . Part 5 is dedicated to new approaches in chain theory and method based on contributions of Paul van Beek and Marcos Fava Neves, and finally part 6 presents papers on innovation and entrepreneurship with contributions from Frances Fortuin, Onno Omta, Sylvia Macchione Saes, Fabio Mizumoto, Gert Jan Hofstede and Jan Omvlee.

Not aiming to exhaust the different topics, we consider that the book raises important dimensions and suggests research veins to be further explored by the readers.

ONNO OMTA
and DECIO ZYLBERSZTAJN
Editors

Part 1

Trust and Culture

- A Non-naive Explanation of Trust
- Managing Trust in Supply Chains: identifying mechanisms to achieve performance

A Non-naive Explanation of Trust

DECIO ZYLBERSZTAJN

PETER ZUURBIER

The paper presents a review of literature of trust and the theory of contracts developing a simplified model to approach trust. Also, selected cases are discussed through the lenses of the theory. Finally the analysis of complex contracts is explored. The main case to be discussed is based on the contract theory of organizations that considers the incentives for assuring contractual effectiveness against the possibilities of hold-ups resulting from contractual incompleteness and opportunism of agents. The key aspect bounding the expected results is the assumption regarding rationality and opportunism, both keystones in the economic theory of organizations.

1. Introduction

In dealing with production coordination, the governance of transactions through the production system emerges as an issue of vital importance. Usually production systems are characterized as complex hybrid forms (Menard, 2000) composed by many individual agents that share common interests in reaching market targets. In order to cooperate some agents delegate decision power to other agents in the same network. They are potentially motivated to cooperate as a way to reach their individual and collective goals. At the same time, agents operating in complex production systems are exposed to potential conflicts, which emerge from difficulties in defining property rights over the residuals generated at the end of the chain.

A realistic approach to such complex contracts should consider both incentives, first to cooperate, and second to compete in sharing the residuals. Part of the literature of complex contractual forms is characterized by a benign treatment of cooperation among agents operating in the chain. The central objective of this paper is to explore the concept of trust between agents in a more realistic and useful way. This is relevant for agents interested in shaping strategies to operate in complex contractual arrangements.

The main case to be discussed is based on the contract theory of organization. This theory considers the incentives for assuring contractual effectiveness against the possibilities of hold-ups resulting from contractual incompleteness and opportunism of agents.

The paper is organized as follows, the second part presenting a review of literature of trust and the theory of contracts developing a simplified model to approach trust. In part three, selected cases are discussed through the lenses of the theory and in part four, chain management aspects are explored.

2. Trust in the Theory of Contracts

The use of the concept of trust, rather than being of semantic interest, is relevant since it can avoid incorrect strategic decisions in organizations. This paper reinforces Williamson's proposal that the term is being mistakenly used with odd consequences for strategists.

The starting point is the assumption of bounded rationality and opportunism, added to incomplete contracting. Whenever agents make safeguards provisions to support future transactions, trust is not being the case – instead, a calculative approach to efficient contracting. As proposed by Williamson (1996), calculative trust is a contradiction. Besides, the responsibility of economists and social scientists dealing with organizations is magnified if one considers the following quote:

> "... the world of commerce is reorganized in favor of the cynics, as against the innocents, when social scientists employ user friendly language that is descriptively accurate – since only the innocents are taken in." (Williamson, 1996, p. 274)

The approach of benign cooperation explanations based on naive trust interpretations is very frequent in the literature of economics of organizations, economic sociology and law and economics. The purpose of this paper is to consider calculative trust, stressing its importance for complex contractual arrangements and to add a critical comment to the models in use.

2.1 Diverse Explanatory Models

This paper reviews three models of trust, departing from the traditional view and adding limits for the use of the concept of trust.

2.1.1 Williamson's Explanation

The Table 2.1. is adapted from Williamson (1975) and explores the basic assumptions of transaction cost economics to deal with forward contracting.

Table 2.1

Opportunism		Bounded Rationality	
		Absent	Present
	Absent	Utopia	General Clause Contracting
	Present	Comprehensive Contracts	Contractual Difficulties

If one considers the presence of opportunism and bounded rationality, then real world contractual difficulties will appear, demanding safeguards to allow for long term contracts to be carried on. If instead, one assumes that complete contracts can be shaped (unbounded rationality), then the problem is limited to drafting comprehensive (complete) provisional clauses to face future outcomes, which are all perfectly anticipated. In the presence of bounded rationality, but assuming no opportunism, all disputes over residuals will be solved based on benign and cooperative modes once the contractual blanks emerge. Finally the absence of both, opportunism and bounded rationality are only compatible with utopian approaches to contracting.

It follows that the possibility of coincidence of both assumptions, namely of unbounded rationality and absence of opportunism brings a problem in dealing with difficulties in the shaping of contracts. The pure assumption of absence of opportunism resolves the problem, but is far from being realistic.[1]

Williamson (1996) defines three categories of trust: calculative trust, institutional trust and personal trust. *Calculative trust* is related to contracts

1 The well known consideration proposed by Williamson, that the condition of opportunism does not assume that every agent will behave opportunistically all the time, but some will sometimes, applies. This is enough to create contractual difficulties.

which are based on safeguards of different shapes, being easily confounded with pure trust. Examples of contracts in this category are the ones based on reputation, which imposes losses to the agents in the case of opportunistic contractual breaches. Being forward-looking, the agents will consider the loss of a flow of future benefits derived from the opportunistic behavior. One can still act opportunistically, weighting costs and benefits of breaking the contracts, preferring in many cases the stability of the contract instead of its rupture, not for benevolent reasons but after weighing benefits and costs. Milgrom and Roberts (1992) stress that reputation effects will be magnified by the spread of information among different agents, even those not actually participating in the transaction.

Institutional trust is the other category, which also has a calculative origin. Agents will not engage in opportunistic behavior since they consider the costs derived from punishment imposed by the institutional environment, the constraints of the legal system or informal social rules rooted in the behavior of agents, in particular in close-knit groups. In that case, the literature frequently conceive situations as trustful by the operation of close-knit groups and the powerful sanctions imposed in case of opportunistic behavior of one of the members. Trust is replaced by the strong role of informal social institutions.

The third concept is *personal or pure trust*, which is the condition in which the agent places confidence in the accomplishment of the contract, even in the presence of incomplete contracting and bounded rationality. This is the situation pictured in Figure 2.1 as utopian contracting.

Williamson uses a simplified contractual schema to stress the importance of calculative trust and to separate this concept from the personal trust.

Based on this schema, some transactions are characterized by the exposure to hazards, related to the potential expropriation of value represented by the investments in specific assets. This is the core of the model of Transaction Cost Economics. If no specific investments are made, no hazards are possible, no safeguards are necessary to support the transaction and no room for building trust exists. If hazards are possible, then two nodes will emerge as possibilities. At node C safeguards are inserted to guarantee the accomplishment of the transaction, such as reputation, other contractual devices and institutional constraints. Again, this node is not compatible with the notion of pure trust, since other mechanisms to support the transactions are explaining the long term orientation of the agents.

Figure 2.2: Modified contractual schema

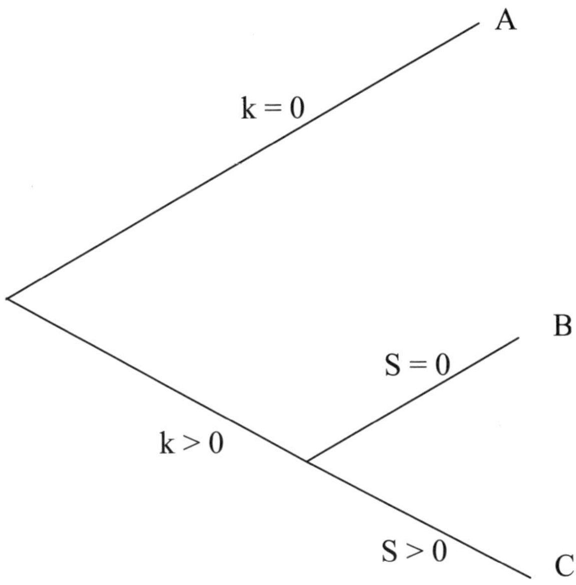

Source: Adapted from Williamson (1985)

At node B, the presence of potential hazards is followed by the absence of safeguards, approaching the situation where personal trust might be considered. However, Williamson precludes this consideration as characterizing pure trust, based on the fact that the contract will be sub-optimal since the price resulting in node B is higher than the one prevailing in node C.

2.1.2 Coleman's Model

The model proposed by Coleman (1996) considers the relation between a trust giver and a trustee. The decision of the first is related to placing trust in the relation and the decision of the trustee is a choice of whether or not to keep the trust. The trustee is trustworthy depending on the expectation with respect to future transactions.

The model is developed based on the definition of a probability p, that the trustee is trustworthy, and the definition of L and G, as being the potential loss and potential gain from breaching the contract.

The decision will be basically derived from the calculated effect of expected gains and losses, as:

(1) $p\ G = (1\text{-}p)\ L$,

where p is the probability that the trustee deserves trust.

If the expected gains of honoring the contract are larger than the expected losses of breaching it, than the rational outcome will be to keep the trusting behavior. Therefore the model invites to compare the magnitude of,

(2) $p/1\text{-}p$ and L/G.

If $p/1\text{-}p > L/G$, then the rational decision is to keep the transaction, otherwise the incentive will be to breach the contract.

The relevant question is how to calculate p, L and G. The decision of placing rational trust will depend on how correct the expectation of p is, or how real it is to consider

(3) $E(p) - p = 0$.

This model allows for the analysis of concrete situations of contractual conditions as proposed by Williamson and Coleman in dealing with calculative trust. One can explore the condition that E(p) approaches p if repeated transactions take place, introducing reputation effects.

2.1.3 Milgrom & Roberts

Models of trust that consider repetitive games are also common in the literature, as can be seen in Axelrod (1984). Again, the repetitive characteristic of the transaction allows for the development of reputation that has been considered as a calculative definition of trust.

Consider the game with two agents, a trustee and a trust giver depicted in Figure 2.3.

Figure 2.3: Reputation model

Trustor		Trustee	
		Honor	Break
	Honor	V,V	L, G+V
	Break	O,O	O,O

Source: Milgrom and Roberts (1992)

In this model, V is the benefit of honoring trust by both players. If the trust giver places trust which is honored by the trustee, then (V,V) represents the resulting profit for both agents. If, instead, trust giver places no trust in the transaction, it is assumed that no transaction will take place, therefore the profit will be (0,0). Finally, if the trustee does not honor the trust placed by the trust giver, then the outcome will be (L, G+V), where L is the loss of the trust giver and G+V is the gain of the trustee.

If the game is played just once, than the equilibrium will be at (0,0) and transaction will not take place. However if the game is repeated N times in the future, then reputation effects might emerge and the Nash equilibrium will be at (V,V), both offering and honoring trust, however on a calculative mode.

2.1.4 Adding Dynamic Considerations

All models dealing with trust, being the ones considering risk elements or the calculative approach, all place importance on the probability of contractual breaches. However, these models consider the probability of hold-up as given. The present study amplifies the dimension of the models by placing the probability of contractual rupture on a dynamic structure, i.e. p is considered endogenous.

The schema defines the expected value of the gains and defines the behavior of the agent with regard to the contractual hold-up as a function of the contrast between the expected gains and the expected losses from the contractual breach. The author defines competent calculativeness as a situation in which the affected parties are aware of the range of outcomes and their probabilities. In a similar way, Coleman defines p as being the known probability that the trustee is trustworthy.

The aspect to be considered in this paper is that, not only E(p) might be always distinct from real and unknown p, but also p is not stable over time, making the definition of the critical value of p related with L and G difficult. The reason for that is the evolution of G over time, considering the possibility of changes in the asset specific commitments providing support for the transactions. As asset specific investments are built, a larger value of the quasi-rents associated to them follows, therefore changing the incentives for a contractual hold-up. Lock in effects might appear, increasing both L and G, but making L/G unknown.

If this assertion is correct, then no provisions for critical values of p can be made, making it more difficult to obtain correct information about p, L and G. Coleman's conclusion that it is possible to build trust as E(p) approaches real p becomes more difficult to attain, since as G changes, and so does p. Therefore it can be said that:

P(breaching) = f (LE, IP, k), where:

LE holds for legal enforcement costs,

IP represents the institutional costs of enforcement and

k is the level of asset specificity, related to the quasi-rents associated to the transaction.

The derived hypotheses are: The larger the level of specific assets, the larger the quasi-rents and the larger the incentives for contractual breaches. The larger LE and IP the larger the probability of observing trust. The basic variables G and L are difficult to calculate, since they change over time, with important consequences for the conclusions presented by Coleman.

3. Case Studies

3.1 Tomato Producers in Brazil

The consumption of tomato paste in Brazil is very relevant for large number of players. The supply needs of local industries are based on a large number of small famers spread in several parts of the country and also imported from other countries. One of the production areas is the São Francisco Valley in the northeast, offering new production areas in the central plains. The production in the northeast used to be based on irrigated areas by small farmers under contract, differently from the new areas where the production is made by large and specialized farmers.

Since the varieties produced for the industry can also be sold in the market for fresh products, some farmers in the northeast have an incentive to break contracts selling to the market when prices move up. The industry is being hit by a considerable number of broken contracts, increasing the transaction costs and showing that the supply strategy should be restructured.

The contracting firms (trust givers) can take the cases to court to enforce the fulfillment of contracts, however at considerable costs, since the production has already been directed to the fresh market causing losses to the industry, increasing the idle capacity and costs associated with bringing the case to courts.

Very frequently, the court decided in favor of the farmers, placing the costs entirely on the industry based on equity principles, the argument being that large companies should not sue unprotected and low income farmers. The concept of "social role of contract" was inserted in Brazilian civil code.

Given the recurrent decision of courts, industries interpreted this as a signal to diversify their supplies, buying pre processed tomato paste from Chile and USA and motivating investments elsewhere in the country. Criticism to this strategy was placed by leaders of farmers, politicians and other authorities. The industry affirmed that is just protecting its interests, being induced to minimize risks of supply resulting from the weak protection provided by court.

In 1999 new specialized and large scale suppliers are moving to central states with projects integrating farming and preprocessing aiming at replacing the imports with domestically produced paste. New organizations are replacing the contracts between the large food company and small farmers, for contracts with a small number of large suppliers, who sell unbranded preprocessed paste.

3.1.1 Alternative Explanations

Considering the modified contractual schema presented in Figure 2.2., the contracts were replaced from node A to node C, since contractual safeguards have been designed to support the transactions. However, safeguards are effective if, and only if, local authorities are willing and have the power to enforce the law. In the present case the interpretation was consistently in favor of the farmers who breach the contract, in fact placing the transaction in node B. By defining the property rights in this manner, the signal provided to farmers is that there are no costs in breaking contracts.

Prices in B should be higher than in C, but in the present case they have been undervalued, since the trust givers were assuming legal enforcement from the courts. The transactions became too costly to be continued in the region, it being safer to import the product, with long term losses to the local farmers.

Considering Coleman's model, the industry undervalued p, the probability of contractual hold-up. The trustees, i.e. the farmers, calculated the expected value of gains derived from the contractual breach to be larger than the losses. In fact the farmers appear not to consider long term effects derived from reputation, since they will no longer be able to supply the industry with the product, so they undervalued the costs.

Looking at the problem through the lenses proposed by Milgrom and Roberts, reputation being considered, the Nash equilibrium should be V,V in Table 2.3. In this case, motivated by reputation, both players will be better off by placing trust in the transaction, an optimal solution emerging. However, this was not the case observed in the contract being described. Ergo the other equilibrium (0,0) appears, since no transaction could take place.

3.1.2 Adding Dynamic Considerations

The present case might illustrate a situation in which the probability p was underestimated in the first transaction. If one assumes that this probability will be reviewed in a Bayesian manner, then the probability function will be different after the transaction takes place.

Taking Equation 2.1, the lack of legal enforcement also contributes to the increase of p, this variable being known as ex-ante, the industry miscalculated its importance, or undervalued it. In this case, at the level of k, asset specificity for the farmer is low, since the production can be diverted to the alternative market. This is not the case for the industry, which depends on the continuous supply to honor its contracts with clients downstream. Since no private institutional costs affects the farmer (low IP) in this case, the industry has two alternative strategies:

a) diversify the source of supply, reducing the risk and demanding less costly safeguards, or

b) based on repeated contracts, find a group of suppliers that will be forward-looking and able to distinguish short term benefits from the long term benefits derived from honoring the contract.

Actually the company followed both strategies, buying from alternative sources and selecting reliable suppliers, being the ones for whom the value of p is smaller than for the original suppliers.

This case shows that contracts have been broken even in the presence of legal constraints. The behavior of the courts, acting based on short term equity principles, added a new source of contractual costs, showing how important the dialogue between justice and efficiency is.

3.2 Brand Name

Brand names are a valuable asset for many product markets. The transaction between the customer and a supermarket is based on the value of the brand. Can this be treated as trust, as it is usually named?

Consider that the consumer has alternatives and chooses based on relevant information about the product. This information might be built after repetitive transactions, resulting in superior reputation of the brand. However, it is very common to find other organizational devices built in order to support the specific transaction, there being hot lines for customers to communicate with the company, label information, and special safeguards for the customer, in case of him not being satisfied with the product.

3.2.1 Alternative Explanations

Brand names are considered highly specific assets characterizing transactions in many industries. To break contracts with clients might bring very high costs of lowering the value of these assets, therefore it is expected that companies will be protected against breaches.

By building specific organization mechanisms to support the transactions, food companies will guarantee that clients feel protected against possible contractual breaches. So, private mechanisms to lower the risk of customers are embedded and function as safeguards for the accomplishment of future transactions. No naive forms of trust are present but instead, typical calculative strategies are observed, with investments to support the transactions.

Considering Coleman's model, consider that credible signals are provided to the customer that permits to build expectations about the value of p, leading to the ex-ante assumption about low probability of hold-up to the part of the industry. Therefore consumers have no trust, but feels protected by a costly mechanism built in order to guarantee the continuity of the transaction. Reputation mechanisms replace trust in the brand.

Introducing dynamic considerations, the role of institutional enforcement becomes more important to protect the consumer against contractual breaches, such as fraud. The evolution of legislation protecting the consumers in different countries functions in a way to substantially reduce the probability of hold-ups, since the penalties might be very high, even in the absence of reputation effects.

4. Conclusions

The efficiency of organizations result from incentives and monitoring costs embedded in contracts between agents. In hybrid contractual arrangements, a complex net of relations are built between agents, each with variable incentives to honor the contracts. Opportunism being absent trust considerations might be considered, indicating no need for enforcement mechanisms.

However, considering the real scenario where transactions are carried out, then naive interpretations of trust are replaced by safeguards provided by contractual clauses, strict enforcement capacity of courts and related institutions and market signals provided by reputation schemes. These schemes are seen in the tomato case, where firms decided to reorganize and move the production out from areas where contracts were facing problems, and are also presenting the efforts that firms make to build organizations in support of brand reputation. In the presence of trust relations, such efforts are not needed.

Pure and noncalculative trust might still be considered by decision makers, but should be recognized as very weak, very fragile and short-lived forms of contractual arrangements.

References

AXELROD, R. 1984. *The evolution of cooperation.* New York: Basic Books.

COLEMAN, J. 1996. *The foundations of social theory.* Harvard.

MENARD, C. 1998. The maladaptation of regulation to hybrid organizational forms. *International Review of Law and Economics*,18-4: 403-417.

MILGROM, P.; ROBERTS, J. 1992. *Economics, organization and management.* Prentice Hall, Englewood Cliffs.

WILLIAMSON, O. E. 1975. *Markets and hierarchies: analysis and antitrust implications.* New York: The Free Press.

______. 1985. *The economic institutions of capitalism: firms, markets, relational contracts.* New York: The Free Press.

______. 1996. *The mechanisms of governance.* New York: Oxford University Press.

Managing Trust in Supply Chains: identifying mechanisms to achieve performance

DANNY P. CLARO

1. Introduction

Coordinated supply chains and networks are ineffective without trust. Even though scholars have extensively covered the matter of trust, there is an ongoing concern among managers: how can firms develop trust and achieve performance? Our chapter aims to review the classic and emerging perspective on trust and propose six mechanisms to build it in a coordinated chain and network context. Coordinated chains and network imply that firms are constantly transacting with each other and need to work closely in order to deliver value to customers. In this context, trust seems essential for their business success.

In this rapidly changing environment, managers seek creative and flexible means to meet competition. In literature, we see reports claiming that many firms have responded to these challenges by developing trust in collaborative relationships with their distribution channels. Trust operates as a governance mechanism that allows companies to share information and that mitigates opportunism in exchange contexts characterized by uncertainty and dependence. By using trust, firms can reduce the transaction costs associated with monitoring, contracting and punishing opportunistic behavior.

The question that may be addressed in this context is: how can firms develop trust and achieve high performance? In this line of thought, we elaborate a central hypothesis about trust and performance. A survey in the Brazilian agrochemical industry has been conducted to test the hypothesis. Agrochemical products (e.g. fungicide and insecticide) are used by growers in their agricultural production. Growers purchase products from agrochemical distributors who also offer after sales technical assistance to the growers. Agrochemical distributors play a critical role in the selling and supporting activities, because products are toxic and require care in the production process. Distributors purchase agrochemicals from manufacturers who are keen to develop close relationships with distributors. The relationship between manufacturers and distributors appear to be an interesting relationship to study trust. For growers to use agrochemical products in a proper way, distributors have to be working closely together with manufacturers. This relationship with manufacturers allows distributors to offer growers the best technical support throughout the use of the product in order to be efficient and avoid any harm to human beings and the environment.

In the next section, the literature about trust is presented. Considering that trust has been extensively discussed in different fields of social science, we intend to concentrate our review on the fields of management and marketing, gaining also insights from social psychology, sociology and economics. Revisiting trust as such offers an important contribution to the body of chain and network literature. In this section, we present six mechanisms that may be employed to build trust. With such a background, the central hypothesis is presented. In section 3, the methodology is presented. Results and Concluding Remarks are discussed at the end of the chapter.

2. Classic and Emerging Perspective on Trust

Trust refers to the extent to which negotiations are fair and commitments are sustained (Anderson & Narus, 1990). The need for trust between partners has been identified as an essential element of buyer-supplier relationships (Anderson & Narus, 1990; Geyskens, Steenkamp & Kumar, 1998; Rousseau, Sitkin, Burt & Camerer et al. 1998). Previous research showed that trust is a basic requirement in the context of buyer-supplier relationships (Morgan & Hunt, 1994). According to Ring and Van de Ven (1992), trust plays a key role in any organizational relationship. Trust enables partners to manage risk and opportunism in transactions (Nooteboom, Berger & Noorderhaven, 1997). There is an element of trust in every transaction, although it varies across the transacting partners (Arrow, 1973). Moreover, trust helps to reduce complex realities more quickly and economically than prediction, authority or bargaining (Powell, 1990).

Trust is a key concept in many research fields, as reflected, for example, in the marketing channels literature (Anderson & Weitz, 1989; Anderson & Narus, 1990; Ganesan, 1994; Morgan & Hunt, 1994; Doney & Cannon, 1997), organizational decision making (Zand, 1972), network literature (Thorelli, 1986; Jarillo, 1988; Powell, 1990; Larson, 1992; Uzzi, 1997; Coleaman, 1988), transaction cost economics (Williamson, 1993; Zajac & Olsen, 1993; Zylbersztajn & Zuurbier, 1999), within individuals in team works (Lewicki, Mcallister, & Bies, 1998; Adler, 2007), public trust (Herder & Brian, 2008) and psychology (Rotter, 1971; Rotter, 1980). Each of these schools of thought uses a different definition of trust. Building on Geyskens, Steenkamp & Kumar's (1998) compilation of definitions of trust, we developed our own compilation that includes the network and other research traditions (Table 1).

Table 1

Study	Research Tradition	Unit of Analysis	Conceptualization of Trust
Anderson and Weitz (1989)	Marketing channels	Sales representative and their suppliers	A firm's belief that its needs will be fulfilled in the future by actions undertaken by their partner.
Anderson and Narus (1990)	Marketing channels	Distributors and their manufacturers	A firm's belief that partners will perform actions that will result in positive outcomes for the firm and will not take unexpected actions that would result in negative outcomes for the firm.
Barney and Hansen (1994)	Management	Organizations	The mutual confidence that no party to an exchange will exploit another's vulnerabilities.
Bradach and Eccles (1989)	Management	Organizations	The positive expectation that reduces the risk that the exchange partner will act opportunistically.
Ganesan (1994) and Doney and Cannon (1997)	Marketing channels	Vendors and retail buyers	The belief that the partner is credible and benevolent.
Granovetter (1985)	Networks	Organizations	Confidence in the general morality of individuals.
Gulati (1995)	Networks	Biopharmaceutical, automotive, new materials suppliers and buyers	The particular level of subjective probability with which agents assess whether another agent or group will perform a particular action both before they can monitor such action and in a context in which it affects their own action.

Study	Research Tradition	Unit of Analysis	Conceptualization of Trust
Hakansson and Snehota (1995)	Networks	Organizations	A context in which the probability that a partner will perform an action that is beneficial or at least not detrimental to the counterpart is sufficiently high as to consider engaging in some form of cooperation.
Klein, Rai and Straub (2007)	Supply chain	Logistics firms	An integrated model of organizational trust, focusing on beliefs: ability, benevolence and integrity.
Kumar, Scheer and Steenkamp (1995)	Marketing channels	Car dealers and car manufacturer	The belief that the partner is honest and benevolent.
Morgan and Hunt (1994)	Marketing channels	Independent retailers and their suppliers	Confidence in the partner's reliability and integrity.
Powell (1990)	Networks	Organizations	Confidence translated into the act of taking as certain those critical aspects of life which in a business environment are rendered uncertain.
Rotter (1971, 1980)	Psychology	Individuals	A generalized expectancy held by an individual that the work, promise or statement of another individual can be relied on.
Sitkin and Roth, (1993)	Management	Organizations and individuals in the medical industry	The belief, attitude or expectation that the actions or outcomes of another individual or organization will be acceptable or will serve the partner's interest.
Thorelli (1986) and Jarillo (1988)	Networks	Organizations	An assumption or reliance on the part of A that if either A or B encounters a problem in the fulfillment of implicit or explicit transactional obligations, B may be counted on to do what A would do if B's resources were at A's disposal.
Uzzi (1997)	Networks	Apparel stores and their suppliers	The belief that an exchange partner would not act in self-interest at another's expense and operates not like calculated risk but like a heuristic – a predilection to assume the best when interpreting another's motives and actions.

Study	Research Tradition	Unit of Analysis	Conceptualization of Trust
Williamson (1993)	Transaction cost economics	Organizations	The rational form of trust fostered by mutual hostages, and building on reputation effects and risk.
Zaheer, McEvily and Perrone (1998)	Management	Electrical and electronic equipment manufacturers	The leap of faith by placing confidence in a referent without knowing with absolute certainty that the referent's future actions will not produce unpleasant surprises.
Zaheer and Venkatraman (1995)	Transaction cost economics	Agency and insurance representative	The extent to which negotiations are fair and commitments are upheld. Trust is a multidimensional concept, significantly developed on affective behavioral and cognitive bases.
Zand (1972)	Management	Individual managers	Actions that (a) increase one's vulnerability, (b) to another whose behavior is not under one's control (c) in a situation in which the penalty (disutility) one suffers if the other abuses that vulnerability is greater than the benefit (utility) one gains if the other does not abuse that vulnerability.

Based on Geyskens, Steenkamp and Kumar (1998: 226)

Before discussing the central hypothesis of this chapter, we discuss the mechanisms to build up trust.

2.1 Mechanisms to Build up Trust

As Table 1 shows, significant differences in assumptions and methods exist between behaviorally oriented and economically oriented organizational scholars (Barney, 1991). On the one hand, behaviorally oriented researchers argue that most exchange partners are trustworthy, that they behave as stewards over the resources under their control and thus that trust in an exchange relationship – even without legal and contractual safeguards – will become common (Das & Teng, 1998). On the other hand, economically oriented scholars respond that it is difficult to distinguish at first between exchange partners that are actually trustworthy and those that only claim to be trustworthy (Williamson, 1993). This limits the scope of trust to that within rational prediction or calculation, wherein partners focus on collecting and processing information to forecast likely outcomes of certain future events (Doney & Canon, 1997). Although rational prediction is clearly an important part of trust, it provides a grossly incomplete understanding of trust on its own. Moreover, some economists recognize that a degree of trust must be assumed to operate, since formal control mechanisms alone cannot entirely stem force or fraud (Akerlof, 1970; Klein, 1996). Following this extensive discussion, six mechanisms to build trust can be identified in the literature.

First, the economic literature suggests that trust primarily involves a calculative process (Williamson, 1996). To the extent that the benefits of cheating do not exceed the costs of being caught, the buyer infers that it would be contrary to the supplier's best interest to cheat, and so the supplier can be trusted (Akerlof, 1970). Therefore, managers have to be able to calculate the costs and rewards of another party cheating or cooperating in a relationship.

Following Wicks, Berman and Jones (1999), we identify two behavioral characteristics that add up to calculative-based trust, namely affection and belief. Affection is an emotion felt by people in a relationship (Rotter, 1980). Trust occurs because an emotional bond is created between individuals, enabling them to move beyond rational prediction to take a leap of faith that trust will be honored (Wicks, Berman & Jones, 1999). Some authors in the marketing channels school view affection-based trust as the benevolence of an individual toward a relationship (Anderson & Narus, 1990; Morgan & Hunt, 1994). Benevolence in a partner is motivated by concern for the well-being of the relationship itself and not by the goal of improving own welfare at the expense of the partners' interests (Ganesan, 1994). The affective aspect of trust has a clear moral element and is influenced by the intentions of the other party (Deutsh, 1969). Therefore, managers can interpret the other party's words and actions, and attempt to determine their intentions in the relationship.

The emotional bond in question is not just in the relationship but is, in large part, a belief in the moral character or goodwill of the trustee in the trusting relationship. Through their shared beliefs, partners can create goal congruence and so reduce the risk of free-riding and other types of opportunism (Bradach & Eccles, 1989). In the marketing channels tradition, belief-based trust is described as credibility (Kumar, Sheer & Steenkamp, 1995). As trust stems from expectations of how another party will behave based on that party's past and present implicit and explicit claims, a manager needs to forecast another party's behavior.

We highlight the affective and belief features because both are critical to build trust. Rational prediction (calculation) helps prevent partners from trusting blindly or foolishly. Affection and belief are necessary for developing and sustaining mutually trusting relationships, as well as for realizing the benefits that flow from trust. Thus, the level of trust can range from a degree of affection-based belief in moral character (e.g., having less than a fully effective deterrent, such as mutually assured destruction), extending up to the point at which trust is so complete as to constitute 'blind faith' in the moral character of the other (e.g., that between parent and child). Based on this understanding, a widely accepted definition of trust refers to the belief, attitude or expectation that the actions or outcomes of another individual, group or organization will be acceptable or will serve the partner's interest (Sitkin & Roth, 1993).

Although this definition embraces the calculative, affective-based and belief aspects of trust discussed previously, for business relationships three other features need specific elaboration. First, trust is directly influenced by the network because trust is socially *embedded* (Granovetter, 1985). Trust exists within a context and is shaped by the dynamics specific to a particular social setting (Powell, 1990). Trust can be transferred from a trusted proof source to another individual or group with which the buyer has little or no direct experience (Doney & Canon, 1997). This transference process allows spreading trust from a known entity to an unknown entity. In his discussion of embeddedness, Granovetter (1985) demonstrated that the models used in classical and neoclassical economics (such as transaction cost economics) are under socialized and omit the role of concrete personal relations and structures (or networks, as discussed previously). He emphasized the fundamental conceptual inadequacy of under socialized approaches to trust (i.e., theories not taking embeddedness seriously), particularly for both describing and creating trusting relations.

Second, trust is *continuous*, as opposed to being a static and discrete concept (Das & Teng, 1998; Wicks, Berman & Jones, 1999). A partner can both trust and distrust people at the same time (Sitkin & Roth, 1993). The development of trust relies on the formation of one partner's expectations about the motives and behaviors of another. Further, trust has a wide spectrum, and it can vary substantially both, within and across relationships, as well as over time. As Bradach and Eccles (1989, p. 108) said, "in dynamic and continuous settings, a record of prior exchange, often obtained secondhand or by imputation from outcomes of prior exchange, provides data on the exchange process. Relationships unfold so that individuals continually update their information base and their decisions to trust".

Finally, trust can be built on the basis of the partners *capabilities*. A manager can assess the ability to meet his or her obligations as well as the partner's expectations. Trust as a derivative of technically competent performance ensures partners that desired outcomes can be obtained. In logistics sector, companies have relied on their ability to exchange information in order to build up trust and achieve performance (Klein, Rai & Straub, 2007). The focus can be turned to the credibility component of trust.

2.2 Trust and Performance

Firms involved in trust relationships are likely to perform well. Trust relationships allow firms to have a shared belief that in the long run, rewards will be distributed fairly among the partners (Barney & Hansen, 1994). There is a general sense that this year's winner could be next year's loser and, consequently, to press one's advantage opportunistically would be unadvisable. Trust is an important lubricant of relationships. It binds parties and has an important future orientation (Ganesan, 1994). Previous studies found that trust guides behavior in some business settings (Morgan & Hunt, 1994; Doney & Cannon, 1997), and when trust is operative the risk of opportunism and market instability is reduced. Moreover, Smith and Barclay (1997) found that trust significantly affects the attitudes and behavior of suppliers toward buyers (i.e., independent sellers).

A high degree of trust between the partners in a business relationship is conducive to coordinative behavior. This assertion follows the findings of Anderson and Narus (1990) and Gulati (1995). Trust encourages effective communication, information sharing and joint pay-offs (Dwyer, Schur & Oh, 1987, Ring & Van de Ven, 1992) and might create a strong social bond (Barney and Hansen, 1994). Thus, trust significantly reduces the perception of risk associated with opportunistic behavior by a partner; it increases confidence that short-term inequities will be resolved over the long term and reduces the transaction costs in an exchange relationship (Ganesan, 1994). Our assumption is that the higher the level of the six mechanisms to build trust, the higher the level of trust in a relationship will be. Therefore, we expect that the higher the degree of the six mechanisms to build trust, the higher the performance of the company. Our central hypothesis may be stated as:

> *Central Hypothesis: The higher the level of the trust mechanisms (H_a: calculative, H_b: affective, H_c: belief, H_d: embeddedness, H_e: continuity and H_f: capability), the higher the firm performance.*

In this study, we included three control variables. Previous research suggests that the buyer-supplier relationship might be affected by the firm size (Lush & Brown, 1996; i.e. turnover and size of the sales force) and dependency (Lush & Brown, 1996). We do not specify hypotheses to each of the control variables, overall we expect a positive relation between firm size and performance. In addition, we expect a negative relationship between dependency and performance. The model is displayed in Figure 1.

Figure 1: The model of trust and performance

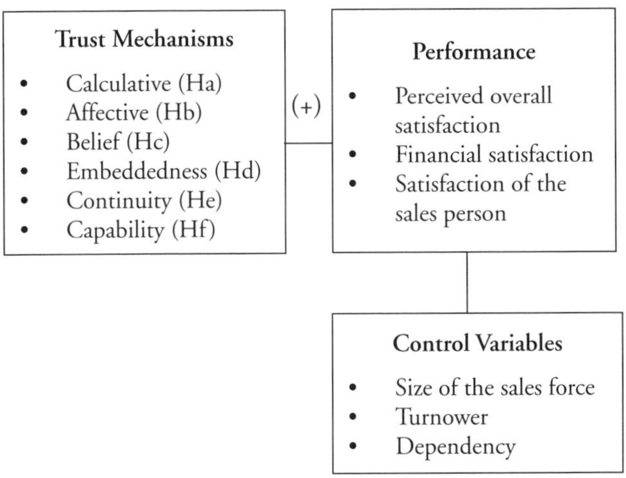

3. Methodology

3.1 Data Collection

The data were collected in the year 2005 in Brazil. Every year, one of the largest agrochemical manufacturers promotes an annual meeting to gather all of its distributors. With the agreement of this agrochemical manufacturer, we presented the research project and invited distributors to fill in the questionnaires. There were over 300 distributors on site coming from all different regions of Brazil. After excluding non-qualifying distributors (e.g., foreign companies), the data collection effort yielded 158 responses of distributor companies, of which 26 were incomplete questionnaires. Our data collection effort resulted in 132 usable questionnaires with a 67% response rate. The sample demographics reflect a diverse representation of respondents' distributors.

A self-administered questionnaire was used that consists of 42 pre-coded questions. For most of the items Likert 5-point response format were used, and a limited number of items were assessed with 2 to 5-point response formats. When responding to the questions about the mechanisms of trust and performance, informants were asked to consider their relationship with the most important agrochemical producer.

Before starting the data collection, we tested the questionnaire in a panel. The input from a panel composed of faculty members and industry experts. It was also particularly helpful in order to create the different measurement scales and individual items. The panel helped improving the wording of some questions and also provided information to develop a list of concepts and definitions, which was included in the introduction letter of the questionnaire.

3.2 Research Instrument

Trust in operational terms refers to the belief that the other partner is honest and sincere and in no circumstances will deliberately do anything that will damage the relationship. Trust is also embodied in a partner's belief that its requirements will be fulfilled through future actions undertaken by the counterpart (Anderson & Weitz, 1989; Barney & Hansen, 1994). We operationalized trust in six mechanisms to build it up. The measure to the *calculative* dimension refers to the activities to calculate costs and rewards. We used 2 items: "sales in relation to the store space allocated for partners' products" and "Consumer flow given partners' products in the store". The measure to capture the *believe* dimension refers to the activities to forecast counterpart's behavior. We used 2 items such as: "The environment to work with this supplier is pretty good" and "We get timely and accurate information from this supplier". The measure to capture the *affective* dimension refers to the activities to forecast counterpart's intentions. We used 2 items such as: "He/she perfectly understands my needs". The measure to capture the *capability* of the partner refers basically to the assessment of the counterpart's ability to meet obligations. There were 5 items such as: "It is good the number of salespeople and technical personnel of the partner assisting us in the business" and "The sales representative of the partner is knowledgeable about the products and is trained to assist us". All of the four measures described above were 5-point Likert scale raging from "Not at all" to "Very Much". The score of each measure was the unweighted average of the corresponding items. We used a 10-point Likert scale to measure the importance of the *network* to the development of the business relationship. We tried to capture 4 relevant themes to the companies in the industry. They were related to competition among distributors of the same agrochemical supplier, competition with other distribution channels, conflict with direct distribution and price setting differences. We decided to keep in the estimation, though this measurement instrument did not perform so well. Finally, the measure to capture the *continuity* dimension of the mechanisms to build up trust refers to an open-ended question as to the number of years that the respondent had done business with the selected agrochemical producer.

This study applies a multidimensional measure of *performance* with a 5-point Likert scale ranging from "not at all satisfied" to "totally satisfied". We measured the satisfaction of the distributor with the contact person in the selected agrochemical producer. Four items were used to this measure. We also measured satisfaction of the distributor with the profitability and margin of the sales of the products of the selected producer. Two items were used to capture the distributors' perception about the financial results. The score of the performance variable was the unweighted average of the corresponding items. Table 2 shows the items used in the data collection.

Three control variables were used in the estimation. To measure *dependency*, we used an open-ended question as to the percentage of the products comes from the selected producer. We used two measures for *firm size*. They were the annual turnover of the company and the size of the sales force.

We checked the reliability of our measurement instruments using Cronbach's alpha, composite reliability (> .67), and extracted variance (> .61) of the measures. In all cases Cronbach's alpha was sufficiently high (> .60) to warrant confidence in the internal consistency of the scales, except one measure of the trust mechanism that is about 0.60. The correlations between the constructs did not suggest problems of pair wise colinearity that would preclude the use of all constructs in one equation (Hair, Anderson, Tatham & Black, 1998). Table 3 displays the correlation matrix and descriptive statistics.

Table 2: Items of likert-scale constructs

Calculative (5-point Likert scale, "not at all"–"very much") α = 0.73

- The investments made to sell the (name of the manufacturer) products increase consumer traffic in our stores.
- The sales of the (name of the manufacturer) products compensates the store space dedicated to this manufacturer.

Affective (5-point Likert scale, "not at all"–"very much") α = 0.76

- My contact person in the manufacturer perfectly understands my needs.
- We have established a mutual understanding in our relationship.

Belief (5-point Likert scale, "not at all"–"very much") α = 0.68

- The environment to work with this manufacturer is pretty good.
- We get timely and accurate information from this manufacturer.

Capability (5-point Likert scale, "not at all"–"very much") α = 0.60

- The commercial, technical and marketing personnel of my manufacturer focus on the products that I sell for them.
- This manufacturer offers an important after sales support to my clients (producers of agriculture products).
- This manufacturer sales approach helps me in selling products.
- It is good the number of salespeople and technical personnel of the manufacturer assisting us in our business.
- The sales representative of the manufacturer is knowledgeable about the products and is trained to assist us.

Embeddedness (10-point Likert scale, "not at all"–"very much") α = 0.58

I exchange valuable information with my network of business contacts about:

- Competition with distributors that sell products of the manufacturer.
- Competition with distributors that sell products of other manufacturers.
- Conflicts with the direct sales channels of the manufacturer.
- Price differences of the same product.

Table 3

	Mean	SD	1	2	3	4	5	6	7	8	9
Performance (1)	4.01	0.57	1								
Calculative (2)	3.76	0.60	.44	1							
Affective (3)	3.81	0.74	.55	.39	1						
Belief (4)	4.22	0.79	.58	.40	.33	1					
Capability (5)	4.32	0.46	.47	.41	.34	.55	1				
Embeddedness (6)	5.28	2.52	-.03	.12	-.10	-.07	-.02	1			
Continuity (7)	7.39	5.60	-.08	-.16	-.10	-.10	.00	.07	1		
Sales force (8)	9.47	8.64	-.14	.03	.00	.00	.00	.15	.11	1	
Dependency (9)	48.13	27.80	.01	.07	-.03	.06	.11	.02	-.19	-.32	1
Turnover (10)	2.78E7	4.37E7	-.07	-.02	-.06	.06	.05	.19	.19	.32	-.02

We conducted a MANOVA Test to evaluate differences in perceptions of the mechanisms to build trust considering the different origin of distributors (i.e. 5 different national regions of Brazilian States). We also conducted a Bonferroni Post Hoc Test to evaluate the difference in performance (Hair et al. 1998). No significant difference was found in our sample, except a difference in perception of calculative mechanism between South and Mid-Western respondents. Overall the great number of estimates (i.e. five mechanisms of trust and the five different national regions), this difference between only 2 regions does not rule out the representativeness of our sample – as one might suggest considering the huge geographic size of the Brazilian territory. Therefore, the test results suggest that the perception of the respondents in our sample is highly generalizable across regions.

4. Results and Discussion

The hypothesis was tested based on Ordinary Least Square Regression[1]. Regression analysis is popular among researchers because it allows for an evaluation of the degree (i.e. coefficient size), nature (i.e. coefficient sign) and optimization (i.e. coefficient of determination, R2) of association between variables (Hair et al. 1998). By computing the unweighted average of the items reflecting each construct, we regressed the six mechanisms to build trust and the control variables on performance (Table 4).

Tests for multicollinearity showed no problem. The indices lied below the threshold values of 10 for the VIF test and 30 for the Condition index (Hair et al. 1998). The explanatory power of the equation supports the further examination of individual coefficients, to check the effects of each mechanism on performance.

[1] We first attempted to use Structural Equation Modeling in Lisrel 10.0 to estimate our model and test the hypothesis. Structural equation modeling is a multivariate technique that combines aspects of multiple regression (examining dependence relations) and factor analysis (representing the construct part of multiple variables) to estimate a series of interrelated dependence relations simultaneously (Hair et al. 1998). However, the large number of variables and the relatively small sample size did not allow for the model to be adjusted. The model did not achieve acceptable Goodness of Fit indices given the number of estimated parameters. We therefore decided to test our hypothesis employing Ordinary Least Squared Regression which is the most commonly used technique in multiple regression analysis (Malhotra, 1999),

Table 4: Results of the model estimation

	Performance	Supported?
Calculative	**.280 (3.19) *****	H_a: Yes
Affective	**.364 (4.39)*****	H_b: Yes
Belief	**.294 (3.34)*****	H_c: Yes
Capability	.062 (.73)	H_d: Not significant
Embeddedness	.048 (.72)	H_e: Not significant
Continuity	.017 (.25)	H_f: Not significant
Size of Sales Force	**-.210 (2.79)*****	No
Dependency	-.081 (1.09)	Not significant
Turnover	-.025 (.35)	Not significant
Adjusted R^2	**.628*****	

***p<0.01, **p<0.05, *p<0.10. Notes: Regression coefficients are standardized coefficients (β) and |t-test| within parentheses.

There are several positive significant effects of the mechanisms of trust on performance. The results show that calculative mechanism influences positively performance (β=.28, p<.001), which is in line with our hypothesis (Ha). This suggests that distributors created an estimation process that the costs of a manufacturer acting in an untrustworthy manner are quite high for firms with good reputation. Manufacturers send strong positive signal when they consistently deliver on its promises to others. Without delivering on its promises it is hard to maintain a preferred position in the market. By assessing carefully the gains and losses of developing a trust relationship, the distributor does not expect any opportunistic behavior of its manufacturer.

The affective mechanism to build trust also influences positively performance (β=.36, p<.001), as hypothesized (Hb). The distributor that is able to interpret the counterpart's intentions performs well. The distributors need to develop an accurate assessment of buyers' interests and values. The manufacturer that holds common goals and policies are able to sign similar intentions. The moral element plays an important role in the relationship and may allow distributors to better forecast long-term actions of the manufacturer.

The belief mechanism to build trust have a positive significant effect on performance (β=.29, $p<.001$), as stated in our hypothesis Hc. Our result shows that distributors tend to believe in the manufacturer and increase performance. Distributors may be reluctant to share information when they believe the manufacturer are more likely to behave in an untrustworthy manner,. The extent to which the manufacturer shares confidential information with its distributor also provides a signal of good faith. The result shows that a positive climate in a relationship allows a distributor to perceive reciprocity and mutuality. Through the belief mechanism, distributors appear to increase the engagement of the manufacturer in the relationship and consequently increase performance.

There is no significant impact of the other mechanisms to build trust on the performance measure. The mechanisms of capability (Hd), embeddedness (He) and continuity (Hf) showed no significant coefficient. Even though literature suggests the importance of these mechanisms, we do not find significant impact of them on performance. One might suggest that, in the particular relationship studied, the focus is heavily placed on the soft side of trust, which calculative, affective and belief mechanisms are of importance.

The control variables of dependency and annual turnover do not have a significant effect on performance. The size of the sales force presented a significant negative coefficient (β=-.21, $p<.001$), opposed to previous research about firm size and performance. Most researchers agree that larger firms have become so by virtue of achievement, which suggests a general intention to invest and take some risks. Interestingly, the distributors appear to lose performance as the number of the sales force increases. One possible explanation is the fact that the industry has gone through a wealthy period in areas were distributors' clients are large producers of soybean. The agribusiness in Brazil faced a great increase in financial results because of international price of such a bean.

5. Conclusion

This chapter aimed to discuss the emerging perspective on trust and develop a model of mechanisms to build trust. We tested the impact of the mechanisms on performance. The findings of our estimated model shows that, even though environment leads to suspicion and doubts, managers in the distribution companies seek trust relationships and try to develop trust using a combination of mechanisms to overcome potential problems (i.e. opportunistic behavior) in trust relationships. Thus, the results of the survey provided important evidence to support the theoretical discussions at hand. Overall, trust showed to be a governance mechanism that efficiently coordinates the activities in the relationship.

The findings of this chapter provide important evidence for the theoretical discussion of trust in business relationships. Our framework of six mechanisms to build trust gives insights on how trust is built. Although our survey does not test the existence of trust, it provides insight into how trust is generated. This study also attempts to measure in the same context six apparently mechanisms to build up trust. The theoretical development and results suggest that the mechanisms by which trust is built are not only based on the calculative dimension. The affective and belief mechanisms appear to play an important role in trust building effort.

Managers may use our study and its empirical evidence as a check on the adequacy of their existing relationships and the type of mechanism they use to develop trust. Firms should weigh the entire set of important relationships to invest more in the mechanisms that lead to performance. Calculating costs and rewards appear to be relevant to develop trust, though not exclusively. Forecasting counterpart's behavior and intentions appear to support the belief and affect mechanisms that support the development of trust. The mere effort of calculating and creating the necessary emotional bonds may lead to an improvement of decision making by managers. It is also important for managers to have accurate perceptions of the impact of trust on performance. We do not claim for managers to develop all relationships based on trust, though the most important may be coordinated by means of trust. The trust is costly to develop and maintain. By considering each of the mechanisms, companies can better do business. If managers either under- or overestimate the positive impact of trust, their efforts will be misguided, eventually dampening performance.

Some limitations of our study must be considered. We used a cross-sectional design, thus preventing the investigation of the dynamic effects of the performance on trust mechanisms. Further work can consider a longitudinal study to investigate the framework at different points in time. In addition, the current study uses OLS regression model to test the hypothesis. Future research may attempt to estimate the equation based on a multivariate technique as Structural Equation Modeling. There is also a need to check the causality of the estimated relationships in the model. There might be a possibility that mechanisms influence each other fostering even more performance. Future research may address these impacts. Our study domain was distributors in the Brazilian agrochemical sector. This might limit the generalization of our conclusions. Further research is encouraged to replicate the research in a different setting, such as another country or product. We concentrated our analysis on some elements of performance. Future research can investigate other objective measures of performance.

References

ADLER, T. R. 2007. Swift trust and distrust in strategic partnering relationships: key considerations. *Journal of Business Strategies,* 24(2), 105-118.

ANDERSON, E.; WEITZ, B. 1989. Determinants of continuity in conventional industrial channel dyads. *Market Science*, 8(4), 310-323.

ANDERSON, J. C.; NARUS, J. A. 1990. A model of distributor firm and manufacturer firm working partnerships. *Journal of Marketing*, 54 (January), 42-58.

AKERLOF, G. A. 1970. The market for "lemons": quality uncertainty and the market mechanism. *Quarterly Journal of Economics*, 84, 488-500.

ARROW, K. 1973. *Information and Economic Behavior*. Federation of Swedish Industry, Stockholm.

BARNEY, J. B. 1991. Firm resources and sustained competitive advantage. *Journal of Management*, 17(1), 99-120.

______; HANSEN, M. H. 1994. Trustworthiness as a source of competitive advantage, *Strategic Management Journal*, 15(Winter Special Issue), 175-190.

BELLO, D. C.; GILLILAND, D. I. 1997. The effect of output controls, process controls, and flexibility on export channel performance. *Journal of Marketing*, 61(January), 22-38.

BRADACH, J. L.; ECCLES, R. G. 1989. Price, authority and trust. *Annual Review of Sociology*, 15, 97-118.

COLEMAN, J. S. 1988. Social capital in the creation of human capital. *American Journal of Sociology*, 94, S95-S120.

DAS, T. K.; TENG, B. 1998. Between trust and control: developing confidence in partner cooperation in alliances. *Academy of Management Review*, 23(3), 491-512.

DEUTSCH, M. 1969. Conflicts: productive and destructive. *Journal of Social Issues*, XXV(1), 7-41.

DONEY, P. M.; CANNON, J. P. 1997. An examination of the nature of trust in buyer-seller relationships, *Journal of Marketing*, 61(4), 35-51.

DWYER, F. R.; SCHURR, P. H.; OH, S. 1987. Developing buyer-seller relationships. *Journal of Marketing*, 51(4), 11-27.

GANESAN, S. 1994. Determinants of long-term orientation in buyer-seller relationships *Journal of Marketing*, 58(2), 1-19.

GEYSKENS, I.; STEENKAMP, J-B. E. M.; KUMAR, N. 1998. Generalizations about trust in marketing channel relationships using meta-analysis. *International Journal of Research in Marketing*, 15, 223-248.

GRANOVETTER, M. 1985. Economic action and social structure: the problem of embeddedness. *American Journal of Sociology*, 91(3), 481-510.

GULATI, R. 1995. Does familiarity breed trust? The implications of repeated ties for contractual choice in alliances. *Academy of Management Journal*, 38(1), 85-112.

HAIR, J. F.; ANDERSON, R.; TATHAM, R. L.; BLACK, W. C. 1998. *Multivariate data analysis*, Upper Saddle River: Prentice Hall.

HAKANSSON, H.; SNEHOTA, I. 1995. *Developing relationships in business network.* New York: Routledge.

HERDER, M.; BRIAN, J. D. 2008. Canada's Stem Cell Corporation: Aggregate Concerns and the Question of Public Trust. *Journal of Business Ethics*, 77, 73-84.

JARILLO, J. C. 1988. On strategic networks. *Strategic Management Journal*, 9(1), 31-41.

KLEIN, B. 1996. Why hold-ups occur: the self-enforcing range of contractual relationships. *Economic Inquiry*, 34(7), 444-463.

KLEIN, R., RAI, A.; STRAUB, D.W. 2007. Competitive and cooperative positioning in supply chain logistics relationships. *Decision Science*, 38(4), 611-646.

KUMAR, N.; SCHEER, L. K.; STEENKAMP, J-B. E. M. 1995. The effects of perceived interdependence on dealer attitudes. *Journal of Marketing Research*, XXXII(8), 348-356.

LARSON, A. 1992. Networks dyads in entrepreneurial settings: a study of the governance of exchange relationships. *Administrative Science Quarterly*, 37, 76-104.

LEWICKI, R.; MCALLISTER, D.; BIES, R. 1998. Trust and distrust: new relationships and realities. *Academy of Management Review,* 23(3), 438-458.

LUSCH, R. F.; BROWN, J. R. 1996. Interdependency, contracting, and relational behavior in market channels. *Journal of Marketing*, 60(10), 19-38.

MALHOTRA, N. K. 1999. *Marketing research: an applied orientation*, Upper Saddle River: Prentice Hall.

MORGAN, R. M.; HUNT, S. D. 1994. The commitment-trust theory of relationship marketing. *Journal of Marketing*, 58(7), 20-38.

NOOTEBOOM, B.; BERGER, H.; Noorderhaven, N. G. 1997. Effects of trust and governance on relational risk. *Academy of Management Journal*, 36, 794-829.

ROUSSEAU, D. M.; SITKIN, S. B.; BURT, R. S.; CAMERER, C. 1998. Not so different after all: a cross-discipline view of trust. *Academy of Management Review*, 23(3), 393-404.

RING, P. S.; VAN DE VEN, A. H. 1992. Structuring cooperative relationships between organizations. *Strategic Management Journal*, 13, 483-498.

ROTTER, J. B. 1971. Generalized expectancies for interpersonal trust. *American Psychologist*, 26(5), 443-452.

______. 1980. Interpersonal Trust, trustworthiness and gullibility. *American Psychologist*, 35(1), 1-7.

POWELL, W. W. 1990. Neither market nor hierarchy: network forms of organization. *Research in Organizational Behavior*, 12, 295-336.

SITKIN, S. B.; ROTH, N. L. 1993. Explaining the limited effectiveness of legalic 'remedies' for trust/distrust. *Organization Science*, 4(3), 367-392.

SMITH, J. B.; BARCLAY, D. W. 1997. The effects of Organizational differences and trust on the effectiveness of selling partner relationships. *Journal of Marketing*, 61(1), 3-21.

THORELLI, H. B. 1986. Networks: between markets and hierarchies. *Strategic Management Journal*, 7, 37-51.

UZZI, B. 1997. Social structure and competition in interfirm networks: the paradox of embeddedness. *Administrative Science Quarterly*, 42, 35-67.

WICKS, A. C.; BERMAN, S. L.; JONES, T. M. 1999. The structure of optimal trust: moral and strategic implications. *Academy of Management Review*, 24(1), 99-116.

WILLIAMSON, O. E. 1993. Calculativeness, trust, and economic organization. *Journal of Law, Economics and Organization*, 36(4), 453-486.

______. 1996. *The mechanism of governance.* New York: Oxford University Press.

ZAHEER, A.; McEVILY, B.; PERRONE, V. 1998. Does trust matter? Exploring the effects of interorganizational and interpersonal trust on performance. *Organization Science*, 9(2), 141-159.

ZAHEER, A.; VENKATRAMAN, N. 1995. Relational governance as an interorganizational strategy: an empirical test of the role of trust in economic exchange. *Strategic Management Journal*, 16(5), 373-392.

ZAJAC, E. J.; OLSEN, C. P. 1993. From transaction cost to transactional value analysis: implications for the study interorganizational strategies. *Journal of Management Studies*, 30(1), 131-145.

ZAND, D. E. 1972. Trust and managerial problem solving. *Administrative Science Quarterly*, 17(2), 229-239.

ZYLBERSZTAJN, D.; ZUURBIER, P. J. P. 1999. *A non-naive explanation of trust: avoiding mistaken decisions for agribusiness chain management.* Séries Estudos Temáticos/USP, 002/99.

Part 2

Collaboration and Vertical Coordination

- Vertical Coordination in the Agrifood Supply Chain: structure and strategy of the agricultural cooperative
- The Road to Institutional Scientific Collaboration in Chains and Networks

Vertical Coordination in the Agrifood Supply Chain: structure and strategy of the agricultural cooperative

JOS BIJMAN

1. Introduction

Over the last decade, agrifood supply chains have been characterized by increasing vertical coordination. The key to vertical coordination is strengthening the link between production, processing and marketing activities in the supply chain. As these activities are usually carried by independent companies, vertical coordination requires some form of contractual agreement or (partial) ownership integration. As traditional market transactions cannot efficiently communicate the appropriate signals to producers and do not lead to consistency in producer responses, organizational solutions such as contracts and partial ownership have been used to strengthen the alignment of individual activities at different stages of the supply chain.

The need to strengthen vertical coordination results from a number of changes in the conditions of agrifood markets: consumers demand higher quality, more food safety guarantees, and more convenience; competition have become stronger due to globalization and saturated markets; the market power of food retail has increased due to more concentration; and all participants in agrifood chains have stepped up their effort in innovation and product differentiation in order to survive in those competitive market conditions. In general, changes in the market conditions urge all chain participants to become more market oriented and more responsive to customer demands.

Cooperatives are typically involved in marketing and processing farm products at the first stages of the supply chain. Consequently, they would seem well-positioned to organize vertical coordination between primary production, processing, distribution and marketing. However, cooperatives have organizational features that may limit their ability to strengthen market orientation and customer responsiveness. Particularly their financial structure and decision-making structure may affect their suitability to play a major role in strengthening vertical coordination. Also their focus on obtaining the best performance in the first stage of the supply chain may cast some doubts on their ability to coordinate the full chain.

Still, cooperatives have developed new strategies and structures to deal with the new supply chain challenges. Given the continuing importance of cooperatives in processing and marketing farm products, they must have found ways to deal with the limitations that could weaken their position in the supply chain. This paper discusses the role of the agricultural cooperative in strengthening vertical coordination. It assesses the strengths and weaknesses of the organizational form, and it presents empirical information on how cooperatives in Europe have responded to the supply chain challenges.

The paper is structured as follows. In section 2 we present figures on the market share of cooperatives in marketing farm products for a number of countries in Europe. Although competition is increasing, cooperatives are holding strong in terms of their market share. In the next section (3) we discuss the traditional motives for farmers to establish and patronize cooperatives. Reducing transaction costs due to uncertainty (or asymmetric information), risks and asset specificity have traditionally been the most important explanations for the prevalence of cooperatives. Then, in section 4 we present the theory on coordination and coordination mechanisms. We argue that coordination among firms, such as those participating in a supply chain, is obtained by particular combinations of four different coordination mechanisms. Next we apply, in section 5, those theoretical notions on (vertical) coordination to the role of cooperatives in the supply chain, and discuss how cooperatives are reinforcing those functions that strengthen vertical coordination. This raises the question how the traditional organizational characteristics of the cooperative support or hamper the ability to improve vertical coordination in the supply chain. Answers to this question, focusing on the ownership and corporate governance structure of the cooperative, are discussed in section 6. Finally, section 7 presents some conclusions on the near future of the role of cooperatives in the agrifood supply chain, particularly on further processes of strategic reorientation and restructuring.

2. Cooperatives in Marketing Farm Products in Europe

Cooperatives have always been important in the European agrifood industry. As farmer-owned firms, providing services for their owners, they have been instrumental in the modernization of European agriculture over the last 50 years. Particularly marketing cooperatives have been crucially important for farmers, who depend for their income on the performance of the cooperative. Indirectly, cooperatives have been important for all farmers because their dominance has forced non-cooperative companies to offer farmers the same price and quality of services. The latter mechanism is the so-called yardstick argument, which is difficult to prove but intuitively appealing.

While marketing coops can be found all over Europe and for all agricultural products, they are particularly strong in North-Western Europe and for commodities like milk, meat, fruit and vegetables, and cereals (see Table 1). Cooperatives also have substantial market shares in the production of animal feeds and the retail of fertilizers, seeds, and farm equipment. Finally, in many countries the provision of agricultural credit is dominated by cooperative banks.

The importance of cooperatives in the marketing of farm products is not just a feature of the past. Comparing the 1995 with the 2003 figures in Table 1 shows that in most countries and for most products, the market share of cooperatives has remained stable or has even gone up.[1] Also when we compare the figures in Table 1 with 1990 figures as presented by Mauget and Declerck (1996) we can draw the same conclusion on the strength of cooperatives in marketing farm products. For instance in the dairy industry, the industry for which most consistent data is available, cooperatives have increased their share of milk processing. France is the exception, as the cooperative share of the dairy market has decreased since the early 1990s.

[1] The figures in Table 1 must be interpreted with care. Not only because the two main publications from wich the figures are taken may have used different sources. Also, measuring the market share of cooperatives is not an easy task as there is no common methodology and there is no governmental body collecting these data. Most figures on market share are estimates by national associations or federations of cooperatives.

Table 1: Market share (%) of cooperatives in marketing farm products, 1995 and 2003

	Milk		Fruit and Vegetables		Meat		Cereals	
	1995	*2003*	*1995*	*2003**	*1995*	*2003*	*1995*	*2003*
Austria	90	94	n.a.	35	50	20	60	60
Belgium	50	50	70-90	85	20-30	25	n.a.	40
Denmark	93	97	20-25	30	66-93	90	87	80
Finland	94	97	n.a.	12	68	74	n.a.	n.a.
France	49	37	35-50	45	27-88	34**	75	74
Germany	20	68	60	30	30	35	n.a.	n.a.
Ireland	100	97	n.a.	75	30-70	70	69	n.a.
Netherlands	82	85	70-96	85	35	35**	n.a.	n.a.
Sweden	99	90	60	45	80	30	75	70
UK	98	55***	35-45	50	20	10-25***	20	25***

Sources: 1995: Van Bekkum and Van Dijk, 1997; 2003: Juliá-Igual and Meliá, 2007; * Source: Duponcel, 2006; ** 1998 data; *** 1999 data; n.a.: not available

Marketing cooperatives can provide different services to their members, thereby limiting or extending their activities to one or more stages of the supply chain. We can distinguish between three categories of marketing co-operatives. First, a number of cooperatives just focus on collecting products and providing an organized market place. The grower-owned flower auction is a typical example of this function. The flower auction is organizing the sales process on behalf of the grower, enabling the latter to fully specialize in production. As the auction is able to attract many buyers, and uses the auction clock for price determination, a transparent and well functioning market results. In the Netherlands the cooperative flower auction is the dominant sales channel, accounting for the marketing of more than 95% of domestically produced cut flowers and potted plants.

A second group of marketing cooperatives consists of organizations that not only collect farm products but also bargain with customers over the proper price. These cooperatives are also known as bargaining associations, although they often perform additional functions such as storage, sorting and grading, and sheltering producers from (too high) market risks (e.g. by pooling seasonal products). This type of marketing cooperatives is used for selling grains and oilseeds, fruits and vegetables, and livestock. The producer organizations that are registered under the EU regulation for supporting the marketing of fresh produce (the so-called CMO regulation) fall within this category. The availability of EU subsidies for special marketing plans for fresh produce has led to an expansion in the number of marketing cooperatives in the fruits and vegetables industry (CEC, 2001; Duponcel, 2006).

The third group of marketing cooperatives consists of the farmer-owned processing companies. The dairy cooperative is a typical example, and can be found throughout Europe (see Table 1). For other farm products, there are major differences in the market share of cooperative processors among European countries. In pork processing, for instance, cooperatives have a dominant position in Denmark, while they have totally disappeared in The Netherlands. Producer-owned cooperatives can also be found in the processing of starch potatoes, sugar beets, olives, fruits and vegetables, poultry, cotton and tobacco (Juliá-Igual and Meliá, 2007). Finally, the European wine industry is well known for its many cooperative wineries (e.g. Chiffoleau et al., 2007).

3. Traditional Motives for Establishing and Patronizing Cooperatives

Traditionally, agricultural cooperatives have been established for reason of reducing risks and transaction costs. While many cooperatives also perform social functions, the economic motives for becoming a member of a cooperative prevail. Schrader (1989) lists the following economic reasons for farmers to engage in collective marketing: resolving market failure; benefiting from economies of scale; capturing profits at another level of the supply chain; assure market access; benefit from reduced risks; building countervailing power; and gaining from coordination. We will briefly discuss these arguments, and illustrate them by referring to a marketing cooperative for fruits and vegetables.

3.1 *Asymmetric Market Power*

Imbalance of market power between farmers and their customers is the result of the large difference in minimum efficient scale of operation in farming compared to marketing or processing. In such oligopsonistic or even monopsonistic markets, farmers are likely to receive a lower price then they would under more competitive conditions. Cooperatives have addressed this asymmetry in market power by jointly purchasing inputs and jointly selling farm products, thereby establishing countervailing power. The marketing cooperative has a number of tools available to enhance the (collective) bargaining power of its members, such as negotiating contracts with buyers; collecting and sorting the products of the members; storing the products and selling in the high price season; and guaranteeing product quality.

3.2 *Asymmetric Information*

Another function of the cooperative related to market failure is reducing information asymmetries. In well-functioning (i.e., competitive) markets participants have full information regarding demand and supply, both on the quality and the quantity of products to be traded. However, this situation of full information disclosure rarely exists in real life, and most transactions are characterized by one party having more information than the other. Situations of asymmetrically distributed information between buyers and sellers can lead to abstention from trade or to the situation where only low quality products are traded. This is the classical information asymmetry problem posed by Akerlof (1970), leading to a loss of welfare. In agricultural markets the problem of hidden information can take the form of producers having better information on the real quality of the product or buyers having better information on final consumer demand.

Marketing cooperative have solved the problem of asymmetric information between producers and buyers in different ways. The problem of hidden information about product quality has been solved by introducing quality grades and standards, and by sorting and grading products into different quality classes. This has reduced the transaction costs (for the buyer) of searching for proper products, thus improving the efficiency of the sales process. The problem of hidden information about consumer demand has been solved by installing market information systems or by hiring a sales agent whose function is not only to find buyers and negotiate a price, but also to collect market information.

When a cooperative appoints a sales agent it may run into a new information problem as it was very hard to evaluate the performance of the agent given the volatility in supply and demand (for instance due to weather conditions) but also given the perishability of the products. For a fruit and vegetables cooperative, having members that supply different products and different qualities, it is even more difficult to asses the performance of the sales agent. Moreover, with such a divers membership the agent cannot satisfy each member equally, which may lead to distrust and conflict. In the Dutch fresh produce industry this double information problem – on market conditions and effort of the sales agent – was solved by establishing a producer-owned auction. By centralizing all supply and demand and by using the auction clock for price determination, the auction cooperative greatly reduces transaction costs between sellers and buyers. In addition to the efficiency obtained in the market, efficiency in production is also enhanced because producers can specialize in on-farm activities.

3.3 Sharing Risk

A cooperative is also an instrument for sharing risk. The more vulnerable producers are to the vagaries of nature or the whims of the market and the more risk averse they are, the more they seek risk reduction strategies. A marketing cooperative can reduce the market risks for the individual producer in several ways. It can reduce market risk by providing its members a guaranteed market. Cooperatives have the statutory obligation to sell any product that complies with the minimum quality standards (unless the bylaws stipulate differently). A private buyer would only buy the amount that was agreed to (in case of a contract), leaving the producer with any surplus for which it has to find another outlet (involving additional transaction costs). In addition, a cooperative may provide insurance to buyer default. In case a buyer is unable to pay (for instance in case of bankruptcy) the individual producer still receives his price and the cost are shared among all members. Moreover, the cooperative may use a pool for selling seasonal products.

While prices vary substantially over the year, the price the producer receives for his products is an average of the prices received for all sales transactions throughout the year. This sales mechanism is common in the potato industry as well as in the hard fruit industry.

3.4 Safeguarding Secific Investments

For many agricultural products there is only a small number of processors, due to the large economies of scale involved in processing (compared to small economies of scale in primary production) and due to the perishability and bulkiness of the farm product. Given these market and product characteristics, durable investments make the farmer dependent on the processor. By establishing a producer-owned processing company, farmers no longer face the risk that an opportunistic processor may take advantage of the farmer dependency. A typical example of this transaction cost reducing effect of (partial vertical integration) can be found in the dairy industry. As efficient milk processing involves significant economies of scale farmers are usually faced with a monopsonistic market structure. Interestingly, the dependency in dairy processing goes both ways. The processing unit is also fully dependent on the supply of milk from the surrounding farmers as other sources of milk are not available or only against high transportation costs. This symmetric dependency has often been mentioned as the explanation for the presence of many cooperatives in the dairy industry (Staatz, 1987).

In conclusion, the common characteristic of these traditional functions is that they reduce costs and solve market failures. By acting collectively, producers save on the costs of collecting market information, selling products, and reducing transaction risk. In addition, producers strengthen their bargaining power by collectively negotiating with buyers of their products and sellers of inputs. While these motives continue to be relevant, over the last two decades additional functions have become important. These new tasks relate to improving and guaranteeing quality, enhancing logistic efficiency, reinforcing information exchange, and strengthening innovation. While traditionally the focus was on cost reduction and bargaining power, these new tasks are more targeted at value creation, either at farm level or at the whole supply chain level. Value creation requires close coordination of the activities by farmers, cooperatives and other participants in the supply chain. The next section presents some basic thoughts on how to obtain coordination.

4. Coordination Mechanisms

Before we asses the strengths and weaknesses of cooperatives in enhancing vertical coordination in agrifood chains, we will first briefly discuss what coordination and more specifically what vertical coordination entails. Coordination is a basic process in society. When individual persons seek to benefit from specialization by focusing on one particular task, thus gaining task-specific knowledge and experience, different individual tasks have to be 'brought together' to obtain a combined result that has a higher value than just the sum of the individual results. Well-coordinated activities lead to efficient use of resources as well as to a good fit between the quantity and quality demanded and produced. The need for coordination is present at different levels of economic activity. It is important within firms, where better coordination leads to higher performance, as well as for the economy as a whole, where better coordination leads to higher productivity, higher efficiency, more customer satisfaction, and more innovation. Most economists focus on the role of markets and prices in obtaining coordination. The price is a 'sufficient statistic' for efficient transactions to take place as it contains the right information for sellers and buyers.

Organization scholars, however, have always claimed the limitation of prices and markets in obtaining coordination (e.g. Simon, 1991). In studying intra-organizational processes they have placed less emphasis on the allocation of resources and more on the interrelatedness of different tasks or activities, and on the organizational structures and organizational processes that support coordination between different tasks.

Coordination can be defined as managing dependencies between activities (Malone and Crowston, 1994). Often this dependency is two-ways: activity A and activity B are mutually dependent (or interdependent). Thompson (1967) distinguishes between three types of interdependence: pooled, sequential, and reciprocal. With pooled interdependence, each part of an organization renders a discrete contribution to the whole and each is supported by the whole. The parts are interdependent in the sense that unless they all perform adequately, the total organization is jeopardized. With sequential interdependence, the output of one part is the input for another part. With reciprocal interdependence the output of each part becomes input for the other parts.[2]

Coordination can be obtained by applying one or more coordination mechanisms. According to Thompson (1967), each type of interdependency requires a different coordination mechanism: with pooled interdependence, coordination by standardization is appropriate; with sequential interdependence, coordination by hierarchical control (called 'plan' by Thompson) is appropriate; and with reciprocal interdependence, coordination by mutual adjustment is called for. The three types of coordination, in the order presented here, place increasingly heavy burdens on communication (information exchange) and decision-making. While Thompson refers to intra-organizational coordination, these concepts of interdependencies and coordination mechanisms also apply to inter-organizational relationships.

Mintzberg (1979) has further elaborated on these coordination mechanisms, distinguishing between mutual adjustment, direct supervision, and several forms of standardisation (of work processes, outputs, skills and norms). Mutual adjustment implies that coordination is achieved by the simple process of informal communication. Direct supervision means that one person issues orders or instructions to several others whose tasks are interrelated. Standardization of work processes leads to coordination because it specifies the work processes of people carrying out interrelated tasks. Standardization of outputs achieves coordination by specifying the results of different tasks. Standardization of skills means that different activities are coordinated by virtue of the training the workers have received. Finally, standardization of norms implies that coordination is obtained by common norms (and beliefs) in the organization.

Combining economics and organization theory results in four basic approaches to obtaining coordination (see Figure 1). The first coordination mechanism consists of price and market, where individual choices are 'guided' by the so-called invisible hand of the market and where the price is the main information carrier. The second coordination mechanism consists of hierarchy, where a central decision-maker directs the activities of individuals

2 What Thompson calls reciprocal interdependence is known in economics as complementarities: the value of performing one activity is a function of the performance of the other activity (Milgrom and Roberts, 1995).

via direct supervision (or administrative control). The third is the community approach, where coordination is obtained through common norms, shared identity, habits and routines, or different standardization processes (Mintzberg, 1979). Finally, the fourth approach to coordination results from direct personal interaction about how to align individual activities, and the bilateral or multilateral agreements made in the group. The latter type of coordination is particularly present in contract negotiations, project teams, and group decision-making.

These four mechanisms can be plotted along two axes. On the vertical axis we find the extent of formalization of agreements, ranging from coordination only by informal norms, shared values, and routines as one extreme to coordination only by formal rules that are bilaterally or multilaterally agreed upon. The distinction between formal and informal institutions of governance has recently received quite some attention in the economic organization literature (e.g. Poppo and Zenger, 2002; Zenger et al., 2002). The horizontal axis indicates the use of outcome-based or behavior-based incentives. On the one hand we find coordination in a pure (spot) market, where price is the only coordination mechanism; on the other hand we find coordination obtained internally in an organization making use of such organizational devices as hierarchy, direct supervision and giving commands. Coordination in real transactions is always the result of a combination of those four mechanisms. Even a spot market includes informal coordination by the users as well as formal coordination through relevant public policies.

This distinction between four different coordination mechanisms helps to better understand how different governance structures (or governance forms) are able to coordinate particular transactions. In Transaction Cost Economics, the central premise is that firms choose (or develop) the most efficient governance structure for their transactions (Williamson, 1985). Depending on the characteristics of the transaction, the partners involved, and the institutional environment in which the transaction is carried out a particular combination of coordination mechanisms will lead to the lowest transaction costs. However, only particular combinations of coordination mechanisms can be found in reality, leading to the assumption that only specific combinations lead to efficient outcomes. The cooperative is a hybrid governance structure (Ménard, 2007) with a particular combination of coordination mechanisms that has proven its viability over the years.

Figure 1: Contract bilateral or multilateral – Four types of coordination mechanisms

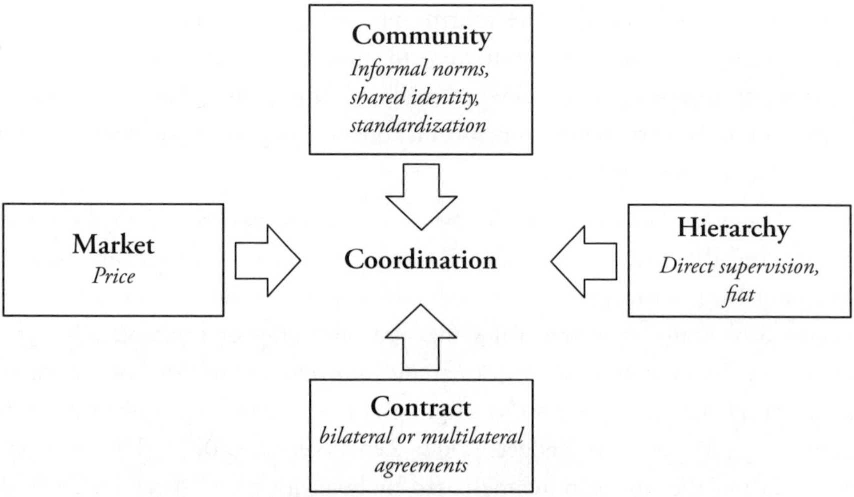

Source: Based on Borgen and Hegrenes, 2005

Coordination requires gathering and processing information, making decisions, and communicating these decisions. The stronger the interdependence among activities carried out by different persons or firms, the greater the amount of information they must process (Galbraith, 1977). Coordination requirements lead to coordination costs, which go up when coordination becomes more difficult. Coordination problems arise due to the lack of shared and accurate knowledge about the decision rules that others are likely to use and how one's own actions are interdependent with those of others (Gulati et al., 2005). Coordination costs are higher in uncertain or volatile environments compared to stable environments. When supply, demand, prices, technology, state policies, or other environmental factors are subject to rapid and unpredictable change, coordination becomes more difficult and therefore more costly. By shifting to (or adding) another coordination mechanism, organizations can reduce the coordination costs.

From this brief discussion of coordination theory we can now draw two conclusions that are relevant for the role of the cooperative in agri-food supply chains. First, when the demand for coordination goes up, for instance when activities by different actors become more interdependent, more information exchange is needed. A coordinator of a complex process/program consisting of different non-standard complementary activities, needs to collect and process detailed information on each of these activities. After taking a decision the coordinator has to provide each actor with the proper information to enable him/her to take the right actions. Second, when the activities of individual actors become more centralized interdependent there is need for more centralized decision-making to make sure that all individual but complementary actions are sufficiently aligned.

5. Vertical Coordination and the Role of the Cooperative

In section 4 we have discussed the issue of coordination in general. However, for this paper we are particularly interested in vertical coordination. Agrifood supply chains are commonly characterized by sequential vertical transactions. The coordination challenge in a supply chain is not only to align the activities of the farmer with those of the processor, and of the processor with those of the retailer, but also to coordinate the transaction between farmer and processor with the transaction between processor and retailer. In other words, the agrifood supply chain is characterized by sequential interdependence.

Vertical coordination in agrifood supply chains (or value chains) has become more important, for a number of reasons (Royer and Rogers, 1998; Galizzi and Venturini, 1999; Hobbs and Young, 2000). First, consumers are demanding higher quality, without willing to pay more. Quality includes food safety, environment friendly, animal friendly, etc. Second, in response to several food crises, governments have introduced more strict food safety legislation. Third, technology has made markets more transparent, has increased competition, and has made supply chains more international. Also advances in logistic technologies have increased competition from distant production areas. Finally, market structures in the food processing and food retailing industry has changed dramatically. Particularly in food retailing, supermarket ownership has become very concentrated (Clarke, 2002). These changing market conditions, new technologies, stricter legislation and more quality conscience consumers has led to strategic reorientation of the agrifood industry. Cooperatives and non-cooperative processing and marketing firms now apply strategies targeted at more innovation, more product differentiation, improved logistic efficiency, higher product quality and more quality monitoring (including guaranteeing food safety). These strategies require more collaboration and coordination among the different participants in the supply chain.

Traditionally, the cooperative as an organizational form is characterized by pooled interdependence: each member has an individual transaction relationship with the cooperative firm but not with each other. Still, the performance in the individual transaction depends on all transactions together, through economies of scale in processing and marketing. When vertical coordination in the supply chain becomes more important, transactions in the cooperative shift from only a pooled interdependence towards a combination of pooled and sequential interdependence. The sequential interdependence appears because the transaction between member and cooperative firm has to be coordinated with the transaction between cooperative and its customer (e.g. a secondary processor or a retailer). Strengthening the coordination between these two sequential transactions is the main challenge for the cooperative in the supply chain.

How do cooperatives deal with this need for more vertical coordination? What new functions have they started? How are they dealing with the increasing coordination costs? Have they implemented changes in their coordination mechanisms? Do cooperatives encounter particular structural barriers to improving vertical coordination in the supply chain? The following section tries to answer these questions on the basis of theoretical and empirical literature on changing strategies and structures of agricultural cooperatives.

5.1 Information Exchange

While collecting and processing market information has always been one of the functions of the cooperative, targeted information exchange has become more important as part of the need to strengthen vertical coordination. Bijman (2002) found that the restructuring of the traditional vegetables auctions in The Netherlands was to a large extent due to the limited options that the auction offered for information exchange between sellers and buyers. The traditional auction functioned well as long as all information was of a generic type, but it was not equipped to transfer information specific to a bilateral trading relationship.

When processors need information on products and production methods, in order to schedule their own processing and marketing activities, cooperative bargaining organizations may be helpful to provide this information. Through having this information collected and exchanged by a cooperative, farmers and processors can economize on coordination costs. Hueth and Marcoul (2003) found that one of the reasons for the existence of bargaining cooperatives in the US vegetables industry is that they are able to share production information with processors that would otherwise be costly to obtain.

Cooperatives have competitive advantages as to solving the problem of asymmetric information about specific product quality characteristics. Producers have better information on product quality, particularly on quality characteristics that are directly related to on-farm production methods, such as in organic production or products of regional origin. The quality of these so-called credence attributes is hard to measure for the buyer. For this reason, buyers may not be willing to pay the appropriate price. When sellers set up a collective marketing organization, this cooperative may use its reputation as a trust-worthy supplier (because it has an ongoing interest in keeping good relations with customers and consumers), to guarantee the promised quality and thus encourage consumer to pay the higher price. As there is no conflict of interest we do not expect producers to cheat on their own cooperative.

Besides providing product and production information to processors, traders and retailers, cooperatives also collect and process market information for their members. Increasingly, this activity also includes collecting and transferring demand information from specific customers. Cooperatives, just like their non-cooperative competitors, are trying to become preferred suppliers of specific processing or retail customers. Once being a preferred supplier, the information exchange function is no longer limited to exchanging general market information, but increasingly includes the specific requirements of those customers.

In sum, we expect that the need for more vertical coordination in agrifood chains leads to the following (coordination) strategies of the cooperative. First, it will lead to enhanced effort of the cooperative in collecting, processing and distributing information. Second, cooperatives increasingly perform a brokerage function between customers and producers, resulting in more restriction for producers on their individual choices on what and how much to produce. Third, cooperatives will try to establish direct trading relations with major retailers, in order to shorten the information chain between producers and final customers/consumers. Fourth, we expect that organic products and products of regional origin, given the information advantage of the producers, are marketed by cooperatives instead of investor-owned firms.

5.2 Quality Assurance

Are cooperatives able to provide the quality assurance that customers demand, and if so, do they have a comparative advantage or disadvantage compared to non-cooperative firms? Processors and retailers increasingly demand the disclosure of detailed information on the production processes applied on the farm; in some countries also legislation requires disclosure. Generally, one cannot expect farmers to be enthusiastic about providing this information, not only because of the paper work involved, but also because it entails a limitation on the freedom to operate the farm. However, when the requirement to disclose detailed information on production methods is issued by the producer-owned cooperative, farmers may be more likely to provide this information because there is no conflict of interest between members and the cooperative.

Quality assurance does not only involve grading and sorting by the cooperative. It also entails helping farmers comply with particular quality requirements. The cooperative, as a member-owned organization, is well-positioned to provide their members with all necessary information and technical assistance. In a number of countries, cooperatives are only to a limited extent involved in providing technical assistance to their members because there is a well-developed public extension service or there is a well-developed private technical consultancy industry (sometimes grown out of a privatized public extension service). However, as coops become preferred suppliers, and production technology becomes less generic, one may expect that cooperatives themselves become involved in organizing technical assistance. Ménard and Valceschini (2005) present a case study of a cooperative in the French tomato industry that defines the quality requirements, provides technical support, collects and selects the products, and takes care of the packaging.

One of the changes in market conditions for agrifood products is the shift from public quality standards to private quality standards (Henson and Reardon, 2005). Large retail companies are known to have individual or collective (such as EurepGAP) quality assurance systems. Often these private standards go beyond the requirements of public standards. This implies that cooperatives supplying to those supermarkets will become involved in helping their members comply with these quality assurance systems.

Verhaegen and Van Huylenbroeck (2002) in their Belgium study on new quality initiatives by agricultural producers found that these producers often set up cooperatives in order to coordinate both horizontally among the producers (to get homogeneous quality products) and vertically between producers and customers (in order to align the supply and demand of high quality products).

5.3 Branding

Producers can improve their communication with consumers and at the same time try to strengthen their competitive position vis-à-vis retailers by building a consumer brand. However, the investments are substantial, long-term and risky. Many cooperatives cannot afford these investments. Still, in some situations it may be easier for a cooperative to establish a brand name than it would be for other firms. In those cases where the quality of the branded product is crucially dependent on the effort of the producer (e.g. in the case of regional specialties or organic products), no other chain actor is willing to invest in a brand name. A brand is a typical example of asset specificity (Klein et al, 1978), which means that production of the branded products and brand ownership should be combined in order to reduce transaction costs (in this case the costs of safeguarding the investments in brand building). For the farmers who produce regional specialties or organic products this all means that they should be the owners of the brand under which their products are sold. Because farmers individually are too small to establish and maintain a brand, they do so collectively in a cooperative. This proposition about the advantage of the cooperative in building a brand for particular products is supported by an empirical study by Raynaud et al. (2005) who found that consumer brands for high quality agricultural products are often owned by cooperatives.

Does the organizational structure of the cooperative affects the marketing of the cooperative's products or the establishment of a brand? Nilsson et al. (2007) have investigated whether being a cooperative has an added value in marketing the products of the cooperative. They found that consumers have positive attitudes towards cooperatives. They suggest there are good options for cooperatives to use their business form as a marketing tool, particularly by established cooperatives, mentioning 'cooperative' in conjunction with other quality attributes, and by local cooperatives trying to build a brand for products of local origin. Beverland (2007) examined the ability of traditional and new generation cooperatives to develop and support market-based assets including brands and long-term relationships with channel buyers in order to develop a sustainable position for their members and increase returns. His findings suggest that traditional cooperatives may be able to develop innovative marketing programs but struggle to support them over the long-term due to problems in ownership structures. The new generation cooperatives studied had more sustained long-term success, as members were able to capture the equity of intangible assets such as brand value, thus ensuring they undertook actions (such as channel support) consistent with building a sustainable long-term positioning.

In sum, we expect that cooperatives will reinforce their effort in building consumer brands as part of the development towards more vertical coordination. In addition, we conjecture that cooperatives with consumer brands will strengthen their control over the production stages of the supply chain in order to protect their brand equity.

5.4 Innovation

Tight coordination between the production activities of the growers and the marketing activities of their customers may improve the efficiency of the supply chain, and may also foster innovation in the chain. Innovations that require adjustments in operations at different stages of the supply chain are so-called system innovations (Teece, 1988). The quintessence of a system innovation is that it can only be successful when different independent actors contribute to the innovation process. In the case of an agrifood chain, new product developments often require a contribution from input suppliers (new inputs), farmers (new farming methods), processors (new processing techniques) and retailers (new marketing approaches). Obtaining such chain innovations requires a coordinator who will take up the task of exchanging information among all partners and making decisions that impact all. The marketing or processing cooperative occupies a central position in the supply chain for coordinating complementary adjustments in production and marketing. In order to perform this coordinator role for chain innovations, the cooperative is likely to apply more centralized decision-making procedures as well as more monitoring of member activities (Royer, 1995).

Cooperatives have a competitive advantage when the innovation consists of a so-called "inherently functional food" (Bröring, 2008). Such functional foods are not just fortified or enriched by simply adding a functional ingredient to a food product during the manufacturing process, but are naturally grown by altering the whole livestock production process. An example is the introduction (in 2007) by the Dutch dairy cooperative Campina of a new milk product with more unsaturated fatty acids. Campina does play a central role in this project as it controls most of the value chain activities. This high level of control seems to be needed in order to account for product quality. Farmers who participate in this program need to obey to a special feeding program which they can source-in from certain "Campina-approved' feed producers. Bröring suggests that to change the behavior and production processes at farm level might have been easier since Campina as a cooperative is jointly-owned by its member-farmers.

We may expect the following developments among cooperatives that pursue innovations in the supply chain. First, they will step up their effort on product innovation, particularly on chain innovations. These types of innovation require strong coordination among the activities and investments at different stages of the supply chain. The cooperative is the central coordinator for this type of innovations. Second, the initiation and implementation of chain innovations require more centralized decision-making, which leads to a reduction of the individual freedom of the participating farmer.

Now let us focus on the type of coordination mechanisms that are applied by the cooperative in the strengthening vertical coordination in the supply chain. Based on the need for more information exchange and more centralized decision-making, we can develop the following propositions. First, we expect that a shift from public standards towards private standards would entail a shift from community coordination towards contractual coordination. While communities reveal community-specific information, contracts are better in exchanging actor-specific information. Also the need for higher quality assurance requires more information exchange. Second, contracts are not only better for bilateral information exchange, they are also better for hierarchical decision-making. Stinchcombe (1985) has argued that contracts are typically hierarchical tools in governing inter-organizational relations. Thus, more vertical coordination will not only lead to a shift from community to contractual governance, but also from market coordination to hierarchical coordination, either in contracts (as a form of hybrid governance structure) or in some for of (partial) vertical integration. It is well known from organization theory that organizations have more powerful control and monitoring mechanisms available than do markets because of their ability to measure and reward behavior as well as outcome (Eisenhardt, 1985). Finally, as product innovation and system innovation has become more important, we would expect to see a shift from market to hierarchy coordination. In sum, to strengthen vertical coordination cooperatives will show a shift from community to contractual coordination and from market to hierarchical coordination (see Figure 1). These shifts have implications for the organization of agricultural cooperative. In the next section we will discuss what changes in the organization (or structure) of the agricultural cooperative can be already seen or can be envisioned for the near future.

6. Cooperative Restructuring to Support More Vertical Coordination

So far we have discussed the supply chain strategies that agricultural cooperatives in Europe are following or are expected to follow in the near future. Decision-making on and implementation of these strategies may be hampered by a number of organizational characteristics of the cooperative. For this reason, several cooperatives have started a process of organizational restructuring in order to enhance market orientation, innovativeness, consumer responsiveness and vertical coordination in the supply chain. Before discussing these restructuring processes we will first briefly introduce the specific organizational features of the farmer-owned cooperative.

6.1 Characteristics of the Cooperative

An agricultural cooperative is a firm that is jointly-owned by farmers. The main purpose of the cooperative is to support these farmers in their individual farming activities. Such services can be supplying inputs (e.g. fertilizers or animal feed), providing rural credit and insurance, marketing farm products, processing farm products, and providing technical assistance. These activities have a minimum efficient scale well beyond what is feasible for the individual farm. By organizing these activities through a jointly-owned firm, farmers benefit from economies of scale while keeping transaction costs low because they have control over the execution of these activities. In addition, by purchasing and selling collectively, farmers have established countervailing power vis-à-vis sellers and buyers that are much larger and therefore have more market power.

A commonly used definition of a cooperative comes from the International Cooperative Alliance (ICA): "A cooperative is an autonomous association of persons united voluntarily to meet their common economic, social, and cultural needs and aspirations through a jointly owned and democratically-controlled enterprise" (see: www.ica.coop.org). This definition indicates one of the most interesting and at the same time most challenging characteristics of the cooperative: its double nature (Draheim, 1955). A cooperative is both an association of members ánd a firm in which economic activities are carried out. The association is the locus of collective action, while the firm provides the actual services to the members. Making this distinction can be helpful to understand the process of cooperative restructuring, as economic conditions and societal trends have differential impact on the association and the enterprise.

Over the years the members of the agricultural cooperatives in Europe have transformed from farming families into farming firms. Members of the cooperative can now be considered as member firms (MFs), who jointly (i.e. through the association) own the cooperative firm (CF). Conceptualizing the CF as a service provider working for the benefit of the MFs does not mean that the CF has no self-interests. Indeed, shifting to a more market oriented strategy implies that the CF no longer considers itself as a purely dependent firm, and increasingly emphasizes its own role and responsibilities with regards to other participants in the supply chain and ultimately to consumers.

In much of the literature on agricultural cooperatives a three-fold relationship between members and their cooperative is used, emphasizing the role of the member of user of the services provided by the CF: user-benefit, user-control, and user-ownership (Barton, 1989). User-benefit means that the members are the primary stakeholders to benefit from the cooperative, and that this benefit is obtained by (individually) using the services of the cooperative. User-control indicates that the rights to decide what strategies and policies the CF will follow ultimately lies with the users. In practice a board of directors, chosen by and from the members, is taking the strategic decisions. User-ownership signifies that the equity capital needed to run the CF is provided by the users.

This distinction in the relationship between members and cooperative is useful to clarify a number of other organizational characteristics of the cooperative. First, there is an order of importance in these three elements; user-benefit is the most important one, while user-control and user-ownership are subordinate to the benefit relationship. Control over and ownership in the cooperative should be considered as tools to obtain the benefits. Second, and most importantly, while the user-benefit relationship is an individual one – as farmers individually patronize the cooperative – the control and ownership functions are performed collectively. The latter means that farmers collectively decide on the activities and investments of the CF, and that the property rights to the assets of the CF are collectively owned. Defining ownership in a firm as the combination of control rights (or decision-rights) and income rights (Hansmann, 1996), one can observe that income rights are held individually, while decision-rights are held collectively. As we shall argue below, these particular organization characteristics have consequences for the extent and content of the vertical coordination strategies by the cooperative.

6.2 Organizational Restructuring

What type of organizational restructuring have cooperatives followed in order to be able to respond optimally to the need for more market orientation and more vertical coordination? This question can best be answered by using the threefold relationship between members and cooperative firm: member-benefit, member-ownership and member-control.

The above described vertical coordination strategies of cooperatives should first be considered as changes in the transaction relationship between MFs and CF. Innovation, quality assurance, market orientation, and customer responsiveness all entail a shift of control over the transaction from the MFs to the CF. A CF that has become a preferred supplier to a large retailer, that has built a consumer brand, and that has invested in a reputation of supplier of high quality products, has a large interest monitor and controlling its supplies. Thus the CF will strengthen its control over the transactions between MFs and CF. This goes beyond monitoring product quality and extends towards monitoring the production processes of the MFs (particularly for products with quality characteristics that crucially depend on the effort of the farmer).

However, the shift from producer orientation to market orientation does not only have implications for the transaction (or patronage) relationship between members and cooperative. It also affects the decision-making processes in the cooperative and it often has implications for the financial structure of the cooperative. This issue of financial structure or ownership structure has been studied by a number authors, notably Cook (1995), Nilsson (1999) and Chaddad and Cook (2004). They all describe the innovative ownership models that cooperatives in Europe and North-America have developed to either strengthen member willingness to invest in the cooperative or invite external investors.

One of these models is particularly interesting for our argument as it not just raises additional equity capital but also entails a shift of decision-rights away from the farmer-members towards the managers of the CF (and the subsidiaries of the CF). In the so-called Coop-Plc model (Harte, 1997; Nilsson, 1999) or Irish Model (Chaddad and Cook, 2004) the cooperative has not only invited outside investors to participate in a subsidiary of the CF, it has also obtained a stock market listing for this cooperative, in order to make the shares tradable. While most or all of the activities and assets are transferred from the cooperative to the Plc-firm, the cooperative remains in place as a shareholder organization, representing its member interests. Although the cooperative initially is majority shareholder, the model opens the option the cooperative becomes a minority owner when the public listed subsidiary is issuing new shares. Examples of this Irish model of cooperative restructuring are the dairy cooperative Kerry (stock listing already in 1986); the supply cooperative IAWS (in 1988); the dairy cooperatives Avonmore and Waterford (both in 1989; in 1997 they merged and became Glanbia); and the dairy cooperative Golden Vale (in 1989; acquired by Kerry in 2001).

Van Bekkum and Bijman (2007) also describe a Finnish model of cooperative restructuring. Three primary products cooperatives from Finland also brought their subsidiaries to the stock market but have retained a controlling stake in these companies through the introduction of a separate class of shares, exclusive to members and which carry stronger voting rights. Two of these cooperatives are minority shareholders in terms of number of shares, but still retain the majority of the votes: Metsäliitto has 38% of the shares of its subsidiary M-real (listed in June 1987), but retained 60% of the voting rights; and LSO Cooperative has 37% of the shares in HK Ruokatalo (listed in February 1997), but 84% of the voting rights. The third example of the Finnish model is the meat company *Atria Group*. The three cooperatives that have founded the Atria Group maintain a majority position both in number of shares (58%) and voting rights (92%).

Introducing these ownership models are a major part of the restructuring processes of cooperatives. Although they are related to the new vertical coordination strategies they are primarily meant to solve financial limitations of the cooperative business form. In this paper we will focus in the restructuring of the decision-making processes, particularly on shifts in the internal governance of the cooperative.

Decision-making in the cooperative is characterized by democratic procedures, in which all members have a vote and all members are eligible to become elected as member of the board of directors. Democratic decision-making has advantages and disadvantages. It has implications for the speed of reaching an agreement and the quality of the decision. Generally, democratic decision-making requires more time to reach a decision compared to autocratic decision-making. Therefore, the latter has coordination advantages compared to democratic decision-making. A second disadvantage of the democratic decision-making process is that it holds the possibility that a majority of the members, contributing only a small part of patronage of the cooperative, imposes policies that exploit a minority consisting of, for instance, large patrons (Staatz, 1987).[3] Democratic decision-making also has advantages, which relate to the quality of the outcome and the effectiveness of implementing decisions. Reynolds (1997) argues that consensus decision-making, which is quite common in boards of agricultural cooperatives, offers the opportunity to combine different perspectives and

[3] In Dutch cooperative vegetable auctions in the 1980s and early 1990s, the majority of small producer-members refused to let the auction facilitate innovative business relationships between particular (groups of) growers and particular clients (Bijman, 2002).

different experiences. In addition, consensus governance makes implementation of policies easier.

How the advantages and disadvantages of collective decision-making in agricultural cooperatives balance out, depends on the competitive conditions. In a stable and/or protected market, cooperatives may have clear advantages. In a more dynamic environment, the disadvantages of the collective decision-making model may become more constraining as to the strategic flexibility that is needed. Slow decision-making becomes more serious when the volatility in the environment increases, such as when market protection is reduced and foreign competitors enter the market. Also when customers demand more innovative products, cooperatives may be at a disadvantage as they have a tendency to avoid new business directions and risky investments (this has been named the 'business as usual' trap; Reynolds, 1997). As new initiatives often have uneven or selective benefits among the membership, the safest option is to avoid rocking the boat.[4] This, in turn, may undermine cohesiveness, as it discourages innovative producers to continue their membership. Producers who have adopted new technologies or production practices want a linkage to value-added processing or marketing systems to maximize benefits of the on-farm innovations.

6.3 *Cooperative Corporate Governance*

Another organizational characteristic of the cooperative that may become a liability in rapidly changing markets is the fact that farmers, as members of the board of directors, take the major decisions. Farmers often lack sufficient knowledge of how and where to guide the CF in terms of marketing and innovation. This problem is particularly serious in large, diversified cooperatives (Cook, 1995). Insufficient expertise may lead to inefficient strategic decisions and to suboptimal control of the management.

As argued above, cooperatives seek to strengthen vertical coordination as part of their strategy to become more customer oriented. This means that in (strategic) decisions of the cooperative, customer interests and member

4 For instance, the large Dutch dairy cooperatives have long refused to accept organic milk. Members that wanted to shift from mainstream to organic milk were forced to leave the cooperative and find another outlet for their milk.

interests will both be taken into account. It is the task of the professional management to ensure that customer interests are sufficiently served, even when they conflict with (short term) member interests. We expect that co-operatives aiming for supply chain integration will experience more difficult decision-making as member interests are no longer the only (or even the main) guiding principle.

When cooperatives become larger and more customer-oriented, the distance between the association part and the firm part of the cooperative increases. Particularly the professional managers of the firm demand sufficient room for entrepreneurial initiatives. This means that the relationship between the board of directors (as representatives of the membership) and the management may change from a situation where the board takes strategic decisions and management takes care of execution, to a situation where management takes the strategic decisions and the board's main function is supervision and ex post control. The new role of the board may become one of endorsing the strategic plans presented by the professional management and then defending these plans among the membership.

Hiring and keeping good managers may be a problem, particularly for a marketing cooperative. First, managers cannot receive incentives in the form of shares in the company. Second, cooperative business may not be perceived as trendy or sexy. Third, because the performance of the cooperative should be measured in terms of member benefit and not in terms of profit, market share or growth, managers cannot easily show there successes in their peer groups. This makes cooperative firms less attractive to certain ambitious managers. Fourth, as cooperatives in general follow prudent growth strategies, often staying close to the activities and products of the members, they are less attractive employers for a particular group of entrepreneurial managers.

Changes in the size and the strategy of the cooperative may have a number of repercussions for managing and controlling the CF. As few empirical studies on this issue have been conducted, we may conjecture the following developments when cooperatives embark on more market oriented strategies. First, the directors, as chosen from among the members, generally do not have the marketing knowledge that is required. Thus, professional marketing management will be hired. Second, even without a strong focus on marketing the large and diversified cooperative requires professional management expertise that board members do not necessarily possess. Third, as the cooperative grows, internationalizes and diversifies, there is a large chance that the interests of the members in all of these activities diverge. As a result, strategic decision-making may become more laborious and/or members become less committed. Fourth, and probably most importantly, when companies become large and diversified they require top-managers of a kind that is only limitedly available; moreover, these managers demand a degree of autonomy from direct interference in company activities by the board of directors. Giving managers higher discretion and more autonomy is in line with traditional organizational theory's prediction that decision-rights should be allocated to those actors that have the knowledge to take those decisions. Having such autonomy is an important element of the intrinsic rewards that top-managers prefer as incentive for their effort. In sum, we expect market oriented cooperatives to hire top-managers which require the board of directors to shift its role from directing towards supervising.

One of the examples of restructuring corporate governance in Dutch cooperatives is the introduction of the so-called corporation model (Figure 2). This model is similar to the above described Irish model, but without the stock listing. However, the main reason for cooperatives to choose the corporation model has not been the need to acquire addition equity capital (as in the Irish case) but has been the perceived need to give the management of the CF more autonomy (and thereby to attract highly qualified managers). In the corporation model the CF takes the legal form of a Plc or Ltd and all of the activities and assets of the cooperative are placed in this Plc or Ltd. The CF is now legally separated from the association, although the association remains the 100% shareholder of the firm.[5] One of the main characteristic of the corporation model, in terms of corporate governance, is that the board of directors of the association is also the supervisory board of the CF; there is no longer a separate supervisory committee at the level of the association. It is a simple model in terms of corporate governance as there is only one supervisory body, which has to take into account both member interests and firm interests. Several large Dutch agricultural cooperatives have obtained this legal structure over the last 15 years, such as Friesland Foods, Campina, and The Greenery.

5 This legal structure makes it much easier for outside investors to invest in the CF.

Figure 2: The corporation model of cooperative corporate governance

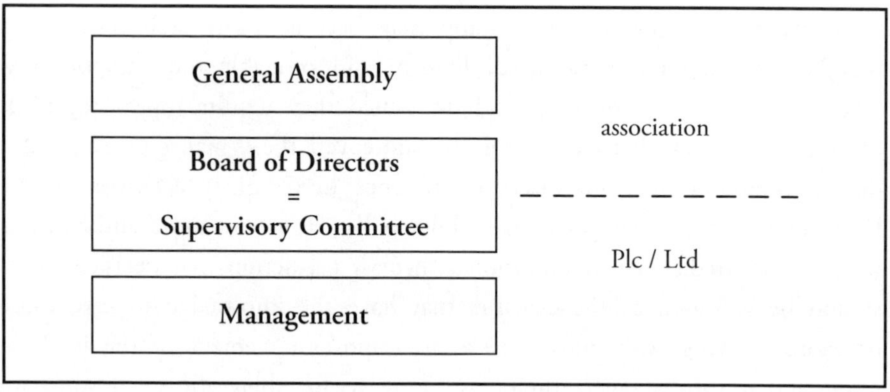

7. Conclusions

In their ambition to respond to retail and consumer demands and better compete with non-cooperative firms, cooperatives in North-West Europe are applying new marketing strategies that require them to strengthen vertical coordination in the supply chain. Stronger vertical coordination entails more and better information exchange as well as more centralized decision-making. In terms of coordination mechanisms this means that the cooperatives are shifting from community to contractual governance and from market to hierarchical governance. The latter also includes giving the management of the CF more decision-rights over logistics, innovation, quality control and sometimes even volume control. This all implies that the CF obtains more control over the transaction relationship between MFs and CF.

Empirical research supporting the above conjectures is very limited. Kyriakopoulos et al. (2004) found that market orientation correlates with differential pricing and cost allocation mechanisms in cooperatives. These mechanisms imply heterogeneity among the membership of the cooperative. In such situations we expect to see a shift from democratic (or community) decision-making towards more hierarchical decision-making. In practice, this means more decision-making authority for the management of the CF. Verhaegen and Van Huylenbroeck (2002), in their study on governance structures for quality food chains in Belgium, found that the higher the investment in the brand, the more decision-making in the cooperative became centralized and the more behavior-type of governance mechanisms were applied by the cooperative in its transactions with the producers.

The current and future shifts in coordination mechanisms, needed to strengthen vertical coordination, raise a number of interesting research questions about the viability of the cooperative model. Does the shift towards more hierarchical and contractual governance mechanisms lead to a loss of social capital, and thereby of member commitment? Is there a trade-off between commitment and coordination? Can we establish a maximum size of the cooperative for which social mechanisms (i.e. community coordination) combine well with the need to strengthen centralized decision-making? Does the brokerage function of aligning producer interests and customer interests lead to lower member trust in the CF, and if so, how can that be countered?

References

AKERLOF, G. A. 1970. The market for “lemons”: qualitative uncertainty and the market mechanism. *Quarterly Journal of Economics* 84: 488-500.

BEKKUM, O. F. van; BIJMAN, J. 2007. Innovations in cooperative ownership: converted and hybrid listed cooperatives. In: RAJAGOPALAN, S. (Ed.) *Cooperatives in 21st Century. The Road Ahead.* Hyderabad, India: Ifcai University Press, p. 34-56.

BEKKUM, O. F. van; DIJK, G. van (Eds.). 1997. *Agricultural co-operatives in the European Union; Trends and issues on the eve of the 21st century*. Assen: Van Gorcum.

BEVERLAND, M. 2007. Can cooperatives brand? Exploring the interplay between cooperative structure and sustained brand marketing success. *Food Policy* 32(4): 480-495.

BIJMAN, J. 2002. *Essays on agricultural cooperatives. Governance structure in fruit and vegetable chains.* Erasmus University Rotterdam, PhD Thesis.

______; HENDRIKSE, G. 2003. Co-operatives in chains: institutional restructuring in the Dutch fruit and vegetables industry. *Journal on Chains and Network Science,* 3(2): 95-107.

BORGEN, S.O.; HEGRENES, A. 2005. *How can transaction cost economics add to the understanding of new contractual formats in the norwegian agri-food system?* Olso, Norwegian Agricultural Economics Research Institute.

BRÖRING, S. 2008. *How systemic innovations require alterations along the entire value chain – The case of animal-derived functional foods.* Paper presented at the 8th International Conference on Management in AgriFood Chains and Networks, Ede, The Netherlands, 29-30 may.

CHADDAD, F. R.; COOK, M. L. 2004. Understanding new cooperative models: An ownership-control rights typology. *Review of Agricultural Economics*, 26 (3): 348-360.

CHIFFOLEAU, Y. et al. 2007. Networks, innovation and performance – Evidence from a cluster of wine cooperatives (Languedoc, South of France). In: KARANTININIS; K.; NILSSON, J. (Eds.). *Vertical markets and cooperative hierarchies.* Dordrecht: Springer, p. 35-59.

CEC – Commission of the European Communities. 2001. *Report from the Commission to the Council on the state of implementation of Regulation (EC) N. 2200/96 on the common organisation of the market in fruit and vegetables.* Brussels (COM(2001) 36 final).

CLARKE, R. 2002. *Buyer power and competition in European food retailing.* Cheltenham: Edward Elgar.

COOK, M. L. 1995. The future of U.S. agricultural cooperatives: a neo-institutional approach. *American Journal of Agricultural Economics* 77 (12): 1153-1159.

DRAHEIM, G. 1955. *Die Genossenschaft als Unternehmungstyp*. Göttingen.

DUPONCEL, M. 2006. Role and importance of producer organisations in the fruit and vegetable sector in the EU, presentation at the CAL-MED second workshop. Washington DC (at: http://ec.europa.eu/agriculture/capreform/fruitveg/slides_en.htm).

EISENHARDT, K. M. 1985. Control: organizational and economic approaches. *Management Science.* 31(2): 134-149.

GALBRAITH, J. R. 1977. *Organization design*. Reading, MA, Addison-Wesley.

GALIZZI, G.; VENTURINI, L. (Eds.). 1999. *Vertical relationships and coordination in the food system*. Heidelberg: Physica Verlag.

GROSSMAN, S. J.; HART, O. D. 1986. The costs and benefits of ownership; A theory of vertical and lateral integration. *Journal of Political Economy* 94(4): 691-719.

GULATI, R.; LAWRENCE, P. R.; PURANUM, P. 2005. Adaptation in vertical relationships: beyond incentive conflict. *Strategic Management Journal* 26(5): 415-440.

HANSMANN, H. 1996. *The ownership of enterprise*. Cambridge, MA/London: The Belknap Press of Harvard University Press.

HARTE, L. N. 1997. Creeping privatisation of irish co-operatives: a transaction cost explanation. In: NILSSON, J.; DIJK, G. van (Eds.). *Strategies and structures in the agro-food industries*. Assen: Van Gorcum, p. 31-53.

HENSON, S.; REARDON, T. 2005. Private agri-food standards: implications for food policy and the agri-food system. *Food Policy* 30(3): 241-253.

HOBBS, J. E.; YOUNG, L. M. 2000. Closer vertical co-ordination in agri-food supply chains: a conceptual framework and some preliminary evidence. *Supply Chain Management* 5(3): 131-142.

HUETH, B.; MARCOUL, P. 2003. An essay on cooperative bargaining in U.S. Agricultural Markets. *Journal of Agricultural & Food Industrial Organization* 1(1): article 10.

JULIÁ-IGUAL, J. F.; Meliá E. 2007. Social economy and the cooperative movement in Europe: input to a new vision of agriculture and rural development in the Europe of the 25. *CIRIEC Working Paper* 2007/06.

KLEIN, B., CRAWFORD, R. G.; ALCHIAN, A. A. 1978. Vertical integration, appropriable rents, and the competitive contracting process. *Journal of Law and Economics* 21: 297-326.

KYRIAKOPOULOS, K., MEULENBERG, M.; NILSSON, J. 2004. The impact of cooperative structure and firm culture on market orientation and performance. *Agribusiness* 20(4): 379-396.

MALONE, T.W.; CROWSTON, K. 1994. The interdisciplinary study of coordination. *ACM Computing Surveys* 26(1): 87-119.

MAUGET, R.; DECLERCK, F. 1996. Structures, strategies, and performance of EC agricultural cooperatives. *Agribusiness* 12(3): 265-275.

MÉNARD, C. 2007. In: KARANTININIS, K.; NILSSON, J. (Eds.). *Cooperatives: hierarchies or hybrids?* Dordrecht, Springer, pp. 1-17.

MÉNARD, C.; VALCESCHINI, E. 2005. New institutions for governing the agri-food industry. *European Review Of Agricultural Economics* 32(3): 421-440.

MILGROM, P.; ROBERTS, J. 1995. Complementarities and fit strategy, structure, and organizational change in manufacturing. *Journal of Accounting and Economics* 19(2-3): 179-208.

MINTZBERG, H. 1979. *The structuring of organizations. A synthesis of the research*. Englewood Cliffs, N. J., Prentice-Hall.

NILSSON, J. 1999. Co-operative organisational models as reflections of the business environments. *Finnisch Journal of Business Economics* 4: 449-470.

NILSSON, J.; RUFFIO, P.; GOUIN, S. 2007. In: KARANTININIS, K.; NILSSON, J. (Eds.). *Do consumers care about cooperatives?* Dordrecht: Springer, p. 225-243.

POPPO, L.; ZENGER, T. 2002. Do formal contracts and relational governance function as substitutes or complements? *Strategic Management Journal* 23(8): 707-725.

RAYNAUD, E.; SAUVEE, L.; VALCESCHINI, E. 2005. Alignment between quality enforcement devices and governance structures in the agro-food vertical chains. *Journal of Management and Governance* 9: 47-77.

REYNOLDS, B. J. 1997. *Decision-making in cooperatives with diverse member interests*. RBS Research Report 155. Washington, DC, USDA/Rural Business-Cooperative Service.

ROYER, J. S. 1995. Potential for cooperative involvement in vertical coordination and value-added activities. *Agribusiness; An International Journal* 11(5): 473-481.

______; ROGERS, R. T. (Eds.). 1998. *The industrialization of agriculture. Vertical coordination in the U.S. food system*. Aldershot, Ashgate.

SCHRADER, L. 1989. Economic justification. In: COBIA, D. W. (Ed.). *Cooperatives in agriculture*. Englewood Cliffs: Prentice Hall, p. 121-136.

SIMON, H. A. 1991. Organizations and Markets. *Journal of Economic Perspectives* 5(2): 25-44.

STAATZ, J. M. 1987. The structural characteristics of farmer cooperatives and their behavioral consequences. *Cooperative theory: new approaches.* J. S. Royer. Washington, DC: USDA, Agricultural Cooperative Service: 33-60.

STINCHCOMBE, A. L. 1985. Contracts as hierarchical documents. In: STINCHCOMBE, A. L.; HEIMER, C. B. (Eds.). *Organizational theory and project management. Administrating uncertainty in norwegian offshore oil.* Oxford: Oxford University Press, p. 121-171.

TEECE, D. J. 1988. Technological change and the nature of the firm. In: DOSI, G.; FREEMAN, C.; NELSON, R.; SILVERBERG, G.; SOETE, L. *Technical change and economic theory.* London/New York: Pinter Publishers, p. 256-281.

THOMPSON, J. D. 1967. *Organizations in action. Social science bases of administrative theory.* New York: McGraw-Hill.

WILLIAMSON, O. E. 1985. *The economic institutions of capitalism. Firms, markets, relational contracting.* New York: Free Press.

ZENGER, T. R.; LAZZARINI, S. G.; POPPO, L. 2002. Informal and formal organization in new institutional economics, In: INGRAM, P.; SILVERMAN, B. S. (Eds.). *New institutionalism in strategic management.* Amsterdam: JAI-Elsevier Science, v. 19, p. 277-305.

The Road to Institutional Scientific Collaboration in Chains and Networks

PETER J. P. ZUURBIER

The 17th century showed some interesting examples of Dutch international business, when some ships landed on the shores of Brazil. Entrepreneurship, strong will and the longing for discovering the world and precious products created the backbone of what may be called afterwards an international strategy. At the heart of the endeavors was a strong network of companies and institutions within the Netherlands to create the (first) multinational company, Verenigde Oostindische Compagnie (VOC, East Indian Company) and later Westindische Compangie (WIC, West Indian Company).

After 1654, the Dutch left, the Portuguese took over again.

After those moments in history the Dutch ships called for Brazilian ports until the day of today. Trade increased rapidly in the last 20 years, Dutch-Brazilian mergers and acquisitions took place, public-private partnerships emerged. Within this context the scientific collaboration got more grounding. The first Wageningen alumni landed in Brazil in the late forties. Scientific linkages became stronger, and finally the Wageningen University-USP-FEA agreement was undersigned in 1996.

Science in the modern life sciences, where agriculture, food, natural resources, health and climate are coming together, has been named as the major production factor in the new bio-based economy. But how does it work and what role do institutions like universities play in this ballgame? In this contribution, an analysis is given of the development of Wageningen University and Research Center. I address the following issues:

- the fundamentals of Wageningen UR
- the creation of Wageningen as an answer to societal demands
- the development from a closed to an open scientific network organization
- the third generation scientific institution and the emergence of research networks and
- the impacts on the collaboration between Wageningen UR and USP.

1. Fundamentals of Wageningen University and Research Center

Wageningen University and Research Center (Wageningen UR) does not exist. From a legal point of view, Wageningen University evolved out of the Wageningen Agricultural University in 1986, formerly called Agricultural College Wageningen, founded in 1918.. The Foundation Agricultural Research Organization (in Dutch: Dienst landbouwkundig Onderzoek) was a part of the Ministry of Agriculture Nature Conservation and Food Quality until 1998. In that year the two big entities got a new leadership for both organizations, leaving the legal entities as they were. This administrative merger resulted into Wageningen UR; the turn-around strategy started in 1998. New institutes were added such as the International Agricultural Center in 2002 and the polytechnic university vanHall/Larenstein in 2004.

Wageningen UR is now one of the largest knowledge institutions in the area of agricultural, animal, food, environmental and related social sciences globally, with 6500 employees, a annual budget of 600 million euro and a strong position in research, education and outreach activities.

In Europe Wageningen became in its domain one of the largest beneficiaries of the EU research funds. The private sector became more and more involved in research focused public-private partnerships and in 2006 the Dutch government prioritized the main research areas for the future. Food and flower were selected as main focal domains for Dutch scientific budget allocation. The question is how this success can be explained?

2. Drivers in the Scientific Domain

In his opening address Hans Wissema (2005) distinguishes various generations of universities. According to his typology, Wissema discusses the first, Medieval, and second, Humboldt, generation of universities. The second one emphasizes the symbiotic integration of research and education, the scientific method, mono-disciplinary specialization and the dominance of the professor as head of his group of students and fellows. Wissema shows the limitations of this type of university, not being capable of adapting to the massive influx of students in the last decades of the 20th century, the demand for multi-disciplinary research, new themes, methods and scientific paradigms and the emergence of specialized research institutes, limiting the monopolistic position of universities in society. These global developments contributed to the search for new modes of functioning internally, new approaches of positioning universities and new relations between universities and society. The impacts became visible in:

- the strong entry of private universities into the academic arena
- new modes of financing of universities from input budgeting to output or result oriented budgeting
- competitive funding of research and
- the need for co-operation between peers to get access to larger funds and grants.

3. Internationalization Within Europe

In this new environment many universities were invited and, some, enforced to cross the institutional barriers. First, for getting access to funding of research and/or education. Second, for offering expertise to new customers; companies and public institutions who were put on distance for long, but now regained interest from the academics; partly to get access to funding as well, partly to get a license for research from these new customers. And from a scientific perspective, collaboration became a necessity, to share expertise and resources for acquiring expensive equipments, laboratories and facilities. In the European Union, this development took place during the eighties and nineties, when European research programs were installed for research. These programs set conditions for getting the funding: collaboration between groups from several European countries became a conditio sine qua non for European research projects. The administrative burden, and transaction costs increased, while the chances for success rate dropped. This intra-European process of internationalization shaped the European research area. The European education area got a huge boosting when the Bologna agreement was accepted, setting the rules for the bachelor-master university programs on a pan-European scale.

4. Internationalization Globally

Due to the globalization in the scientific community, enhanced by information and communication technology and scientific interest into conducting larger research programs and staff mobility, internationalization got an extra impulse. In some cases, universities established campuses in other countries. In some other cases, universities established joint degree programs or licensed programs out to other universities. In this fast evolving environment, universities that did not participate in international research and/or educational programs lost the pace of scientific advancement. For the individual researcher or professor, it hardly became possible to cover all the transaction costs for getting informed about new tenders, calls or research agenda setting for research programs. Funding agencies persisted on strong project management; a task too large and complex for many individual scholars. New services entered the scientific market place; internal consultants, EU help desks, program info centers and subsidy brokers, who offer help by no cure no pay to get the funding right.

By these developments the need for getting better informed, building up new partnerships and staying on top of the scientific market asked for professionals located at funding agencies, at universities and intermediate institutions.

5. Agricultural Research and Development

From a sector point of view, agricultural research and development, as an umbrella concept covering all the related thematic areas like animal sciences, food and nutrition sciences and environmental sciences was faced with the dynamics at large in the scientific community and had to redefine the context for research.

Basically, agricultural research were meant for increasing agricultural productivity and generating income for farmers and the rural community. This could bring about alleviation of poverty and keep prices of agricultural products for the urban population relative low. Already in the nineties the International Food Policy Research Institute (IFPRI) concluded that the proportion of official development assistance devoted to agricultural decreased rapidly. At he same time, the concentration in the various sector of the private industry, such as the food manufacturing, seed, machinery and biotechnology sectors, increased and enabled these companies to focus on the intellectual property rights as a base of income. In Brazil, Embrapa as a State company for agricultural research, directly linked to the Ministry of Agriculture, expanded and contributed largely to the diffusion and adoption of innovations in the farming community. In the Netherlands, the reverse took place; public spending for agricultural research and education diminished and the public agricultural extension service was privatized and became a irrelevant factor.

6. Re-Inventing the Knowledge Asset

Due to the afore mentioned developments in the scientific arena and the specific developments in agricultural research, education and outreach, the Dutch government deciced to re-invent the knowledge assets in the agri and food cluster in the late nineties. As mentioned, the collusion of Wageningen University and the Agricultural Research Organization became a cornerstone of the new dynamics. However, more had to be done. Three main new strategies evolved:

1. the third generation public – private networks and
2. the global-local strategy and

7. The Third Generation Public-Private Networks

Due to pressure from society and the budget restrictions for public funded research, the Dutch government took an initiative in the nineties to start with top-technology centers, or centers of excellence. In the last fifteen years and more specifically, the last five years some of these institutes were established in the agri- and food cluster.

Here we mention the Top Institute Food and Nutrition and Green Genetics (GG).

8. Top Institute Food and Nutrition

In the face of today's challenge to make the healthy choice the easy choice, it is vital for the food industry and research organizations to pool knowledge and resources for multidisciplinary research. The Top Institute (TI) Food and Nutrition, formerly known as Wageningen Center for Food Sciences (WCFS), is a unique public/private partnership that generates vision on scientific breakthroughs in food and nutrition, resulting in the development of innovative products and technologies that respond to consumer demands for safe, tasty and healthy foods.

The justification for establishing the Institute was the result of an analysis of the interactions along the value chain: from societal needs via consumer needs to science (Figure 1).

The analysis of How to make better food was affected by factors that are affecting the Food Industry, such as the high speed of innovation, globalization in the food industry, differentiation of products to segments and the fast life cycle of food items.

Encouraged by this analysis and by government signals carrying a positive attitude towards co-financing a Top Institute, the initiators founded a public-private institute in 1997 to accelerate the food innovation process in the Dutch food industry.

Now the institute has an annual 40 million € budget and a critical mass of 200 scientists, seconded from various research institutes.

The financing is assured since then by the food companies (27%), participating research institutes (24%) and the Dutch government (48%).

Figure 1: Main drivers for better food

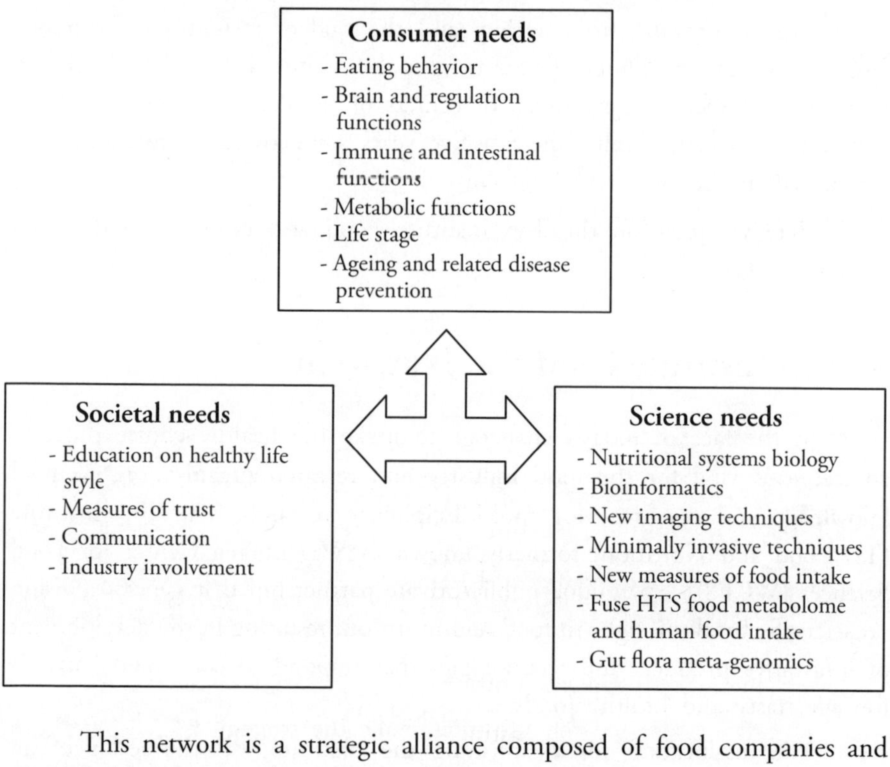

This network is a strategic alliance composed of food companies and research institutes, with a strong focus on fundamental research at pre-competitive level.

The institute is a virtual organization. Research groups are doing their work in their own research institute labs.

The virtual organization is output-driven, as defined by scientific publications, citation index scores, patents and, not the least, partners satisfaction. So far 540 scientific publications and 35 patents were delivered.

Because of the virtual nature and strong focused lines of research programs and projects, access to combined facilities and expertise of partners became a cornerstone for speeding up the knowledge base of the Institute. The virtual nature of the organization enables a high level of flexibility where appointments are defined by the length of the project awarded. For the scientist working in this environment offers them the highest level of competence and sharing of knowledge.

The Institute committees and Board facilitate the process of orchestrating the research process based on market trends, strategic considerations and innovation challenges, translated to 'knowledge needs'. Priorities and selection of research programs are decided upon by the partner companies and research institutes.

Now, in 2008 the main themes are:

- nutrition and health including nutrigenomics
- functionality and safety and
- microbial functionality and structure.

According to the partners the Critical Success Factors for the success of the Institute are:

- All-in partnership (no tickets but passe-partout)
- Virtual institute structure
- Integrated knowledge and value chain from the start
- Long-term research strategy of industrial partners
- Substantial financial contribution by government
- Industry & research institutes make the strategy
- Facilitating role of government and,most important,
- Trust and confidence in the partnership

9. Green Genetics

The Netherlands has a long tradition on breeding vegetables and flowers. This tradition goes back to the 19th century, when the first breeding companies start to produce and sell new variety seeds.

The importance of the seed industry today is shown in Figure 2.

Figure 2: Export of seed products (2006)

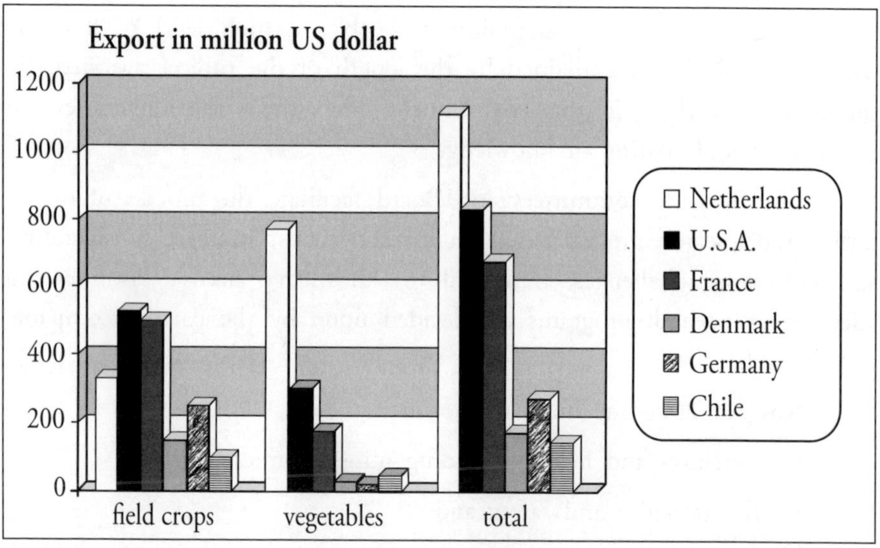

New varieties have improved traits e.g. such as higher yield, resistances to pathogens and insects, improved quality (taste, health) and/or resistances to a-biotic stress (e.g. drought). The demands from downstream the value chain are translated to producers/growers and translated, next, to breeding companies. The economic value is immense as the following example shows.

Tomato seed

Price per seed €0,20

Tomato fruit value per seed €16,00

Grower pays per kg seed €50.000,00

Value per kg seed for grower €3.500.000,00

Value per kg seed for retailer €7.000.000,00.

The value adding by breeding companies is restricted by the time lapse: it takes 5 to 9 years to bring new varieties to the market, due to the length of time for breeding and the administrative procedures in most countries to get a license to market the new product. On top of that, the vegetable market contains numbers of products of which the most important ones are tomato, lettuce, bell peppers and melon.

Not surprising, that individual companies in the vegetable seed industry look for ways how to speed up the time-to-market.

This brought some companies to establish alliances and/or mergers. Nowadays 40 companies play a major role globally. The largest are Seminis Vegetable Seeds, Vilmoin Clause and Cie., Syngenta, Takii, Sakata, Nunhems, Rijk Zwaan, ENZA Zaden, Bejo Zaden and De Ruiter Seeds. Not surprisingly, due to the Dutch network of seed companies, that some of these established a network in 1989: BioSeeds-Keygene in the field of molecular plant biotechnology. This upstream stage in the value chain could hardly be covered by the individual companies, due to expertise, high costs and uncertainty. This network has resulted in a strong position in applied genetics and molecular breeding, a patent position in molecular technologies and traits and a leading position in the application of molecular markers in breeding. By consequence, new cultivars were developed by using these technologies.

So, the first stage of building a stronger industry network started by an alliance of companies.

The next stage in the process of network development became visible when the Dutch government established the Dutch Genomics Initiative. The Netherlands Plant Genomic Network focused on

- environmental quality, linking scientists that work on genomics of various plant-pathogen interactions, and
- Consumer and Industrial Quality, gathering scientists working on the transcriptome, proteome and metabolome of plants in relation to aspects of quality, health and storability.

The Center for Biosystems Genomics (CBSG) facilitates the network that is composed of several Dutch universities and research institutes, the potato breeding and processing industry, tomato breeding industry and Keygene, the consortium of seed companies. Unraveling the tomato genome became one of the challenges. The potential benefits for the seed companies were obvious: a complete understanding of the function and structure of the genome enables companies to improve their varieties also by non-GMO interventions.

The next stage in the development of the seed network was the establishing of Green Genetics, a Top Institute that develops and applies genetic information for the creation of crops with improved performance and improved quality. This virtual organization has been composed by innovative companies active in breeding, tissue culture, biotechnology and genetic services such as bio-informatics companies. Top universities and research institutes are accomplishing the scientific function.

One of the characteristics is the governance of the network. Industrial partners have the 50% majority vote in decision-making although their financial part is less (23%). Industry determines the research themes and projects and are responsible for the economic value creation. The government assures a long term coverage of the budget (50%), and the research partners cover the rest (22%). The total annual budget is 50 million euro.

The core focuses on expertise development and capacity building in the three basic disciplines: genetics, phytopathology and physiology. The core program will disburse approximately 20% of the TTI budget (15% for research and 5% for education) and comprehends a limited number of integrated research and education projects.

Summarizing, TTI Green Genetics is a virtual institute that uses the existing infrastructure of the research partners. It consists of a public-private partnership in which industry together with the top-level research groups of Dutch universities and technology and service providers co-operate in a coherent program.

The (small) organization itself is responsible for acquiring and managing research and educational projects.

Most of the actual research activities (of both the core and the cluster projects) take place at the research groups' locations.

The industrial partners lead the consortium and have a 50%+ vote in all decision-making bodies.

The total organization and office costs are budgeted at a maximum of 5% of the total budget.

The legal form of TTI Green Genetics is a not-for-profit foundation according to Dutch law.

10. The Two Examples Compared

The comparison of the two examples show some interesting results.

	Institute for Food and Nutrition	Green Genetics
Governance	Public-private partnership; virtual institute	Public-private partnership: virtual network
Role of government	Strong: facilitator and sponsor	First moderate, now strong as facilitator and sponsor
Asset	Fundamental knowledge on food-health interaction	Fundamental knowledge on structure&function of genetics
Demand driven	By society and consumers	By vegetable customers in the value chain
Innovation system	Semi-closed innovation: open within the network	Semi-closed innovation: open within parts of the network
Critical factor	Time-to-market from scientific output to product innovation	Volatility in customer demands

The examples described here, offer ground for the following hypotheses.

First networks do evolve over time, based on a perceived benefit, are volatile by nature and change their profiles depending on dynamics in the network environment.

Second, the more pre-competitive the binding asset, the easier the access for participation by the private partners. However, the strength of weak ties might inhibit a strong basis for the network. This might invite public partners to step in. Their role mainly is to facilitate the establishment of the network, reducing financial risks and uncertainties.

Last, the performance of networks depend partly on some critical factors. Based on the examples the following factors might be distinguished. The success depends on:

- Industry & research institutes make the strategy
- Long-term research strategy of industrial partners

- Facilitating role of government
- Substantial financial contribution by government
- Trust and confidence in the partnership
- All-in partnership
- Virtual institute structure
- Integrated knowledge and value chain from the start.

11. The Global-local Strategy

Most universities have an operational international strategy. This strategy offers students and staff exchange, and exchange of scientific information and material.

Sometimes this strategy has been officially put in a memorandum of understanding (Mou). Some institutions are proud having hundreds of these documents, whatever the impacts are.

There are few institutions with a profound view on how to establish a strong loosely-coupled network of science and society. Some privatized universities are implementing a global horizontal network of campuses, either virtual or physical. All under the same name or logo, using the same curricula, setting the same quality standards and having the same objective. Within Brazil famous examples are COC, Ibmec and FGV. In the Netherlands private universities falling in the category of global institutions are Webster and Rochester.

Public universities are in most cases slower in adapting to the new environment. Some of these established new campuses, facilitated by national educational reforms and policies. Within Brazil, the University of Sao Paulo was offered the opportunity to expand the number of campuses within the State of Sao Paulo.

Another strategy universities deployed in recent years, was the establishing of research institutions, centers or networks, mainly within the university. This border spanning activity served the purpose to elaborate on a society or science relevant theme, build critical mass and going beyond the traditional departmental borders. A nice example is PENSA, embedded within the Faculty of Economy and Administration of the USP, and established and developed by Decio Zylbersztajn.

A third strategy goes beyond the university borders, the national borders and the temporarily consortia timelines. This strategic partnership on an institutional level falls into the category of pre-joint ventures and or pre-mergers. This strategy is emerging in some places in the world. In business, this phenomenon is rather familiar. For example, two companies establish a joint-venture: the first company has a particular product portfolio and the other company a particular distribution channel. Within the joint-venture the two "mother" companies create a autonomous joint-venture to access the market with the product portfolio.

In the academic market place, cross-border joint-ventures come rather close to the third generation public-private networks. However, these networks do have a rather geographical narrow scope. In the global-local framework, geographical borders are becoming irrelevant, however the institutions do not. This strategy captures the best of two worlds: the "mother" universities invest into newly established joint-venture and build up competitive advantage by offering services on a regional or on a global scale, capitalizing on the string of cutting edge knowledge and technologies that originate in the "mother" institutions.

12. Impacts on USP-FEA and Wageningen UR Collaboration

The collaboration between USP-FEA and the department of management Studies of Wageningen University started in 1994, when Prof. Decio Zylberstajn and the author met at a IAMA congress. The emergence of the relationship offered opportunities to meet in Brazil, the Netherlands and several other places in the world, where the demand for knowledge on chains and networks existed.

The PENSA program at USP-FEA created a vehicle for institutional collaboration, undersigned in 1996 and renewed after every 5 years.

The establishing of the Agro Competence center (ACC/AKK) in the mid nineties offered an additional opportunity to identify research project on chains and networks in the Netherlands, Brazil and other places in the world. More and more scientific articles were published, the Chain Conferences in Wageningen and the PENSA Chain Conference in Brazil brought many people from all places of the world together to share experiences, improve methodologies and expand the theoretical stock of knowledge.

Based on personal relationships and trust, the chain and network paradigms became more and more familiar in science and in industry. Nowadays, the concepts have been embedded in practice, business models and science.

The examples described in this article give evidence of the impacts of the rich content of chain and network concepts and theories and the value for practice in the private and public arena.

13. Conclusion

Chain and network concepts became the carrier for the collaboration between Wageningen University and USP-FEA. The theoretical underpinning offered by neo-institutional economics, social capital theory, strategic management paradigms offered a wealth of ideas, experiments, workshops, publications and debates. The strong collaboration showed the basic fundamentals of scientific advancement: trust and curiosity. Does that mean that the PENSA- Wageningen model will evolve into a stronger relationship? Well, due to the relationship, Wageningen UR and USP built up a stronger nexus in 2007. USP offered at the Campus Esalq office space for the Latin America Office of Wageningen UR. This office has the objective to built large research programs on themes that are relevant both for the strategic partners and Wageningen UR. In the Brazilian environment, it is not surprising that large programs on biofuels and natural resources are underway. USP and Wageningen UR are getting more and more involved into the strategic partnership model. The future? A joint venture between both institutions on Biofuel Research?

Part 3

Quality and Safety

- Best Practice Quality Systems in Food Chains
- Public and Private Mechanisms in Food Safety
- Designing Risk Profiles in Food Supply Chains; an Assessment of Classification Criteria

Best Practice Quality Systems in Food Chains

WIJNAND VAN PLAGGENHOEF

JACQUES TRIENEKENS

ONNO OMTA

1. Introduction

Concerns about quality and safety in agri-food supply chains have been raised among consumers, especially due sector-wide crises, such as the BSE crisis. The EU and the national governments have reacted on the above mentioned crises by setting up regulations for quality and safety of agri-food products. Furthermore, retailers have introduced quality management standards in which they impose quality requirements on their suppliers. However, concerns have been raised about the (administrative) burdens being placed on firms, because firms must comply with many private and public quality regulations. In order to reduce the compliance burdens, European governments want to assign the private sector more responsibility for compliance. In order to comply with the quality requirements, closely coupled agri-food supply chains have emerged in which a platform is established for open communication about specifications and chain process improvements which results in a mutual commitment for each other's quality requirements. Moreover, the exchanges of outcomes of quality tests and inspections, results in more possibilities for enforcement of quality requirements. This paper aims at recommendations for managers and policy makers for establishing self regulated and integrated quality management systems in agri-food supply chains. The study is a follow-up study of a large scale survey performed in three food chains.

1.1 Theoretical Model and Survey

Plaggenhoef (2007) developed a research model for integration and self-regulation of quality management in food chains, building on (elements of) various theoretical streams from literature: Supply Chain Management (SCM), Transaction Cost Theory (TCT), Quality Management theory, Contingency theory and theory on Self Regulation.

SCM (Vorst, 2000; Trienekens and Beulens, 2001; Cooper et al., 1997; Lambert et al., 1998; Vorst, 2004) emphasises the importance of information exchange by means of ICT which can be regarded as a catalyst for successful integration of supply chain processes. TCT (Williamson, 1991, 1996; Barney & Hesterley, 1999; Rindfleisch & Heide, 1997) underlines the impact of transaction specific investments (TSIs) as needed for the integration of quality management. Due to strong collaboration in chains supported by these investments, opportunistic behaviour of the chain partners is to a large extent prevented. Furthermore, external drivers (media attention, legislative demands, changing consumer demands and societal demands for corporate social responsibility) put pressure on firms to integrate their quality management. From a Contingency Theory perspective (Lawrence and Lorsch, 1967; Zajac and Shortell, 1989; Powel, 1992) a firm that faces more external pressures will be more inclined to integrate its quality management systems with its suppliers and buyers whereby the importance of the own quality strategy for the success of this integration is emphasised. As was already argued, the integration of quality management with suppliers and buyers is expected to have a positive impact on self regulation (Havinga, 2006; King and Lenox, 2005; De Bakker et al, 2007; Amstel et al., 2006) (in this study explained by the constructs commitment and enforcement), because firms get common goals and transparency in the chain, which enables them better to control each other. Quality Management theories (Spiegel, 2004; Luning, 2002; Sousa and Voss, 2002) are used in our research model to define the most important elements of quality management in a supply chain perspective. Due to intensive collaboration in the chain, for example, on quality management, higher performance for the individual firms in the chain is expected. Literature on buyer-supplier relationships frequently states that increased performance is likely to be best achieved by means of committed suppliers and buyers. For measuring performance of a firm buyer satisfaction and revenue growth of the firm were used. These thoughts are summarised in Figure 1.

Figure 1: Theoretical model (Plaggenhoef, 2007)

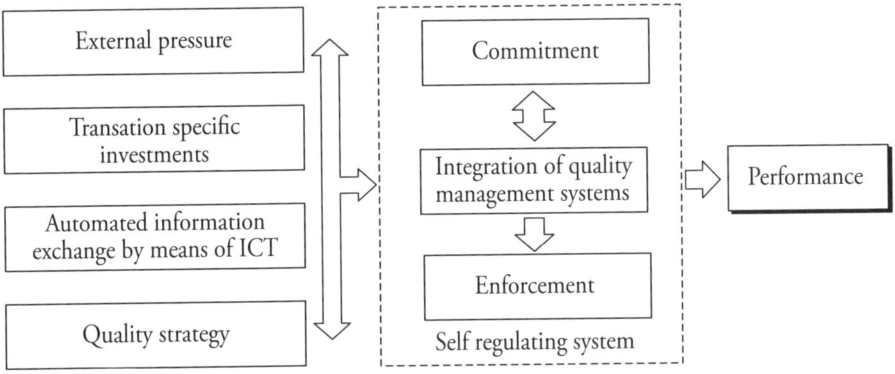

In this paper we address three research questions:

1. Which (internal and external) factors have an impact on the integration of quality management systems in agri-food supply chains?
2. How do integrated quality management systems affect self regulation and performance in agri-food supply chains?
3. What is the best way to create self regulated quality management systems in agri-food supply chains?

2. Methodology

An important feature of the study is that it collects data from both the supplier and the buyer side of the firm and includes two successive stages in each chain (primary producers and traders and/or processors). This approach ensures the proper implementation of the SCM approach. Until now, most studies were limited to data collection in the firm or solely about the suppliers or buyers.

The poultry meat chain, the fruit and vegetable chain and the flower and potted plant chain were chosen because:

1. These chains are valid representations of the agri-food sector, they are characterised by a large diversity of marketing channels and products.

2. All these chains are of great interest for the Dutch economy, especially with regard to export
3. All the three chains pay a lot of attention to quality management.

A survey was conducted among primary producers, processors and/or traders in the three chains. The primary goal of the survey was to investigate the relationships in the theoretical model.

In total 585 firms reacted to the survey. Table 1 shows the distribution of the respondents across the chains involved. Data were analysed with multiple regression, confirmatory factor analysis and structural equation modeling (Plaggenhoef, 2007). Based on the analysis of the survey, it turned out that the general research model was highly generalisable for the different kinds of firms involved in the study. Therefore, it could be regarded as a robust model for studying quality management and self regulation in agri-food supply chains. However, the measured levels of quality management in the flower and potted chain was significantly lower compared to the poultry meat en the fruit en vegetable chain. An explanation is that food safety does not play a role in the flower and potted plant chain.

Table 1: Number of firms per chain

Firm	Number of firms			Total
	Poultry meat	Fruit and vegetables	Flowers and potted plants	
Primary producers	116	151	102	369
Traders/processors	34	98	84	216
Total	150	249	186	585

The study has shown that if firms perceive stronger external pressures, their quality management systems will be more integrated with suppliers and buyers (see Figure 2). Many of the pressures are not aimed at specific firms, but often influence all firms in a supply chain. However, incorrect actions of only one firm in the supply chain may result in increasing external pressures on all firms in the chain. By integrating quality management systems in agri-food supply chains, managers try to prevent this.

Taking a closer look at "external pressures", Interestingly, legislative demands have hardly any impact on the integration of quality management systems with buyers and suppliers, while *media attention, societal demands for corporate social responsibility* and *changing consumer demands* have a great impact.

TSIs and integrated ICT systems (for example 'tracking and tracing systems') also contribute to the successful integration of quality management systems. Integration and collaboration on quality lowers the risks for opportunistic behaviour. Firms send an important signal to other parties in the chain that the relationship is highly valued by TSIs and integration of quality management systems. Interestingly, the quality strategy of the focal firm has an impact on the integration of quality management with the suppliers, but not with the buyers. The most likely explanation is that firms are able to impose their quality requirements upstream, but not downstream in the chain. When selecting suppliers, the firm is able to let its interest for quality management play an important role, whereas this is much more difficult in the choice of its buyers.

The study showed empirical evidence that integrated quality management systems are strongly positively related to self regulation, see Figure 3. Due to the integration of quality management systems a platform is established for open communication about specifications and chain process improvements which results in a mutual understanding and commitment for each other's quality requirements. Moreover, the exchanges of outcomes of quality test and – inspections, results in more possibilities for enforcement of quality requirements.

Another finding of the study is that integration of quality management leads to higher performance. Firms that have integrated their quality management systems with their suppliers and buyers achieve higher levels of performance (both for buyer satisfaction and revenue growth, performance indicators used in the survey). This effect is achieved by commitment of the parties in the chain and not by means of enforcement. A policy that is focused too much on enforcement and sanctions has no effect in the supplier model and works even detrimentally in the buyer model. Enforcement has the potential to result in conflicts with suppliers, especially if sanctions are imposed that are perceived to be unjust or unreasonable. However, although a large majority of firms will comply with quality requirements as well as possible and too strong enforcement is de-motivating for them, a certain level of enforcement is needed for firms that will behave opportunistically.

Figure 2: Factors influencing integration of quality management with the supplier (left) and buyer (right); no line means no significant relationship

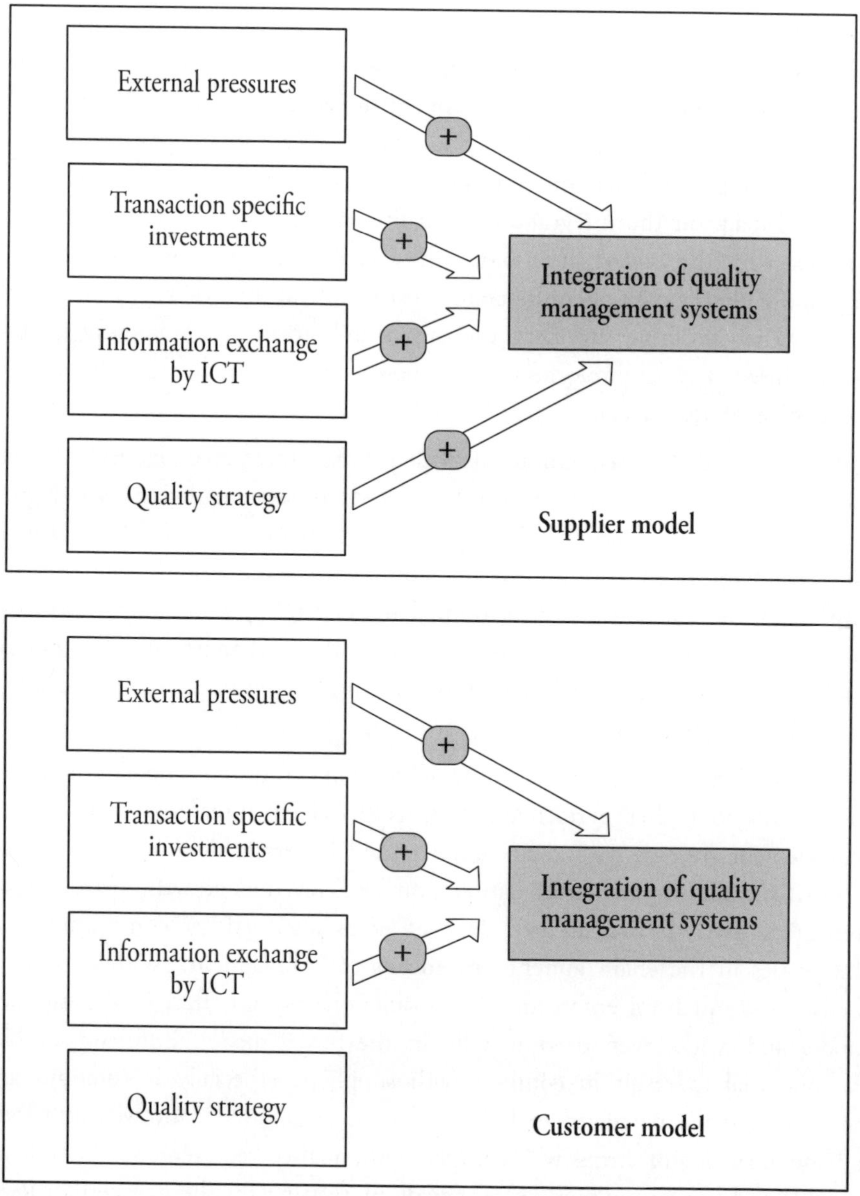

Figure 3: Impact of integration of quality management on self regulation and performance of firms in agri-food supply chains (dashed arrow means weak significant relationship)

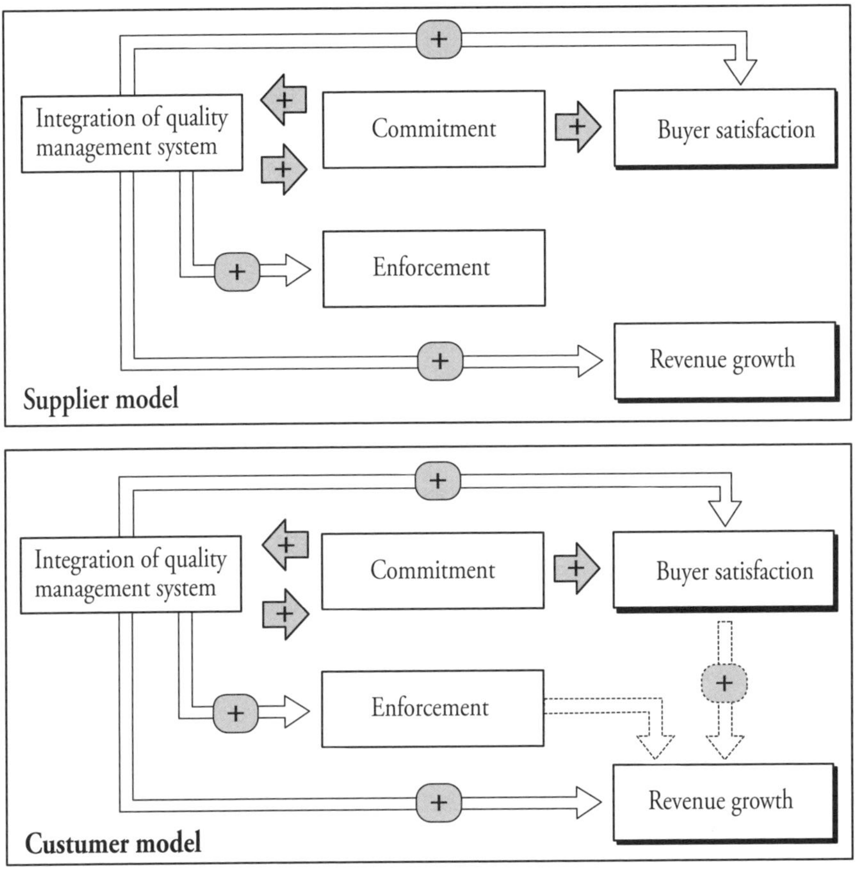

3. Research into Best Practices

Based on these outcomes of the survey 14 in-depth interviews were held with key stakeholders of the three chains. These were stakeholders that were well-informed about best practices in quality management in these chains. The interviews were carried out from July to September 2006. Willingness to participate in an interview was asked in a personal phone call in which the objective of the interview was explained. None of the potential experts refused. For each chain involved in this study the objective was to interview at least:

- One primary producer
- One trader and/or processor
- One person employed at an interest organisation (e.g. Products Board or trade association)
- One certifier

The study successfully achieved this objective, however, in the poultry meat sector no certifier was included, because the interviewed poultry farmer had a very broad knowledge of the sector and could easily make comparisons between different quality management systems.[1] Another reason was that two representatives of the Product Boards of Livestock, Meat and Eggs (PVE) were involved, assuring the 'helicopter' view in this chain. In total, fourteen people were interviewed. Their working experience ranged from two years to thirty years, with an average of nineteen years. For these experts quality management was their full time job, assuring that experts were well informed about quality management and self regulation. Firms included in the study were relatively large firms from an agri-food perspective. Those firms often have more resources available to build 'best practice' quality management systems and to deliver products to buyers that have very stringent quality requirements. The outcomes of the in-depth interviews are presented according to the research model presented in Figure 1.

3.1 Factors Influencing Integration of Quality Management

The main factors influencing integration of quality management, as described in the research model were:

- External pressure
- Transaction specific investments (TSIs)
- Information exchange by ICT
- Quality strategy.

[1] In the past this poultry farmer was involved in different research activities, has been asked as a speaker on several congresses and attended many meetings in which representatives of the poultry chain were invited.

The outcomes for these factors in the in-depth interviews are discussed below.

External Pressure

For most experts in the in-depth interviews it was difficult to give examples of 'best practices' on how to deal with external pressures on individual firms. The business environment was regarded as unpredictable and firms had only limited influence on it. Moreover, most pressures from the business environment were often not targeted at one specific firm but groups of firms or even a whole sector.

Nine of the fourteen experts mentioned that in many sectors quality management systems exist that deal with specific quality requirements. Compliance with such systems can be regarded as a 'best practice' for dealing with the external pressures. In the fruit and vegetable chain an example is Nature's Choice initiated by the British retailer Tesco. In this system, besides the requirements that are comparable with Eurep-GAP (a common retail standard in fresh produce chains), firms must have a plan for managing the business environment, including detailed actions, such as, protecting and encouraging wildlife diversity. Pollution control and energy use are also important parts of the scheme, with specific controls on discharges to local watercourses, and energy use reviews by independent third parties. Participating in sector-wide initiatives can be regarded as another 'best practice' for dealing with certain pressures. These initiatives are usually developed by interest organisations or Product Boards.

Transaction Specific Investments (TSIs)

At least eight experts mentioned TSIs in quality conscious personnel to effectively deal with the specific quality requirements of their buyers. For example, a pepper grower who was delivering to Tesco trained his personnel in the detection, recognition and report of harmful insects and plant diseases.

One expert from the flowers and potted plant sector mentioned the participation in a highly specialised quality system of a grower association as an example of a TSI. Before a grower can fully participate in the quality system a learning trajectory is started. During the learning period the grower pays only 20% of the quality costs. When the grower has reached the desired quality level.

Information Exchange by ICT

In each chain investigated, large integrated ICT systems exist between buyers and suppliers. Four experts mentioned that especially the large traders and or processors are initiators of these standardised ICT systems. For example, a big fruit and vegetable trader has developed an Internet based system to which suppliers deliver requested quality data. The outcomes of quality tests and inspections are (anonymously) published on a web site on which firms can log in and compare their own scores with the scores of others. For many firms benchmarking is an extra stimulus to try to be the best performing firm in their sector.

Five experts emphasised that quality management systems should not be stand alone systems in the chain, but should be integrated with e.g. production management. For example, the quality management system of a slaughterhouse also includes information monitoring, for example, on which feed and medicines were used during the growing period of chickens at the farms. Due to this integration of quality management, firms gain more insight in their production processes, which increases and provides more possibilities for improvement.

Quality Strategy

One expert stressed that a firm should have a clear strategy on which position quality management should take relative to the other activities of a firm. If quality management is integrated with the commercial, financial and personnel strategy of the firm, it will more easily be supported by the personnel and it will not be regarded as a bureaucratic burden. If the main interest of a firm is to obtain a quality certificate, but it does not have an appropriate quality strategy, the quality management system will not be successful in the long term.

Often awareness of the importance of quality management starts at the strategic level, and goes down through the whole firm or chain. The personnel will find it in their working instructions and the management will have to give good examples to its personnel.

3.2 *Self Regulating Behaviour*

The in-depth interviews paid paramount attention to self regulation and its dimensions, *commitment* and *enforcement*. Attention was also paid to the roles of industry organisations, certifying organisations and interest organisations, such as Product Boards and trading associations, in designing self regulated quality management systems.

Commitment

For many traders and/or processors it is a challenge to tie the best performing suppliers on quality to their firm. Three traders and two primary producers emphasise the presence of supplier panels. These panels serve as communication channels between suppliers and buyers and are very useful for increasing commitment.

In this study (Plaggenhoef, 2007) commitment consists of the individual dimensions 'knowledge and clarity of regulations', 'the (im) material (dis) advantages of regulations', 'the degree to which regulations are accepted', the willingness to comply with regulations' and 'the chance of discovering and sanctioning by third parties'. These are discussed in detail below. This discussion reveals the experts' opinions about how self regulation should be improved.

The Knowledge and Clarity of Regulations

Four experts mentioned that most private quality systems in agri-food chains are accredited systems, which means that the regulations and procedures are clearly described and are supervised by an independent Council of Accreditation. According to them, in this way, it is completely clear to firms what the requirements of private quality management systems are. Five experts mentioned that, however, the public regulations from the government were sometimes difficult to understand.

The (im) Material (dis) Advantages of Non-compliance

Experts like the idea and the emerging practice in which good performing firms on quality are inspected less frequently by the VWA than bad performing firms. If the costs of these controls are charged to firms it introduces a bonus-malus principle for compliance with quality requirements. This approach could increase the motivation of firms to adopt quality regulations, because they know that compliance with the (private) quality management systems will result in lower inspections.

Three experts mentioned that legislative demands on quality management result in (logistic) problems in the production processes. An expert from a big poultry processor reported that legislative demands on inspections constrained his production process. For example, in The Netherlands a maximum of 9,000 chickens per hour is allowed to be slaughtered, because otherwise controlling agents are not able to control the total flow. This is quite low compared to Belgium and Germany, where 11,000 and 12,000 chickens per hour are slaughtered.

The Degree to Which Regulations are Accepted

Audits make quality requirements more acceptable to firms. If a firm has a certified quality system, the audit is a learning process, in which auditors take the total structure of the firm into account. For example, how processes are organised and how information is communicated within the firm. An auditor is not regarded as a police officer, but as an improver of the firms' processes. Experts would like governmental agencies to work like auditors, because the added value of an auditor is that he helps the entrepreneur to find the balance between the quality requirements and how these requirements should be met within the firm.

The Willingness to Comply with Regulations

Three experts mentioned that The Netherlands has an important competitive advantage for the introduction of self regulation. In almost all agricultural sectors there is an extensive network of industry organisations, Product Boards and other kinds of associations which represent many firms. These organisations are often active in translating new or changed legislation to their members. This results in a higher willingness to comply with quality regulations.

The Chance of Discovery and Sanctioning by Third Parties

The VWA expert reported that based on Regulation EU 882/2004[2] it is necessary to be transparent about the outcomes of inspections of con-

2 http://eur-lex.europa.eu/LexUriServ/site/nl/consleg/2004/R/02004R0882-20060525--nl.pdf.

trolling agencies. In fact this regulation introduces among others a kind of societal control by the public. The Ministry of Agriculture, Nature and Food Quality and the Ministry of Health, Welfare and Sport have decided that the fruit and vegetable sector will be a pilot sector to work out this EU regulation. The VWA has launched a web site in which all the results of the residual controls are published with the names of the traders and retailers ('blame-and-shame' approach). If the products fail, it is mentioned on which aspects and whether these aspects are harmful to human health. This approach may increase the efforts of firms to comply with quality management regulations.

The expert further warns that when the government introduces more frequent inspections for bad performing firms and less frequent inspections for good performing firms, the probability of finding an offence will become much higher. When these outcomes are published it might seem that the number of non-compliances in The Netherlands is high, especially if these outcomes are used for comparisons across countries.

Enforcement

Regarding enforcement, experts pointed out that almost all big market parties, especially retailers, have summarised their quality requirements for suppliers in certified systems. Independent auditors take care of the compliance with such systems and in case of repetitive non-compliance firms will lose their certificate.

However, in case of very stringent quality regulations firms might fake compliance with regulations by manipulating measurements. When faking compliance, it might seem that these stringent regulations are having some effect, but in practice they do not.

The dimensions of enforcement in this study are 'creditability' and 'sanctioning' (Plaggenhoef, 2007).

Creditability (Chance of Control, Chance of Detection and Chance of Selection)

The expert from the VWA stated that for the introduction of reliable self regulation it is necessary for certifiers to employ highly qualified independent auditors. Auditors should have the time, knowledge and experience to judge the system on its contents. This enables them to make a judgement on whether all hazards are clearly identified, whether these hazards are really hazards, and whether corrective and preventive actions are needed. According to the expert of the VWA some quality systems deal with the transfer of responsibility to the suppliers and not really with the assurance of quality itself. Another point of attention with regard to the creditability according to this expert was that the government takes care of exact compliance with requirements, whereas in many private quality management systems the certificate is obtained if a firm complies with a certain percentage of the requirements.

The experts further argued that certifiers know firms and develop relationships with them in which improvement of quality management is very important. As a result they have more insight in the problems and can help to resolve problems.

Sanctions

According to the expert from the VWA the introduction of a Council of Accreditation is a critical success factor for the introduction of self regulation. The commercial relationship between firms and certifiers could hamper certifiers in their sanction possibilities. If a certifier states that a certain firm does not deserve the certificate the firm might go to another certifier. According to an expert from the VWA this could be quite simple for firms, because there is a strong competition between certifiers. However, two experts explicitly mentioned that the common sanction for repeated non-compliance is withdrawal of the certificate or exclusion from delivery, which is much more effective for a firm than a fine. In this regard, retailers themselves are very keen to enforce quality regulations.

According to a firm expert the VWA should not worry about the strictness of sanctions in certified quality management systems. However, firm experts warn that the government should take care of firms that operate at the bottom of the market where certificates have less value.

3.3 Performance

Performance was measured by using an operational indicator, buyer satisfaction and a financial performance indicator, revenue growth of the focal firm. Both are discussed below.

Buyer Satisfaction

Eight experts explicitly mentioned that in business relationships with strongly integrated quality management systems firms take the initiative to make customised appointments to monitor, to align and to improve the production processes.

As already stated, six experts mentioned that firms choose to co-operate with firms that have a similar attitude toward quality management. These firms are often in close contact with each other to achieve common goals. Within these relationships clear appointments are made about the way these goals should be achieved.

Three experts mentioned that for achieving buyer satisfaction, commitment is much more important than enforcement. If the relationship is good, problems are usually solved in good harmony.

Revenue Growth

Most experts found that, besides bringing gains to the company, quality management systems result in higher costs due to costs for auditing, administration and training. Quality management systems cost money, particularly in the implementation phase. Moreover, the exact revenues of good quality management are often difficult to quantify. One expert thought that the relationship between revenue growth and integration of quality management was behaving according to the law of decreasing margins. Thus, if a firm improves from a bad level of quality management, the revenue growth will be great. However, if a firm has already achieved a high quality level, improvements will not contribute much to revenue growth any more.

4. Implications for Managers and Policy Makers

4.1 Implications for Managers

The recommendations for managers are focused on establishing "best practices" in quality management. Managers in agri-food firms might ask themselves questions such as: "How should we start or strengthen the integration of quality management with our buyers and suppliers?", "What factors do influence (and how strongly) the integration of quality management with our suppliers and buyers and How can we benefit from integration of quality management systems?" The present study has identified a number of important implications, summarised below:

4.1.1 Jointly Dealing With Pressures

Managers should realise that in order to deal effectively with pressures from the business environment, firms should integrate their quality management systems with other firms in the chain. The main reason for this is that failure of the quality management system of one firm affects the reputation of all firms in the chain. In strongly integrated supply chains, ideally, the goals of the entire chain become the common objectives of each firm, but also, more information and control actions will become available to the firms in each stage of the supply chain to enforce quality regulations. In this way, integration of quality management increases compliance behaviour. However, managers should realise that they can use their buying power to impose their quality strategy on their suppliers, but it seems to be less possible to impose their quality strategy on their buyers.

4.1.2 Collaboration to Improve Performance

Managers active in agri-food chains should strive for integration of quality management with their buyers and suppliers, because it is advantageous for firms. It turns out that firms that have higher levels of integration of quality management achieve higher levels of performance in terms of buyer satisfaction and revenue growth. To achieve a high level of performance, and especially buyer satisfaction, it is necessary to find committed parties in the chain that share the firm's objectives with regard to quality management. Commitment can be regarded as the 'glue' that holds together successful buyer supplier relationships. Commitment can be enlarged by:

- Maintaining high quality standards and link up the own firm with exchange partners that have similar visions on quality management.
- Communicating timely quality information and by intensifying the relationships through personal contacts and visits with suppliers and buyers.

- Sharing the benefits from better quality management throughout the supply chain and stimulating the notification of problems without directly imposing sanctions.
- Enforcement of quality requirements should be avoided as much as possible. Strict enforcement does not lead to higher performance in most cases because:
- Strong enforcement of quality regulation has the potential to be destructive and initiates dysfunctional conflict behaviour, especially if sanctions are imposed that are perceived to be unjust or unreasonable. Therefore, stringent enforcement may ruin the necessary (long-term) relationships on quality management in agri-food supply chains.
- If buyers use strong sanctions for non-compliance with quality requirements, suppliers might be faking compliance behaviour and will not notify their buyers in case of quality problems, because they are afraid of stringent sanctions.
- Stringent enforcement by frequent or many controls de-motivates firms that are performing well and results in high and unnecessary monitoring costs for the enforcing firm.

4.1.3 Better use of Quality Data

Managers should be aware that due to the compliance with quality requirements, they possess a rich source of information about their quality performance over time. At the moment these quality measures are often only used to verify compliance. Analysing this data deeper might reveal the roots of quality problems and indicate ways to solve these problems.

4.1.4 Aligning Quality Strategy With Firm Strategy

Managers should develop a clear strategy that positions quality management within the other activities of the firm. If quality management is integrated with the commercial, financial and personnel strategy of the firm, it will not be regarded as a bureaucratic burden and can be better aligned in the firm's processes. Motivation of the personnel could be further improved by developing effective procedures that are short and practical. If the only interest of a firm is to obtain a quality certificate, not supported by an appropriate quality strategy, the quality management system will not be successful in the long run. Therefore, managers should take care that quality management is 'alive' within the firm and should avoid practices that might decrease the perceived importance of good quality management by their employees. Examples are enhancing the quality systems just before auditing or selling products that do not meet the quality requirements in times of product shortage. Such practices may be interpreted by personnel that quality management is just another management fashion, to which they should pay only limited attention.

4.2 Implications for Policy Makers

The study has also derived important implications for policy makers. These recommendations mainly focus on facilitation and improvement of self regulation in agri-food supply chains. Policy makers might be interested in the answers to questions such as: 'What hampers the self regulation of quality management in agri-food supply chains?', 'How can we improve quality management of firms in agri-food supply chains?' and 'What is the role of the government with regard to inspections of quality management in the near future?' This study provides the following implications:

4.2.1 Application of Control-on-Control'

Within the concept of *'control-on-control'* the government should retain ultimate responsibility for quality assurance, especially with regard to the mandatory legal European requirements. '*Control-on-control'* is likely to increase the overall level of quality management in agri-food firms. Good performing firms will become even more motivated to improve their quality management, because the governmental inspection frequency of their firms will decrease, lowering the administrative and financial burdens of the inspections. Bad performing firms will be controlled more frequently. Even if the vast majority of firms do the right thing, there is always the chance that irrational, incompetent and stubborn firms will produce serious harm. No less than in other walks of life, there are firms that are simply resistant to new chances. While relatively small and operating at the bottom of the market, these minority of firms cannot be ignored. For such firms, direct inspections offer the most efficient way of ensuring a basic level of quality management. As a result the effectiveness of the governmental inspections will increase, because the government is 'fishing where the fishes are'. The government should stress this higher effectiveness of the *'control-on-control'* approach to other governments in Europe. This is also important in order to avoid unjust comparisons with other EU countries that control all firms. Because bad performing firms are inspected more frequently, it might falsely be suggested that the number of non-compliances in The Netherlands is high. Fair comparisons are extremely important for Dutch agri-food supply chains, because most Dutch agri-food chains are highly internationally oriented.

4.2.2 Uniform Certification Procedures

Policy makers should realise that even the traditional *'command-and-control'* approach of governmental control is not a kind of golden standard for a 100% compliance with quality regulations. Fraud will always be possible. However to minimise the chance of fraud, the procedures should be clearly described and supervised by an independent Council of Accreditation. This prevents the commercial relationship between audited firms and certifiers from hampering certifiers in their evaluation. *'Control-on-control'* might even be more effective in preventing fraud -because certifiers know firms and develop relationships with them in which improvement of quality management is very important. As a result they have more insight in the problems and can help to resolve problems a firm has in complying with regulations better than governmental agencies. Moreover, a common sanction for repeated non-compliance with certified quality management systems is withdrawal of the certificate or exclusion from delivery. This is a severe sanction, because firms that are excluded from their chains no longer have the possibility to deliver to their buyers, which is a more stringent sanction than a fine.

4.2.3 Innovative Approaches

The present study showed that not *legislative demands*, but more consumer oriented measures such as increasing *media attention* and *societal demands for corporate social responsibility* have the most important impact on the integration of quality management in agri-food supply chains. Therefore, policy makers should focus on innovative approaches that positively emphasise the efforts of firms to deliver safe and high quality foods, for example:

- Create awards for firms with 'best practice' quality management systems comparable to the corporate social responsibility award of the Ministry of Agriculture, Nature and Food Quality. Winners receive a lot of positive attention in the media.
- Develop a 'score card' including a number of criteria on which the quality management of firms should objectively be assessed. Based on this score card of quality performance a ranking list of firms can be composed and published. It is expected that this ranking list will start a kind of competition among firms in order to achieve a higher ranking. Of course, this list has to be updated regularly, for example, once a month. This score card could possibly be connected with existing private initiatives such as the Action Plan for Salmonella and Campylobacter and Food Compass.
- Extend the publication of the inspection results on the Internet page of the Dutch Food and Non-Food Authority to all agri-food sectors, instead of only the fruit and vegetable chain. In order to safeguard their quality reputation firms may intensify the integration of quality management with their suppliers and buyers as a means of complying with quality management regulations (shame-and-blame approach).

4.2.4 Commitment Instead of Enforcement

Commitment and not enforcement lead to better performance with regard to quality management. This also has consequences for the government. At the moment, the government works according to the inspection principle, which means that many details are checked extensively. Firms perceive this as an enforcement based way of working. In order to change this perception, the government should work according to the auditing principle. The added value of an auditor is that he helps the entrepreneur to find a balance between the quality requirements and the way these requirements should be met within the firm and this is perceived as a commitment based way of working. In this way, the inspection of quality requirements will be perceived more positively by firms.

4.2.5 Retain the Advantages of 'Control-on-Control'

Finally, regarding the possibilities of effective sanctioning in private quality management systems, policy makers should be sure that they do not develop too stringent requirements for self regulating systems if they transfer part of their responsibilities to the market, because they are afraid that something will go wrong. Recent research has shown that self regulation in other sectors such as health, higher education and environmental management did not lead to lower administrative burdens for firms (Dorbeck-Jung et al., 2005). Regulations of the government were replaced by all kinds of regulations of private organisations. Because these organisations formulate and implement their regulations from a specific interest, there is less room for own initiatives of firms. Firms face many costs in order to show that they comply with all these new regulations. If this happens, the expected advantages of self regulation will be gone for firms. In order to prevent this, an independent organisation, comparable with a Council of Accreditation or Product Board could judge whether or not these (administrative) regulations are justified.

5. Concluding Remarks

This paper discussed the results of fourteen in-depth interviews that were held with experts in three food chains on integration of quality management systems. It provides a number of additional qualitative insights to the survey performed in previous research, by focusing on the 'how' and 'why' questions to better explain the relationships found. The questions were open-ended, because then the expert would not be hindered by any framework or bias of the researcher. From these interviews it became clear how firms have implemented self regulating 'best practices' quality management systems in agri-food supply chains and helped to formulate practical recommendations for managers and policy makers. During the interviews it became apparent that it is not always clear what belongs to quality management systems and what not. The boundaries between quality management systems and other systems of the firm are blurring. Information structures that were created for the transfer of information about quality compliance are increasingly used for the transfer of all kinds of product and process related information. One should note that the term 'best practice' quality management system depends on the market a firm is operating in. At the bottom of the market in particular quality regulations are regarded as something firms have to comply with and the perception exists that firms should do as little as possible for the assurance of quality.

Regarding self regulation, the in-depth interviews were useful, because self regulation is quite a broadly defined term in current management and policy research. The discussion of the outcomes of the interviews shed light on the two main dimensions of self regulating behaviour, commitment and enforcement. During the interviews, it turned out that firms would like the implementation of 'control-on-control' as soon as possible. The main reason was that their quality efforts would be rewarded, because they would get a lower inspection frequency of governmental agencies. In addition, many experts believed that certifiers are able to implement and to supervise the quality management systems better and that certifiers had enough sanction possibilities for firms that tried to cheat the 'rules of the game' in quality management systems. The commercial relationship, the education of the auditors and the necessity of accredited systems were important points of attention to take into account according to the VWA.

References

AMSTEL VAN-VAN SAANE, M.; DRIESSEN, P.; GLASBERGEN, P. 2006. *Eco-labeling and information asymmetry: a comparison of five eco-labels in the Netherlands.* Institutional Mechanisms for Industry Self-Regulation; Harvard: University; Boston: United States of America, pp. 24.

BARNEY, J. B.; HESTERLY, W. 1999. Organizational economics: understanding the relationship between organizations and economic analysis. In: STEWARD, R. C.; HARDY, C. (Eds.). *Studying organization. Sage publications*, p. 109-141.

COOPER, M. C.; LAMBERT, M. D.; PAGH, J. D. 1997. Supply chain management: more than a new name for logistics. *The international Journal of Logistics Management*, 8(1): 1-13.

DE BAKKER et al. 2007. Nieuwe rollen, nieuwe kansen (in Dutch). LEI, The Hague, The Netherlands, 104p.

DORBECK-JUNG, B. R., HEFFEN, M. J. OUDE, Vrielink-van; REUSSING, G.H. 2005. *Open normen en regeldruk* – Een onderzoek naar de kosten en oorzaken van irritaties bij open normen in de kwaliteitszorg (in Dutch). University of Twente, Enschede, The Netherlands.

HAVINGA, T., 2006. Private regulations of food safety by supermarkets. *Law & Policy*, 28(4).

KING, A.; LENOX, M. 2005. *Industry self-regulation without sanctions:* The chemical industry's responsble care program. Academy of Management Journal, forthcoming.

LAMBERT, M. D.; COOPER, M. C.; PAGH, J. D. 1998. Supply chain management: implementation issues and research opportunities. *The international Journal of Logistics Management*, 9(2): 1-19.

LAWRENCE, P. R.; LORSCH, J. W. 1967. *Organization and environment: Managing differentiation and integration*. Harvard University. Boston: United States of America, 279p.

LUNING, P. A.; MARCELIS, W. J.; JONGEN, W. M. F. 2002. *Food quality management.* Wageningen Academic Publishers, Wageningen, The Netherlands, 323p.

PLAGGENHOEF, W. 2007. *Integration and self regulation of quality management in Dutch agri-food supply chains; a cross-chain analysis of the poultry meat, the fruit and vegetable and the flower and potted plant chains.* PhD thesis Wageningen University, The Netherlands, 305p.

POWELL, T. C. 1992. Organizational alignment as competitive advantage. *Strategic Management Journal*, 13(2): 119-134.

RINDFLEISCH, A.; HEIDE, J. B. 1997. Transaction cost analysis, past, present and future applications. *Journal of Marketing*, 61: 30-54.

SOUSA, R.; VOSS, C. A. 2002. Quality management re-visited: a reflective review and agenda for future research. *Journal of Operations Management*, 20: 91-109.

SPIEGEL, van der M., 2004. *Measuring effectiveness of food quality management.* Ponsen & Looijen, Wageningen, The Netherlands, 182p.

TRIENEKENS, J. H.; BEULENS, A. J. M. 2001. Views on inter-enterprise relationships. *Production Planning and Control*, 12(5): 466-477.

VORST VAN DER, J. G. A. G. 2000. *Effective food supply chains.* Generating, modelling and evaluating supply chain scenarios, Wageningen University, Wageningen, The Netherlands, 305p.

______. 2004, Supply chain management: theory and practices. In: CAMPS, T.; DIEDEREN, P.; HOFSTEDE, G. J.; VOS B. (Eds.). *The emerging world of chains and networks.* Bridging theory and practice. Reed Business Information B.V., Gravenhage, The Netherlands, pp. 105-146.

WILLIAMSON, O. E. 1991. Comparative economic organization: The analysis of discrete structural alternatives. *Administrative Quarterly*, 36: 269-296.

______. 1996. *The mechanism of governance.* Oxford University Press, New York: United States of America.

ZAJAC, E. J.; SHORTELL, S. M. 1989. Changing generic strategies: Likehood, direction and performance implications. *Strategic Management Journal*, 10(5): 413-430.

Public and Private Mechanisms in Food Safety

Eduardo Eugênio Spers

Decio Zylbersztajn

The guarantee of good quality food is a growing focus of governments, companies and the standardization, certification and trade agents. Their efforts are addressed to influence the consumer's perception over the many attributes of a food product, with special attention to the nutrition and safety aspects. The warranty of quality suggests voluntary standards by companies and more regulation by the government. The public and private mechanisms have been analyzed separately in marketing and regulation literature. The analysis of the interactions among these mechanisms provides conflicting and extreme visions like the private food quality and safety mechanism being substituted by the public and other where the performance of the state is unnecessary due to the consumer's trust in the reputation of a brand or organization. A third vision happens when the regulation is complemented with the use of private strategies and vice versa. The objective of this chapter is to propose a model generated from the framework of game theory and hedonic demand analysis of attributes to evaluate these interactions.

1. Introduction

Food safety attributes are not always easy to observe. In many cases public regulations are necessary to monitor the quality of food in the market. Private mechanisms are also relevant, and they are expressed in the form of reputation of brands. Both public and private mechanisms to guarantee quality attributes are not independent. The question of whether they are complements or substitutes is relevant for firms to decide strategies and governments to define public policies.

Public and private mechanisms are usually analyzed separately in the literature of food safety and quality. Conflicting views appear as reputation mechanisms are substituted by regulatory measures or else, when regulation is complemented by reputation. According to Cohen (1998, p. 47), two research areas are relevant in dealing with adaptations of firms to legal changes. First, external incentives such as the incorporation of social norms, social pressures, and reputation mechanisms. Second, internal incentives that the organization possesses to adapt to legal changes. This chapter focuses on the first area, analyzing how consumers perceive the external incentives to the adoption of a public mechanism such as norms and State monitoring as well as the incentives to adopt a private mechanism such as quality brand advertising. The aim is to characterize the interaction of public and private mechanisms in terms of complementarity and substitution.

The guarantee of food quality is a growing focus of governments, companies and standardization agents. Efforts are addressed to control the attributes of a food product, with a peculiar care of the nutrition and safety characteristics. Guaranteeing quality is gaining notoriety as food consumption is being better appraised for the rulers, consumers and companies. This better evaluation suggests more voluntary quality assurances for companies and more regulation for the government (Caswell, 1998, p. 409).

To understand how these private and public mechanisms interact in terms of complementarity or substitution is important (Lazzarini, 2002, p. 2). If a substitution exists, a private company could invest on branding when the public monitoring is not present to ensure consumers high safety perception. Instead, if a complementarity exists, a private company needs some kind of public monitoring.

Trust is commonly seen as a substitute for complex contracts in interorganization transactions, whereas in an alternative perspective, formal contracts are seen as a complement (Poppo and Zenger, 2002, p. 707). Different levels of incentives exist, tacit or imposed, to the adoption of a quality guarantee system, through economic units, norms and regulators. These incentives help in understanding the adoption of private strategies and public policies.

Pressure for more regulation appears as a consequence of low trust in institutions and limited rationality by consumers when they overestimated, underestimated and did not understand certain risks and benefits in food consumption. This justifies why this article focuses on consumers to evaluate the private and public mechanisms. Which combination, intensity or situation of public and private mechanisms should be used to provide incentives to consumers' high safety perception? The main goal of this chapter is to propose the discussion about the complementary and substitution relationship among the public and private mechanisms regarded in food safety.

The chapter is structured into four sections including this introduction. Initially, the food safety issue is characterized, and the adoption of public and private mechanisms in Brazil is discussed. In section three, a theoretical model is proposed based on the consumer's perception, hedonic model and game theory. Finally, the conclusions are presented in section four.

2. The Enforcement of Food Safety

Food safety is the consumer's warranty to acquire food with quality and health attributes (Spers, 1993) Institution changes like new industrialization processes, new consumer demands, industrialization and urbanization, increase in competitiveness, development of scientific research, decrease in income expenses on food and globalization demands increasing the consumer, government and private organizations' interest for safety and quality

The food segment has been focused on by a growing and successive crisis of credibility, fear and insecurity due to accusations of contaminations and adulterations. Another factor that contributes to this distrust is the little understanding about developments obtained by process and genetic engineering. Although there are benefits, some consumers and nongovernmental organizations believe that these technologies can be dangerous if more intensively explored. The communication between the producing system and the final consumer becomes more dynamics and complex. Demand for food information grows as the consumer's knowledge and involvement increase with regard to constant changes in their attributes, process, and conservation. New attributes such as the genetic modified organism (GMO) could cause misunderstanding, distrust and overestimating their effects.

Distrust regarding State enforcement of health and consumption of healthy foods have worsened with the crisis of mad cow disease. Industries and distributors try to increase their trust by a non-commercialization of GMOs. Companies are accused of not appropriately informing the consumer about scientific improvements and risks, creating negative perception and antipathy.

Meat is a source of protein and important vitamins and minerals. However, if produced and marketed in an incorrect way by private companies, it can cause alimentary intoxication and, consequently, loss of value and reputation to the final consumer. In the case of Brazilian beef, the healthy profile is emphasized as a "green" cattle (that grows in the fields), different from those intensive processes that led to the mad cow disease, which opens discussions about the State's effectiveness in guaranteeing consumer's safety (Enriquez-Cabot and Goldberg, 1996).

Understanding how consumer perception behaves over government enforcement policies and private branding strategies could help in an appropriate introduction of effective communication over food safety aspects.

3. A Model for Transaction between a Consumer and a Food Company

The proposed model is based on the consumer's perception regarding public and private mechanisms' attributes, which occurs in different intensities between consumer and company. A hedonic model measures the preference of different attributes of public and private mechanisms, and game theory evaluates these mechanisms' decisions, which allows the achievement of a Pareto situation.

In Lancaster (1971), goods are not directed objects of their preference but have associated a group of relevant attributes. The utility function is a set of attributes (Aj = (oh) or characteristics obtained through several products.

Analyzing the process of meat purchase, Barcellos and Callegaro (2002) interviewed 400 consumers in a Brazilian city, and, through factor analysis, they reduced the variables in information quality indicators. Keeping constant the information about the animal and the product and choosing a specific type of meat, the consumer preference structure could be defined by the monitoring attributes (or public mechanism) and brand (private mechanism). We use these results as an assumption to the proposed model.

In the hedonic model, the product i is defined as a combination of attributes Aj = (oh + ai+1 +... + ai+n), which is produced in a technological structure of production T. When the quality attributes are not perfectly observed by the consumer in purchasing, as is the case of most food safety attributes, an organization O, in a certain market j, could offer the same product i with a different combination of attributes that varies from Aj′ with low quality to Aj with high quality. As it follows along the chain value, the product i suffers transformations at a cost Zi that will be offered to the final consumer who perceives a benefit or a value Vi in the product i (Besanko, et al, 2000, p. 395).

Preference of a product i will be a function of Vi; the value or medium benefit perceived by the consumer in relation to the product i; pi is the market price paid and received by the product i, and Zi is the medium cost of production of the product i. In a transaction among a consumer C and an organization O, which accomplishes the offering of a product i, the total value is divided between the consumer and the organization. In this case, (Vi-pi) is the medium value received by the consumer C, and (pi-Zi) is the medium profit received by the organization O.

Assuming the existence of different technological combinations of production T, that are different combinations of attributes Aj, the product i will provide different benefits to the consumer C, which vary from a value Vi to vi (assuming Vi > vi). For instance, the consumer perceives, in the acquisition of a certain meat that contains attributes that guarantee a higher level of safety and quality, also a higher value than other meat that does not possess these attributes nor has a lower level of the same attributes.

If organization O offers a value Vi, it is reasonable to suppose that their technological structure of production T has a higher cost, because it incorporates additional procedures to food safety guarantee. Considering different quality patterns, the structure of production cost could vary from Zi to zi (assuming Zi > zi).

Even if there are variations in perceptions over the attributes of benefits among different segments of consumers, we suppose that part of the population is willing to pay for a better quality pattern and consumer C does not buy the product in case he or she notices a low quality (Vi-pi) < 0.

According to Baird et al. (2000, p.6), a strategic problem begins when two people interact and both have to decide what to do without knowing what the other is accomplishing. The adoption of a norm related to food safety is accomplished by how rigorous the State is in enforcing and punishing organizations and how technically and economically difficult the norm to be adopted is. Both have to decide the enforcement they will exercise without knowing the other strategy. This behavior will also depend on the legal environment. We may suppose that the organization will adopt the higher quality norm in case the punishment imposed by the State is higher.

Laffont and Tirole (1993, p. 211) argue that a monopolist who does not suffer any type of regulation will have two incentives to adopt high standards of quality and safety. When the quality is observed by consumers before the consumption, when it has a reduction of sales and when the income of the monopolist's price exceeds the marginal cost. When the quality is observed by consumers only after their consumption, the monopolist has the incentive to provide a high-quality pattern, unless the consumer repeats the purchase. In this case, the private mechanism appears as reputation and branding. The public and private mechanisms are alternatives and could interact between themselves in terms of complementarity or substitution.

Like other economic models, game theory simplifies a certain social situation, and it has been used in the field of organizations, law (Katz, 1990) and consumer behavior (Gunnthordsdottir, 2002). The application of this theory will accomplish the understanding of how economic units behave due to a varied combination of public and private mechanisms.

Three elements are necessary to a game: (1) the players, in the case of private organizations and the consumers; (2) the available strategy, to buy or not, to offer higher or lower quality and accomplishing the public mechanism or not or adopting a private mechanism; and (3) the compensation that each player receives for a possible strategy, differences between value perceived and price for the consumer and between price and cost for the company. The premises to formulate the game are described next.

In case an organization offers a product of high quality, it will receive pi-Zi, and the consumer C will perceive a value Vi-pi when purchasing the product. In another situation, where the organization offers a product of low quality, the consumer will receive a value vi-pi and the organization pi-zi. Although the company offers high or low quality, if the consumer C does not buy the product, both will receive zero. Evaluating the payoffs between the consumer and the organization (C,O), the Nash Equilibrium occurs in a situation in which the Pareto is lower if the game has been played in a single time (Figure 1). As the quality and safety are not noticed by the consumer, the game can be seen in a simultaneous way; in other words, the consumer does not see the movement of the organization.

Figure 1: Payoff between Organization "O" and Consumer "C"

		Organization O	
		Offer high quality	Offer low quality
Consumer C	Buy	V_i-p_i , p_i-Z_i	v_i-p_i , p_i-z_i
	Not buy	0 , 0	0 , 0

Where:

p_i = price of the product i;
V_i = Consumers' value received from a product i with high-quality attributes;
v_i = Consumers' value received from a product i with low-quality attributes;
Z_i = Organizations' cost of producing high-quality product i;
z_i = Organizations' cost of producing low-quality product i.
Considering $V > v$ and $Z > z$

To increase welfare, it would be desirable that the balance of the game happens in the strategy of "buying" and offering a "high quality." For this, we suppose the presence of government or a regulator R, with a public mechanism of monitoring that could detect, with a probability s, and not to detect with a probability (1-s), the offers of a low-quality product.

3.1 Introduction of the Public Mechanism

The government is present in the economy to enforce property rights and the execution of the contracts (Klein and Leffer, 1981, p. 615). It has the function of guaranteeing, through the public mechanisms of inspection and punishment, the execution of the necessary activities that reach a safety level demanded by the society. When establishing regulations and norms, two types of costs happen, one enforcing and another monitoring. Therefore, to minimize their costs, they should decide which governance structure would be more efficient, in other words, at a smaller transaction cost.

The presence of public mechanisms related to enforcing food safety (Turner, 2000, p. 43) is growing. Some examples are (1) rules or labeling the minimum and maximum limits of vitamins, minerals and additives, (2) limits of pesticides, residues and pollutants, (3) structures of monitoring and regulation agencies and lawsuits, (4) information about new complex technologies, (5) non-tariff barriers and (6) practices of controlling food production processes and conservation, identifying the origin and the history of a product, like traceability, which is used in meat. To export bovine meat, the producer needs to have the Brazilian System of Bovine Identification and Certification (SISBOV) and the Federal Inspection System (SIF) for food products of animal origin.

Norms and regulation instruments in a market are introduced due to the presence of asymmetry in information between buyers and sellers. In the case of food consumption, there are difficulties in verifying many of the intrinsic safety attributes; for instance, organic production and the presence of residues forbidden or above the tolerated limit. Besides, there cannot be consensus among consumers, government and private companies about which should be the best level of food safety enforced.

The literature justifies the need for a governmental intervention (Mercuro and Medema, 1997; Viscusi, 1985; Buzby, 1998; and Posner, 1998) from demand type, imperfect competition, public property rights, externalities, incomplete market and imperfect information. If there is a market failure, it is necessary to identify appropriate governmental mechanisms (Stiglitz, 2000, p. 249) and food safety, depending on the case, that may be related to one or more of those failures.

Henson and Traill (1993) argue that for a perfect market operation, in the case of products that involve risks, may have a divergence between private and public or social food safety levels: (1) perception of the consumer's risk may differ from specialists; (2) imperfections in offering information about food safety; (3) failure of price system, reflecting the total costs and benefits, and (4) unfair distribution of costs and benefits associated with changes in safety levels.

Law (2001) argues that government intervention in the US food sector was an answer to a higher transaction cost imposed by the need of information and changes in regulation that passed through the federal level.

The lack of property rights regarding food safety consumption shows the need for the State performance (Demsetz, 1967). Safety could be demanded and offered in different property levels. If there is a market failure, different private and public desires regarding the level of quality and safety allow opportunistic behavior. An organization could restrict knowledge or information about their product quality to difficult consumer perceptions.

Food safety is a service offered by an organization that chooses the level of offering and different patterns of quality attributes. The regulator defines these patterns in services that are difficult to be specified through rules, and, when health attributes are evolved, it could generate controversies. It becomes more difficult with the introduction of new services and constant innovations related to production and conservation. The regulator needs to define the minimum quality pattern that could be accomplished and enforced by periodic inspections and fines (Kahn, 1998, p. 22). The market failure regarding asymmetrical information is evidenced by several authors (Law, 2001; Akerlof, 1970; Katz, 1998 and Stigler, 1961). The presence of incomplete contracts and asymmetrical information also allows opportunistic behavior, and so the government's intervention and enforcing is needed.

Public choice studies the political process (Buchanan, 2000, p. 153). Not always the law can be formulated with one or some consumers' or companies' desires, because their interests would not be necessarily equal to that of most. The regulatory agencies could work exclusively to a particularly group of interests (Buchanan, 2000, p. 331). Therefore, it is important that, even when formulating public mechanisms of regulation, the existence of lobby and corruption could affect their accomplishment and efficiency in generating welfare. An organization can be detected by a regulatory agency as offering low quality but not punished due to the existence of corruption. Organizations could lobby for a superior quality standard regulation, because they have better condition or higher competitive advantage to accomplish producing these pattern products (Law, 2001, p. 9).

Organization O, which wants to offer high quality, could have problems due to the impossibility of guaranteeing a hundred percent safety. The adoption of practices for a higher level of safety could allow them to avoid punishment, since the probability of s would be null and (1-s) equal to 1. Being s is also considered quality of inspection; if organization O, is discovered by regulator R, as offering a low quality, it will receive a fine m (Figure 2).

If zi + sfi (Zi (or sfi (Zi – zi), the Nash result balance will be higher for consumer C in purchasing the product and for organization O that offers high quality, then, a desired situation occurs. However, if sfi < Zi – zi, the consumer and the company will need another mechanism to reach the result of superior Pareto-like reputation.

Figure 2. Payoff with introduction of regulator "R"

		Organization O	
		Offer high quality	**Offer low quality**
Consumer C	**Buy**	V_i-p_i , p_i-Z_i	v_i-p_i , p_i-z_i-$s_i m_i$
	Not buy	**0 , 0**	**0 , 0**

Where:

s_i = probability of discovering lower quality of product i or enforcement efficiency;

m_i = fine paid for low quality by organization O;

$F = s_i m_i$

$s_i m_i \geq Z_i - z_i$ or $F \geq Z$

3.2 Introducing the Private Mechanism

Safety could be managed, quality becomes important, costs exist, and their profitability affects food companies. Some damages and costs caused by contaminations are related to the quantity of product loss, legal actions, compensations to consumers, corporate and brand image, consumer's trust, crisis administration and the impact on other companies that produce similar products.

The food sector is worrying and investing in the quality management of their products. Besides the harmful aspects mentioned, some benefits motivate investments in product attributes, consumer's and supplier's credibility, brand protection and in the desire for obtaining competitive advantage.

There are internal motivations to adopt a private mechanism to control quality, which is difficult to measure and could vary from company to company. These incentives are the improvement in production efficiency, management and quality controls, consumer service, facility of a new partner introduction in the chain, identification and solution of problems, market share and consumers' maintenance. Some private companies have property rights over goods and attributes regulated by law that identify certain quality patterns accepted and perceived by the market as brand and seals.

Increasing market complexity and competition could represent the decline in loyal consumers. Some consumer segments that have fewer brands loyal demand more investments in communication. In meat, the perception among different quality attributes is difficult, and, therefore, they have no reasons to be loyal to a certain brand. Brands are tools to conquer meat consumers' trust, which could tranquilize them while all other problems are solved by a brand owner (Spers and Zylbersztajn, 1997).

Private companies need a brand that could generate enough sense of trust to obtain consumers' loyalty from valued attributes as safety. According to Arnold (1992), the aim of an organization is to create value to consumers' minds by product or service. This means products and messages like brand private mechanisms that induce purchase in the future.

Considering now that organization O and Consumer C interact repeatedly and the future payoffs are adjusted with a discount factor that could have several interpretations, it can be considered as an indicator of degree of interaction or purchase frequency in the future. The problem of moral hazard can appear as consumer ignores quality choice. The infinite repetition of that interaction strategy is necessary to guarantee the desired market efficiency (high-quality product) and could support the perfect (therefore, sequential) strategy balance. The supply of high quality will be part of the perfect balance of the repeated subgame (Abreu, 1988 and Burguet, 1996) if, i.e.,

$$\frac{p-Z}{(1-\delta)} \geq p - z - sf + 0$$

That is equal a:

$$\delta \geq \frac{(Z-z-sf)}{(p-z-sf)} \quad (1)$$

Simplifying the analysis, normalizing p = 1; Z < 1 and (1 – Z) the margin sale, denoting F = sf as the expected level of punishment, assuming z = 0, equation (1) would be

$$\delta \geq \frac{(Z-F)}{(1-F)} \quad (2)$$

Based on Figure 3 AB (assuming Z = ½), CB (F > Z) and AD (δ > F), we can solve the game and verify the combinations that culminate in a balance where consumer C buys and organization O offers high quality. If sf = F δ Z, the regulation guarantees by itself the supply of high quality.

Figure 3: Balance for Z = ½, in agreement with different levels of F and δ

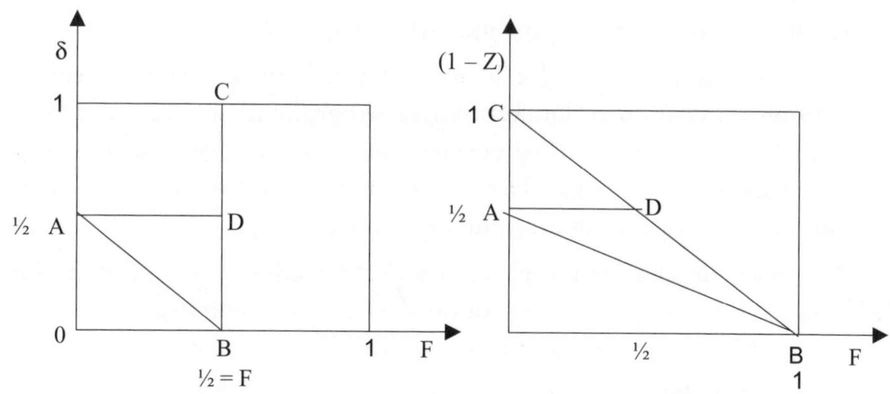

As δ increases, or the value of the future earnings is larger than ½, the reputation or private mechanism alone guarantees the high quality, since public mechanism is smaller than ½. Public mechanism substitutes the private guaranteeing the desired balance, whenever it goes larger than ½, and in case it is smaller, since δ is equal to ½, the complementarity between public and private mechanisms will happen. If F or δ go simultaneously smaller than ½, the purchase will not be executed, since equation (2) does not match. In all cases, the not buying is also a perfect balance of the subgame, because it is part of the Nash equilibrium of repetitive game. Therefore, the repetition is not enough to attempt high quality.

In case of incentives for the adoption of public mechanisms by an organization, a more complex and possible way to work with the problem is to input the role of brand. In Klein's and Leffer´s approach (1981), the brand is used to avoid competitors' entrance, once it imposes unrecoverable costs in certain markets. Otherwise, there would not be a prize (p-Z) to be arbitrated.

The brand can signal quality in a situation where consumers could form expectations over a product (or attributes) through a communication strategy (Tirole, 2002. p. 107-108). If the firm sells a product with more advertising, a larger price is necessary to guarantee its quality (Klein and Leffler, p. 632). According to Horstmann and MacDonald (1994, p. 578), neither introductory price nor advertising serves as signs of product quality.

We assumed that brand or quality stamp is a private mechanism that can facilitate perceptions of high product quality when generating reputation and future purchases. Brand loyalty concept is assumed here as being a proxy to measure the discount factor δ. According to Chaudhuri and Holbrook (2001), brand loyalty can be measured to identify trust and affection.

Concluding, some hypotheses could be proposed if regarding public and private mechanisms in the different levels of consumer perception of product quality.

4. Concluding Remarks

Food safety involves several agents: government, organizations and consumers. The relationship among those agents is dynamic and must be analyzed together.

The increase in safety perception by consumers reflects government action of increasing enforcement; and organizations could apply more efficient mechanisms of product differentiation. On the other hand, the government could increase consumer's sensibility and concern regarding safety aspects through educational programs.

Studies with this proposed model could capture regional differences. In some regions, depending the level of consumer perception of safety, the use of a public or private mechanisms could be substitute or complementary. Applications in other problems that involve both private and public strategies such as environmental and social subjects could be useful.

References

ABREU, Dilip. 1988. On the Theory of Infinitely Repeated Games with Discounting. v. 56, n. 2, *Econometrica*, march, p. 383-396.

AKERLOF, George. 1970. The market for "lemons": quality uncertainty and the market mechanism. *Quarterly Journal of Economics*, v. 84, Aug., p. 488-500.

ARNOLD, David. 1992. *The handbook of brand management*. The Economist Books, International Management Series. Massachusetts: Perseus Books. 259p.

BAIRD, Baird Douglas G.; GERTNER, Robert H.; PICKER, Randal C. 2000. *Game theory and the law*. Harvard University Press. Cambridge, Massachusetts, London, England. 330p.

BAKER, A. B.; CROSBIE, P. J. 1993. *Measuring food safety preferences*: identifying consumer segments. working paper. Santa Clara: Santa Clara University. 34p.

BARCELLOS, Marcia Dutra de; CALLEGARO, Carlos Alberto Martins. 2002. *A importância da informação como indicador de qualidade: o caso da compra de carne bovina em Porto Alegre*, Anais: Encontro Nacional de Pós-Graduação em Administração (ENANPAD). Salvador, Brazil. 15p.

BESANKO, David; DRANOVE, David; SHANLEY, Mark. 2000. *Economics of strategy*. 2. ed. John Wilcy & Sons, Inc. 644p.

BUCHANAN, James M. 2000. Politics as public choice. *The Collective Works of James M. Buchanan*. Liberty Fund, Indianapolis, IN. 497p.

BURGUET, Roberto. 1996. Optimal repeated purchases when sellers are learning about... *Journal of Economic Theory*, v. 68, n. 2, Feb., p. 440-415.

BUZBY, Jean C.; FOX, John A.; READY, Richard C.; CRUTCHFIELD, Stephen. 1998. Measuring consumer benefits of food safety risk regulation. *Journal of Agriculture and Applied Economics*, v. 30, July, n. 1.

CASWELL, Julie A. 1998. Valuing the benefits and costs of improved food safety and nutrition. *The Australian Journal of Agricultural and Resource Economics*, v. 42, n. 4, p. 409-424.

CHAUDHURI, Arjun; HOLBROOK, Morris B. 2001. The chain of effects from brand trust and brand affect to brand performance: The role of brand loyalty. *Journal of Marketing*, v. 65, Apr., n. 2, p. 81-93.

COHEN, Mark A. 1998. *Monitoring and enforcement of environmental policy*. Trabalho de pesquisa. Vanderbilt University. Nashville, TN, August, 59p.

ENRIQUEZ-CABOT; GOLDBERG, Ray A. 1996. *Technology crises and the future of agribusiness: BSE in Europe*. Case study. Harvard: Harvard Business School. 41p.

GUNNTHORSDOTTIR, Anna; McCABE, Kevin; SMITH, Vernon. 2002. Using the Machiavellianism instrument to predict trustworthiness in a bargaining game. *Journal of Economic Psychology*, v. 23, Feb., p. 49-67.

HENSON, S.; TRAILL, B. 1993.The demand for food safety. Market imperfections and the role of government. *Food policy*. p. 152-162.

HORSTMANN, Ignatius J.; MacDONALD, Glenn M. 1994. When is advertising a signal of product quality? *Journal of Economics & Management Strategy*. v. 3, n. 3, Fall, p. 561-584.

KAHN, Alfred E. 1998. *The economics of regulation: principles and institutions*. Massachusetts: Institute of Technology. v. 1, 199p.

KATZ, A. 1990. The strategic structure of offer and acceptance: game theory and the law of contract formation. *Michigan Law Review*, n. 89, p. 216-295.

KLEIN, Benjamin; LEFFER, Keith B. 1981. The role of market forces in assuring contractual performance. *Journal of Political Economy*, v. 89, n. 4, p. 615-641.

KREPS, David M. 2001. *Game theory and economic modelling*. Oxford: Clarendon Press. 195p.

LAFFONT, Jean-Jacques; TIROLE, Jean. 1993. *A theory of incentives in procurement and regulation*. The MIT Press Cambridge, Massachusetts, London, England, 705p.

LANCASTER, K. 1971. *Consumer demand*: a new approach. New York: Columbia University Press.

LAW, Marc, T. 2001. The transaction cost origins of food and drug regulation. ISNIE Congress.

LAZZARINI, Sergio G.; MILLER, Gary J; ZENGER, Todd R. 2002. *Order with some Law:* complementarity vs. substitution of formal and informal arrangements. São Paulo: IBMEC working paper. 52p.

MERCURO, Nicholas; MEDEMA, Steven G. 1997. *Economics and the law:* from posner to post-modernism. Chapter 3: Public choice theory. Princeton, New Jersey: Princeton University Press, p. 84-100.

POPPO, Laura; ZENGER. 2002. Todd. do formal contracts and relational governance function as substitutes of complements? *Strategic Management Journal*, p. 707-725, v. 23, n. 8, 2002.

POSNER, Richard A. 1998. *Economic analysis of law*. Chapter 13: The choice between regulation and common law. 5. ed. Aspen Law & Business. A Division of Aspen Publisher, Inc. p. 401-424.

SILVA, Carlos Arthur B. da; BATALHA, Mário Otávio (Coord.). 1999. *Estudo sobre a eficiência econômica e competitividade da cadeia agroindustrial da pecuária de corte no Brasil.* Relatório final. Consórcio Funarbe – Universidade Federal de Viçosa e Universidade Federal de São Carlos. Brasília, Julho, 184p.

SPERS, Eduardo Eugênio. 1993. A segurança alimentar ao longo da cadeia. *Conjuntura alimentos*, v. 5, n. 1, Fev. p. 18-26 .

STIGLITZ, Joseph E. 2000. Economics of the public sector. 3. ed. New York/London: W. W. Norton & Company. 823p.

TIROLE, Jean. 2002. *The theory of industrial organization*. 13 ed. Cambridge: The MIT Press. 479p.

TURNER, Alan. 2000. The future of food law. *Food Manufacture*, v. 75 n. 2, Feb., p. 43-45.

UNNEVERHR, Laurian J. 2000. Food safety issues and fresh food product export from Ldcs. *Agricultural Economics*, v. 23, Sept., n. 3.

Designing Risk Profiles in Food Supply Chains; an Assessment of Classification Criteria

MIRANDA P.M. MEUWISSEN[1]

MONIQUE C.M. MOURITS

MARIA DE GRAAF

RUUD B.M. HUIRNE

Abstract

Risk profiling in food supply chains is often hampered due to a lack of data. This prohibits the development of actuarially sound and fair risk pooling systems. In this paper we study risk classification of animal feed companies and pig farms for feed crisis and epidemic disease risks respectively. Data are generated through expert elicitation, simulation modelling and "circumstantial evidence" from literature. Results show that risk profiling of animal feed companies is possible, but classification criteria mainly relate to structural business characteristics such as plant size and type of feed produced for which relatively little impact on animal feed producers' risk prevention behaviour can be expected. With regard to pig farms, the design of risk profiles seems more promising as there are relatively many classification criteria that show a relationship with the level of risk–though transaction costs can be substantial. Results are useful in current supply chain debates on extending risk pooling opportunities for feed producers' product liability risks and farmers' damage from livestock epidemics.

1 Business Economics, Wageningen University, Hollandseweg 1, 6706 KN Wageningen. Contact author: miranda.meuwissen@wur.nl, tel: +31 317 483857, fax: +31 317 482745.

Keywords: Risk classification; Livestock epidemics; Animal feed crises; Conjoint analysis; Stochastic simulation

1. Introduction

Governments increasingly urge food supply chain participants to design private (or public-private) risk financing solutions for catastrophic risks. For instance, in 1998, Dutch arable farmers, after having faced extreme levels of rainfall, were largely compensated by the government (Van Asseldonk et al., 2002). Afterwards, however, they were urged to design some form of insurance for extreme weather events. Similarly, Dutch swine farmers in the period 1997/98, while facing a relatively large outbreak of classical swine fever, received millions of Euros of compensation from European and Dutch governments (Meuwissen et al., 1999). Very soon after the end of the epidemic however governments required the pig sector to put more capital into the so-called animal health fund to ensure the availability of more sector capital for future epidemics. A further example of decreasing government support can be found in the area of animal feed contaminations. While in 2002 during the MPA (medroxy-progestron-acetaat) crisis in the Netherlands the Dutch government compensated pig farmers whose pigs had to be destructed, this was left to supply chain partners themselves during the 2006 dioxin crisis (Meuwissen et al., 2009).

In searching for private or public-private risk financing solutions such as insurance or mutual funds there is a need to adequately deal with the problem of adverse selection (Rejda, 1998). If not dealt with properly, premiums paid do not sufficiently reflect the risks of the pool. As an answer, insurance companies classify insureds into various risk profiles and set premiums and eligibility criteria accordingly. Alternatively, adverse selection can be dealt with by making the risk financing scheme compulsory. Still, risk classification is then often regarded as important to ensure fairness among pool members.

These issues are certainly not typical for food supply chains, i.e. they equally apply to e.g. automobile, property and health insurance schemes. What is however typical for food supply chains is the relatively limited amount of data about such risks as livestock epidemics as these are generally rare events. Even more, due to the dynamic risk environment of food supply chains, historic data are often of relatively little value. These issues hamper the establishment of statistically founded risk classification methods and therefore the design of actuarially sound and fair risk financing schemes.

In order to accommodate the development of risk financing schemes for catastrophic risks in food supply chains, this paper studies the feasibility of risk profiling through a combination of expert elicitation, literature review and simulation modelling. Experts are interviewed through standard questionnaires and conjoint analysis. We focus on catastrophic risks of animal feed crises and swine epidemics, both in the Netherlands. More specifically we assess the classification of animal feed companies and pig farms respectively. Risk financing schemes to which these classifications might apply include feed producers' recall or product liability insurance schemes and animal health funds for veterinary costs and business interruption losses of swine epidemics respectively.

2. Risk Profiling Experiences in the Past

With regard to insurance schemes covering feed crisis risk generally some level of risk classification is implemented by means of company visits by insurance company experts during which a number of criteria are checked. Company visits are mostly used for determining a feed company's eligibility for insurance; they do not lead to detailed class rating of premiums to be paid.

In the field of livestock epidemics the majority of financing discussions in the past focused on farmers' compulsory contributions to the animal health fund. For instance, during the years 1999-2004, maximum sector contributions were negotiated to be Euro 227 million. For the period 2005-2009 this was Euro 125 million and negotiations for 2010-2014 are underway. Also, the type of damage covered has frequently been discussed. At the moment, for instance, stakeholders debate whether or not to extend the fund's coverage with market losses for farmers who face protective vaccination programmes during an epidemic. Besides, also discussions on risk classification have regularly been undertaken. So far, however, there was only a very brief period, i.e. in 1999 right after the end of the 1997/98 outbreak of classical swine fever, during which risk classification was actually in place. Classification criteria then included farm location and number of animal contacts with other farms. Due to heavy sector criticism this class rating only held for

1 year and was fully abandoned afterwards. Other EU countries, such as Belgium, enforced similar types of classification and still apply them (Van Asseldonk et al., 2006a).

In both stages of the chain, i.e. animal feed production and farm-level animal production, stakeholders currently initiate debates on risk profiling. In the animal feed sector it is believed that more transparent, objective and risk-based classification criteria could enlarge the insurability of the sector. In livestock production some degree of risk classification is perceived to increase the level of fairness in existing animal health funds.

3. Materials and Methods

3.1 Longlist of Potential Risk Factors

Both for contamination risks in animal feed as well as for epidemic disease risks in livestock we started by putting together a longlist of potential risk factors. For animal feed risks we distinguished between 11 factors. These include among others the type of feed produced, i.e. compound feed versus wet feed, the specific sector compound feed is produced for (e.g. cattle or pig production), company size and country of origin of the feed ingredients. Factors are listed in the first column of Table 1.

With regard to epidemic disease risks we listed 31 factors, grouped into 5 categories, i.e. farm location, farm animal contacts, other farm contacts, farm hygiene and farm type. Factors are listed in the first column of Table 2. Farm hygiene, for instance, includes factors on whether a farm has a hygiene barrier, strictly separated clean versus dirty routing and uses own or somebody else's trucks for transporting pigs.

Table 1: Longlist of potential factors influencing the risk of animal feed crises in the Netherlands and related findings from literature[1,2]

Risk factors and levels	Reported risk and company characteristics
1. Type of animal feed: compound (C) versus wet (W)[3]	- **[Risk, 0]** Reported crises (1997-2008)[c]: total = 6. C = 3, W = 1, C+W = 2. - **[Risk, +]** Modelled risk analyses:[d,h] expected occurrence of contamination = 1 per 5 years (C+W). Expected # contaminated farms per crisis = 659 (C) and 117 (W). Worst case figures are 2,210 and 331 respectively. - **[Company, 0]** Production[e,h]. Total = 17.5 mln ton kg. C = 71%, W = 29%. - **[Company, +]** Number of companies. C > 80, W > 35, C+W>4.
2. Type of compound feed: cattle (Ca) versus pig (Pi) versus poultry (Po) versus other (O)	- **[Risk, -]** Incidences[f]. EWS (2003-06): total = 9 cases. Ca = 3, Pi = 1, Po = 1, O = 4. DUS (2004-05): total = 7 cases. Ca = 2, Pi = 2, Po = 2, O = 1. - **[Company, 0]** Production: total (2003) = 12.2 mln ton kg. Ca = 26%, Pi = 43%, Po = 26%, O = 5%. - **[Company, -]** Companies producing 1: 2: 3: 4 types of feed = 13%: 9%: 16%: 62%.
3. Company size of compound feed producers: large (L) versus small (S)[4]	- **[Risk, +]** Experts have different opinions[h]. 1/3: P(L) = P(S), 1/3: P(L) ≈ 2 x P(S), 1/3: P(L) ≈ 10x P(S). - **[Company, 0/+]** Company size: L = 75%, S = 5%, others in between.
4. Compound feed ingredients	- **[Risk, +]** Risk scores per ingredient[a]: e.g. wheat = 82, soya bean industry products = 255. - **[Company, -]** Compound feed composition: multiple ingredients, e.g. pig feed ≈ 2% beet molasses, 4% peas, 4% barley, 3% maize industry products, etc.; about the same for all companies.
5. Country of origin of compound feed ingredients	- **[Risk, 0]** Incidences[f]: somewhat higher risk for Asian countries. - **[Company, -]** Companies' sourcing policy: they mostly compete for the same ingredients from the same suppliers (75% originates from USA, Thailand and Malaysia).

Risk factors and levels	Reported risk and company characteristics
6. Separated production lines (compound feed): yes versus no	- [**Risk, +**] Production line design ranked 12th (from 21 attributes) in conjoint study on chemical risks in compound feed production of dairy chains[g]. - [**Company, +/0**] Factor is measurable. No sector data available.
7. Quality assurance systems: GMP+ versus GMP+ and more	- [**Risk, +**] Quality assurance systems ranked 2nd for chemical (21 attributes) and microbiological risks (23 attributes)[g]. ISO9001 and ISO22000 include additional food safety enhancing aspects, such as improved management and quality system layout[b]. - [**Company, +/0**] Factor is measurable. No sector data available.
8. Member of TrusQ or SafeFeed: yes versus no	- [**Risk, -**] Both organisations aim to deepen GMP+ practices. No longitudinal impact analysis available[h]. - [**Company, +**] Members: >75% of animal feed companies in the Netherlands.
9. Tracking and tracing system: yes versus no	- [**Risk, +**] Adequate systems can substantially reduce the impact of crises[b]. - [**Company, -**] Company systems must fulfil legal requirements[b].
10. Farm types supplied: production (multiplying, dairy, hens) versus meat (fattening, beef, broilers)	- [**Risk, +**] Expected impact of feed contaminationd: m, d: 5% with growth disruption and downgraded quality during 5-10 days; d: 2% with no collection of milk during 7 days; f, be: 15% with culling of whole herd. - [**Company, 0/-**] Supply of m/f, d/be: companies supply both subsectors, for h/br: 50% of companies is specialised towards one subsector (mostly hens).
11. Export to US: yes versus no	- [**Risk, +**] Perceived as risky due to US claiming culture (personal communication, 2007) - [**Company, 0/-**] Only applicable to premixes and additives (< 5 companies), not for compound feed and wet feed.

1 [Risk] and [Company] denote findings with respect to feed risks and company characteristics respectively. Attached scores +, 0 and – indicate whether these findings support clear, undecisive or weak differences between factor levels respectively.

2 Sources: (a) Hazard classifications Product Board Animal Feed (www.pdv.nl); (b) Meuwissen et al., 2003; (c) Meuwissen et al., 2009; (d) Meuwissen et al., 2008; (e)

Organisation of wet feed producers (www.opnv.nl); (f) Rapid Alert System Feed and Food (ec.europa.eu/food/food/rapidalert), EWS = early warning system, DUS = database unwanted substances; (g) Valeeva et al., 2005; (h) Van Asseldonk et al., 2006b; (i) Velthuis et al., 2006.

3 Wet feed includes feed such as wheat starch, brewers' grains, sugar beet pulp, potato cutting and whey.

4 Large and small companies produce > 1 million ton kg and <100,000 ton kg of compound feed per year respectively.

Table 2: Longlist of potential factors influencing the risk of introduction and spread of swine epidemics in the Netherlands and experts' evaluation of riskiness (n = 28). Scores are from 1 (very low risk) to 9 (very high risk)[1]

Potential risk factors	Riskiness for introduction		Riskiness for spread	
	Mean (sd)	Ranking[2]	Mean (sd)	Ranking[2]
Farm location	**5.6 (2.4)**		**6.3 (2.5)**	
1. Farm density in region	6.6 (2.1)	8	7.0 (2.1)	6
2. Animal density in region	5.6 (2.4)	15	5.2 (2.2)	14
Farm animal contacts	**7.5 (2.0)**		**7.3 (2.2)**	
3. Import of animals	7.7 (1.9)	1	5.8 (3.0)	7
4. Number of contact addresses	7.2 (2.0)	2	7.2 (2.1)	1
5. Frequency of animal contacts	6.2 (2.1)	5	6.8 (1.9)	2
6. Import, but from single permanent contact	6.1 (2.3)	6	5.3 (2.9)	8
7. Distance of animal contacts	4.6 (2.4)	10	5.0 (2.4)	9
8. Supply of breeding animals to multiplying farm	4.5 (2.2)	11	4.3 (2.4)	16

Potential risk factors	Riskiness for introduction		Riskiness for spread	
	Mean (sd)	Ranking[2]	Mean (sd)	Ranking[2]
9. Supply of piglets to fattening farm	6.4 (2.0)	3	6.4 (2.1)	4
10. Supply of fattening pigs to slaughterhouse	3.2 (1.9)	22	3.6 (2.3)	21
Other farm contacts	**5.7 (2.0)**		**5.7 (1.8)**	
11. Trucks from rendering company	6.3 (1.7)	9	6.3 (1.9)	11
12. Veterinary practitioner	5.4 (2.2)	16	6.0 (2.2)	13
13. Off-farm manure transports	4.7 (1.9)	20	5.0 (2.0)	18
14. Artificial insemination	4.2 (2.1)	23	5.0 (2.3)	18
15. Supply of wet feed	3.4 (1.8)	25	3.8 (1.6)	24
16. Supply of compound feed	3.1 (1.6)	26	3.6 (1.8)	26
Farm hygiene	**6.4 (2.3)**		**6.5 (2.0)**	
17. Hygiene barrier	7.4 (1.7)	4	7.3 (1.7)	3
18. Strictly separated clean versus dirty routing	7.0 (2.3)	7	6.9 (2.4)	5
19. Animal transport by farmers' owned trucks	5.0 (2.4)	12	5.0 (2.5)	15
20. Animal transport by transport company	5.0 (2.4)	12	5.6 (2.3)	10
21. Fences around premises	4.8 (2.4)	17	4.8 (2.3)	17

Potential risk factors	Riskiness for introduction		Riskiness for spread	
	Mean (sd)	Ranking[2]	Mean (sd)	Ranking[2]
Farm type	4.8 (2.11)		5.2 (1.9)	
22. Free range and organic farms[3]	6.6 (1.8)	13	6.6 (1.8)	12
23. Farms with a diversified business[4]	6.6 (1.8)	14	6.3 (2.0)	14
24. Mixed farm with cattle and/or sheep	6.2 (1.6)	18	6.0 (1.9)	17
25. Hobby farm	5.9 (2.4)	19	5.3 (2.4)	20
26. Fattening farm	5.3 (1.9)	21	4.0 (1.9)	25
27. Multiplying farm	4.5 (1.7)	24	5.4 (2.4)	19
28. Closed farm, stables not on one site	3.6 (1.3)	27	4.0 (2.0)	25
29. Breeding farm	2.6 (1.7)	28	4.6 (2.7)	22
30. Closed farm, stables on one site	2.6 (1.6)	28	2.9 (1.6)	27
31. Artificial insemination company	2.5 (1.9)	29	4.2 (2.9)	23

1 Category scores, i.e. for farm location, farm animal contacts etc., are from 1 (very low importance) to 9 (very high importance)

2 Based on weighted means.

3 Including outdoor housing of pigs.

4 Such as camping, kennel or selling from home.

3.2 Contamination Risks in the Animal Feed Sector: Conjoint Analysis

After having composed the longlist of risk factors, the importance of the various factors was studied by conjoint analysis. In a conjoint analysis experts evaluate combinations of risk factors, so-called profiles. Evaluation scores can then be used to assess the importance of each individual factor and the utilities of underlying factor levels. As standard conjoint analysis can deal with a maximum of about 6 factors (Hair et al., 1998), a literature review was carried out to shorten the longlist from 11 to a maximum of 6 factors. In reviewing the literature we focused on the relationship of factor levels with the level of risk and specific company characteristics.

As the right-hand column of Table 1 shows, factor levels of 4 factors show relatively strong differences in risk and company characteristics: factor 1 (type of animal feed; compound versus wet feed), factor 3 (company size; large versus small), factor 6 (separated production lines; yes, no) and factor 7 (number of certificates; GMP+ versus GMP+ and more). These are included in the conjoint profiles. For the other factors, sometimes a difference was found in the level of risk, such as for factor 4, i.e. compound feed ingredients, but not in related company characteristics: feed companies hardly differ in this respect. Alternatively, for some factors, e.g. factor 8 (membership of TrusQ or SafeFeed), companies are different, but literature does not support differences in the level of risk. Factors 10 (farm types supplied) and 11 (export to US) are still included in the conjoint profiles because of their relevant relationship with the level of risk and as there is at least some degree of measurability.

Factor levels of the 6 selected risk factors, i.e. type of animal feed, quality assurance, separated production lines, distribution of products to the US, company size and type of farms supplied, were combined into 10 so-called "full profiles". Profiles were designed according to a fractional factorial process and assuming a main effects model, i.e. without interaction between risk factors. See Figure 1 for an example of such a "full profile". Profiles were then presented to experts in a questionnaire which was pretested by a feed company expert of an insurance broker. This insurance broker also provided names and addresses of experts to be surveyed. In spring 2008, questionnaires were sent to 28 quality managers of animal feed companies in the Netherlands. A cover letter explained the aim of the survey, i.e. to identify feed industry's risk profiles potentially to be used in insurance schemes covering damage of feed crises. Experts evaluated conjoint profiles on a scale from 1 (very low preference) to 7 (very high preference). In addition they indicated their own company's characteristics for each of the factor levels. After 1 month 14 fully-filled questionnaires were returned and used for further analyses. During this month no feed crises occurred. Table 3 (second column) shows that most respondents are from relatively large companies producing mostly compound feed and paying relatively much attention to quality assurance.

Figure 1: Example of conjoint profile presented to animal feed experts

Situation 1

1. Only compound feed
2. GMP+ and more
3. No strictly separated production lines
4. No distribution to the US
5. Annual production < 100,000 ton
6. Only supply to production farms

My preference for this type of animal feed company is:						
Very low			Moderate			Very high
1	2	3	4	5	6	7

3.3 Epidemic Risks in the Pig Sector: Expert Elicitation and Risk Modelling

In order to elicit experts' opinion about the risk factors related to swine epidemics as shown in Table 2, a structured questionnaire was sent to selected experts. Experts were from farmers' organisations, veterinary practices and governmental departments. The majority of experts had been closely involved in the 1997/98 outbreak of classical swine fever and the 2001 outbreak of foot and mouth disease. A cover letter explained the aim of the questionnaire, i.e. to design risk profiles of pig farms potentially to be applied in the pig sector's animal health fund or any future insurance schemes covering epidemic disease damage in the pig sector. Experts were first asked to assess the riskiness of each factor in relation to the *introduction* of an epidemic disease into the Netherlands. These questions were on a Likert-scale ranging from 1 (very low risk) to 9 (very high risk). They were also asked to indicate importances for the 5 categories of risk, again on a scale from 1 (very low importance) to 9 (very high importance). Similar questions were then asked with regard to the *spread* of epidemic diseases in the Netherlands. In total, in spring 2002, 30 questionnaires were sent and during a one-month period

23 questionnaires were returned and used for further analyses. During this period no epidemic diseases occurred.

Besides this round of questionnaires, we also deployed a simulation model entitled InterCSF (Mangen et al., 2001) to further study the influence of some of the risk factors listed. InterCSF is a stochastic model which mimics the spread of classical swine fever epidemics in the Netherlands. Factors studied include: (i) farm and animal density (compare factors 1 and 2, Table 2); (ii) weekly number of transports of live animals to other farms (factor 5); (iii) distance of these transports (factor 7); and (iv) farm type of primary infection (factors 26 and 27). In this paper, InterCSF-results refer to direct damage figures per classical swine fever epidemic in the 50% and the 95%-percentiles.[2]

4. Results

4.1 Risk Factors Related to Animal Feed Crises

Through the conjoint method insight is not only obtained in the relative importances of selected risk factors but also in preferences (utilities) for underlying factor levels. As higher utilities indicate lower levels of risk, Table 3 shows among others that the production of compound feed is perceived to be less risky than the production of wet feed. Also, smaller companies are perceived to be less risky than larger companies. In case of a contamination, large-scale companies may easily lead to widespread distribution of contaminated products and therefore damage (see also reported findings from literature in Table 1).

The relatively high risk of wet feed is not in line with literature but may be due to the unbalanced panel of experts mostly representing compound feed producing companies. As wet feed is "not their business", related risks may be perceived as relatively high. This unfamiliarity may also explain the high importance of supplying products to the US as a risk factor. Other relative importances, i.e. for the factors on quality assurance, design of production lines, company size and farm types supplied, are perceived to be lower and are more or less in the same range. Scores may reflect the fact that these factors are more or less "common business" and already assured.

[2] Meaning that 50% of damage outcomes were below the 50%-percentile and 5% of outcomes exceeded the 95%-percentile.

Table 3: Characteristics of feed companies in sample, relative importances of risk factors and utility scores per factor level (n=14).

Risk factors and levels	Company characteristics	Relative importances per risk factor	Utility scores per factor level
1. Type of animal feed		0.32	
- Compound feed	14		0.78
- Wet feed	2		-0.78
2. Supply to US		0.30	
- Yes	0		-0.80
- No	14		0.80
3. Quality assurance systems		0.11	
- GMP+	3		-0.31
- GMP+ and more	11		0.31
4. Separated production lines		0.11	
- Strictly separated lines	6		0.19
- Not strictly separated lines	8		-0.19
5. Company size		0.08	
- >100,000 ton kg per year	12		-0.11
- <100,000 ton kg per year	2		0.11
6. Farm types supplied		0.07	
- Production farms	14		0.13
- Meat farms	14		-0.13

A comparison of the characteristics of the companies in our sample and utility scores per factor level shows that experts generally perceive their companies to have relatively limited risks. Only for company size and design of production lines, more companies can be found in the higher risk level than in the lower risk level. This picture is confirmed when we use utility scores to actually classify the 14 companies in relation to each other: 10 companies are classified as "low risk" and 4 as "high risk".[3]

3 "Low risk" includes relatively high utility scores, i.e. aggregated risk score of a company ≥ group mean of the 14 companies. "High risk" includes relatively low scores, i.e. ag-

4.2 Risk Factors Related to Livestock Epidemics

Among the 5 categories of factors presented to the experts, the highest importance is attributed to farm animal contacts (scores of 7.5 and 7.3 for risks of disease introduction and spread respectively) and farm hygiene (scores of 6.4 and 6.5 respectively). Farm type was perceived to be the least important. These results show that the ranking of risk categories is the same for risk factors related to disease introduction and spread. The same largely holds for the perceived riskiness of the factors within each of the categories. For instance, in the category of farm location, farm density is perceived to be more risky than animal density, both for the risk of introducing a disease as well as for the risk of spreading it. In relation to animal contacts, risky factors are the import of animals, number of contact addresses, frequency of animal contacts and the supply of piglets to fattening farms. Supplying pigs to slaughterhouses is not perceived to be very risky, not for disease introduction nor for the spreading of a disease (ranked 22nd and 21st respectively). In the group of "other farm contacts", risks are perceived to be higher for trucks from rendering companies and visits from veterinary practitioners than for trucks delivering animal feed. For farm hygiene, factors related to hygiene barriers and separated clean versus dirty routing are perceived as more relevant than issues of transport. In the category of farm type, none of the types mentioned is in the "top 10" of risk factors. Still, results show that free range and organic farms, farms with diversified businesses and mixed farms are perceived to be more risky than specialised pig farms such as breeding, multiplying and fattening farms and artificial insemination companies.

InterCSF simulation results largely support expert opinions. For instance with regard to the relevance of farm density, differences between sparsely populated livestock areas (SPLA) and densely populated livestock areas (DPLA) are illustrative. In the default situation, direct damage of classical swine fever epidemics are Euro 18 million versus Euro 206 million in the 50% and 95%-percentiles respectively (Table 4). Distance of animal contacts, which was not in the experts' top 5, also in simulation does not show a very strong influence when comparing "shorter" and "longer" distances. For

gregated risk score of a company < group mean. If classification is based on factors 2-6, i.e. excluding type of feed, classification of companies does not change.

farm type, simulation results show that if an epidemic starts at a breeding farm, damage is expected to be much higher than when an epidemic would start at a multiplying or fattening farm. Experts however seemed to believe that breeding farms' higher attention for risk prevention measures outweigh the risk related to their higher number of animal contacts.

Table 4: Direct damage of classical swine fever epidemics in the Netherlands for default situation and impact of risk factors (million euro)[1]

	Sparsely populated pig area[2]		Densely populated pig area[2]	
	50%	95%	50%	95%
Default situation	**2**	**18**	**96**	**206**
Number of transports per week (live animals to other farms)[3]				
- Less	1	6	76	141
- More	4	22	156	283
Distance of transports (live animals to other farms)[4]				
- Shorter	3	18	115	253
- Longer	4	42	110	274
Farm type of primary infection[5]				
- Breeding	6	48	117	249
- Fattening	1	5	87	187

1 Assuming basis EU control strategies without vaccination. Damage includes organisational costs and the value of destructed herds.

2 The sparsely populated area has 9,826 pigs and 32 pig farms per 10 km. In the densely populated area these are 464,754 and 592 respectively (2002 consensus data Animal Health Service).

3 Default settings are on average 0.77 and 0.62 transports per week for breeding and multiplying farms respectively. In the "less" scenario 0 transports take place. In the "more" scenario, numbers are on average 2.4 and 1.1 respectively.

4 Default settings are 95% of transports < 50 km. In the "shorter" and "longer" scenarios these are 95% < 20 km and 75% < 50 km respectively.

5 Default settings assume a multiplying farm to face the primary infection.

5. Towards More Risk Classification in Food Supply Chains?

Results of this paper show that despite limited data, quantitative support for risk profiling is possible. Starting from longlists of potential risk factors related to animal feed contamination risks and swine epidemics, results of expert elicitation, simulation modelling and "circumstantial evidence" from literature reduces these lists to 6 and 7 factors respectively (Table 5). When discussing their appropriateness for future risk profiling in food supply chains however several issues are relevant, which are as follows.

At first, do selected risk factors show a strong *relationship with the level of risk*? For animal feed crises, literature shows relationships with risk for 8 of the 11 factors. For further analyses however 2 factors were no longer considered, i.e. compound feed ingredients and the availability of a tracking and tracing system, as for these factors companies are hardly any different. A full-profile conjoint analysis supported the relevance of the 6 prioritised risk factors. The somewhat lower score for the risk factor of company size relates to some indecisive findings in literature and the relatively low importance of this factor in conjoint analysis. With regard to epidemic disease risks experts fairly much agreed on which 7 risk factors show the strongest relationship with the risk of introducing a disease into the Netherlands and the risk of spreading it. Expert opinions were underpinned by the results of the classical swine fever simulation model.

Secondly, *can companies be sufficiently differentiated*? For animal feed risks, this item was already part of selecting risk factors for the conjoint analysis. For 2 of the prioritised risk factors in Table 5, i.e. supply to the US and farm types supplied, feed companies are expected not to strongly differ as hardly any company exports to the US and almost all companies supply feed to all farming sectors. With regard to differentiating among farms, lowest scores are given for frequency of animal contacts and a farm's hygiene barrier. These are legally determined issues and not much difference among farms is to be expected.

A third item is to which degree risk classification criteria can *induce behavioural changes* in the supply chain, e.g. towards more risk prevention. Table 5 show that prioritised risk factors score relatively low on this item as for many factors, e.g. region of location, company size and type of clients, structural business changes would be required. On the contrary, behavioural changes for risk factors such as importing animals, proper usage of hygiene barriers and number of quality assurance schemes seem to be more straightforward to implement.

Furthermore, as a fourth aspect, *transactions costs* of implementing a risk profiling system should ideally be relatively limited. Table 5 shows that, due to detailed registration systems, transaction costs for most risk factors are expected not to be substantial. Hygiene barriers and routing in pig farms score relatively poor as actual usage of these facilities is difficult to measure. Also regions' farm density scores relatively low as definitions of regions can be cumbersome and, as an alternative, farm densities need to be determined per individual farm taking into account a certain radius around each farm.

Table 5: Prioritised risk factors for animal feed crises and livestock epidemics and evaluation of potential for risk classification (++: factor scores well, --: factor scores poor).

	Relationship to risk	Differences between farms/plants	Behavioural impact	Limited transaction costs[1]
Animal feed crisis risk				
- Type of animal feed	+	+	0	++
- Supply to US	+	-	0	++
- Quality assurance systems	++	+	+	+
- Strictly separated production lines	+	+	+	+
- Company size	0/+	+	-	++
- Farm types supplied	+	-	0	+
Epidemic livestock disease risk				
- Import of animals	+	+	+	+
- Number of contact addresses	++	0	+	+
- Frequency of animal contacts	++	+	+	+
- Supply of piglets to fattening farm	++	+	0	+
- Farm density in region	+	+	--	0
- Hygiene barrier	++	0	+	--
- Strictly separated clean vs dirty routing	+	+	+	-

1 A + and – indicate relatively low and high transaction costs respectively.

All in all, considering the scores in Table 5, some level of risk profiling seems to be possible for epidemic disease risks in pig farms. Prioritised risk factors show relatively strong relationships with the level of risk and for most of them behavioural changes are feasible. Room for finetuning can be found in performing risk analyses on various types of hygiene barriers and to study the appropriate radius around farms for determining "farm density in the region". With regard to designing risk profiles for animal feed companies, the case of risk classification seems somewhat less strong. Risk analyses not always point into the same direction, such as with company size, and for some risk factors companies are hardly any different. Also, as many factors relate to structural business characteristics there is not much behavioural change to be expected.

Results are useful in current supply chain debates on extending risk pooling opportunities for feed producers' product liability risks and farmers' losses from livestock epidemics. Eventual implementation of (some degree of) risk profiling however will depend on the objectives of stakeholders involved. Although a clear relationship with risk will always be important, stakeholders who want to stress incentives for risk prevention might opt for other criteria than those who want to minimise transaction costs. Results also illustrate that some risk communication among supply chain partners is needed to achieve broadly accepted risk profiling systems. Compound feed producers for instance seem to misperceive risks related to the production of wet feed.

References

HAIR, J. E.; ANDERSON, R. E.; TATHAM, R. L.; BLACK, W. C. 1998. *Multivariate data analysis*. New Jersey: Prentice Hall.

MANGEN, M. J. J.; JALVINGH, A. W.; NIELEN, M.; MOURITS, M. C. M.; KLINKENBERG, D.; DIJKHUIZEN, A. A. 2001. Spatial and stochastic simulation to compare two emergency vaccination strategies with a marker vaccine in the 1997/98. Dutch classical swine fever epidemic. *Preventive Veterinary Medicine* 48, 177-200.

MEUWISSEN, M. P. M.; HORST, S. H.; HUIRNE, R. B. M.; DIJKHUIZEN, A. A. 1999. A model to estimate the financial consequences of classical swine fever outbreaks: principles and outcomes. *Preventive Veterinary Medicine* 42, 249-270.

MEUWISSEN, M. P. M.; VAN ANDEL, A. A.; VAN ASSELDONK, M. A. P. M.; HUIRNE, R. B. M. 2009. Supply chain damage due to animal feed contamination; scenario analyses for processing industries. *British Food Journal*, forthcoming.

MEUWISSEN, M. P. M.; VAN ASSELDONK, M. A. P. M.; Huirne, R. B. M. 2008. Liability risks in agri-food supply chains: the case of wet feed. *Paper presented at the EAAE-meetings*, Gent, Belgium, Aug. 27-29.

MEUWISSEN, M. P. M.; VELTHUIS, A. G. J.; HOGEVEEN, H.; HUIRNE, R. B. M. 2003. Traceability and certification in meat supply chains. *Journal of Agribusiness* 21, 167-181.

REJDA, G. E. 1998. *Principles of risk management and insurance*. New York: Harper Collins.

VALEEVA, N. I.; MEUWISSEN, M. P. M.; OUDE LANSINK, A. G. J. M.; Huirne, R. B. M. 2005. Improving food safety within the dairy chain: an application of conjoint analysis. *Journal of Dairy Science* 88, 1601-1612.

VAN ASSELDONK, M. A. P. M.; MEUWISSEN, M. P. M.; HUIRNE, R. B. M. 2002. Belief in disaster relief and the demand for a public-private insurance program. *Review of Agricultural Economics* 24, 196-207.

VAN ASSELDONK, M. A. P. M.; MEUWISSEN, M. P. M.; HUIRNE, R. B. M. 2006b. *The production of compound feed in the Netherlands: an analysis of contamination risks*. Institute for Risk Management in Agriculture, Wageningen UR, The Netherlands.

VAN ASSELDONK, M. A. P. M.; MEUWISSEN, M. P. M.; HUIRNE, R. B. M.; WILKENS, E. 2006a. European public and private schemes indemnifying epidemic livestock losses: a review. In: HOAG, D. L.; THILMANY, D. D.; KOONTZ, S. R. (Eds.). *The economics of livestock disease insurance:* concepts, issues and international case studies. p. 115-125.

VELTHUIS, A. G. J.; VAN ERVE, C.; MEUWISSEN, M. P. M. 2006. Modelling the recall costs of consumption milk in relation to time. In: BIJMAN, J.; OMTA, S. W. F.; TRIENEKENS, J. H.; WIJNANDS, J. H. M.; WUBBEN, E. F. M. (Eds.). *International agri-food chains and networks*: management and organization. Wageningen Academic Publishers. p. 259-268.

Part 4

Sustainability and Governance

- The Importance of Socioenvironmental Certification in Agri-chains
- The Evolution of Sustainability Management Research
- Netchain Leadership in the U.S. Ethanol Sector
- Corporate Governance and Corporate Responsibility
- Relating International Ethanol Supply Chain Performance to Their Governance Structures

The Importance of Socioenvironmental Certification in Agri-chains

SAMUEL RIBEIRO GIORDANO

This article discusses the importance of certification of agribusiness products that aim to secure and maintain Brazilian competitiveness in international markets.

International consumers perceive that production processes in agriculture may cause serious damage and pose a big threat not only to the environment, but also to the people involved in these processes. Because of these negative impacts, several agribusiness companies and cooperatives have changed their productive processes to achieve more sustainable ways of production. The development of sustainability certification involving social and environmental assessment for agribusiness products can thus provide the needed guarantee to consumers as well as enhance the competitiveness of Brazilian agricultural food products.

The Brazilian experience with coffee and forestry production may help develop the concept of socioenvironment concern for other crops and the rising star of the Brazilian agrichains, the biofuels.

The central question of this paper is how to develop a sustainability seal in agriculture and how to clearly present its benefits, especially to Brazilian consumers. The international consumers seem to be pushed to a sea of seals. Showing the benefits of seal implementation along the agrichain is a major challenge. The international consumer is the focus but the domestic consumer cannot be forgotten.

1. Concept Relevance

Consumers of raw or industrial agribusiness goods demand more and more products that have been produced using good socioenvironmental practices.

In several countries such as the USA and the EC and also in Brazil, consumer rights advocates ask for a minimum guarantee of environment-friendly procedures for use in production processes. Thus, many segments in the agribusiness sector such as the distributors and retailers started to attach seals that inform consumers that these products were produced employing good socioenvironmental practices.

Actually, these measures were in anticipation of the demand from consumers. They offered to the consumers a guarantee assuring their products to reduce risks arising from pressures imposed by the international environmentalist movements.

The Brazilian agribusiness followed the same steps, specially the sectors dedicated to biofuels. They are looking now for a certification process involving stakeholders who participate in the production process, from the field to the gas stations. In this way, the productive sectors imagine that these procedures will be more easily recognized by society and consumers.

Adopting classic practices of monitoring and control, a certification process aims to make more visible to society the socioenvironment actions and measures made by the agribusiness segment. At the center of this subject is a movement to engage the consumers in the chain process of socioenvironmental responsibility. By acquiring products with a determined custody chain, the costumer will be an important part of the process, injecting financial resources and ensuring that the system is working.

In the case of biofuels, consumers will certainly look for guarantees from the field to the gas station and coffee drinkers will assess socioenvironmental responsibility from the bean to the cup.

2. Status of the Problem and State-of-the-art Trends

Agricultural production and agribusiness are extremely important economic activities in Brazil. They occupy a large part of the national territory, affecting directly and indirectly a significant part of the Brazilian population.

The well-being of rural workers and producers and their families, along with the conservation of natural ecosystems and their biodiversity, depend directly on agricultural operations developed with adequate criteria of socioenvironmental performance.

The socioenvironmental behavior codes and certification are important tools to achieve sustainability objectives.

The regulating agents can be either the government or national or international organizations Coordination is, very often, made by a dominating company or through organizing mechanisms accorded between the players. Many discussions and recurring questions refer to the costs involved in such certifications. These costs tend to be shared and transmitted to the several segments involved in the production system. There are sectors that affirm that consumers will pay for this bill and the direct costs will be passed straight to them. But there are those who feel that all segments involved in the certification process (input suppliers, rural producers, industry, wholesale, retail, and sector engaged in the quest for quality procedures) should share the bill and divide costs among them all.

One example of this is the fate of nations that lost in World War II, specially Germany and Japan. These nations were destroyed by the conflict but they saw the need to put its economy together, its agriculture and its industry, aiming to improve the quality of life of its citizens. This collective effort lasted for 25 years and represented a cost that a whole generation paid for, so that the present generation could afford a high pattern of life today. Actually, this post-war generation of men and women invested their time, their handiwork, their financial resources, and their goodwill on the future generations. These countries developed learning curves that allowed automobiles to be popularized through production lines at low cost and reasonable quality. This effort took more than 15 years. Common sense dictates that the certification process had its origins in beliefs and political struggles, but its origins appeared to be related to economic motivation. According to CONROY (2007), with the advance and diffusion of electrical energy and electric appliances, the insurance companies started to make demands from industry, asking for a certification that assured that the appliances would not cause death by electric shock. The insurance companies were worried that if there were high incidence of these accidents, their economic capacity could be compromised.

In Brazil, the key question is: Isn't it about time to invest efforts on learning, knowledge, and financial resources to ensure that the next generations will have a sustainable means of production and credibility in the international markets in order to sell food and fiber goods with added value? For Brazil, it is no longer enough to be the first exporter in several rankings of commodities, if heavy investments and efforts in education are not made. Only education at all levels can save Brazil from losing its place in the ranking of competing nations. The socioenvironmental practices and investments will be directly proportional to investments made in education.

The guarantee that will be given to international and local consumers, through a good socioenvironmental practice certification, demand that this effort be made now.

This change of attitude toward responsibility brought about much debate. The debate should involved questions related to carbon and also the difficult dialogue about ways to sustain human development as population growth rate increases. Collective actions taken today could generate positive externalities to the group of players included in the agribusiness systems. This transformation will certainly bring benefits into the future. The certification as a tool of modification created with local criteria and as the fruit of ample discussion and understanding could help enhance the sustainability process of Brazilian agribusiness. Agribusiness is the big business of the present Brazil and will continue to be so in the future, for a long time. The focal point of this article is about the importance and benefits of socioenvironmental certification for the Brazilian agribusiness.

2.1 The Concept of Certification

According to the Brazilian Association of Technical Standardization (ABNT, 2006), the certification is a set of activities developed by an organization, independently of the commercial relation, that aim to attest publicly, by a written certificate, that such a product process or service is complying with specified requirements.

These requirements can be national or international. The certification activities can involve: documental analysis, auditing /inspections in the organization, sampling and testing of the product in the market, or the industry aiming to evaluate compliance with standards and its maintenance.

In its broad concept, the certification is the definition of the attributes of a product, process, or service and the guarantee that they fit in predefined standards. In this way, the certification involves standards in the private, public, national, or international spheres and a certifying organization with the power of monitoring and excluding those who do not comply with the accorded rules (institutional environment) (NASSAR, 2003). In other words, the certification is one step ahead of mere standardization, from the point of view of the agribusiness system.

Standardization is a way of reducing transaction costs. These costs are relative to the functioning of the economic system. They involve the identification of the suppliers, the distributors, the contracts among them, their control and effective compliance, the characteristics of the products, incentives and bonuses, associated services, and more. In looking at this question more deeply, this issue is all about information exchange (FARINA, 2003).

The certification is a detailed standardization that has exclusion instruments. More specifically, the socioenvironmental certification is necessary to differentiate products that were produced according to the three principles of sustainability: environmentally adequate, socially fair, and economically feasible. The certification should express the interests of these three points (PINTO, 2000).

It is important to note at this point that the certification is a process. As such, it should not be thought of as isolated and punctual attitudes. It should encompass a group of actions that start with the awareness of the problem, passes through technical standardization, and advances toward the operational, administrative, and recording procedures and also relationship with society. The certification is the result of a process of (re)organization of the company/organization, achieved by the efforts made by different levels of its administration. It is definitely not a shelf product. The certification improves the image of the organizations and facilitates the buying decision of costumers. In this period of humanity called Technical-Scientific-Informational (SANTOS, 1994), there is an acceleration of time speed. The informational exchange is done at light speed. With technological advance, speed and time change in an exponential manner. Buyers and sellers cannot anymore, within the globalization process, make inspections and verifications of the food they exchange. In this way, they need mechanisms that can transfer efficiency for their operations.

The standardization of categories and attributes of food are basic elements and should be accepted by both negotiating sides. This information can be given through a seal issued by a certifier accredited by a third party organization. The knowledge of this information leads to an enhancement of the market and the transparency of its functioning (FARINA, 2003). The monitoring that leads to certification aims to guarantee consumers and buyers about the attributes of the product or process. These actions can make the market clearer, reducing the disparity of information. When the seller provides these information, it is easier to manage the processes and offer guaranties of the attributes of products or processes are easily exchanged.

From the consumers' point of view, the certification seal of a product should, by principle, furnish information and guarantees of attributes of the product or process commercialized .The seal expresses the products' or processes' compliance with the rules and standards, it being an information transmitter to the consumers. In parallel with this concept is introduced the concept of behavior code. Being a voluntary adhesion code audited by sampling, the code confers also a sealing, without being characterized as a certification.

One of the greatest problems of certification of products and processes and its sealing is that there recently appeared a lot of different seals for products in the market. The consumer, in many cases, does not have enough time or enough information about the seals to differentiate them from the others. If the consumer cannot identify clearly the purpose of the seal, it can backfire. Imagine a consumer with limited information confronted with a product in the supermarket shelf that bears four different seals. It is not a definite truth that a seal-bearing product will add value to the consumer. The belief goods can be satisfied with the introduction of the seal, but it will be effective only to a determined public that knows and values its attributes.

In the last 10 years, this point evolved, with the regulation of labels. The industry was forced to put at least the chemical composition in the labels, the origins of the fat, the presence of gluten, fenialanin and other 'problem maker' products to sensible consumers. Even though these measures, the Brazilian consumer faces choices that cannot always be correctly identified due to failure of health authorities or the industry or the self-interest in getting more acquainted with the products. In some cases, the consumer faces the key factors of the certification and sealing is the information passed to the consumer. Without this key, a product can bear more than 20 seals without attracting the attention of the consumer. It should be also considered that many industries are not yet concerned with social communication and public relation campaigns, in the belief that the seal will speak by itself, which is definitely not true.

2.2 *Types of Certification*

Two criteria can be used to characterize the certification (NASSAR, 2003): by the regulating agent and by the certification objective.

a) Certification by a Regulating Agent

The regulatory agents can be government or national organizations. In the case of French wines, for instance, it is made a collective certification, regulated or not, by a certifying organization. This is precisely the case of guaranteed and controlled denominations of origin (DOCG) in Italy, with Tuscany wines, specifically in the subregion of the Chianti. There is also the internal or self-certification occurring in self-transactions of a company aiming to reduce its transaction costs. In this model can be fitted many supermarket networks. Bellow can be seen the different types of certification used in Brazil.

- Purity seals. The Brazilian Industry Association of Coffee established a purity seal guaranteeing the auditing of factories and analysis of coffee samples bought randomly in commerce to attest the purity of the product. They are interested in proving that within the package is only coffee and not other mixtures. The success of this seal led to the recent creation of another one, by the same association. Called the Quality Seal, it aims of this new to reduce disinformation about the quality of coffee inside the package. Any roaster can adhere to this program by brand. If he wants to work with one or two brands of his company and not all of them, he can. The seal gives consumers these six characteristics of the blend:
  - the species of the coffee, *Arabica* or *Robusta*;
  - the grade of roasting, very dark, light to dark;
  - the body, inexistent, light to full bodied;
  - the aroma, inexistent, subtle to intense;
  - the flavor, intense, medium, discreet; and
  - the grinding, very fine, fine to coarse.

The Brazilian experience in the coffee industry should be mentioned by its importance in paradigm setting in the sector.

- Product Quality Seal. There are many seals of this kind and Qualité France (QF) can be mentioned. In Europe, the QF is the only organization that certifies the quality of agribusiness products through rigid procedures every 3 months in the product acquiring process, in the blending, in the roasting, in the air freezing, and in the packaging.
- Geographical Origin Seal. The Caccer Seal, for instance, guarantees the quality of the coffee produced in the central savannahs of Brazil (Cerrados) under a sustainable model encompassing the environment, the economy, and the social aspects.
- The Forestry Seal FSC. The Forest Stewardship Council attests that the wood (or other forestry input) used in a product originated from a sustainable production forest that was adequately managed in an environment-friendly, socially fair, and economically feasible system and in compliance with the country's laws.
- Organic or Biological Production Seals. The seal certifies that the sealed product does not contain chemicals and it guarantees that it is the result of agricultural practices whereby the quality of the natural environment,the nutritional and biological quality, and the life quality of those who live in the country and cities are assured.
- Seal ISO-14.001 This group of ISO rules are standards related with environmental management systems and others, which are specific tools to set environmental policies aimed to reach goals and objectives.

b) Certification by Objective

The certification can aim to attain various aspects such as certification of processes, certification of products, and multistakeholder certification.

The process certification aims to guarantee that the production process of a good or a service met the standards established by an independent third party so that a certain characteristic can be assured to the consumer. The ISO Standards are an example. In the automotive spare parts industry, the total quality process of ISO 9.000 certification leads to a level of total absence of defective parts in the fabrication process. In this way, the automobile industry does not need to replace defective spare parts. In its productive process, measures were taken to avoid these cases.

Another example of process certification for services are the banks' credit cards with ISO 9.001 certification of total quality. They guarantee the services provided by banks in avoiding fraud, cloning, and maintaining good relationship with consumers. Sometimes, other services such as life insurance, health insurance against accidents, luggage losses, and other types are offered. In the agribusiness systems, there are processes of environmental certification called ISO 14.000. This group of rules covers standards related to environmental management systems. They are specific tools to set environmental policies aimed to achieve specific objectives . The standards consist of doing good agricultural practices designated to minimize the negative impacts of agricultural production on the environment. Even though it is an interesting inside-the-organization instrument used to monitor and control the quality of supplier-consumer relations, several environmentalist groups criticize the way the series 14.000 are developed, as well as the use of certification by certified companies (PINTO, 2000).

In the food industry, Brazil has the norm ISO 22.000. It aims to demonstrate that the industry has competence in controlling risks and ensuring safety in food and that it is constantly looking after safety, so that this aim matches the clients' and law requirements. The benefits obtained with the implementation of an ISO 22.000 system are as follows:

- Improvement in productivity due to optimization of the processes and resources involved, reducing losses and enhancing safety through the application of efficient mechanisms of control.
- Improvement in the awareness and avoidance of compromise with collaborators with respect to the company's objectives and principles of food safety;
- Reduction of the complaint index, attaining a better image of the company for its consumers.
- More consistency in the traceability mechanisms of the products, inputs, and ingredients along the productive chain, guaranteeing more trust and control of resources.
- Reduction of interface problems in the segments of the productive chain.

A system like the ISO 22.000 can cover all agribusiness systems beyond the main parts (production–agriculture and animal industry–distribution–final consumer), and those that support the chain (packaging industry, transport logistics, additives, cleaning products, and others). This norm is aligned with ISO 9.001:2000, and there is an intimate compatibility between them and other systems normally used by companies and organizations.

The certification of products, as was earlier seen, started with electrical appliances.

The certification can signal to the consumer that the products fit the purpose for they are designed or it could, as in the past, certify that electrical appliances would not cause death by electrical shock to the consumer.

Since they are certified, the products can bear a certification seal. They should be utilized accordingly with the instructions and technical specifications so performance can be attained.

In general, they are oriented to the consumers' market, presenting a direct message from the supplier to the consumer. The case of agricultural products precedes in many years the industrial revolution certification at the beginning of the 20th century. It is worthwhile to mention the history to learn something from the past. The Douro Denomination region (north Portugal), where the port wines are made, was the first agricultural region in the world to receive geographical denomination by boundaries. A Royal Bill established by the Marquis of Pombal on September 10 1756 denominated a region situated northeast of Portugal, in the Douro River basin. This region is surrounded by mountains, giving it particular soil and climate characteristics. With a total area of 250,000 hectares, the region had 38,588 hectares of vineyards. It was subdivided into three distinct subregions, not only due to weather factors, but also for socioeconomic reasons. This process of geographical denomination started because the port wines had a good value at the time and represented a considerable parcel of the regional and national income of Portugal. Being a unique product, it represented Portugal's expression in the world its culture, environment, technology, agriculture, soils, winds, rains, the economy, and society itself. With so many attributes and a growing demand in the world market, a fraudulent process was carried on. Falsified products started to appear in Portugal and even in Holland. This was a threat to the economic, social, and environmental patrimony of Portugal. The consequences were immediate with falling prices in England, its major client. The producers were accused of doing the fraud. This process mobilized especially the big wineries that pressed strongly the Marquis de Pombal government to institutionalize the General Agricultural Wine Company of the High Douro. This regulatory process had two objectives: to assure the quality of the product to avoid fraud and to regulate production, commerce, and prices. The productive region is delimitated with 335 stone marks establishing the Feitoria designation, a pattern that stood for best quality wines and the only ones that could be exported to England. This product was also known as fine wine. The regulations were set and severe punishment was applied if the rules were broken. Today, this wine has kept its reputation due to measures taken in the 18th century (GIORDANO, 2007).

In the case of Italian and French wines, a collective certification is done, regulated or not, by a certifier organization. In this case, there was a series of graduations, more or less rigid, established in common with the whole European Community. This is the case of the Denomination of Origin Controlled and Guaranteed, the AOCG (Apellation d'Origine Controllé et Garantie) in France or its equivalent entity in Italy, the DOCG (Denominazione di Origine Controlata i Garantita).

c) The Multistakeholder Certification

This certification involves all sorts of participants in the processes risk takers such as shareholders, managers, consumers, workers, and citizens in general. In this way, certification is legitimized because all parts involved were consulted and heard prior to certification.

The awareness of environmentalist and social movements of consumers in the USA and Europe developed with the consumption of goods coming from the Third World. After the 21 Agenda were elaborated in the United Nations Summit Environment Conference in Rio de Janeiro in 1992, it was observed that criticism and boycott of these products would be useless. It was necessary to present viable alternatives to existing models. The development should look for a more harmonious and equal conciliation between the economic, social, and environmental interests.

The Forest Stewardship Council (FSC) certification, with its seal FSC for forestry products, was a pioneer initiative of socioenvironmental multistakeholder certification to promote the responsible management of forests in the world. Through a process of consultations, the FSC establishes international patterns to ensure responsible management of forests. The FSC accredits independent third-party organizations that can certify forest companies and forest processors of forest products with the FSC patterns. The seal provides international recognition to companies that responsibly manage the forests and permits its consumers to recognize the products and the producers who support initiatives in sustaining the forests.

The FSC provides marketing programs and information services that contribute to the mission of promoting a responsible forestry system in the world. In the last 13 years, more than 90 million hectares were certified in more than 70 countries with the FSC patterns. On the other hand, thousands of products were produced using certified wood with the FSC seal. This program operates in 45 countries by means of national initiatives and organizations. In Brasil, IMAFLORA—Instituto para o Manejo Florestal e Agrícola makes this operation. FSC in Brazil has the denomination of Conselho Brasileiro de Manejo Florestal—FSC Brasil. It is an independent and non-profit nongovernment organization, recognized as the Civil Society Organization of Public Interest (OSCIP-Organização da Sociedade Civil de Interesse Público) (IMAFLORA, 2005).

3. Examples of Certification in Brazil

Profiting from the experience held by IMAFLORA in forest and agricultural certification, Brazil already has a committed group in this organization that can face the biofuel certification. There are some signals made by the EU and the USA, besides the traditional market of Japan, showing that biofuels mixing in varied proportions with fossil fuels will be a reality. Many governments are already changing their regulation toward this issue, turning mandatory the addition of biofuels to fossil fuels to signal the public that efforts are being made to reduce emissions of carbon to the atmosphere. The fear of global climate changes and the need to make something tangible will probably intensify actions to enhance these mixtures. Today, international markets do not have enough ethanol or vegetable oils to satisfy world demand in case regulation of fuels gets tight. It seems that regulations get tighter and tighter as public opinion gives pressure in this direction. As a means to avoid cartels and possible monopoly, the EU authorities and the UN officials started a steep campaign attacking all biofuels indiscriminately. The main accusation is that biofuels are responsible for the rise in food prices in the world. If it considers the corn used for production of ethanol in the USA, it may have some validity. But Brazilian ethanol is made of sugar cane that does not compete with food areas in Brazil. In the last 5 years, Brazil is enhancing significantly its grain production and, in 2008, it is expected to have a record 140 million tons. The convenient 'forgiveness' toward oil prices that rose from 30 to 130 dollars per barrel in the last 5 years, raising the production cost of agriculture worldwide, is not even mentioned.

The IMAFLORA program of agriculture certification is a chapter that represents Brazil in the Sustainable Agriculture Network (SAN), which defines criteria of social, environmental, and economic performance to assess agricultural production.

The agricultural certification looks for contribution to the preservation of natural resources and the well-being of rural workers, producers, and their families, stimulating responsible production and done according to socioenvironmental criteria.

The certified organizations that use the seal 'Rainforest Alliance Certified' in its products and marketing folders allows consumers to identify products made under responsible production.

Responsible production is understood as a series of techniques and appropriate systems adapted to the socioenvironmental reality of each region.

It should be emphasized that responsible production may not be completely confirmed, but it has in its principles sustainable development; it is the main reference and the bearing to be followed.

The agriculture certification process assesses any farm of any scale (small, medium, or large) in the country. In this way, it covers sugar cane mills, huge coffee and orange states, and from small communities to agrarian reform projects to familiar producers.

The certification processes can be realized individually or in groups (associations, cooperatives, or independent groups). Besides the certification of the production unit, the agriculture certification program can also certify industries and processors that use certified inputs, through the custody chain that guarantees the traceability of the product from its origin to the final destination.

The agriculture certification program offers two kinds of certification:

1. Certification of the farm: directed to the input production units.
2. Certification of the custody chain: assesses operations in the processing, selling, buying, and distributing steps of the chain of products that came from certified production. The custody chain certification can trace the origins of the inputs from the farm to the final consumer.

When certification is approved, the use of the seal is charged yearly. The amounts depend on the scale of the project assessed and are paid directly to the RAS Secretariat in New York.

The certification can be done by the user, with a self team or by an independent organization, outsourced, that will be responsible for the auditing and fiscalization that will guarantee compliance with applicable rules. In both cases, there are expenses to cover the inspection trips of the technical teams to various places and also the fees of the team members.

The first alternative is also called self-verification and can cause some discomfort in the market and society, since this kind of verification is seen as a partial and biased process.

The second alternative of outsourcing an independent organization to make verifications can give more trust and security for the system. It may be more expensive than the self process. In all cases mentioned, the costs will fall over the certification contractor. These costs can sometimes be reduced by the use of policies directed to support the production of smallholder and familiar units.

3.1 Possible Benefits of the Seal

a) Benefits to the Producer

The certification can assure the efficient application of control systems and quality guarantee in the organization, reducing losses and production costs. In this way, the competitiveness of the certified organizations is enhanced as against those who are not certified. The certification can also make the clients more satisfied and helps to sell products and introduce them to new markets.

b) Benefits to the Exporter

If the certification is made by an organization, e.g., ABNT (Brazilian Association of Technical Normalization) that has agreements with other countries, there is no need to have a new certification in the destination country. Such mechanisms are important to reduce transaction costs. In the same way, if there is equivalency in the normalization of the certification in the originating country as well as in the country of destination, the exporter is protected against technical barriers to commerce.

c) Benefits to the Government

The certification is an instrument that can be used by the government to create an adequate technical infrastructure to help develop the technology and raise the quality level of domestic products.

The certification can also prevent unnecessary protocols and help in the development of better policies to the consumers.

d) Benefits to the Final Consumer

The final consumer of food, fibers, and biofuels can be benefited if he or she knows that there are organized production control processes related to socioenvironmental issues.

4. Relevant Application in the Agrifood Chain Strategy

With regard to the application of certification in agrifood and biofuels, several positive aspects can be mentioned. Of course, the certification is not a guarantee that everything is all right, but it helps a lot to improve some managerial aspects of the agrifood chain as can be seen below (GRI, 2008).

a) Improvement of the Organization's Image

- Improvement of the image of the agrifood chain
- Improvement of the institutional environment

- Promotion of the image of the organization as socioenvironmentally responsible
- Improvement of the regional image of the chain
- Application of monitoring actions based on normatization with quality patterns
- Improvement of credibility in public opinion regarding the chain
- Reducing society's prejudice against agrichain socioenvironmental impacts
- Compliance with socioenvironmental responsibility role of the chain
- Compliance with the rules of environmental authorities
- Compliance with social aspects of labor and workers
- Awareness of socioenvironmental concerns
- Production of food and fiber in a more secure way
- Improvement in motivation to follow patterns that may result in better financial performance

b) Improvement in Processes

- Normatization of processes along the agrichains
- Improvement in the management of the organizations involved with certification
- Improvement of safety in the processes as a result of auditing systems
- Improvement in the awareness of managers in following established patterns
- Compliance with international standards
- Improvement in the capacity and qualification of agents involved in the process
- Facilitation in the environmental licensing process

5. Conclusions and Suggestions

In a general way, there is a positive perception with regard to the certification of agents involved in production in Brazil. Still to be discussed are issues of certification cost and the definition of how the distribution of these costs would be along the agrifood chain.

This issue could be the subject of a more profound research to gain an understanding of the custody chain. It is important to mention that certification is a process and not an isolated action. In Brazil, collective actions are somewhat difficult to execute because of the national culture of lack of association, but there is nothing that cannot be surpassed, if the incentives given are fair. In the same direction, other subjects that can be explored are public opinion perception, awareness and knowledge about certification in general, seals, and specific seals according to objectives. The results would help design social communication plans to achieve better results.

Other interesting topics of research may include the methodological steps or operational procedures to certify the custody chain of agribusiness products.

One of the key questions that could be asked now is: Is it not about time for Brazil to make investments in knowledge, knowhow, education, and conscientization to guarantee to the next generations a means of sustainability and good reputation in the food, fiber, and biofuel production systems? As the world gets more and more competitive, it is not enough for Brazil to use comparative advantages of land, weather, water, and photosynthesis. The investments in socioenvironmental practices must be done now. Actually, this change in posture toward responsibility needs ample debate to comprehend the issues related to carbon emissions until the difficult subject of the ways the nation need to go to reach a sustainable and responsible path toward human development. Collective actions taken today can generate positive externalities to the whole body of actors who work hard in the agribusinesses systems. For sure, these transformations will benefit future generations. The certification as a tool of change created with rationality and as fruits of ample agreement can guarantee the continuity, in the present and in the future, of the great business of Brazil, which is agribusiness.

References

ABNT. Certificação. <http://www.abnt.org.br/certif_body.htm>. Accessed 9 Jan. 2008.

ABRAMOVAY, R. 2004. Entre Deus e o diabo: mercados e interação humana nas ciências sociais. *Tempo Social, Revista de Sociologia da USP*, v. 16, n. 2, São Paulo.

BACCHI, M. R. P.; MIRANDA, S. H. G.; BARTHOLOMEU, D. B. et al. 2007. *Estudo, diagnóstico econômico, social e ambiental e perspectivas do cumprimento do Código Florestal Brasileiro pelo setor sucro-alcooleiro* no Brasil. Relatório de Pesquisa. Piracicaba: Cepea.

CONCEIÇÃO, J. C. P. R; BARROS, A. L. M. de. 2005. *Certificação e rastreabilidade no agronegócio: instrumentos cada vez mais necessários*. Texto para Discussão n. 1122, Instituto de Pesquisa Econômica Aplicada (Ipea), Brasília.

CONROY, M. E. 2007. Branded! How the "Certification Revolution" is Transforming Global Corporations. New Society Publishers, Gabriola Island, Canadá.

DANKERS, C. 2000. Environmental and social standards, certification and labelling for cash crops. Relatório FAO – Food and Agriculture Organization of the United Nations, Roma. <http://www. fao.org/docrep/006/y5136e/y5136e00.htm>. Accessed: 19 mar. 2008.

FARINA, E. M. M. Q. 2001. Challenges for Brazil's food industry in the context of globalization and Mercosur consolidation. *International Food and Agribusiness Management Review*, v. 2, issue 3-4, p. 315-330.

FARINA, E. M. M. Q. 2003. Padronização em sistemas agroindustriais. In: ZYLBERSZTAJN, D.; SCARE, R. F. *Gestão da qualidade no agribusiness:* estudos e casos. São Paulo: Atlas. p 18-29.

GIORDANO, S. R. 2007. *Territorial marketing and controlled origin denominations*. Working paper not published.

GIORDANO, S. R.; REZENDE, C. L. 2003. *Cadernos da universidade illy do café*. São Paulo: Universidade illy do Café/PENSA-FIA-FEA-USP. p. 58-68.

GRI. Diretrizes para padronização de relatórios de sustentabilidade: Informações gerais. Produzido por BSD BRASIL. <http://www.bsd-net>. Accessed: 12 mar. 2008.

IMAFLORA, Agriculture Certification Program. <http://www.imaflora.org/?fuseaction=content&IDassunto=14>. Accessed: 14 mar. 2008.

IMAFLORA, Brasil Certificado: a história da certificação florestal no Brasil. 2005. Edição Imaflora, Piracicaba.

ISEAL Alliance. 2006. *Code of good practice for setting social and environmental standards*. Public Version 4 – January.

ISO. <http://www. iso14000.com/>. Accessed: 13 fev. 2008.

NASSAR, A. M. 2003. Certificação no agribusiness. In: ZYLBERSZTAJN, D & SCARE, R. F. *Gestão da Qualidade no Agribusiness: estudos e casos*. São Paulo: Atlas. p. 30-46.

PINTO, L. F. G. 2004. Fundamentos da certificação sócio-ambiental. *Certificação sócio-ambiental do setor sucroalcoleiro*. Imaflora, 2004.

QUALITE FRANCE at <http://www.qualite-france.com/homePage_frameset.html>. Accessed: 12 mar. 2008.

REZENDE, C. L.; FARINA, E. M. M. Q. 2001. Assimetria informacional no mercado de alimentos orgânicos. In: *Seminário Brasileiro da Nova Economia Institucional*, 2. Campinas. Anais: CD-Rom.

SANTOS, M. 1994. *Técnica, espaço, tempo*. Globalização e meio técnico-científico informacional. São Paulo: Hucitec. 190p.

The Evolution of Sustainability Management Research

H.J. (Harry) Bremmers

In this contribution the development of sustainability management research is sketched, for a period of 15 years (1993 – 2008). The goal is to evaluate previous research, assess gaps in knowledge development, and to formulate a research agenda for the near future. It aims to provide a basis for intensified cooperation with scientists for the University of Sao Paulo, Brazil. Such cooperation could counteract environmental depletion.

In our research upon till present, different research perspectives have been adopted: transaction cost economics (TC), agency theory, stakeholder theory and the (resource based) dynamic capability approach. They will serve to explain the different phases of sustainability policy, as well as the progress of our own research.

The TC-approach serves to explain the public policy agenda in 1945-1975 (which we call the permissive period). Facilitating economic growth was the first concern after WW2 in Europe. When during the repressive period (1975-1995), environmental impacts (especially soil pollution) came to the surface, instruments were created to rule out future impacts: information processing and control through environmental care system deployment. Government acted as a principal, limiting the behavioral alternatives of the agents (private companies). Next, stakeholder theory can serve to explain public policy in the globalization period (1995-2006). It provided a basis for the analysis of factors influencing not only internally oriented, but also externally oriented environmental care. The first addresses the deployment of (elements of) in-company care systems. The second cooperation in the supply chains and networks (inside-out), as well as their influence on business strategy (outside-in). In the globalization period (2006-2009), dynamic capability theory serves to explain sustainability policies and management from a longitudinal perspective. We now try to explain capability deployment as a result of a public policy, available resources and strategic fit of company and environmental goals (or its absence). Not generic policy prescriptions like in previous research, but contingencies should guide public-private interaction. To detect contingent pathways towards sustainability is our concern for the future.

1. Introduction

The fifteenth anniversary of collaboration between Sao Paulo and Wageningen coincides with 15 years of research by the Business Administration Group on the factors that explain the management for the environment, called nowadays: sustainability management. Environmental management, as a concept, has broadened the view on the position of firms in their business network. Starting in 1993 and subsequently published (Bremmers, 1995) environmental management research addressed different topics following social urgency and scientific interest of members of the Management Studies Group (WUR). This interest was dynamic, not static, as a result of world-wide contacts and emerging environmental research agendas, of which our contact with Sao Paulo is a prominent one. The goal of this contribution is to provide a synopsis of 15 years of research which contributed to environmental care and pro-activeness of firms, and, on the basis of identified gaps in it, formulate a scientific basis for future research and cooperation. In first instance, an isolated and defensive view was adopted ("how will/should firms respond to governmental requirements"). In later years, the view was broadened towards supply chain and network issues, explain pro-activeness instead of mere compliance, and to strategic issues instead of pure process control. The paper intends, by ex-post analyzing the different viewpoints which were adopted, to sketch the development of our thinking on sustainability issues. This reflection will enable us to formulate a research agenda for the near future.

The proceeds of this contribution is as follows. § 2 will address the policy and theory developments during the period. § 3 will reveal highlights the research which was carried out. In § 4, a renewed research agenda will be proposed.

2. Policy and Theory

During a period of 15 years, major shifts have taken place in public policy to enhance sustainable business management. In the same time period, changes can be observed in the theoretical perspectives which are used to explain public policy and firms' environmental management. First we will focus on the policy shifts (§ 2.1), next we will address the theoretical angles from which reality has been addressed (§2.2).

2.1 A Shifting Public Policy

The post-war period can be divided into four stages which we cal(led) (Haverkamp et al., 2005): the permissive period (1945-1975), the repressive period (1975-1995) the integrative period (1995-2006), and added in this contribution the globalization period (2006-2009).

The permissive period (1945-1975) is characterized by public authorities focusing on post-war recovery (at the expense of the environment) rather than environmental protection. As a result, damages to the environment with respect to water pollution, air (acidification) and soil could take place without practical limitations or public scrutiny. Companies could be made liable for environmental damages but these damages were hidden, and if exposed, were not scrutinized for the benefit of economic growth. P stood for Profit, not Planet or People.

In the repressive period (1975-1995), a scattered and vast legal system was created, addressing different environmental compartments like air, soil, noise and water. Environmental impacts of the previous era were discovered. The intention was expressed to clean up all environmental waste, while at the same time the costs of repair would be claimed in law-suits from the private sector. A barrier in holding pollutants responsible (and let them pay) for actions in the past was vested in the proof that had to be delivered of "knowing or being able to know", at the time of occurrence, that pollution would lead to clean-up in the future. In many cases, such proof could not be delivered. In 1994, major claims against Shell and Philips PLC were rejected by the lack of knowledge on environmental impacts by the companies in the late sixties. New legal instruments were created, the most important being the Environmental Care Act (ECA, 1992). The ECA provided a legal framework for governmental agencies to plan and control environmental improvement. Plans were made to oblige 10 000 – 12 000 companies to implement a full environmental case system (ECS). At the end of the repressive period, severe doubts were expressed of the feasibility of these plans, given the administrative burdens and usefulness of such a vast implementation of environmental care. Summarizing, in the repressive period, the P of Planet came high on the political agenda, at the expense of Profit.

In the integrative period, convergent business, environmental and social goals came high on the political agenda. For this era, cooperation -rather than conflict- between private enterprise and public authorities is characteristic. Governments is regarded as a stakeholder and ally in business restructuring. Not only government is involved in sustainability management, joint action in supply chains and networks is proposed (see for instance the energy reduction program of SenterNovem, in carrying out covenant MJA2). Gradually, environmental management is not regarded as an alien activity, but integrated in the generic risk management activities of firms (Bremmers and Hagelaar, 2001). Structural adaptation of business processes is a leading topic now. For this to make happen, public-private agreements (covenants) are concluded upon. If pollution prevention pays, firms will benefit from investments in pollution prevention, rather than end-of-pipe measures only. In the integrative period, Profit and Planet are not seen as conflicting interest fields, but are seen as interconnected areas.

In the globalization period (2006-2009) we have come to the conviction that environmental problems are globally interconnected. People are the gate towards sustainability. They store knowledge from the past and hold the key to environmental sustainability. People are also the primary cause for environmental depletion. Changes in behavior are necessary on a personal as well as a managerial level. Meat production in the Netherlands for instance (85kg/person/year), is based on the usage of soy beans and other crop (imported national consumption and export of meat: 3.2 bln kg/year), which in the end causes de-forestisation (1 mln hectares of tropical rain forest converted already into monoculture areas). Social circumstances and income inequality force the rapid deforestation, climate change, and global warming are a living proof of market failure. Problems can only be solved by means of exchange of technological innovation and long-term cooperation. A globally reinforced strict environmental policy is necessary to reduce the negative impacts of market failure. Profit, people and planet are seen as interconnected.

2.2 Shifting Theoretical Viewpoints

In this sub-paragraph, we address 4 research perspectives which can explain the focal interests of the four periods discerned:

- transaction cost theory

- agency theory
- stakeholder theory
- capability approach/resource based view

As indicated, in the next (§ 3) we use these perspectives to organize our own research with respect to environmental and sustainability management.

Transaction Cost Theory

Different policy aims can be explained from different theoretical angles. The policy focus of the permissive period can best be explained from a transaction cost perspective. Transaction cost economics, with R.H. Coase (1937) and O.E. Williamson (1975) as most prominent contributors, asks itself: why do firms (more general: hierarchies) exist (see also Zuurbier and Bremmers, 1997). Cost differences between centralized and decentralized decision making determine the choice for intervention (legislative coercion) or freedom. The permissive period fosters a choice for free enterprise; costs (including transaction costs) of governmental interference were deemed to be bigger than costs of damage and repair. The fundamental idea of societal order is therefore neoclassical of a kind. At the pole "leaving the environment to the market" resource depletion is trusted to encourage technological progress (Anderson and Leal 1991). However, externalities (like air and water pollution or ozone layer breakdown) will be internalized only if customers differentiate products on the basis of sustainability aspects and attach a premium to them (Prakash, 2002). Moreover, this "neo-classical" approach to the environmental problem presupposes unlimited resource-substitution possibilities, a "time-less" world in which technological innovation is produced instantly and at will, and a voluntary internalization. Self-regulation as such does not make companies survive in a competitive environment, since it costs money without need or reward (Rumelt 1991, Reinhardt 1999). The argument that environmental measures induce competitive advantages (Porter 1980, Porter and Van der Linde 1995, Schmidheiny 1992, Waddock and Graves 1998, Hart 1995, Esty and Porter 1998, Shrivastava 1995) and (therefore) to extra company value (Dowell et al. 2000, Konar and Cohen 2001) only holds if:

- companies malfunction in the first place and have not exploited all opportunities a competitive market offers (see: Porter & Van der Linde 1995, Caves & Porter 1977)

- or by the sake of market-imperfections which protect resources, including capabilities, from competing (copying) adversaries in the market.

Costs of governmental intervention being high and market opportunities of environmentally sustainable behavior being hidden or absent, induce free exploitation of the Planet to benefit of Profit. However, reliance on self-enforcement led to an estimated $ 75 bln of soil pollution cleanup costs, which still have to be paid (among other: Bremmers, 2001, 2002).

Agency Theory

Agency theory can explain the interactions between a superior (i.e., the government) and a subordinate (i.e., private business) to come up to the principal's goals and intentions (Jensen and Meckling, 1976). The adverse consequences of information-asymmetry (a market imperfection), goal dis-congruence and divergence of risk preferences are addressed by means of governance instruments. To limit the space of maneuvering of the agent, bonding is an important instrument (see: Epstein and O'Halloran, 1994; Spiller and Tomassi, 2005). Governmental actions include setting generic and specific (i.e., in environmental permits) rules and regulations. Bonuses and penalties ('carrot and stick'-policy) are a second instrument that is employed. Creating transparency by means of environmental reporting a third. Environmental reporting fills the information gap between citizens, government and private sector. Nowadays, environmental reports serve not only national functions, but are also internationally renown instruments for creating transparency of multinational enterprise. International standards for reporting were among other developed by CERES (Global Reporting Initiative (GRI)),[1] see Braakhuis red., 1995; Bremmers, 2000).

Agency theory views the relationship between principal and agent as conflictous (Eisenhardt, 2000; Gusc, 2007). A lack of trust is compensated by improving transparency and control. Systems are forced to be implemented to control environmental impact. Public-private control has the character of a double agency relationship. First, central government will delegate authority to lower public bodies (Spiller and Tomassi, 2005); next lower governmental bodies (like municipalities, water authorities, provinces) will influence firm behavior by continuous interaction and information exchange (executive leg-

1 www.ceres.org/reporting/globalreporting.html.

islation, monitoring and control). Our research has therefore also addressed the role of lower governmental bodies, especially in relation to SMEs for which local authorities are more important than central authorities.

Stakeholder Theory

The Dutch institutional environment – especially in the integrative period – is characterized by influence of ngo's on environmental performance of companies, as well as public-private agreements with respect to measures for improving sustainable business management. Environmental problems have been internalized in many companies, the focus shifted from ex post reaction to ex ante prevention, and from environmental to risk management (Bremmers and Hagelaar, 2001). Stakeholders include internal and external participants which influence the firm's goal achievement and/or are influenced by the firm in their own goal achievement (see for instance: Carrol, 1979). With respect to environmental issues the government is traditionally the primary – non-commercial – stakeholder. Also supply chain participants (buyers and suppliers) play a key role in enhancing sustainable business behavior. Competitors in the business environment form a benchmark, especially for SMEs. Adjusting to the stakeholder environment can be achieved by (among others) improving the supply chain information system and/or by integrated (supply-chain wide) auditing and licensing. In doing so, cost-efficiency, transparency and sustainability can be improved (Bremmers and Omta, 2004; Bremmers et al., 2007). The environmental optimism is reflected in Ecological Modernization Theory. It aims to understand, interpret and conceptualize ecology-inspired and environment-induced processes of transformation and reform in the core practices and central institutions of modern society (Mol, 2004, p.93; also Van Tatenhove and Leroy, 2003; Arts and Van Tatenhove, 2005).

Capabilities Approach

Capability theorizing finds its origin in the resource based view (see for instance: Prahalad & Hamel 1990, Wernerfelt, 1984 etc.). Building (environmental) dynamic capabilities (Teece et al., 1997) is of great importance for sustained and embedded environmental management. Capabilities link the resources of a firm to its stakeholder environment. The capability approach has found multiple applications in the social sciences (compare: Klassen and Whybark, 1999; Russo and Fouts, 1997; Van Kleef and Roome, 2007; Fortuyn, 2006). Building capabilities costs time and effort. For supply chain wide environmental management information & communication (IC) as well as cooperation capabilities are of immanent importance. Technically, the development of capabilities is necessary to accelerate knowledge-building by knowledge-exchange (a key factor for creating competitive advantage; Boiral 2002, Nonaka and Takeuchi 1995, Subramaniam and Youndt 2005). Economically they are needed to solve the problem of value displacement. This problem occurs if measures in one stage of the supply chain have a positive or negative impact (costs, value-added etc.) in other phases. For redistributing costs and benefits negotiations within the supply chain are necessary. In our view, the governance-gap between 'market' and 'hierarchy' can only be bridged if information and communication capabilities are developed that facilitate cooperation in supply chains & networks.

3. Shifting Research Focus

Research in sustainable business management requires combining a theoretical framework (§ 2) with a research field (empirical object). Fields for environmental research are given in Figure 1.

Figure 1: Research fields

breath of environmental involvement			
network	branchwide process innovation	public-private agreements on environmental management practice	environmental image management
supply chain	tracking and tracing of causes of environmental impact	coordination with suppliers and/or buyers of environmental action	Life cycle assessment & management
incompany	good housekeeping measures	functional integration of environmental management	renewal of machinery environmental marketing strategy
	operational	*organizational*	*strategic*
			managerial focus

The vertical axis in Figure 1 contains the breath of the environmental focus. While our research in the early nineties was limited to in-company environmental management, in later years it became more and more supply chain- and network-oriented. The horizontal axis regards the managerial tasks which are under study. A prominent way to improve such managerial performance is the inclusion of certified environmental management systems in the organization, like ISO14000 series (for instance: Halkos and Evangelinos 2002, Zutshi and Sohal 2004). Implementing such systems could act as a barrier for beyond-compliance performance, since they stimulate primarily process- instead of product-innovations (Prakash, 2002).

3.1 *Focus 1: Environmental Reporting*

The effect of environmental impact on financial reporting was addressed in 1995 (Bremmers, 1995). The choice for this research topic can be explained from a transaction cost perspective. From a market perspective, transaction costs should be reduced to the minimum, to reduce the costs of information gathering (and of opportunistic behavior in transactions like acquiring shares, companies or exchange of tangible and tacit assets). Provision of company information in financial and environmental reports illuminates the 'black box' which a firm is from the perspective of the shareholder. From a corporate perspective, a displacement of risk takes place: from firm to shareholder. It is therefore not only economically efficient (limiting transaction costs and improving the functioning of markets) but also morally right to provide information about effects of business operations on different levels (including non-financial levels). Environmental damages and risks impede on the value of assets and liabilities governed by management on behalf of stakeholders. To investigate such effects, the economic-proprietress-concept of Beckman (1988) was used as a starting point. In the economic-proprietress-concept the volume risk on a substantial and transactable right is the criterion for disclosure of assets. The limited possibilities for valuing intangible assets (like environmental systems, patents, or created goodwill) have as a consequence that improvements in business operations to internalise external effects have immediate negative consequences on visible performance, and, consequently, strengthen the inclination to act myopic: short term gains are preferred above long-term environmental sustainability. Our advice was to alleviate the legal possibilities to activate expenditures on behalf of the environment.

3.2 Focus 2: Environmental Care

The second research focus regards the organizational managerial perspective. The breath is in-company. It can best be explained from an agency theoretical viewpoint. As indicated, the principal (society) limits the managerial alternatives of private firms, to protect the environment. The Dutch government was among the first in Europe to stress self-responsibility of companies to take care of their environmental impact. Environmental care has therefore become of great importance to many Dutch companies (Haverkamp, 2007; De Bakker, 2001; Wijen, 2002; De Bruijn and Hofman, 2000; Van Berkel and Van Kampen, 1999). In 1995, we carried out a written survey to investigate the state-of-the-art of environmental care implementation in the Netherlands. As could be expected at that time, coming up to the wishes of the 'principal' (government) is the primary motive for environmental care system implementation.

Table 1: Motives for environmental care

	(1) Most important motive	(2)	(3)	(4) Least important motive
improving sales	31	12	38	144
improving image	21	34	44	126
improving efficiency	30	50	42	103
improving quality	54	46	36	89
lower environmental impact	31	44	26	124
compliance	99	44	28	54
other	2	1	4	218

Source: Bremmers et al. (1996)

Moreover, it was argued that the role-perception of management is a crucial factor in the adoption of environmental care. It was advised that public policy should take account of the conditions under which firms operate. Lack of profitability in the repressive period would lead to the adoption of strategies which improve financial performance, at the expense of the environment, should public pressure be alleviated. It explains why product development and environmental marketing strategies were not prominent topics by then. We concluded that governmental agencies were insufficiently aware of the contingencies under which corporations operate. Such contingencies were addressed in follow-up research (see § 3.4).

3.3 Focus 3: External Drivers for Environmental Management

The third focus takes the stakeholder theory as a starting point (For instance: Clarkson, 1995). The managerial tasks (see Table 1) that are studied are mainly organizational, while the breath is supply-chain oriented. Our efforts have been directed at categorizing and explaining managerial behavior from drivers outside the firm: its stakeholder environment. Companies are, to a smaller or larger extent, entangled in a web of relationships, forcing them to adopt the norms and practices in the business network (outside-in). But they also can be change-oriented and put their own goals and standards first, relying on unique resources, to adjust their environment inside-out (Porter and Kramer, 2006). Stakeholder scrutiny limits the managerial space to maneuver (DiMaggio and Powell 1983). The government, being the main stakeholder, limits managerial slack by rulemaking (environmental book-keeping, reporting, licensing etc.) and enforced adoption of care systems. Goals of stakeholders (for-profit and not-for-profit) can be in conflict with each other. If they converge, "pollution prevention pays".

We made a distinction between internally oriented EMSs and externally oriented EMSs (Bremmers et al., 2006). The results of analyses on a of a large survey carried out in 2002 suggest, that small and medium-sized companies are able to accommodate to demands with respect to the implementation of internally oriented care systems (I-EMSs). I-EMSs focus at the single firm or location. In general, they are predominantly influenced by governmental and other 'non-commercial' stakeholder groups. For the implementation of externally oriented EMSs (E-EMSs), which focus on the supply-chain and network, qualitative rather than quantitative relationship characteristics between companies and the government are important. Moreover, commercial stakeholder groups (such as uppliers, clients and competitors) influence E-EMS levels significantly. The results showed also, that companies react differently to stakeholder demands. One key variable is company size. Size is a control variable which will influence other key drivers for sustainability. Table

2 shows, that especially in the category 50-250 employees the influence of the government is relatively high. Surprisingly, this middle-sized category is 'accommodative', rather than 'pro-active'.

Table 2: Stakeholder influences and size (5-point scale), SD in parentheses); N = 337, 75 and 24 respectively

	≤ 50	51-250	>250	KW*(p)
Government	3.53 (1.13)	4.04 (.751)	3.69 (.928)	.002
Competitors	1.63 (.817)	1.84 (.823)	1.79 (.509)	.017
Suppliers	1.98 (1.034)	1.96 (.738)	2.29 (.955)	.206
Clients	2.41 (1.255)	2.62 (1.1)	2.48 (1.22)	.031
Environmental organizations	2.00 (1.13)	2.15 (1.036)	2.17 (.868)	.140
Inhabitants	2.63 (1.247)	3.05 (1.129)	3.13 (.947)	.007
Intermediaries	1.41 (1.260)	2.25 (1.320)	2.34 (1.433)	0.00

*/Kruskal Wallis significance
Source: Bremmers et al, 2007

In an extensive longitudinal research by Haverkamp (2007), it is shown that especially externally oriented capabilities for environmental management (cooperation with suppliers and buyers, as well as product redesign) has hardly improved in the Dutch food and beverage industry in the period 2002-2005. What then drives companies towards environmental pro-activeness and beyond-compliance environmental performance?

3.4 *Capability and Sustainability*

The next phase in our research is currently unfolding (2006). It aims at explaining the process of acquiring dynamic capabilities as dependent on business strategy (Miles et al., 1978) and available resources (RBV). Strategy is the inside-out response to a dynamic and demanding business network. A sustainability strategy will have to be in concordance with the generic business strategy. For instance, defender firms will focus more on cost savings by means of control of material flows, while prospector firms will focus their attention on strategic advantages of image building and reputation. If sustainability and business strategy do not converge, governments will have to play an active and restrictive role. The current research embraces the idea that self-enforcement will, in many cases, not pay and will not be taken up voluntarily. 'Different governmental policies for different firms' will have to be the adagio. Alignment, fit, or convergence can be studied at three levels: strategic, structural and operational (see Figure 2).

Figure 2: Aligning sustainability strategy with business strategy

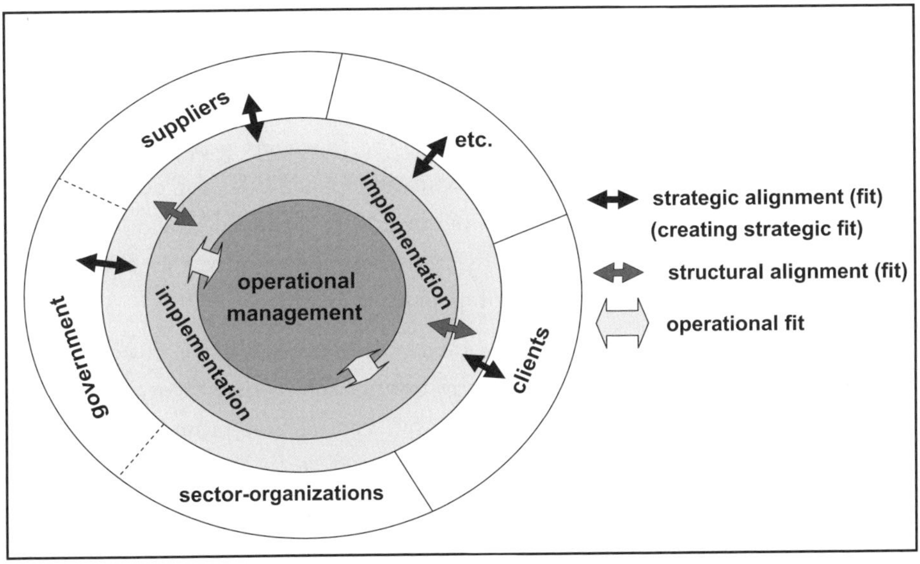

The problem we address in future is filling the knowledge gap of the relationships between (1) the level of transparency (2) network embeddedness and institutional environment and (3) the quality of environmental sustainability management of major food companies. Given the depletion of ozone layer, disappearing rain forest, accelerated usage of fossil fuels it should be admitted that the optimistic viewpoint of ecological modernization and cradle-to-cradle management find their natural limitations where the market does not attach prices to natural impact. A contingency approach is needed, whereby behavioural and structural characteristics of sub-sectors guide public policy towards a differentiated response. We call the approach we develop "dynamic behavioural fingerprinting". It designates that each company or group of companies has its own characteristic way of dealing with sustainability problems. The capabilities it has developed in the past determine to a large extent how it is going to behave in the future. Different levels of capability acquisition require different policies from public authorities. For some companies and subsectors, coercion is needed, other can function well in a cooperative atmosphere, a third category can be left free. Ecological Modernization is uniform in its efforts to improve the natural environment: cooperation is a win-win strategy. Our viewpoint is more differentiated, but therefore also less easy to propagate.

4. Final Remarks

Three research topics guided us in the past:

- creating transparency to improve the functioning of financial markets. Reducing transactions costs and possibilities for opportunistic behavior can be achieved by means of financial, including environmental, reporting. Transaction cost theory serves as a scientific basis. It fosters profit, not people or planet.
- improving environmental care by means of coercive governmental interference. It fosters hierarchy, not market. Agency theory has served as a theoretical basis. Planet is put central, not profit or people.
- stakeholder management, to solve conflicts between profit and planet. Stakeholder theory was used as a primary source for scientific underpinning. It bares the optimism of cooperation between government and the private sector. Profit and planet are put central. The viewpoint is static and "generic", trying to come to advice for a wide range of firms with different characteristics and capabilities. Moreover, the time dimension of firms' capability deployment is forgotten.
- Looking at the gaps in the research upon till now, our research agenda for the future should include the study of:
    - harmony and conflict of interests of profit, planet and people,
    - with the awareness of the historical (dynamic) context of the firm,
    - focusing on capabilities, rather than costs, instruments or interests,
    - the result should be a differentiated view on applicable policies to improve sustainability management.

References

AMIT, R.; SCHOEMAKER, P. J. H. 1993. Strategic assets and organizational rent. *Strategic Management Journal* 14(1): 33–46.

ANDERSON, T. L.; LEAL, D. R. 1991. *Free market environmentalism.* San Francisco: Research Institute for Public Policy/Westview Press.

ARTS, B.; TATENHOVE, J. van. 2005. *Political modernization.* Springer, Netherlands: Institutional Dynamics in Environmental Governance.

BAKKER, de F.; NIJHOF, A. 2001. Responsible chain management: a capability assessment framework. *Business Strategy and the Environment* 11(1): 63-75.

BECKMAN, H. 1988. *Economische beschikkingsmacht:* Grondslag voor vermogensverantwoording en winstneming. MAB: 325-341.

BERKEL, van R.; VAN KAMPEN, M.; KORTMAN, J. 1999. Opportunities and constraints for product-oriented Environmental Management Systems (P-EMS). *Journal of Cleaner Production* 7(6): 447-455.

BOIRAL, O. 2002. *Tacit Knowledge and Environmental Management Long Range Planning* 35 (3): 291-317.

BRAAKHUIS, F. L. M.; GIJTENBEEK, M.; HAFKAMP, W. A. (Eds.). 1995. *Milieumanagement: van kosten naar baten.* Alphen aan den Rijn, Samson H. D. Tjeenk Willink.

BREMMERS, H. J. 2002. Bodemverontreiniging: een bodemloze put? (Soil pollution, an infinite burden?) *Tijdschrift Bodem* (12)5, Oct. 179-181.

______. 1995. Milieuschade en financieel verslag (Environmnetal damage and financial reporting; commercial edition). *Kluwer Juridisch,* serie Recht en Praktijk, Sept. 1995, 392 p.

______. 2000. *Milieuverslaggeving* (Environmental Reporting). Elsevier Bedrijfswetenschappen, The Hague.

______. 2001. Verslaggeving van bodemverontreiniging – geen vuiltje in de bodem? (Reporting on soil pollution) *Tijdschrift voor milieuaansprakelijkheid*: 145-150.

BREMMERS, H. J.; HAGELAAR, G. 2001. Van milieu- naar risicomanagement (From environmental to risk management). Tijdschrift Bedrijfskunde. *Journal of Business Administration* 73: 78-85.

BREMMERS, H. J.; HAGELAAR, G.; REGT, M. C. de. 1996. Bedrijfssituatie en milieuzorg (Company characteristics and environmental management). *Milieu-Tijdschrift voor Milieukunde* 1: 12-19.

BREMMERS, H. J.; KEMP, R.; HAVERKAMP, D. J.; OMTA, S. W. F. 2006. Do stakeholder groups influence environmental management system development in the Dutch agri-food sector? *Business Strategy and the Environment* 16: 214-231.

BREMMERS, H. J.; OMTA, S. W. F.; HAVERKAMP, D. J. Explaining environmental management system development: a stakeholder approach. *International Food and Agribusiness Management Review* 7(4), Dec. 2004.

BREMMERS, H. J., OMTA, S. W. F.; SMIT., M. E. 2003. *Managing environmental information flows in food and agribusiness chains end-rapport* (parts A, B, C). Research report, WUR.

BRUIJN DE, T. J. N. M.; HOFMAN, P. S. 2000. Pollution prevention and industrial transformation: Evoking structural changes within companies. *Journal of Cleaner Production* 8: 215-223.

CARROLL, A. B. 1979. A three-dimensional conceptual model of corporate performance. *Academy of Management Review* 4(4): 497-505.

CAVES, R. E.; PORTER, M. E. 1977. From entry barriers to mobility barriers: conjectural decisions and contrived deterrence to new competition. *The Quarterly Journal of Economics* 91(2): 241-262

CHRISTMANN, P.; TAYLOR, G. 2003. Environmental self-regulation in the global economy: the role of firm capabilities – Multinationals, *Environment and Global Competition*. JAI Press.

CLARKSON, M. B. E. 1995. A stakeholder framework for analyzing and evaluating corporate social performance. *The Academy of Management Review* 20(1): 92-117.

COASE, R. H. 1937. The nature of the firm. *Economica* 4: 777-95.

DOWELL, G.; HART, S.; YEUNG, B. 2000. Do corporate global environmental standards create or destroy market value? *Management Science* 46(8): 1059-1074.

DIMAGGIO, P. J.; POWELL, W. W. 1983. The iron cage revisited: Institutional Isomorphism and Collective Rationality in Organizational Fields. *American Sociological Review* 48(2): 147-160.

EISENHARDT, K. M.; MARTIN, J. A. 2000. Dynamic capabilities: what are they? *Strategic Management Journal* 21: 1105-1121.

EPSTEIN, D.; Sh. O'Halloran. 1994. Administrative procedures, Information and Agency Discretion. *American Journal of Political Science* 38(3): 697-722.

ESTY, D. C.; PORTER, M. E. 1998. Industrial ecology and competitiveness. *Journal of Industrial Ecology* 2: 35-43.

GRANOVETTER, M. 1973. The strength of weak ties. *The American Journal of Sociology* 78(6): 1360-1380.

GRAY R., Kouhy, R.; LAVERS, S. 1995. Corporate social and environmental reporting. *Accounting, Auditing and Accountability Journal* 8(2): 47-77.

GUSC, J. 2007. Headquarters – *Subsidiary relationship governance in emerging markets of Central eastern Europe*. Phd-thesis, Wageningen University, Netherlands.

HALKOS, G. E.; EVANGELINOS, K. I. 2002. Determinants of environmental management systems standards implementation: evidence from Greek industry. *Business Strategy and the Environment* 11(6): 360-375.

HART, S. L. 1995. A natural-resource-based view of the firm. *The Academy of Management Review* 20(4): 986-1014.

HAVERKAMP D-J. 2007. Environmental management in the Dutch food and beverage industry. Phd-dissertation, Wageningen University, Netherlands.

HAVERKAMP, D-J.; BREMMERS, H. J.; ROOIJ, M. de. 2005. Milieuzorg geketend of milieuzorg in ketens? (Environmental management chained or in chains?). *Bestuurskunde* (14): 29-35.

JENSEN, M. C.; MECKLING, W. H. 1976. Theory of the firm: Managerial behavior, agency costs and ownership structure. *Journal of Financial Economics* 3(4): 305-360.

KLASSEN, R. D.; WHYBARK, D. C. 1999. The impact of environmental technologies on manufacturing performance. *The Academy of Management Journal* 42 (6): 599-615.

KLEEF, J. A. G. van; ROOME, N. J. 2007. Developing capabilities and competence for sustainable business management as innovation: a research agenda. *Journal of Cleaner Production* 15(1): 38-51.

KONAR, S.; COHEN, M. A. 2001. Does the Market Value Environmental Performance? *The Review of Economics and Statistics* 83(2): 281-289.

MILES, R. E., SNOW, C. C., MEYER, A. D. and Coleman, H. J., Jr. 1978. Organizational strategy, structure, and process. *Academy of Management Review* 3(3): 546-562.

MOL, A. P. J.; LAUBER, V.; LIEFFERINK, D. 2004. *The voluntary approach to environmental policy*: joint environmental policy-making in Europe. University Press.

NONAKA I., H. TAKEUCHI. 1995. *The Knowledge-creating Company: How Japanese Companies Create the Dynamics of Innovation.* Oxford: University Press.

PETERAF, M. A. 2006. The cornerstones of competitive advantage: A resource-based view. *Strategic Management Journal* 14(3): 179-191.

PORTER, M. E. 1980. *Competitive strategy.* New York: The Free Press.

PORTER M. E.; KRAMER, M. R. 2006. Strategy and society: the link between competitive advantage and corporate social responsibility. *Harvard Business Review* 84(12): 78-92.

PORTER, M. E.; VAN DER LINDE. 1995. Green and competitive: ending the statement. *Harvard Business Review* 73: 20-134.

PRAHALAD, C. K; HAMEL, G. 1990. The core competence of the corporation. *Harvard Business Review* 79-91.

PRAKASH, A. 2002. Green marketing, public policy and managerial strategies. *Business Strategy and the Environment* 11(5): 285-297.

______. Why do firms adopt "beyond-compliance" environmental policies? *Business Strategy and the Environment* 10: 286-299.

REINHARDT, F. 1999. Market failure and the environmental policies of firms: economic rationales for "beyond compliance" behavior. *Journal of Industrial Ecology* (3): 9-21.

ROCHA, C.; BREZET, H. 1999. Product-oriented environmental management systems: a case study. *The Journal of Sustainable Product Design* (4): 30-42.

RUMELT, R. P. 1991. How much does industry matter? *Strategic Management Journal* (12): 167-185.

RUSSO, M. V.; FOUTS, P. A. 1997. A resource-based perspective on corporate environmental performance and profitability. *The Academy of Management Journal* 40(3): 534-559.

SCHMIDHEINY, S. 1992. *Changing course:* a global business perspective on development and the environment. MIT Press.

SHRIVASTAVA, P. 1995. The role of corporations in achieving ecological sustainability. *The Academy of Management Review* 20: 936-960.

SPILLER, P. T.; TOMASSI, M. 2005. The institutions of regulation. an applicatioon to public policies. In: MÉNARD, C.; SHIRLEY, M. M. (Eds.). *Handbook of new Institutional Economics.* Springer Verlag.

SUBRAMANIAM M.; YOUNDT, M. A. 2005. The influence of intellectual capital on the types of innovative capabilities *Academy of Management Journal* 48(3): 450–463.

TATENHOVE VAN, J. P. M.; LEROY, P. 2003. Environment and participation in a context of political modernisation. *Environmental Values* 12(2): 155-174.

WADDOCK, S.; GRAVES, S. B. 1998. The corporate social performance: financial performance link. *Strategic Management Journal* 18 (4): 303-319.

WERNERFELT, B. 1984. A resource-based view of the firm. *Strategic Management Journal* 5(2): 171-180.

WIJEN, F. H. 2002. *Stakeholder influence and organizational learning in environmental management.* PhD dissertation, University of Tilburg, Tilburg

WILLIAMSON, O. E. 1975. *Markets and hierarchies.* New York: Free Press.

WILLIAMSON, O. E. 1985. *The economic institutions of capitalism.* New York: Free Press.

ZUTSHI A., SOHAL, A. 2004. Environmental management system adoption by Australasian organisations. *Technovation* 24(4): 335-357.

ZUURBIER, P. J. P.; BREMMERS, H. J. 1997. *Analyzing farmer-coop relations: an adjusted TCE-approach.* First Brazilian Workshop on Agri Chain Mangement, D. Zylbersztajn and M. Neves (Eds.), Universidade de São Paulo, Pensa: 68-85.

Netchain Leadership in the U.S. Ethanol Sector

MOLLY J. BURRESS

MICHAEL L. COOK

1. The Significance of Ownership in Supply Chain Analysis

Vertical coordination and integration studies in the area of biofuels have tended to rely on traditional industrial-organization driven supply chain analysis models. Traditional models often consider industry structure and firm behavior without regard to multiple roles of owners in the value chain. This chapter addresses the evolution of the ethanol value chain from a broader perspective which we call netchain ownership analysis. Netchain analysis considers horizontal, vertical and diagonal relationships across networks (Lazzarini, Chaddad and Cook, 2001). Our analysis includes special consideration of the role of producer-ownership in the biofuels sector as previous studies have shown the allocation of ownership may have an effect on the ability of the chain to generate optimum surpluses (Hendrikse and Bijman, 2002).

The U.S. ethanol industry has experienced a dramatic transformation from a highly concentrated, investor-owned sector to a more atomistic sector. Significant farmer investment is one factor that contributed to this change in market structure. We investigate the driving factors underlying producer investment as well as the challenges faced by producers in vertically integrating. We find a subset of producers were able to overcome these constraints by negotiating a unique nexus of contracts to form a highly-integrated value chain rooted in producer investment and producer control. We concentrate on one investment model that seems to have been successful due to high levels of mutual adjustment across several coordination mechanisms. We conclude by considering what the success of this highly integrated model suggests in terms of strategy recommendations for producer groups.

2. Netchain Analysis of Producer-Owned Organizations: Shifting Perspective from the Farm to the Factory

Historically, research on producer-owned marketing cooperatives has focused on incentives for cooperation among producers and the maximization of rent generation at the farm level. Operating on a service at cost principle, the cooperative's primary function has been to pass revenues to the member in proportion to patronage.

However, producers have been increasing their risk exposure through higher levels of upfront, proactive risk capital investment in processing ventures. Many new ownership models distribute revenues in proportion to investment or tie patronage rights to investment. Therefore, producers are beginning to adopt a more sophisticated multi-level rent generation mentality. In these instances, producers evaluate the performance of their investment in terms of an organization's 1) ability to maximize rent generation at the individual farm level and 2) ability to maximize rent generation at the firm level (Cook and Plunkett, 2006). Instead of focusing solely on farm-level profitability, producers are increasingly providing risk capital to their organizations intending to generate rents at the cooperative level. Producers engaged in the formation of new ventures for the extraction of rents at multiple levels has been referred to as collective entrepreneurship (Cook and Plunkett, 2006). Although the cooperative structure is retained in many of these organizations, we also witness the formation of similar ventures under alternative legal models such as limited liability companies (LLCs) or public limited companies (Chaddad and Cook, 2004; Cook and Chaddad, 2004).

The proliferation of highly integrated models of producer-ownership has challenged researchers to shift the primary focus of their analysis from the farm and to consider multiple rent generation opportunities throughout the value chain. Scholars have also begun to document factors affecting producer's ability to vertically integrate (Hendrikse and Bijman, 2002; McKee and Boland, 2007; Burress, Cook and Klein, 2008).

While producer assumption of ownership rights may lead to more efficient production from the perspective of quality and availability of raw material inputs, we must not assume a producer ownership advantage to apply across variables. For example, producers are better-positioned as owners to improve the quality of raw inputs or to introduce new qualities to the inputs which may result in higher revenue margins due to increased consumer prices (Sexton and Iskow, 1988). This argument is often put forth with respect to organizational structures in which producer ownership rights are coupled with the right and obligation to deliver (Burress, et al., 2008). In addition, producer-owned organizations may be less vulnerable to price fluctuations in commodity markets as producers of the commodity inputs are highly skilled in risk management practices. However, producers may be at a disadvantage in terms of their ability to market their products while competing with large, established competitors. In addition, they may lack the adequate scale to engage in costly research and development activities.

We find evidence in the literature that suggests producer-owned organizations may confront distinct challenges as they vertically integrate through multiple production levels. These challenges may be rooted in their ownership structure, specifically as a function of the owner's previous experience, knowledge base, and existing networks. As farmers, producers possess knowledge, experience and expertise related to crop production. From a resource-based view of the firm, it is evident producers' human capital asset base may put them at a disadvantage when forming processing facilities and competing with firms whose owners and organizers have developed distinct expertise in processing and marketing. While these assets may be purchased on the market, it is not clear that producers have experience in the recruitment of upper management or the willingness to pay for such expertise during the initial stages of new venture development.

Well-documented in the literature on cooperative development are producers' challenges with respect to accessing managerial expertise, incorporating new technology, gaining credibility and legitimacy, surviving start-up with low levels of working capital, and establishing of marketing and distribution networks (Cook, 1994). We explain reasons for each of these challenges according to a resource-based view of the firm (Peteraf, 1993).

3. Challenges Faced by Producer-Owners in Vertical Integration

3.1 Expertise Unrelated to New Venture, Unlikely to Hire Expertise

Producers who seek to vertically integrate possess expertise in the area of crop production. However, they may be less knowledgeable in managing processing facilities, especially at the scale necessary for efficiency (Western Plains Energy, 2002). In addition, producer-owners may be less likely to compensate board members and management at competitive levels. Thus, not only do producer-owners not possess adequate expertise in the areas in which they intend to vertically integrate, but studies suggest producers have demonstrated the tendency to be unwilling to compensate board and management at levels competitive with investor-owned firms in order to attract expertise (Dunn, et al., 2002). In a study of California-based cooperatives, Lang and Spatz found producer-owned firms of comparable size compensated their board members at about an eighth of the rate of compensation paid to board members in investor-owned firms (1995).

3.2 Problems Incorporating Unproven Technology, Especially when Designing New Facilities

Given producers' limited knowledge of the construction and design of processing facilities, several scholars have indicated severe difficulties among producer-owned organizations in the timely realization of plant goals related to operational capacity. Construction and design difficulties have resulted in delayed profitability of new ventures as well as venture failure (Trucano, 1997). Newly developed, "unproven" technologies related to plant design seem to increase the probability of start-up difficulties in producer-owned ventures (McKee and Boland, 2007). Newly developed technologies often represent an attractive opportunity for producer-owned groups to generate high revenues associated with new materials and processes. However, commercialization of production with new technologies often involves unforeseen complications that can bankrupt new producer-owned organizations experiencing capital constraints.

3.3 Lack of Existing Marketing and Distribution Networks

Producer-owners are also subject to the familiar "chicken and egg" problem that thwarts many start-ups: it is difficult to develop market prospects prior to beginning production (Gompers, Lerner and Scharfstein, 2005). However, a lack of previous experience in the processing industry often means producer-owners are one step further removed from developing relationships with potential buyers. In addition, producer board directors may be at a disadvantage in terms of their ability to evaluate marketing relationships developed by hired management teams (Solberg, 1999).

Cooperatives often attempt to overcome these disadvantages through marketing agencies in common, dedicated supply agreements to a single buyer, and niche marketing. Niche marketing strategies are often reliant on consumer demand for local products, products of a specific origin, or products with unique characteristics. Dedicated supply agreements establish a ready-market for products, but may not offer the highest returns in the long run. Marketing agencies in common, or cooperation among cooperatives for the purpose of marketing, may be the most attractive alternative in the long run. However, this level of coordination may involve prohibitive start-up costs for new ventures. Thus, marketing agencies in common are often the product of established producer ventures (Bleyl, 2006). United Sugars is an example of a common marketing agency developed through collaboration among producer-owned sugar beet cooperatives in the U.S. (Torgerson, 2000).

3.4 Producers Lack Legitimacy without an Industry Track Record

Establishing legitimacy has been suggested to have a positive effect on a firm's ability to attract resources and its ultimate survival (Aldrich and Fiol, 1994). Successful farmers are often instrumental in the development of producer-owned ventures as project champions (Tong, 1997). Their reputation as talented businessmen and willingness to invest in the venture often lends legitimacy to the new project, especially from the perspective of their peers. Legitimacy can then act as a self-enforcing mechanism, attracting additional resources to the firm (Deeds, Mang and Frandsen, 2004). Indeed, the process utilized by new generation cooperatives in attracting upfront risk capital contributions from producers performs a dual role of capitalizing the company while sending a strong signal to creditors of the producers' credible commitment to the venture (Trucano, 1997). The role of producer investment as a mechanism to lend legitimacy to new ventures is supported by theories from the entrepreneurship literature that backing from venture capital organizations increases legitimacy (Chang, 2004).

However, in the case of producer-owned organizations, the self-reinforcing nature of investor legitimacy encounters limitations when a producer group seeks support from lenders. Legitimacy gained among peers does not always translate into an ability to raise funds from financial institutions. Producers are at a disadvantage when they are unable to demonstrate experience or expertise related to the proposed venture (Reuber and Fischer, 1994; Shane and Cable, 2002). As producers' operational plans become further removed from their area of demonstrated expertise, willingness of lenders and other capital providers to finance may diminish. This can result in undercapitalized start-up ventures.

3.5 Low Working Capital Increases Risk for Failure

While cooperative leaders recognize they may be undercapitalized, this does not always translate into recognition of the critical nature of working capital (Chaddad and Cook, 2004; Chaddad, Cook and Heckelei, 2005). The expectation that processing facilities and marketing activities can be developed quickly and efficiently has led many organizations to severely underestimate their working capital needs. Initial revenues generated in processing are expected to mitigate undercapitalization. Thus, any delays or setbacks in design, construction, or marketing subject the organization to substantial risk. These working capital problems may not be unique to producer-owned groups. However, producer-owners are at a disadvantage relative to incumbent firms in determining the reliability of their working capital forecasts as new entrants to the processing industry. In addition, working capital needs are particularly difficult to judge in agricultural processing industries due to high seasonal variations and potential unexpected crop loss.

Producer-owned organizations have mitigated working capital constraints by returning to their members for multiple share offerings (Thyfault, 1996). However, this strategy is not entirely reliable if the venture is experiencing start-up problems. Setbacks can reduce producer confidence in the business plan. And, as raw material providers to the processing facility, processing or marketing difficulties will lead to lower prices returned to the producers for their raw material deliveries. If producers receive low prices for their commodity inputs, this decline in revenue may reduce their ability to invest additional capital regardless of their willingness to invest. And, in the event producers seek lender financing for additional share offerings, lenders will be less likely to provide financing if they are aware the share offering was initiated as a result of venture setbacks.

3.6 *Risk Management and the Incentive to Overcommit*

As producers, farmers are familiar with the need to manage commodity risk. However, they may overestimate their ability to manage risk related to inputs and products not related to their on-farm business. In other words, experience in managing risk related to fertilizer, corn and soybeans may not prepare farmers to manage risk in natural gas and ethanol marketing.

In addition, by investing in a processing facility, certain producers may increase their risk exposure. Failure to deliver can result in fines to the producer, whereas widespread failure to deliver among cooperating producers can result in venture failure. Crop losses as well as producer over-commitment can translate into an inability to uphold raw material delivery obligations. Over-commitment is especially dangerous for successful cooperatives that consistently pay above-market prices to member-producers, as access to premiums creates an incentive among members to commit to deliveries beyond their production capacity.

3.7 *Market Power Drives Demand for Integration but Signals High Entry Barriers*

Market power is often cited as a significant factor leading to the development of producer cooperatives (Sexton and Iskow, 1988; Hansmann, 1996). Depressed prices hypothesized to be a result of market structure represent a strong motivator for newly forming producer-owned ventures. Within the ethanol sector, researchers have presented evidence supporting the possibility of both upstream and downstream market power being exercised in the seed sector and processing sector, respectively (Saitone, Sexton and Sexton, 2008).

While issues of significant market power motivate horizontal integration, they may also signal challenges to vertical integration due to the presence of a strong, established competitor in the industry. Downstream integration into the processing sector or upstream integration into the seed sector may necessitate competing with established, competitive firms. Issues concerning market structure indicate producer-groups may be at a disadvantage in vertically integrating by establishing a new venture due to higher entry barriers relative to competitive industries.[1]

[1] Given high entry barriers, producer-owned organizations have been founded on either a "beat 'em" or "join 'em" strategy. While both strategies recognize the structural issue of market power, the beat strategy is often ruled out due to the associated high

4. Current Value Chain Integration Approaches to Minimize Producer-Owner Challenges

We are currently witnessing the development of innovative netchain strategies that directly respond to the challenges faced by producers as they seek to generate rents at multiple levels. One example of an innovative netchain strategy that ameliorates these challenges is a model developed in the U.S. Ethanol Industry. The specific example we explore in this article is a complex set of agreements negotiated between corn producers and an ethanol company named POET. We refer to this complex set of agreements as the POET model. We examine the strategies used by producer-owners who took a proactive approach to developing joint investment networks coupled with supply chain management agreements.

The POET model lends itself to analysis due to the highly integrated nature of the agreements among investors and the high level of standardization of these agreements across the plant partner network. While the current analysis focuses on the POET model, we recognize components of this approach are utilized by producer organizations in the ethanol sector and other sectors with varying levels of integration. Within the ethanol and biodiesel sectors, the success of the POET model has inspired second-movers to follow suit[2] (Missouri Soybean Association, 2005).

4.1 Producer-Ownership: Transformation of the U.S. Ethanol Sector

In the 1990s, the U.S. ethanol sector was dominated by investor-owned firms. The concentration ratio of the top four firms was estimated at 73%, with approximately 60% of capacity being owned by Archer Daniels Midland (Hendrickson and Heffernan, 2007). Farmer ownership was negligible. By 2007, however, the U.S. ethanol sector had witnessed a dramatic

entry barriers. The join strategy is the rationale used for developing dedicated supply agreements with recognized industry leaders.

2 Subsequent to POET's success with supply chain integration through producer-ownership, additional actors in the biofuels industry have sought to develop similar joint investment arrangements with producer groups. An example would include Archer Daniels Midland's 2005 joint investment in biodiesel with Missouri producers.

turn. The concentration ratio of the top four firms is now estimated to be a mere 31.5% (Hendrickson and Heffernan, 2007). The Renewable Fuels Association estimates about 42% of ethanol plants are farmer-owned. These producer-owned plants account for about 39% of ethanol production capacity in the U.S. (Renewable Fuels Association, 2008).

Ethanol Plants, 1999-2007:
Farmer vs. Non-Farmer Ownership

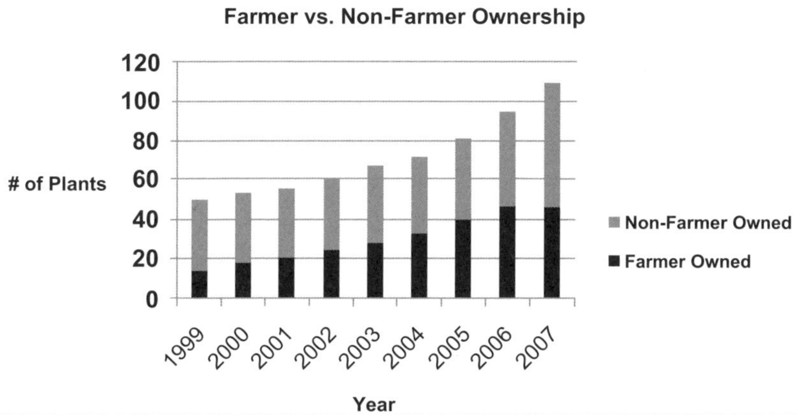

Undoubtedly, this transformation was affected by exogenous factors. Volatility in fuel prices and environmental concerns encouraged investment in ethanol production facilities. In addition, state and federal incentives supported industry growth. These incentives include production incentives, excise tax exemptions and use mandates (Food and Agricultural Policy Research Institute, 2008). Two factors may have acted to increase producer-ownership relative to investor ownership: 1) state incentives directed at small-scale ethanol processing facilities or those owned by agricultural producers and 2) uncertainty with respect to continued state legislative support.

Examples of states actively promoting farmer ownership of ethanol production facilities include Missouri and Minnesota. Missouri established a fuel ethanol incentive to fund the provision of subsidies to processing facilities maintaining at least fifty-one percent producer ownership (Missouri Revised Statutes). Minnesota has enacted similar provisions. After the sale of a farmer-owned cooperative to an investor-owned firm, Minnesota strengthened their commitment to farmer-owned ethanol processing facilities by requiring repayment of state funds distributed in the previous two years if farmers lose majority control of the processing plant (Minnesota House of Representatitves, 2003; Morris and Hill, 2006).

Much of the state and federal support was uncertain in the decades during which farmer ownership grew, decreasing the likelihood that non-farmer investors would be willing to invest. Minnesota, whose producer payment program allowed payments of 20 cents per gallon up to a maximum of 15 million gallons per year, was drastically cut after budget constraints in 2003: producer payments dropped to 10 cents a gallon for a maximum of 3 million gallons (Minnesota House of Representatitves, 2003; Morris and Hill, 2006).

Producers' willingness to invest in ethanol production facilities was driven by depressed corn prices and interest in developing alternative markets for corn (Livingston, et al., 1998). This offensive strategy would incite significant structural changes in the organizational models of producer ownership as their rent generation strategy shifted from 1) a single rent generation approach focused on returning revenues to the farm level to 2) a dual rent generation approach in which producer members sought to generate returns at the farm and firm levels.

How were producers able to effectively organize and invest in plant ownership to contribute to radical industry transformation the ethanol sector? Certain contractual arrangements employed by industry leaders were able to ameliorate constraints of producer integration into the ethanol value chain and, as a result, unlock significant pockets of wealth across the midwest United States. Producers now saw an opportunity to leverage wealth that had been harboured in land equity for risk capital investment in processing facilities (Stroburg, 2005). We analyze the components of these contractual arrangements by describing the mechanisms used by an industry player successful in negotiating alliances with producer-owners: POET.

4.2 The POET Model

One of the largest ethanol producers in the world, POET currently operates 26 ethanol plants in the United States. From these plants, POET markets approximately 1.5 billion gallons of ethanol and 3.5 million tons of distillers grains a year (Dolan, 2008). Other leading U.S. ethanol producers include Verasun with a 1.64 billion gallon capacity and Archer Daniels Midland whose current capacity of just over 1 billion is expected to reach 1.65 billion gallons by 2010 (Archer Daniels Midland Company, 2008; Renewable Fuels Association, 2008; Verasun, 2008).

4.3 The Evolution of POET: From Family-Owned Construction Company to Integrated Venture Management

POET originally formed in 1991 as a family-owned company to design and build ethanol plants.[3] U.S. crop producers were interested in investing in ethanol plants in their local area as a way to increase revenue from corn. As POET and farmer-investors began to recognize their mutual interdependencies, they developed a unique business model that allowed for rapid expansion of the ethanol supply chain while minimizing many of the challenges producer-owners were experiencing in attempting to vertically integrate from crop production into ethanol processing and distribution. The basic design elements of this model include raw material delivery agreements, joint risk capital investment, production network management, integrated risk management, coordinated technology development and commercialization, and consolidation of marketing and distribution. These mechanisms work to ameliorate constraints of producer integration into the ethanol value chain.

4.3.1 Raw Material Delivery Agreements

It is important to note that many producer groups investing in ethanol processing facilities developed ownership models that tied risk capital investment and raw material delivery rights to ownership. In other words, producers joined together to buy shares to finance design and construction of the processing facility. These ownership shares were tied to delivery agreements stipulating the owners' obligations for corn delivery to be used in the ethanol plant. The legal entity utilized by producer groups was typically a cooperative, especially New Generation cooperatives, a limited liability company, or a combination of legal forms. Corn delivery agreements arranged and promoted by local farmers represented a dedicated, stable supply of raw material inputs for developing processing facilities.

4.3.2 Joint Risk Capital Investment

Producers utilized strong local ties and dense networks to generate a pool of interested capital providers. Producers' actions in establishing venture legitimacy and attracting credible commitments at the local level was often

[3] Broin and Assoicates was the original company name. All Broin Companies changed their name to POET in 2007. To avoid confusion, we refer to this company as POET even if the activities we are referring to were conducted when the company was still registered as Broin.

the first step in the development of new ethanol plant ventures. However, many producer groups found it difficult to fulfil their equity requirements when restricting ownership to producer-owners (Livingston, et al., 1998; Thongchua, Powell and Lawless, 2002). Therefore, they developed multi-tier and multi-class organizations to increase the pool of potential investors. Multi-tier and multi-class structures made it possible to vary investor rights with respect to residual distribution, raw material delivery obligations, voting rights, and board representation. In addition, a multi-tier approach, utilizing a cooperative as a major investor in an ethanol-producing limited liability company allowed new ventures to access favourable tax treatment and production incentives.

Table 1: Example POET Plant Ownership Arrangements[1]

Location	Initial Primary Producer Group Investor	Primary Investor Ownership Interest	Broin Ownership Interest (POET)	Board Appointments Controlled by Broin (POET)
Big Stone, SD	Northern Growers	77%	22%	2/7
Macon, MO	Northeast Missouri Grain Processors	82%	9%	1/7
Bingham Lake, MN	Southwest Minnesota Agrifuels Cooperative	64%	35%	N/A
Chancellor, SD	Great Plains Ethanol	40%[2]	16%	2/9
Wentworth, SD	Lake Area Corn Processors[3]	88%	12%	2/7
Glenville/Albert Lea, MN	EXOL	100%	0%	N/A
Coon Rapids, IA	Tall Corn Cooperative	59%	32%	N/A

Sources: (Thongchua, et al., 2002; Western Plains Energy, 2002; Krumpelman-Farmer, 2005; Campbell, 2006; Lake Area Corn Processors, 2006; Great Plains Ethanol, 2007; Great Plains Ethanol, 2008; Hagy, 2008; Northern Growers LLC, 2008).

1 The percentages noted here were calculated based on Securities and Exchange filings, case studies, and other documents as noted in sources. For the most part, these percentages reflect initial equity investments. Therefore, current equity investments may have changed.

2 The forty percent figure is representative of Class A Shareholders. Class A shares are linked to corn delivery agreements.

3 The forty percent figure is representative of Class A Shareholders. Class A shares are linked to corn delivery agreements.

In an effort to complete their equity drives, farmers actively sought non-producer investment from private investors, local electric cooperatives, local grain elevators, and plant design firms (Krumpelman-Farmer, 2005). Investment by ethanol plant design firms contributed directly to capital financing needs (See Table 1). In addition, an investment on the part of leading design-engineering firms in the ethanol industry helped to establish legitimacy with creditors and other investors as to the viability of producers' business plans (Campbell, 2006). Finally, investment by the design-build firm signalled POET would have a long-term involvement in the governance of the organization through share ownership. This long-term involvement in governance was expected to have a positive impact on firm performance due to POET's extensive industry knowledge, contacts and information. POET's ownership stake also allowed newly developing plants to cite the success of existing plants under POET management as a proxy for their expected progress when seeking lender financing.

Larger investors were cautious to invest in the ethanol industry in the 1990s and early 2000s as a result of low margins in the ethanol industry in the late 1980s (Leonard, 2006). Producers, however, presented themselves as investors knowledgeable with respect to the prospects of the developing ethanol industry. In addition, farmers' dual rent generation approach made an investment in ethanol feasible. If margins were low at the firm level, farmers still benefitted at the farm level due to their delivery agreements to deliver raw inputs to the processing facility. In addition, farmers' ability to generate local investor networks proved essential to the development of POET's ethanol production network. While maintaining relatively low equity stakes, POET was able to deliver capital and legitimacy to farmer-owned ventures, grow their plant network, maintain control rights over the future direction of the facilities they built, and limit their risk capital exposure. Current POET equity in partner plants ranges from three to twenty-six per cent (Dolan, 2008).

4.3.3 Optimization of Production Network through Management Agreements

While eager to invest in ethanol production facilities, farmer-owners recognized their limitations in terms of recruiting and monitoring capable management teams (Western Plains Energy, 2002). In 1994, farmers began to negotiate management agreements with POET. POET plant management agreements gave producer-owners access not only to POET's extensive industry knowledge, but also to structural and process improvements being implemented across the plant network. In this manner, the value of enhancements developed and tested at one POET plant could be captured across the plant partner network. By 2008, twenty six plants had negotiated management agreements with POET (POET, 2008).

While managerial and technological knowledge is non-rivalrous in terms of use within the partner network, it is rivalrous in exchange (Antonelli, 2007). The ability of plant partners to extract monopolistic or entrepreneurial rents from these innovations depends on their ability to exclude non-network firms' access to proprietary knowledge. Therefore, plant partners have developed strict intellectual property right protections to increase the appropriability of returns to innovative management systems as well as technological advances. Property right protections utilized to localize returns to the plant partner network include non-disclosure, non-compete and confidentiality provisions in employee contracts.

Close working collaboration with POET in the design, construction, management and governance has enabled farmers to mitigate start-up concerns with respect to equipment problems and working capital concerns. Even when engaging in new plant development, producer-owners have access to reliable information on which to base their prospectus as the developing plant shares components of its engineering design and management with POET plants across the network. This coordination maximizes the ability of those involved to forecast working capital needs and minimizes the potential for construction and equipment problems that may constrain working capital accruement.

4.3.4 Integrated Risk Management and Input Cost Reduction

The precursor to POET Risk Management was formed in 1995 to deliver risk management services for corn and natural gas. Plants participate by entering into Corn and Natural Gas Price Risk Management Agreements. This organization, while operating under the POET name, remains independently owned by Commodity Marketing Co., Albert Lea, MN. However, Commodity Marketing Co. has carried out risk management for all POET-managed plants since 1998.

Risk management agreements allow partner plants protection against volatile commodity markets while lowering the costs associated with maintaining redundant in-house staff to carry out this function. While individual ethanol producers can contract similar risk management services, the plant partner network offers additional advantages. Horizontal integration of risk management across the plant network allows POET plants the possibility of pooling risk across facilities.

4.3.5 Coordination of Technology Development and Commercialization

In addition to management agreements, farmers have successfully collaborated with POET in technological development at multiple levels within the value chain: in raw material delivery, in ethanol production, and in co-product processing. Given difficulties experienced by previous producer-investors in the processing industry, the ability to engage in continuous collaboration with POET engineering experts on production efficiency and the development of new production technology is attractive to producer groups. POET benefits by maintaining a plant network receptive to rapid commercialization of new technologies developed.

However, receptivity is not limited to plant testing and adoption of technologies to be commercialized. Due to POET's extensive collaboration with farmers, POET retains the capacity for close collaboration with producers in the development of technologies that rely on farm-level trials. For example, POET is currently collaborating with producers to discern the most efficient process for harvesting corn cobs for utilization in newly developing cellulosic plants (Sioux City Journal, 2007).

The primary contractual arrangements governing network technology development are technology and patents rights license agreements which producer organizations have negotiated with POET Research. These agreements give individual plants the right to utilize technology developed throughout the POET plant network while limiting the appropriability of these technology developments to ethanol plants outside the network. POET's first commercial ethanol production facility in Scotland, SD is now the headquarters of POET Research which coordinates research and development work with respect to ethanol production. POET Nutrition[4] engages in research on distiller's grains. The extensive collaboration carried out as a result this netchain strategy has also allowed the POET network to be seen as an attractive partner for organizations such as DuPont, Novozyme and the U.S. Department of Energy. POET is currently collaborating with the U.S. Department of Energy on research and development leading to the construction of a cellulosic ethanol facility in Emmitsburg, Iowa (Bevill, 2008).

4.3.6 Consolidation of Marketing and Distribution

Agreements with POET for the marketing of distillers grains and ethanol products allow producer-owners another mechanism to integrate their processing facilities into distribution networks. Dakota Grains Marketing Association, now POET Nutrition, was developed in 1995 as a marketing agency for distillers grains. In addition to developing market access for producers, POET has developed branded Dakota Gold distillers grain products to increase producer revenues from ethanol co-products. POET Nutrition supports these marketing activities with their research on the nutritional benefits of Dakota Gold products.

In 1997, POET established Ethanol Products, LLC to market ethanol and carbon dioxide released during the fermentation stage of ethanol production. Ethanol Products is also able to act as a collective bargaining agent to supply denaturant to plants. Producer groups facilitated the development of Ethanol Products through minority share interests in the organization (Lake Area Corn Processors, 2006). Marketing services are contracted by plants through ethanol marketing and service agreements. These marketing and service agreements are not limited to partner plants, those plants having negotiated a management agreement with POET. Independently managed plants have also chosen to enter into ethanol marketing agreements to secure market access, as well as information regarding marketing prospects and the feasibility of a certain location (Western Plains Energy, 2002). For new ethanol production facilities, signing a marketing agreement is often essential to securing lender support (Informa Economics, 2007). Therefore, while POET ethanol marketing agreements are an integral part of many plants' success during operational phases, the marketing agreement may also serve a critical role during development phases as well.

4 POET Nutrition was formerly known as Dakota Gold Research Association, founded in 2002.

The involvement of POET in ethanol marketing through Ethanol Products, LLC gives potential producer investors access to superior information regarding ideal plant locations. Individual producers may exhibit heterogeneous preferences with respect to a building location if they are to bear a share of raw material transportation costs (Tong, 1997). However, these heterogeneous preferences can be unified with evidence that a specific location will improve market access and reduce transportation costs associated with product marketing.

Figure 1: POET model: mutual coordination within the U.S. ethanol value chain

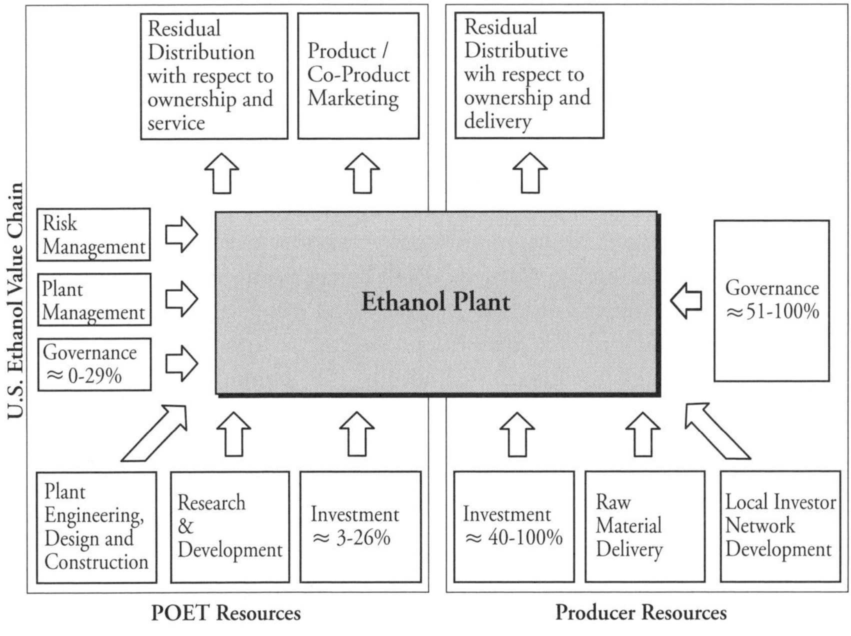

5. Producer Strategies for Achieving Vertical Integration in the Ethanol Supply Chain

In the past, producers looking to invest in ethanol production facilities have retained several different companies to perform services for their new venture. Managing multiple contracts for feasibility studies, design-build agreements, management agreements, and product marketing may prove difficult for producers stepping outside their area of expertise. In addition, retaining multiple companies presents the possibility for multiple conflicts of interest.

One strategy producers have found to overcome start-up challenges is to join a network of plants operating as an integrated system. Certain producer groups have been successful in developing individual components of this approach in the past. For example, the Renewable Products Marketing Group, founded by a group of farmer-cooperatives, was able to successfully negotiate ethanol producing marketing agreements and reduce input costs by collectively purchasing raw materials (Informa Economics, 2007). However, the POET model represents an opportunity to utilize the integrated systems approach across multiple functions with lower upfront transaction costs. Key design mechanisms of this approach have been adapted by producer-owned organizations to achieve scope economies in transaction cost management.

Farmers present themselves as desirable partners in the development of new ethanol production facilities because they are able to secure a reliable corn supply and utilize their networks to attract wiling investors. The POET model facilitates this investment by contributing essential knowledge and services with respect to plant design, governance, management, procurement, risk mitigation, research and development, and product marketing. This seems to constitute a win-win solution for many producers and other local investors. By investing alongside farmers, POET has been able to retain control rights across the majority of their plants. Local producers and investors, by contributing the majority of investment capital to these operations, ensure that residual earnings are distributed locally (see Figure 1).

6. Future Perspectives for Research

POET is an example of a construction company that grew into a chain management service provider for multiple farmer-owned ethanol ventures. The POET model represents one example of an integrated system that was negotiated to respond to several challenges producers experience when attempting to vertically integrate (see Table 2). Future research should seek to identify additional challenges that thwart producers' ability to access rents at multiple levels in the value chain. Hopefully, further identification of these challenges will allow us to explore additional mechanisms producer-owners may utilize to improve supply chain integration.

We find the ability of this integrated systems approach to improve access to debt capital and increase venture legitimacy for new producer-owned ventures particularly intriguing. While the POET case has demonstrated the potential of this model for rural development and local ownership in the context of the United States, it will be interesting to see whether similar models can be developed to support enterprising producers in low-income countries. We look forward to exploring supply chain innovations instigated by various supply chain actors and in a variety of industries within agro-food-energy networks.

Table 2: Mechanisms for value chain optimization among producer-controlled entities in the U.S. ethanol sector: the POET model

Value Component	Producer Challenge	POET Model	Contractual Mechanisms
Stable Raw Material Supply	Producers experienced depressed corn prices and were searching for alternative avenues to market their crop.	Producers buy the right and obligation to deliver corn.	Corn Delivery Agreements
Joint Risk Capital Investment	Producers with no proven track record in the ethanol industry lack credibility, legitimacy with creditors.	POET facilitates plant development and retains governance control by contributing low levels (3-26%) of risk capital to plant construction.	Joint Investment through Shareholder Agreements
Coordination in Plant Location	Transportation costs create heterogeneous preferences among producers with respect to plant location.	POET works with investors to conduct feasibility studies in conjunction with new plant design, considering the impact of new plant location on product marketing across the network.	Design Build Agreement–with POET Design and Construction
Co-Optimization of Production Networks	Limited management expertise at processing level puts producers at a disadvantage among large, established competitors.	Integrated plant management across 26 plant network allows for procedural and structural improvements to be disseminated. Attempts are made to retain exclusive command of proprietary managerial and technological knowledge.	Plant Management Agreement with POET Plant Management Non-disclosure, non-compete and confidentiality provisions
Integrated Risk Management	Producers bear significant risk due to price volatility in commodity markets. Vertical integration represents an attempt to extract value from depressed commodity prices.	Non-redundant risk management staff in combination with pooled risk management across facilities acts to provide another level of risk protection against commodity volatility.	Corn and Natural Gas Price Risk Management Agreement with POET Plant Management

Value Component	Producer Challenge	POET Model	Contractual Mechanisms
Collective Research, Development, and Commercialization	New technology utilization is perceived as a high risk strategy as attempts to scale up technology have proven crippling to newly forming producer-owned groups.	The POET network structure affords the capacity to conduct research and disseminate procedural and technological improvements across the netchain.	Design Build Agreement–with POET Design and Construction
			Technology and Patents Rights License Agreement with POET Research
Consolidated Marketing and Distribution	Producers possess little previous industry experience and thus possess few network ties and information to establish distribution networks for products and co-products.	New plant openings are coordinated within an established system managing logistics, market development, and market information for ethanol, CO2 and denaturants.	Ethanol Marketing and Service Agreement with POET Ethanol Products
			DDGS Marketing Agreement with POET Nutrition

References

ALDRICH, H. E.; FIOL, C. M. Fools rush in? The institutional context of industry creation. *The Academy of Management Review* 19, n. 4 (1994): 645-670.

ANTONELLI, C. *Localized technological knowledge: pecuniary knowledge externalities and appropriability.* Jena, Germany: Max Planck Institute of Economics, 2007.

ARCHER Daniels Midland Company. *Annual Report.* Decatur, IL, 2008.

BEVILL, K. *Poetry in motion.* Ethanol Producer Magazine, July 2008.

BLEYL, S. *Marketing successes: renewable products marketing group. Tools for agriculture: Managing the Risk*, Conference sponsored by USDA Risk Management Agency, USDA Office of Energy Policy and New Uses and the Farm Foundation, Kansas City, MO, June 27, 2006.

BURRESS, M. J.; COOK, M. L.; KLEIN, P. G. The clustering of organizational innovation: developing governance models for vertical integration. *International Food and Agribusiness Management Review* 11, n. 4 (2008): 49-75.

CAMPBELL, D. Fuel farming: missouri farmers harvest bumper crop of ethanol, raising spirits and cash. *Rural Cooperatives* Sept.-Oct. 2006.

CHADDAD, F.; COOK, M. L. Understanding new cooperative models: an ownership-control rights typology. *Review of Agricultural Economics* 26, n. 3 (2004): 348-360.

CHADDAD, F. R.; COOK, M. L. The economics of organization structure changes: a US perspective on demutualization. *Annals of Public & Cooperative Economics* 75, n. 4 (2004): 575-594.

CHADDAD, F. R., COOK, M. L.; HECKELEI, T. Testing for the presence of financial constraints in US Agricultural Cooperatives: an investment behaviour approach. *Journal of Agricultural Economics* 56, n. 3 (2005): 385-397.

CHANG, S. J. Venture capital financing, strategic alliances, and the initial public offerings of internet startups. *Journal of Business Venturing* 19, n. 5 (2004): 721-741.

COOK, M. L. The role of management behavior in agricultural cooperatives. *Journal of Agricultural Cooperatives* 9 (1994).

COOK, M. L.; CHADDAD, F. R. Redesigning cooperative boundaries: the emergence of new models. *American Journal of Agricultural Economics* 86, n. 5 (2004): 1249-1253.

COOK, M. L.; PLUNKETT, B. Collective entrepreneurship: an emerging phenomenon in producer-owned organizations. *Journal of Agricultural and Applied Economics* 38, n. 2 (2006): 421-428.

DEEDS, D. L., MANG, P. Y.; FRANDSEN, M. L. The influence of firms' and industries' legitimacy on the flow of capital into high-technology ventures. *Strategic Organization* 2, n. 1 (2004): 9-34.

DOLAN, K. Mr. Ethanol Fights Back. *Forbes*, Nov. 24, 2008.

DUNN, J. R., et al. *Agricultural cooperatives in the 21st Century*. Washington, DC: United States Department of Agriculture, Rural Business–Cooperative Service, 2002.

Food and Agricultural Policy Research Institute. *State support for ethanol use and state demand for ethanol produced in the Midwest*. Columbia: University of Missouri, November 2008.

GOMPERS, P.; LERNER, J.; SCHARFSTEIN, D. Entrepreneurial spawning: Public Corporations and the Genesis of New Ventures, 1986 to 1999. *The Journal of Finance* 60, n. 2 (2005).

GREAT Plains Ethanol. *Securities and Eschange Commission Form 10-Q*. Chancellor, SD, 2007.

______. *Securities and Exchange Commission Form 10-K*. Chancellor, SD, 2008.

HAGY, W. F. Presentation at the 2008 Farm to Fuel Summit, Federal Energy Programs Session, Orlando, Florida, August 1, 2008.

HANSMANN, H. *The ownership of enterprise*. Cambridge, MA: Harvard University Press, 1996.

HENDRICKSON, M.; HEFFERNAN, W. *Concentration of agricultural markets*. Columbia, MO: Department of Rural Sociology, University of Missouri, April 2007.

HENDRIKSE, G. W. J.; BIJMAN, J. Ownership structure in agrifood chains: the marketing cooperative. *American Journal of Agricultural Economics* 1, n. 84 (2002): 104-119.

INFORMA Economics. *Business Models for Ethanol and Biodiesel*. Washington, DC: Prepared for the United States Department of Agriculture, January 2007.

KRUMPELMAN-FARMER, E. The investment horizon issue in user-owned organizations. Ph.D. Dissertation, University of Missouri, 2005.

LAKE Area Corn Processors. *Securities and Exchange Commision Schedule 14A*. Wentworth, South Dakota, 2006.

LANG, M. G.; SPATZ, K. *Cooperative director compensation*. Rural Cooperatives Center, University of California, Davis, Department of Agricultural and Resource Economics (1995).

LAZZARINI, S.; CHADDAD, F.; COOK, M. L. Integrating supply chain and network analyses: the study of netchains. *Journal on Chain & Network Science* 1, n. 1 (2001): 7-22.

LEONARD, C. *Energy concerns make ethanol a hot investment*. Seattle: The Seattle Times, February 28 2006.

LIVINGSTON, K., et al. *Northeast missouri grain processors, Inc. Community Case Study*: University of Wisconsin Center for Cooperatives, February 1998.

MCKEE, G.; BOLAND, M. American Crystal Sugar Company: making ethanol from sugar beets? *Agricultural Marketing Resource Center, Value-added Business Profile, Iowa State University* (2007).

MINNESOTA House of Representatitves (2003) House File 994.

MISSOURI Revised Statutes Chapter 142, Motor Fuel Tax, Section 142.028.

MISSOURI Soybean Association. *Missouri's largest biodiesel production facility announced: biofuels LLC, ADM, Ray-Carroll county grain growers and MFA oil announce intention to join to help meet nation's energy needs with farmer's harvest*, April 25 2005.

MORRIS, M.; HILL, A. *Ethanol opportunities and questions*. Fayetteville, AR: National Sustainable Agricultural Information Service, National Center for Appropriate Technology, 2006.

NORTHERN Growers LLC. *Securities and exchange commission form 10-K*. Big Stone City, SD, 2008.

PETERAF, M. A. The cornerstones of competitive advantage: a resource-based view. *Strategic Management Journal* 14, n. 3 (1993): 179-191.

POET (2008) Meet Poet: History/Legacy.

RENEWABLE Fuels Association. *Changing the Climate: Ethanol Industry Outlook 2008*. Washington, DC, 2008.

______. Industry Statistics, 2008.

REUBER, A. R.; FISCHER, E. M. Entrepreneurs' experience, expertise, and the performance of technology-based firms. *IEEE Transactions of Engineering Management* 41, n. 4, Nov. (1994).

SAITONE, T. L.; SEXTON, R. J.; SEXTON, S. E. Market power in the corn sector: how does it affect the impacts of the ethanol subsidy? *Journal of Agricultural and Resource Economics* 33, n. 2 (2008): 169-194.

SEXTON, R.; ISKOW, J. *Factors critical to the success or failure of emerging agricultural cooperatives*: California division of agriculture and natural resources. Giannini Foundation Information Series, 88-3, 1988.

SHANE, S.; CABLE, D. Network ties, reputation, and the financing of new ventures. *Management Science* 48, n. 3 March (2002).

SIOUX City Journal. *Poet testing equipment to harvest corn cobs for ethanol.* Hurley, SD, Novermber 4 2007.

SOLBERG, D. *The disappearing farm:* can cooperatives keep rural people rooted in the plains? Leeds, ND: High Country News, June 21 1999.

STROBURG, J. *Industrial use of soybeans in Iowa.* American Agricultural Economics Association, Pre-Conference Workshop, Providence, Rhode Island, July 23, 2005.

THONGCHUA, N., POWELL, M.; LAWLESS, G. *Southwest minnesota agrifuels cooperative*: University of Wisconsin Center for Cooperatives, Case Study Prepared for the North Central Initiative for Small Farm Profitability, 2002.

THYFAULT, C. Developing new generation co-ops: getting started on the path to success. *Rural Cooperatives* 63, n. 4 July/August (1996).

TONG, L. *The property rights fundamentals of a new form of agricultural collective action: the new generation cooperative.* Master's Thesis University of Missouri, 1997.

TORGERSON, R. Cooperative marketing in the new millennium. *Rural Cooperatives* January/February (2000): 7-8.

TRUCANO, M. *Southern minnesota beet sugar cooperative: a history of the early years.* Renville, MN: Southern Minnesota Beet Sugar Cooperative, 1997.

VERASUN (2008) About Verasun Energy.

WESTERN PLAINS ENERGY, L. L. C. *Securities and Exchange Commission Form 424B3 – Prospectus [Rule 424(b)(3)].* Hoxie, KS, 2002.

Corporate Governance and Corporate Responsibility

CLÁUDIO A. P. MACHADO FILHO

This paper discusses some convergences among the concepts of corporate governance and corporate responsibility in the process of creating and sustaining the reputation capital of companies. The intangible assets are part of the competitive strategy of firms in an environment of global changes. Insofar as the velocity of the acquisitions of tangible assets increases and the production process is becoming globally "standardized", firms that wish to sustain a distinct competitive advantage (differentiation) are induced to protect, explore, and improve their intangible assets. While tangible resources are more easily "imitable" by competitors, the intangible resources of leadership and reputation are more difficult to be replaced or imitated. Therefore, the management of corporate identity involves the corporate management of tangible and intangible factors, aiming to create an interconnected network of perceptions about the image and reputation of the firm in the public's mind, including clients, suppliers, employees, and society in its broadest form.

Specifically, this essay focuses on the governance challenges in the agrifood chain, in order to manage the intrinsic risks of reputational damage. Departing from the decision making process in a single corporation, the expansion towards a chain or network perspective increases complexity into the decision making process. How do managers and boards of companies coordinate the decision making process, internalizing the concept of sustainability, considering not only their own companies but also upstream and downstream counterparts?

An overview of the main theoretical perspectives related to these issues will be presented. The long ongoing debate about the role of companies in the society will be drawn out, adding to the discussion, the institutional perspective.

1. Introduction

The increasing global concern about the corporate responsibility of business is particularly sensitive in the food agrichains. From seeds to fork, the several segments of the food chains present specific challenges in terms of environmental and social issues. Major companies in this process are challenged to globally address these issues, adapting their broad strategies to specific local institutional conditions. This is already a major challenge. Local companies, connected to food agrichains have also increasing challenges, not only to mitigate their own risks but also to explore the opportunities of the global market.

But increasing complexity in the global market should be considered. We are in a world of instant communication; where financial markets are integrated; where the investors activism and their concerns about quarterly results is emphasized; where the flow of capital presents increasing volatility, impacting different countries, markets and firms; where close and family run companies are discovering the opportunities of the market capital to finance their investments. In other words, the real capitalism is widely spreading through different societies.

Many developing countries are increasingly internalizing the concepts of good corporate governance practices (transparency, accountability, fairness, responsibility and so on), through corporate governance codes, legal environment protecting minority shareholder rights, and self enforced market mechanisms to minimize information asymmetry among principals and agents and to provide a benign environment to the development of capital markets.

Besides the clear advantages of this process, it might pose contradictory or at least challenging elements to the managers' and boards' decision-making. In terms of sustainability considerations, how to balance short term financial results and long term value creation for the firm? What are the parameters? What are the trade-offs? How can the managers and boards address some critical social and environmental decisions? Sometimes these decisions add irremediable sunk costs to the bottom line. How must management address these decisions and how must they to communicate these? How can management convince shareholders, market analysts, employees about the rationale of some decisions from a long term value creation perspective?

The tensions are concrete. Managers are being called to respond to growing demands from stockholders and a wide range of other stakeholders ranging from clients, suppliers, communities, NGO's. These growing demands range from short to long term perspectives. Growing demands range from economic, environmental and social aspects of sustainability. The issue of corporate responsibility is no longer regarded as an altruist-philanthropic initiative.

It is moving toward the core strategic decisions of many companies, where corporate reputation, risk management, license to operate, corporate diplomacy become key elements of the daily strategic decision and operations.

In terms of agrifood chains, we present the hypothesis that the concept of strictly coordinated subsystem (Zylbersztajn & Farina, 1998) will be increasingly implemented in the marketplace. The logic is that the specificities surrounding several aspects of sustainability among different parts of chains tend to grow, leading to different governance mechanisms in the inter-firms along the chains.

Another hypothesis is that there might be an increase in the collective actions of agrifood companies to address issues of sustainability. Some pre-competitive arrangements, (vertical or horizontal) might be an efficient response to the challenges ahead. Not only in terms of sharing costs to common initiatives but also to shared knowledge and technological transfer in order to achieve effective results. And as a consequence, to have a more sounding voice about the responsible role of agrifood businesses to deal with the expectations of external common stakeholders and the general society as a whole. In doing that, the chances of reaching a better reputational capital increases.

2. Corporate Governance and Responsibility

In the heart of governance practices is the need to reduce the "Agency Costs", to reconcile the undertaking's long-term interests. From the seminal work of Spence and Zeckhauser (1971) and Ross (1974), the scholars of the science of organizations started giving more attention to the development of "Theory of Agency" developed later by Jensen and Meckling (1976), Fame and Jensen (1983). The agency problem is an essential element within the company's contractual view, brought by Coase (1937). The agent-principal relationship is always conflicting when a certain individual – agent – acts on behalf of the other, the one named "principal", and the objectives of both do not fully coincide.

The issue of property and control separation within modern organizations was brought to discussion by Berle and Means (1933), and today it has a central position in the development of the theory of organizations, as emphasized by Demsetz and Lehn (1985).

Thus in a relationship principal/agent, for instance, employer/employee, shareholders/executives or institutors/executives, the "principal" tries to implement an incentive and monitoring structure aimed at aligning the interests of the agent to its interests.

The relationship between value maximization, stakeholder theory and corporate objective function is complex. The social responsibility actions, based on the stakeholder theory would be justified considering that managers should make decisions taking into account the interests of several stakeholders involved, not only the financial claimants (shareholders), which means addressing the interests of employees, communities, customers, government agencies, and so on. As Wood (1991, p. 695) in Jones, Marc (1999) points out: "The basic idea of corporate social responsibility is that business and society are interwoven rather than distinct entities; therefore, society has certain expectations for appropriate business behavior and outcomes."

Jensen (2000), in a critical article disagree strongly from the stakeholder theory, that considers that firms should not assume only one single value objective function of seeking value maximization. Jensen reinforces the logic of companies to follow only one single objective finction.

Another critic of stakeholder theory comes from Sternberg (1999), sustaining that stakeholder theory has been presented as a corrective model of the perceived mistakes in the issues of corporate governance and business ethics, and has been so widespread that it is becoming the new orthodoxy. However, in the same direction of Jensen's critics, Sternberg calls the attention of an implicit deviation of stakeholder theory: with no way to keep score, managers become unaccountable for their actions. The managers might mask their ineffective decisions under the multiple objectives of stakeholder theory, causing a strong problem of agency, since whatever the actions and decisions they do, there is some justification.

In Sternberg's words (op.cit.), "Far from being a source of improvements, this most distinctive stakeholder doctrine is fundamentally misguided, incapable of providing better corporate governance, business performance or business conduct. It is intrinsically incompatible with business and all other substantive objectives, and systematically stakeholding undermines both private property and accountability, it can be used to rationalize almost any kind of government intervention, no matter how intrusive or restrictive".

The interesting point, however, is that Jensen's and Sternberg's arguments are not necessarily against the social actions by companies. On the contrary, such actions might pragmatically be used strategically by firms to create reputation capital that helps in the process of seeking value maximization of the firm. The basic point, however is that value seeking should continue being the *only objective function of firms*, according to these authors.

According to Jensen, "Since a firm cannot maximize value if it ignores the interest of its stakeholders, enlightened value maximization can utilize much of the structure of stakeholder theory by accepting long run maximization of the value of the firm as the criterion for making the requisite tradeoffs among its stakeholders. Managers, directors, strategists and management scientists can benefit from enlightened stakeholder theory as well".

Jones, Marc (1999) summarizes the arguments in favor and against the activities of social responsibility by the profit organizations, considering ideological and pragmatic aspects:

a) Arguments pro social responsibility actions by companies

The arguments that support social responsibility actions are based on ethics (ideological) or rational instruments:

The ethical arguments are derived from religious principles, philosophical references or prevailing social norms (Andrew, 1989 in Jones, Marc, 1999). These arguments suggest that a firm should behave in a social responsible manner *because it is morally correct.* These arguments have a strong normative component.

The instrumental argument for pro social responsibility is based on some kind of calculative assumption that the social responsible behavior somehow will benefit the company as a whole, at least in the long run (T. Jones, 1995). Fombrum (1996, 2000), Pava & Krausz (1995), points that such actions can help the company minimize risks of reputation losses while creating a good platform to explore business opportunities, differentiating the firm's image from less social aware competitors.

b) Arguments against social responsibility actions by companies

The arguments against social responsible actions are based on the institutional function of organizations and the property rights perspectives.

The argument based on the concept of institutional function (Leavitt, 1958 in Jones, Marc (1999) assumes that other organizations such as government, unions, churches and other civil organizations exists exactly to deal with the kind of function requested by social responsible actions. Another point is that managers of profit companies do not possess the abilities and/or time to implement such kind of public actions.

The argument based in the property rights perspective (Friedman, 1962 in Jones, Marc, 1999), has its roots in the neoclassical economic analysis. This perspective sustains that managers have no other right but to try maximizing the shareholder value. According to Friedman (1962), "there is one and just one social responsibility of companies – use its resources in activities projected to raise the profits, in accordance to the rules of open and free competition, without fraud. Few tendencies can be so damaged to the fundamentals of our free society as the acceptance by the executives of other social responsible duties than generate as much money as possible for the shareholders" (under the strict rules of the game). Acting another way would constitute a violation of legal, moral and fiduciary responsibilities, characterizing an agency conflict.

c) The convergence of arguments pro and against

Certo and Peter (1993) try to summarize the convergence of arguments favorable and against the involvement of companies in activities of social responsibilities: "The classical approach considers companies as economic entities while the contemporary one considers companies as members of society. However, in many cases, both approaches drive to the same conclusion. For instance, when the activity is enforced by law or when the activity might bring profits, both approaches support the involvement in the social action.

Zylbersztajn (2000) analyzes the spontaneous cooperative action among profit organizations and society: "These actions will be justified by the maximization optic when the firm can benefit from a positive social environment, enhancing its image and increasing the value of the firm in the long run. In other situations, it can represent a deviation among the objective functions of shareholders and managers. Finally, the social actions might result from a proposal of shareholders that derive utility from these practices".

In the first case, considering the value maximization approach, the company would have economic gains by the increase of reputation capital.

Also, when the shareholders derive utility from social actions, even without economic gains, there is no problem of alignment of interests between principal and agents (agency costs). The agency problems emerge only when the kind of social action does not imply economic gains, and when the shareholder does not derive utility from the action.

With the intensification of the market integration process, in many situations, the determinant factor for survival of companies could depend on the development and sustenance of a favorable reputation (GRAY and BALMER, 1998; ANDRIOF and McINTOSH, 2001). This perception begins to manifest both in the management community and in the academic arena. As Teece (1998) emphasizes, the competency of knowledge and other intangible resources have emerged as a key factors in competitiveness in developed nations.

According to Teece (op. cit), the intangible assets increasingly become the basis of differentiation in many sectors. Consequently, greater emphasis has been given to the aspects linked to reputation, consumer loyalty and technological knowledge, among others. That is, at present, given the greater technological and marketing ease of replicating practices and behaviors, the factor of differentiation for obtaining competitive advantages becomes, in large measure, the public's perception of the firm's reputation.

Petrick *et al.* (1999) considers that reputation can be viewed as the product of a competitive process in which the firm signals its distinct characteristics for the public (internal and external), in order to maximize its moral and socioeconomic status. The reputation capital is that portion of the firm's market value that can be attributed to the perception of the firm as a corporation that exercises good conduct in the market.

The entrepreneurs' concern is a result of firms' growing exposure to public opinion, by the communication media, which transmits information to the most remote locations in real time, helping to disseminate a good reputation or destroy it in a very short period of time.

In essence, the reputation capital of a firm is made up of several dimensions that mold the image of a given corporation. Several authors have suggested that the "reputation social capital" of the firm can have an effect on sales, disseminating the premise that the reputation capital of the firm affects its market value, due to the adverse publicity (JONES and RUBIN, 1999). Consumers, employees, and suppliers tend to punish firms engaged in socially irresponsible practices. The positive effect of the good social reputation is also emphasized. Chauvin and Hirschey (1994) point out that:

"If investors believe that consumers will prefer to buy goods and services from good employers, this can reflect the estimate of the effect that the firm's reputation in the work market can have on sales."

Schwartz (*apud* JONES and RUBIN)[1] affirms that "actions that improve the public image of a corporation can change advantageously the curve of demand for the products of that corporation". Corning (1999) comments that the management of reputational capital is vital in a period in which the media holds so much influence over consumers, investors, and other interest groups, and that a bad media campaign can have the power to destroy the reputation capital of an organization. As a result, the public relations departments of an organization have become increasingly important, especially in situations where the firm is the target of a prolonged negative campaign. Brickley et al. (2000, p. 2) points out:

> ... the reputation of the firm for ethical behavior, including its perceived integrity in dealing with clients, suppliers and other parties, is part of the value of its name (*brand name capital*); thus, this is reflected in its assessment (just as individual human capital is based in part on its reputation for ethical behavior). Hence, private markets propitiate potentially important incentives to ethical behavior, by imposing costs on organizations and individuals that break established ethical standards.

According to this hypothesis, firms that develop socially questionable behavior in their arena, whether in the ethical or legal sense, intentionally or not, can attract media attention, which, in turn, can cause irreversible damage to the firm, compromising its very survival, as in some events linked to environmental spoliation, exposing the surrounding community to risk, practices harmful to employees, to cite a few examples. On the other hand, the socially positive practices can obtain the contrary effect, calling the attention of public opinion, clients, consumers, and government in a positive manner.

1 SCHWARTZ, R. A. Corporate Philanthropic Contributions. In: JONES, Kari; RUBIN, Paul H. Effects of Harmful Environmental Events on Reputation Firms. working paper, *Social Science Research Network Electronic Library*, abr., 1999. Available in: <http://papers.ssrn.com.taf?abstract_id158849>. Accessed September 3, 1999.

Gibson (2000) exemplifies the case of Johnson & Johnson, which in 1982 took 31 million packages of Tylenol capsules off the market, when it was discovered that someone had sabotaged the firm by injecting poison (cyanide) into a few boxes. The firm's reaction was open, public, and cost more than 50 million dollars. But the firm maintained the name of its product, and reconquered its market share in a short period of time. In 2002, the firm was sixth in the ranking of "World's Most Admired Companies" – *Fortune,* 2002).

A favorable reputation, for example, can communicate to the consumers or clients the quality of the firm's mix of products, allowing it to exercise premium prices for its products and services. Similarly, the good reputation can raise firm employees' self-esteem, which translates into greater productivity, and also facilitates the firm's access to better credit conditions (GARBETT, 1988). Klein and Leffer (1981) argue that brand or corporate image serve as an entry barrier for competitors, since it imposes sunk costs to the entry in the marketplace. For many products, quality is not evaluated until the product is consumed. Therefore, companies with a well-established reputation of good quality and ethical procedures might signal the quality before the buying process (WEIGELT and CAMERE, 1988, p.448).

Fombrun (1996.) defines corporate reputation as the "net affective or emotional reaction" (good or bad, weak or strong) of clients, investors, suppliers, employees, and the public in general in relation to the company's name. Corporate identity is defined as the set of principles and values of the managers and employees of the firm.

In the daily life of the organization, corporate identity appears in the form of the administrative practices employed in the firm's internal and external relations. Within our society, which is based on language, names are attributed to everything that can be perceived or recognized, to distinguish one thing from others in the world (TADELIS, 1999). The same occurs with firms. From the moment a firm is established, it begins to be recognized by its name, which is uniquely associated to its characteristics and past performance. The name, or indeed, the reputation conferred by this name is an intangible good of this company.[2] The firm is recognized by its name and

2 The intangible assets of the firms are not, in general, visible in their balance, and their value is calculated solely on the occasion of the sale of the firm, subtracting the net tangible value from the price of sale. This goodwill captures the value of the intangible assets, where the value of the firm's reputation is included.

by its presentations, forming mental images that lead to the formation of corporate reputation in the perception of people, as illustrated in Figure 1:

Figure 1: Interrelation between identity and corporate reputation

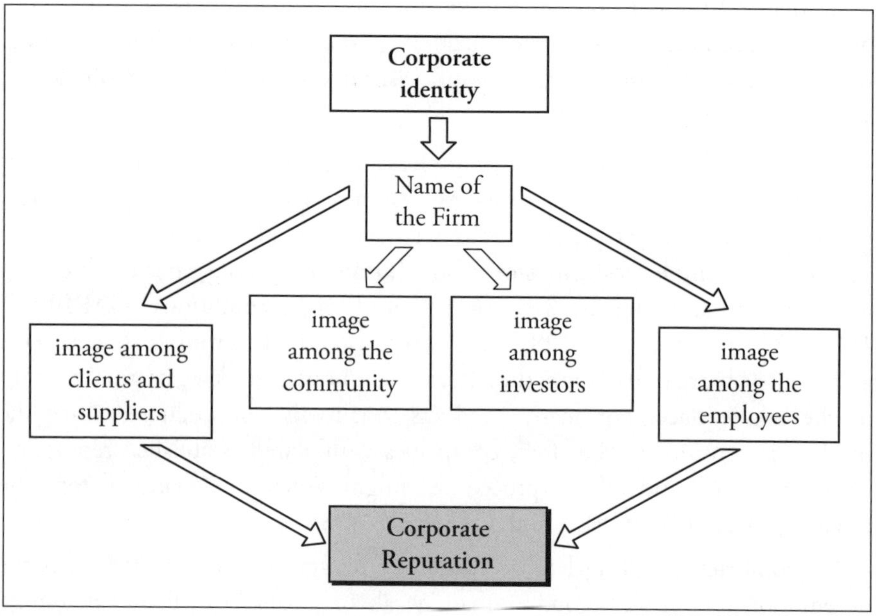

Source: Adapted from Fombrun, 1996

Though Fombrun (op. cit) offers an operational description to analyze the interrelations between the various component factors of reputation, the authors do not advance into a deeper theoretical analysis to explain the behavior of agents in their trade practices. This reference is important to explain in what situations reputation is more or less important from the strictly economic viewpoint, an analysis from which possible unethical behaviors on the part of the agents derive. Hence, aspects linked to credibility, trust, and responsibility is analyzed based on models of *game theory, transaction cost economics (TCE), agency, and stakeholder theory.*

The viewpoint provided by the New Institutional Economics is relevant to the present work because it relates the premises of agent behavior (especially opportunism) to the efficiency of the governance structures that emerge, given the institutional system in effect. Zylbersztajn's (2000) highlights the relationship of ethics with the institutional aspect and conduct of companies:

> ... even if the solution of the issue of ethical relativism could be achieved by departing from a common cultural standard, it should be asked how can one induce organizations to adopt certain ethical standards. This is the question of central importance for administrators and scientists of organizations in general. If *unethical* behavior adds costs to transactions, since voluntary cooperation is not always achieved, what are the prescriptions that can be made to mitigate the problem, either in the public or the private sphere? How can societies, and within them organizations, incorporate ethical principles, which ultimately are cost reducers?

One of the behavioral assumptions of TCE (inserted in the context of the New Institutional Economics), opportunism, is fundamental to the present work. Institutions that minimize opportunistic behaviors, in many situations, minimize unethical behaviors and reduce transaction costs among economic agents. One of the most important control mechanisms for opportunism is the development of reputation, measured as the present value of a future flow of resources stemming from the value of brand name and public image.

Jones and Rubin (1999) declare that the definitions of reputation in the literature and the concept of reputation effect refer basically to the reputation of the firm in the market of products, dealing with employees or suppliers, and to the reputation of the administration in the market of capitals. Chauvin and James (1994) note that in all the theoretical works on reputation, it has economic value because it improves the efficiency of the markets. The economists have sought to describe and model the methods involved to mitigate the problem of information asymmetry and of opportunistic behavior. If a firm deviates from a commitment to quality, the consumers punish the firm with less willingness to pay for the product (considering the premise that the consumer is able to evaluate the quality parameters). The net present value of future profits declines and, consequently, the market value of the firm.

In another context, if the firm deceives its supplier in some way, for example, it will likely have to incur higher costs to obtain the supply commitment in the future. Firms that deceive their employees may have to offer higher salaries or bonuses to attract future employees in a competitive job market. Hence, reputation can be considered an entry cost of a firm in the market, in which subsequent profits represent the present value of the return of the investment in reputation and ethical conduct. Also in relation to the investors, the involvement of a firm in a negative incident (for example in environmental aspects) can lead them to reassess their beliefs in the capacity of the firm to deal with the resulting losses. Furthermore, the investors can assess the possibility of implementing stronger regulatory actions that could affect the profits of the firm in the future. Miles and Covin (2000, p.302) present the hypothesis of the existence of a positive correlation between reputation, environmental performance, and financial performance:

> ...firms that try to cheat, by not complying with the regulations are frequently exposed, either by the regulators or by public opinion, and are typically forced to pay fines and/or suffer erosion of their competitive positions due to damage to their reputation.

Jones and Rubin (1999) sum up the possible situations deriving from reputation effect, according to the traditional theoretical framework of the reputation approach:

1) A negative incident can result in a drop in reputation of the firm for its clients, employees, or suppliers. Depending on the nature of the implicit agreement, the loss of reputation may be a result of:

- A deviation from expected behavior;
- The revision on the part of consumers, employees, or suppliers of the odds likelihood of the firm cheating.

2) The firm can also suffer loss of market value if the events lead to a loss in belief in the capacity of its managers on the part of investors. This fact can be the result of:

- An increased perceived risk of future incidents and/or
- A perceived increment in risk of increasingly restrictive regulations.

Jones and Murrell (2001) hold that "trust" is the reputation that the firm enjoys for having a reliable behavior. Thus, actions of social responsibility can be indicators of the *trustworthiness* of the firm. Conceptualizing trust as the reputation of the firm, Jones (1995) essentially establishes that the indication of corporate social responsibility improves the performance of the firm: "The ability of the firm to signal its reputation for non-opportunistic behavior (by means of joint actions with shareholders) can lead to an improvement of performance in the business activity".

The explanation is that if corporate social responsibility is a signal *of what* is important to the firm, then it is reasonable to propose the hypothesis that this signal can be used by the various agents (employees, clients, suppliers, investors, and creditors) to form the impressions on values, beliefs, direction, and general conduct of the firm. Jones (1995) develops a model that integrates the economic theory and ethics, concluding that firms that conduct business with the various stakeholders on the basis of "trust" have incentives to demonstrate commitment to ethical behavior. Ethical behavior will provide the firm with a competitive advantage, as long as it develops lasting and productive relationships with these stakeholders.

Fombrun (2000) synthesizes that the socially responsible activity helps the firm reinforce its connection to the local community and to the employees. On the other hand, the construction of reputation capital also improves the ability of negotiating more attractive contracts for the firm with suppliers and government, in addition to, in certain circumstances, a propitiating premium prices for the products of the firm and lower capital costs. The author refers specifically to the activities of philanthropic social responsibility as a creator or maintainer of reputation capital from two aspects: a) Creating competitive advantage, improving the capacity of the firm to attract and maintain resources; b) Minimizing risks of reputation losses. The model expressed in Figure 2, based on Fombrun (2000), summarizes the logic of the increase of firm value from socially responsible actions.

Figure 2: Model of value creation by means of actions of social responsibility

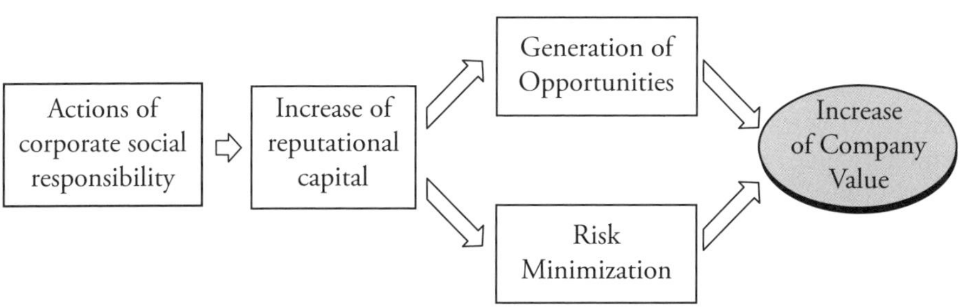

Source: Adapted from Fombrun, 2000

The logic presented in the model is that the firms that practice social responsibility can obtain reputation capital gains, launching business opportunities, reducing potential risks of their conduct in the market, preserving or generating an increase in the value of the firm.

Nonetheless, Fombrun emphasizes that one cannot establish a direct correlation between the Corporate Social Performance (CSP) and the Corporate Financial Performance (CFP), arguing that the activities that generate corporate social performance do not directly affect financial performance, but affect the stock of reputational capital and, consequently, the financial value of the intangible assets of the organization. Chauvin and Hirschey (1994), hold that philanthropic action has a positive effect on the market value of firms. Investors are more inclined to trust their resources to firms that enjoy a higher reputation, due to the lower perceived risks and potential opportunities of marketing created. The firms are responding to consumers' insistence on dealing only with firms that display a good image, and corporate philanthropy is one of the means of creating that image.

> "...giving to charity increases demand or decreases demand elasticity for a firm's product" (NAVARRO apud JONES e RUBIN, 1999).[3]

The action of the media and the risks of legal actions have led organizations to adopt codes of conduct, in order to avoid eventual losses of reputation value, caused by scandals or legal actions. Williams and Barret (2000) studied the relation between firms that practiced philanthropic acts and the restoration of image, shaken by eventual illegal acts that were practiced. According to the results of the study, the philanthropic actions served to restore partially the damaged image of firms that practiced illegal acts. Philanthropic actions are inserted in the vision of the stakeholder theory, that firms have social responsibilities in relation to an ample group of agents, among which are the communities that can benefit from the actions of corporate philanthropy.

3 NAVARRO, Peter. Why do Corporations Give to Charity? JONES, Kari ; RUBIN, Paul H. Effects of Harmful Environmental Events on Reputation Firms. *Workingpaper. Social Science Research Network Electronic Library*, abr., 1999. Available in: < http://papers.ssrn.com.taf?abstract_id158849>. Acesso em: 03 set.1999.

3. Final Remarks

This essay discussed the economic variables related to the questions governance, social responsibility and reputation of organizations. It approached these themes from the viewpoint of the New Institutional Economics, as a theoretical framework for the discussion of the motivations for social responsibility of organizations. Social responsibility is associated with the creation of image and reputation that serve as strategic intangible assets of organizations.

The intangible assets are part of the competitive strategy of firms in an environment of global changes. Insofar as the velocity of the acquisitions of tangible assets increases and the production process is becoming globally "standardized", firms that wish to sustain a distinct competitive advantage (differentiation) are induced to protect, explore, and improve their intangible assets. While tangible resources are more easily "imitable" by competitors, the intangible resources of leadership and reputation are more difficult to be replaced or imitated. Therefore, the *management of corporate identity* involves the corporate management of tangible and intangible factors, aiming to create an interconnected network of perceptions about the image and reputation of the firm in the public's mind, including clients, suppliers, employees, and society in its broadest form.

Our hypothesis is that some factors can minimize the possibility of opportunistic actions of agents. For example, in markets that have a restricted circle of agents, the *institutional environment* in which the transaction is inserted can inhibit opportunistic attitudes, under pain of *loss of reputation,* given the recursive character of the transactions. Both the formal institutions (formal laws and rules of conduct, forms of legal punishment) and the informal institutions (informal rules of conduct, culture, coercion of the social groups to the actions of the individuals) determine the greater or lesser possibility of agents to act opportunistically. Therefore, by minimizing this form of action, they minimize the transaction costs. That is, the effective institutions are those that, in some form, minimize the possibility of opportunistic actions among agents, minimizing transaction costs. Seen from another perspective, it can be stated that in these environments, socially responsible behavior, in ethical/legal dimensions, makes it possible for the firms to gain (or at least not lose) reputation. Finally, this essay brings together and summarizes the relationship among reputation, corporate social responsibility actions and economic performance, opening room for several in depth studies in order to test the different underlying hypothesis derived from the literature review.

References

ANDRIOF J.; McINTOSH, M. *Perspectives on corporate citizenship*. UK: Warwick Business School, 2001.

AKERLOF, George A. The market for lemons: quality, uncertainty and the market mechanism. *Quarterly Journal of Economics*, [S.L.]: 488-500, ago, 1970.

BECHT, M., BOLTON, P., ROELL, A. Corporate governance and control. NBER in *Working paper series*, 2002 Disponível: <http//www.nber.org/papers/w9371>.

BRICKLEY, James; SMITH JR., Clifford; ZIMMERMAN, Jerold L. Business ethics and organizational architecture. *Social Science Research Network Electronic paper Collection*. [S.L.]: nov., 2000. Disponível em: <http://papers.ssrn.com/paper.taf?abstract_id250947>. Acesso em: 16 dez. 2000.

CHAUVIN, Keith W.; HIRSCHEY, Mark. Goodwill, profitability and market value of the firm. *Journal of Accounting and Public Policy*. [S.L.]: v.13, p. 159-180, 1994.

CHAUVIN, Keith W.; JAMES, Guthrie. Labor market reputation and the value of the firm. *Managerial and Decision Economics*. v. 15, p. 543-552, 1994.

CORNING, Beth. Great reputations. *Accountancy. [S.L.]:* v. 123, p. 38-39, mar., 1999.

FOMBRUN, Charles. *Reputation: realizing value from the corporate image*. Boston: HBS Press, 1996.

FOMBRUN, Charles et al. Opportunity platforms and safety nets: corporate citizenship and reputational risk. *Business and Society Review*, Malden, MA: Blackwell Publishers, 105: 1 p. 85-106, 2000.

FORTUNE. *World's most admired companies*. Switzerland: v. 145, n. 5, Europe edition, 11 mar., 2002.

FREEMAN, R. Strategic management: a stakeholder approach. Pitman, Boston, 1984, in: JONES, Marc T. The institutional determinants of social responsibility. *Journal of Business Ethics* 20, p. 163-179, 1999.

FRIEDMAN, M. *Capitalism and freedom.* Chicago: University of Chicago Press, 1962.

GARBETT, T. *How to build a corporation's identity and project its image.* [S.L.]: Lexington Books, 1988.

GIBSON, Kevin. The moral basis of stakeholder theory. *Journal of Business Ethics.* Netherlands: Kluwer Academic Publishers, n. 26, p. 245-257, 2000.

GRAY, Edmund R.; BALMER, John M. T. Managing corporate image and corporate reputation. *Long Range Planning.* [S.L.]: out., 1998, p. 695-702.

JENSEN, Michael. Value maximization, stakeholder theory and the corporate objective function. *Harvard Business School Working Paper* 00-058, April 2000.

JONES, Kari; RUBIN, Paul H. Effects of harmful environmental events on reputation firms. working paper. *Social Science Research Network Electronic Library*, abr., 1999. Disponível em: <http://papers.ssrn.com.taf?abstract_id158849>. Acesso em: 3 set.1999.

JONES, Marc T. The institutional determinants of social responsibility. *Journal of Business Ethics.* Netherlands: Kluwer Academic Publishers, v. 20, p. 163-179, 1999.

JONES, M. Instrumental stakeholder theory: a synthesis of ethics and economics. *Academy of Management Review.* [S.L.]: v.20, p.404-437, 1995.

JONES, Ray; MURRELL, Audrey. Signaling positive corporate social performance. *Business & Society*, [S.L.]: Sage Publications, v. 40, n.1, p. 59-78, Mar., 2001.

KLEIN, Benjamin; LEFFER, Keith B. The role of market forces assuring contractual performance. *Journal of Political Economy*, v. 89, n. 4, p. 615-641, 1981.

KREPS, David M. Corporate culture and economic theory. In: WILLIAMSON, Oliver. *The mechanisms of governance.* New York: Oxford University Press, 1996.

MACHADO, C. A. P. *Responsabilidade social corporativa e a criação de valor para as organizações: um estudo multicasos.* São Paulo, 2002. Tese (Doutorado) – FEA-USP.

MILES, Morgan; COVIN, Jeffrey. Environmental marketing: a source of reputational, competitive and financial advantage. Netherlands: Kluwer Academic Publishers. *Journal of Business Ethics*, ed. 23, p. 299-311, 2000.

MILGROM, Paul; NORTH, Douglass; WEINGAST, Barry. The role of institution in the revival of trade. In: WILLIAMSON, Oliver, E. *The mechanisms of governance.* New York: Oxford University Press, 1996.

MILGROM, Paul; ROBERTS, John. *Economics, organization and management.* New Jersey: Prentice Hall, 1992.

NAVARRO, Peter. Why do corporations give to charity? JONES, Kari; RUBIN, Paul H. Effects of harmful environmental events on reputation firms. *working paper, Social Science Research Network Electronic Library*, abr., 1999. Disponível em: <http://papers.ssrn.com.taf?abstract_id158849>. Acesso em: 3 set.1999.

NORTH, Douglass C. *Custos de transação, instituições e desempenho econômico.* São Paulo: Instituto Liberal, 1994. 38 p.

______. *Institutions, institutional change and economic performance.* Cambridge: Cambridge University Press, 1990.

PETRICK, Joseph et al. Global leadership skills and reputational capital: Intangible resources for sustainable competitive advantage. *Academy of Management Executive.* [S.L.]: v. 13, n. 1, p. 58-69, 1999.

SCHWARTZ, R. A. Corporate philanthropic contributions. *The Journal of Finance*, v. 23, p. 479-497, 1968.

SMITH N. Craig. Corporate citizenship and their critics. In: MAIGNAN, Isabelle. Consumer's perceptions of corporate social responsibilities: a cross-cultural comparison. *Journal of Business Ethics.* Netherlands: Kluwer Academic Publishers. v. 30, p. 57-72, 2001.

STERNBERG, Elaine. The stakeholder concept: a mistaken doctrine. *Foundation for Business Responsibilities*, Issue n. 4, Nov. 1999.

TADELIS, Steven. What's in a name? Reputation as a tradable asset. *The American Economic Review*, [S.L.]: p. 548-563, Jun. 1999.

TEECE, David J. Capturing value from knowledge assets: The new economy, markets for know-How and intangible assets. [S.L.]: *Californian Management Review*, v. 40, n. 3, Spring 1998.

WEIGELT, Keith; CAMERER, Colin. Reputation and corporate strategy: a review of recent theory and application. *Strategic Management Journal*, v. 9, n. 5, sept.-out. 1988, p. 443-454.

WILLIAMS, Bernard. Formal structure and social reality. In: WILLIAMSON, Oliver E. *The mechanisms of governance*. New York: Oxford University Press, 1996.

WILLIAMS, Robert J; BARRET, Douglas. Corporate philanthropy, criminal activity and firm reputation: Is there a link? *Journal of Business Ethics*. Netherlands: Kluwer Academic Publishers, v. 26, p. 341-350, 2000.

WILLIAMSON, Oliver E. *The mechanisms of governance*. New York: Oxford University Press, 1996.

WINKLEMAN, Michael. The right stuff. *Chief Executive*. [S.L.]: p.80-81, April 1999.

ZYLBERSZTAJN, Decio. A Organização Ética: um ensaio sobre as relações entre ambiente econômico e o comportamento das organizações. *Working paper*, FEA/USP, 2000.

Relating International Ethanol Supply Chain Performance to their Governance Structures

EMIEL F.M. WUBBEN[1]

1. Introduction

The first decade of new millennium presents the rapid development of new international biomass value chains. This systems innovation is steered by a set of partly contrasting drivers. First, international treaties, as the Kyoto Protocol, urge countries and companies to quickly reduce emissions worldwide.

Second, agricultural policies aim at reducing fossil fuel dependency and enhancing value creation by promoting biomass substitution. Third, commercial factors such as productivity differences pressure for international value chains to optimize costs, time, value creation, and value appropriation. Fourth, sustainability issues, such as energy balances and land protection bring in unsettled but important boundaries to the realization of the market potential. Fifth and final, what is popularly called the competition between food, fuel, and feed, presents us all with the difficult optimization of creating biomass for primary crops, processed food, bio-based materials, bio-based chemicals, feed, fibers and compost, power, heat, and bio-fuels.

At international policy level the ambition is formulated to substitute 30% of fossil inputs by sustainable biomass in 2030 (LT-Vision PGG), with an emphasis on bio-fuels. Compared to heat, power, and chemicals/materials, bio-fuels are expected to contribute most in terms of fossil

[1] Management Studies Group, Wageningen University. Hollandseweg 1, 6706 KN Wageningen, the Netherlands. +31-317-484428. Email: wubben@wur.nl

substitution, energy savings, and emission reduction. Bio-fuels may ease the pressure on petrol for which the prices in the international markets show, for years, a constant rise with a peak at 140 Dollar per barrel in June 2008. Ethanol dominates bio-diesel in (international) bio-fuel markets. Analyzing the behavior of the international ethanol supply chains may help international business, developing efficient ethanol supply chains. When one adds the lack of reliable literature on the issue of building and managing international bio-fuel chains, then the relevancy of this subject for the international community is evident. The production of ethanol as well as the international commercialization of this product is mainly concentrated in Brazil and United States, producing respectively approximately 46% and 40% of the total world production. When one adds to this that Brazil has the lowest cost in the world, is globally the prime exporter of ethanol, and aims at expanding is its ethanol production, than it is also evident why we would like to investigate the international ethanol supply chains originating from Brazil for this book.

The aim of this chapter is to contribute the literature on managing international ethanol supply chains by analyzing and comparing the structure and performance of the international ethanol supply chains from Brazil to other countries. In particular we will answer the following research question: In order to facilitate the further expansion of international business of ethanol how can international ethanol chains be efficiently organized? We will analyze a series of Brazilian supply chains on their performance, governance structure, strategic alliances and asset specificity to arrive at conclusions on the type of organization that is driving the best performing chain.

The paper is organized as follows. Following this introduction, we will first specify the concepts from the areas of governance structures, alliances, transaction costs theory, and performance measurement. Next, we will introduce the object of research. This followed by the application of the stated four areas of research. We will combine the research in an integrating analysis and close with a concluding section.

2. Theory

This paragraph details the concepts that explain the relation between the organization of international supply chains and their performance. The main theories that have a direct relation to the organization of international supply chains are governance literature, transaction cost economics, and strategic alliance literature. It is expected that the differences in performance of ethanol supply chains can be explained by the differences in governance structures. The differences in governance structures are expected to be explainable by differences in strategic alliances and investments in specific assets for each chain. Evidently performance measurements will be tackled to find adequate indicators of international supply chain performance.

Conform Lazzarini, et al (2001) we define supply chains 'as a set of sequential, vertically organized transactions representing successive stages of value creation'. Supply chain management aims at the integration of planning, co-coordinating and controlling the activities. Supply chains are managed to improve its performance maximizing the satisfaction of all the stakeholders involved. Their goals are mainly related to the function of adding superior consumer value at less cost to the supply chain (Camps 2004; Alvarado and Kotzarb 2001; Omta, Trienekens, et al 2001).

Whenever the literature relates to international supply chains, all concepts refer to a chain developed between two or more countries and managed across borders. Akkermans and Bogerd et al (1999) arrived at the conclusion that the main reasons for not establishing effective international supply chain management were; (1) lack of management attention and (2) dominance of functional thinking. Oppen (2002) calls governance structure as a critical issue for the success of management in international chains. One may find the following reasons explaining the importance of governance in international supply chains (Humphrey and Schmitz, 2001):

- Market access for the lead firm to the exporting or importing country;
- Certain forms of governance bring along a fast track to production capabilities;
- Chain governance is dominant in the distribution or appropriation of the realized gains;
- The degree of chain integration influence the international diffusion of policy initiatives.

A governance structure in this study is any arrangement downstream or upstream a chain combining contracts and administrative entities developed in a formal or informal way. There are many theories concerning the categorization of governance structures. Williamson (1998) mainly divides it in two categories: market and hierarchies. Besides the role of markets and hierarchies, a growing body of literature substantiates the idea of an intermediary class of governance structure; hybrid forms (Ménard 2004). Hybrid forms could be defined as agreements among autonomous entities doing business together mutually adjusting with little help from the price system and without a unified ownership. Usually the basic rule for choosing between market or organizations follow the logic of; the higher are the levels of asset specificity, uncertainty/complexity and frequency, the higher are the costs of transaction across markets (Douma and Schreuder, 1998). Legally there are roughly three types of governance structures; First, transactions are usually carried out in spot market when it is low expected uncertainty/complexity and low asset specificity for both parties in the transaction; Second, transactions go via long-term contracts when asset specificity is high for both parties, requiring relatively low levels of uncertainty/complexity; and, third, vertical integration is preferable under high uncertainty/complexity, given low asset specificity and low frequency of interactions, or for all cases of high uncertainty/complexity where high asset specificity is relevant for at least one party.

When we go from the general concept of chain governance to look at more specific explanations, we now focus on organizational structures, i.e. the ways companies can cooperate with each other. We refer to this as strategic alliances, broadly defined as coalitions occurring among (parent) firms. There are various degrees of vertical integration can be placed on a continuum between market based transactions and hierarchical modes of full integration (Gulati and Singh, 1998; Hagedoorn and Sadowski, 1999; Ring and Van de Ven, 1992).

Figure 1: Strategic alliance options with parent firm (Adapted from Lorange and Roos, 1992)

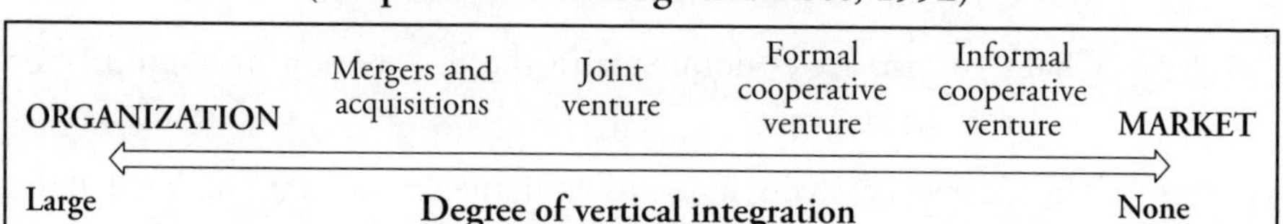

Merger and acquisitions represents full vertical integration among the activities of two or more companies. A joint venture involves the creation of a legally separate company of which the alliance partners are normally founding shareholders (Faulkner, 1995). Next, we relate to a formal cooperative venture when two or more firms that have the same core business are willing to cooperate via a written contract. But these firms may also choose for a more flexible, informal cooperative venture based on trust

Finally, going from the general concept of chain governance to its explanatory items, we now focus on asset specificity, by which we can link up to the transactions costs in the actual deal-making. The term transaction cost refers to the comparison of costs for a market transaction versus the costs of company-internal transactions. The production costs are assumed to be irrelevant, for equal for all alternative forms of transactions. The comprehension of transaction cost is crucial for the understanding of governance perspectives in a supply chain (Williamson 1999; and Coase 1937). There are three critical factors having direct influence on the transaction cost's level, that is uncertainty/complexity, frequency and asset specificity. Here we focus on asset specificity, a term already referred to above, because asset specificity is the most predictable factor of TCE. Moreover, asset specificity is the main feature commending internal organizations (Farina and Zylbersztajn 1997). For that reason Williamson proposes the development of an assessment of asset specificity in terms of comparative measures taking into account the six types of assets: Human assets; physical assets; site specificity; buyer-dedicated assets; brand name capital; and temporal specificity of assests. Although that is a considerable simplification, the key advantage is that rank ordering usually is enough for a comparative analysis among organizations (Williamson 1998).

There are few review studies in the area of supply chain performance measurements (Beamon 1999; Aramyan, Ondersteijn, et al 2006; Lee and Billington 1992). Performance measurement is the process of quantifying actions. There are many types of supply chain measurements, but none of those alone present all the preferred characteristics. For example, supply chain models usually do not include important aspects, such as flexibility of the chain. Arguing that the existing performance measures for supply chains are not adequate, Beamon (1999) advocates the use of a mixed measurement system. Persson and Olhanger (1998) and Beamon (1999) thereby empathize the following three types of measures: resource; output; and flexibility.

Having listed the prime concepts of this research, it is expected that the differences in performance of ethanol supply chains can be explained by the differences in governance structures. The differences in governance structures are expected to be explained by differences in strategic alliances and investments in specific assets for each chain. We will investigate each of these items as the expectations are still to be confirmed. The international supply chain will be the term used in this research. The international supply chain in this study goes from the sugar cane grower in Brazil to the customer abroad.

3. Ethanol Supply Chains

It is relevant to differentiate between different types of ethanol, because a specific type of ethanol brings about a specific supply chain with different stakeholders. Here we focus on ethanol from agricultural sources, especially sugar cane juice. When one look at the composition of ethanol, for the international market we focus on anhydrous alcohol, that is ethanol that is at least 99% pure, almost free of water. Nationally, however, until 1996 hydrous ethanol dominated the market for it was the cheaper to produce. The fall in market share of hydrous ethanol was turned into growth again by 2003. Finally, when looking at the end-user the focus is on automotive fuel alcohol, which can be used either in blends or as 100% substitute for gasoline. To summarize this chapter looks at anhydrous ethanol from sugar cane for fuel purposes.

The production of ethanol for automotive fuels accounts for some 80 percent of the global total ethanol production. Nevertheless, Just some countries produce ethanol at a substantive levels, with Brazil is the biggest producer followed by United States. Together the two countries account for over 80 percent of total ethanol-for-fuel production (see Figure 2).

Parallel to the production, the consumption shows similar figures. Brazil and the USA. Are the major users of ethanol, followed by the EU, Canada and China. National mandatory legislation for the use of biofuels in various countries stimulates international trade to compensate for local demand and supply unbalances.

Figure 2: World and Regional Fuel Ethanol Production (Adapted from IEA 2004 and Murray 2005)

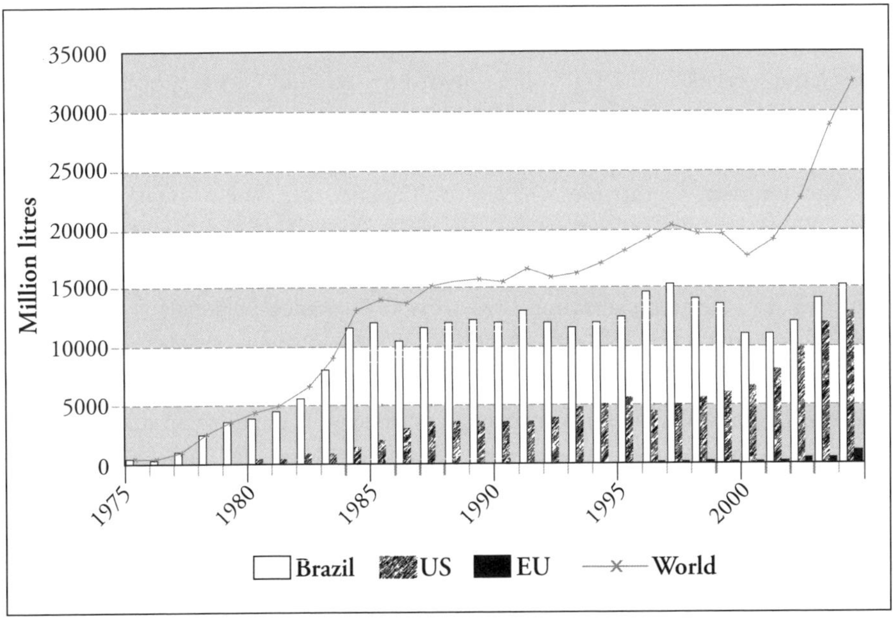

* Production from US are mixed with Canada ethanol production, however Canadian production correspond to less than 4% of the total given amounts.

It is possible to divide the fuel ethanol trades in three main periods. In the 1980s there was a regular trade flow of wine alcohol from the EU to the countries of the Caribbean (Caribbean Basis Initiative), where this product was refined and shipped on as a motor fuel to U.S. In this period Brazil also exported fuel ethanol to the U.S. The second trade flow, in mid 1990's, consisted of synthetic alcohol, methanol from South Africa to Brazil, agricultural alcohol from U.S. to Brazil and ethanol from EU (via CBI) to U.S. The current trade flow, which started in this millennium, has Brazil as the leader export country and U.S. and the EU as net importers. Nowadays Brazil is the biggest producer of ethanol, consumer and exporter in the world.

In Brazil, large-scale production of fuel ethanol began in 1975, with the launch of the so-called National Fuel Alcohol Program (Proalcool). The main reason for the development of the fuel ethanol market was the country's dependency on import petrol, which became apparent with the oil crises in 1973 and 1979. Proalcool brought various forms of support in the ethanol market. Ever since, the fuel ethanol is derived from sugar cane. Anhydrous ethanol started to be blended with gasoline, in increasing rates, as an octane enhancer to substitute MTBE. After the second petroleum crises in 1979, the hydrous ethanol was popularized as a 100% substitute of gasoline, jointly with sales of dedicated cars. This program lasted until the end of 1990's, with the liberalization of the market. Companies have to depend on their own efficiency-ratios instead of depending on governmental arrangements. Also ethanol prices are freed floating, driven by market forces, although tax incentives and subsidies for commercialization still exist. Nowadays, sugar cane crops are harvested in 5.4 million hectares, which corresponds to 9% of the national cultivated area (Carvalho 2005). On average, some 52 percent of the Brazilian sugar cane was used for ethanol production. The activities involving sugar cane account for 2.3% of Gross Domestic Product (GDP). Besides, from these activities generate more than 3.5 million direct and indirect jobs (Shikida and Alves 2001; Procana 2006b). Already in the 1980s the production goal was at 10.7 billion liters of ethanol. Production peaked at 15 billion in 1998, after which the market stagnated and production fell until below 11 billion liters again by 2001. However, the period 2001-2006 showed a steep growth till almost 16 billion in 2005.

Berg (2004) listed three key success factors explaining the over-whelming success of the Brazilian biofuel program. The first key success factor is abundance and cheapness of the feedstock sugar cane. Sugar cane can be harvested in many tropical regions. Moreover, its productivity per hectare is very high, roughly 7000 liters of ethanol per hectare, compared to 4000 liters of ethanol on the basis of corn. In addition sugar cane under Brazilian conditions has the lowest production cost for ethanol in the world, ranging between 18 to 23 dollars cents per liter, dependent on the region. Already before the enormous rise in grain prices, the per liter price on the basis of corn (USA) was more expensive, with wheat (EU) more than 100 percent more expensive. The second key success factor is the technology. The technology for breaking down the molecules of sugar cane is much simpler than for wheat, beet and barley. The later crops but also rice, soybean, trees, and starches have to go through the hydrolysis-step, making it more resource-inefficient (Mazaferro 2004). Furthermore, in Brazil the technology involved in the production of ethanol from sugar cane has gone down a learning curve of some thirty years. The third, key success factor is governmental support, as already mentioned. As strated, the Brazilian government, with the help of the World Bank, developed a supportive framework towards building up an ethanol market. This allowed the enlargement of the sugar cane cropped area, construction of new plants and changes of industrial equipments to utilize ethanol as a fuel. Important was the early support via the state-owned company Petrobras, that gave guarantees for buying predeterminate amounts of ethanol (Marjota-Maistro 2002).

According to Procana (2006) there are 304 units producing sugar and/or ethanol, 227 only in the Centre/South region. There are three different types of units processing sugar cane; sugar mills, sugar mills with distillery plants and independent distilleries. The majority of the units nowadays produce sugar and ethanol. The 304 units are spread over two sugar cane subsystems in Brazil; Centre/South and North/Northeast, mainly in areas previously used for cattle. The first subsystem is far more competitive (productivity) than the second. Within the Centre/South region, Sao Paulo is the main centre of the sugar cane activities. Some determining factors for this hegemony are the location near by the major consumer centers, good biophysics conditions, and the economic concentration on the sugar cane activities (Shikida and Alves 2001; Amaral, Neves, et al 2003).

In 1990 the estimated ethanol production costs in Brazil were around US$ 0.23/liter. With 77% of operating costs, that is 55% of total costs, the feedstock accounts for the main portion of the total costs for producing fuel ethanol. Over the past decade, there have been substantial efficiency improvements in technologies involving ethanol and sugar cane production and more widespread adoption of electricity cogeneration from bagasse (residue from sugar cane). Both improvements have lowered production costs further (IEA 2004). Recent production cost estimates for ethanol are US$ 0.18 per litter. Costs for anhydrous are several cents higher, due to the dehydration process extra costs (Macedo 2002).

Total exports of ethanol for fuel, beverages and industrial usages, has been (far) below 1 billion liters until 2003. By 2004 we see a jump of export levels to appr. 2.5 billion liters annually, most probably due to the rise in fuel ethanol exports. The costs for exports, comprise of transportation cost (freight) in Brazil, an average of the distances between the mills located near Sao Paulo and the Port of Santos, terminal costs at the Port of Santos, international transportation to, for example, the Port of Rotterdam (The Netherlands), insurance costs, import tariffs, and harbor costs. These export costs, apart from trade margins, minimally add over US$ 0.10/ liter to the production costs. Since 2000, the Brazilian ethanol export prices have varied a lot, according to the interviews, from US$ 0.20/liter up till US$ 0.55/liter.

The Brazilian ethanol export chain comprises of at least seven main players, that is; commercial groups, traders, transportation companies, harbors, storage companies, inspection companies and customers abroad. We will detail each stakeholder in this supply chain. First, notice that commercial groups usually collaborate with traders to export ethanol. Among the commercial groups that have

been exporting there are 6 standing out; Copersucar, Cosan, Crystalsev, Bioagência, SCA (Sociedade Corretora de Álcool) and J.Pessoa. Each commercial group has its own sugar/ethanol mills associates. Their main role is to sell the ethanol from its associates. To export ethanol these companies tend to collaborate with traders. The most well known and active traders are Alcotra, Petrobras, Vertical, EdFMan, Coimex, Dreyfus and Bauche. The role of the traders in the ethanol chain can easily be explained as they have easier access on storage capacity and on the international market demand. The traders may also act as an inspector, controlling the whole operation.

The transportation companies transport the ethanol from the mills to the harbor, primarily by means of trucks. In the period of our field research only one company utilized trains, for a small percentage of total volumes. Moreover, a small amount of ethanol has been transported by pipes.

Concerning the Brazilian harbors, the main points for ethanol export are the ports of Santos and Paranagua. Stolt and União are the largest firms who store the ethanol in their private tanks located in these ports.

Another important stakeholder in the international ethanol market is the inspection company, the major firms being Intertek and SGS. The inspection companies operate from production control up to the shipment of the product: starting in the plants with the quantification and analysis of the stock and the production, inspecting the trucks going to the terminals, examining tanks, lines and pumps, chemically analyzing the product, and finally in the ships, checking the reservoirs and the whole on-board system before receiving the cargo, and also the quantification and chemical analysis of the alcohol shipped.

The last stakeholders in this chain, the customer abroad, is quite difficult to detect. Among the Brazilian ethanol sellers, there is quite some confusion regarding the final destination of the ethanol. Sometimes they do not know the final destiny of the commercialized ethanol, as there are many intermediary spots (e.g. Port of Rotterdam). It is known that the main destination for the carburant alcohol is the western coast of USA, especially to big distributors as Chevron, Shell and BP (Hoffman 2003). There are some tracks showing some carburant ethanol going to Sweden, France, Germany, India, Niger and Venezuela.

As mentioned before, the ethanol export market in Brazil is growing fast, but there many constraints that Brazil is facing for exporting its ethanol, the main one being logistic problems. There are three main reasons for the logistic problems: (1) dependency on roads, (2) lack of terminals and (3) lack of port infrastructure (BNDES 2003). The trend for the next years, if no investments will be made, is that logistic problems will increase. However, the government and Petrobras are keen on tackling these problems by rising infrastructure investments.

4. Methodology

In this research we used both data sources and knowledge sources (Verschuren and Doorewaard, 1999). Triangulation is the most reliable way to secure internal validity. (Paulien, et al, 2002). A triangulation of sources, method and data type was often possible, enabling the enhancement of the quality of the results from this research. More specifically, we collected information from literature, documents, media, and individual people:

- Individual people for this research are experts on the ethanol chains and/or from the involved firms. The method of data gathering used in this case was life interviews, conversations by telephone and emails. In total 13 people were interviewed, 2 contacted by phone and 10 contacted by email.

- Industry journals (e.g. Jornalcana and Visão Agrícola) and internet websites (e.g. Unica, Procana and Brazilian Ministry of Agriculture) were used for public and scientific information.
- Documents were gathered in the form of files, research reports and annual reports (e.g. Anuário da Cana).
- Finally, literature was used, in particular books, scientific articles and conference papers.
- In order to increase the external validity of the results from this research attention was paid to choose a significant sample in terms of representation. In order to analyze the Brazilian international ethanol chains a sample of five ethanol chains is chosen. There are three factors that led to the choice of these five chains:
  1. Significance for the international market;
  2. Location; and
  3. Exports

Regarding the significance for the international market, the selected 5 chains represent more than 60% of the Brazilian ethanol exports and 44% of the national production. Together, the five chains comprise of 83 sugar and ethanol mills. The related ethanol mills and commercial companies are located in the Centre/South region of Brazil, which is the most important centre in this field. The same location, in this case the same region, means a similar logistic structure available for everyone. The third factor is meant to sample chains with a proven track record in the international business. The majority of the chains from the sample have been exporting at least since 2002. The names of the organizations and related chains are not made explicit as that was irrelevant for answering the research question, and some interviewed organizations preferred not to be quoted.

5. Results

5.1 Governance Structures

For this research for the level of vertical integration we selected four measures taking us along the international ethanol supply chain. The first and most important measure is on the relation between the mills and commercial groups. As stated in the literature section there are roughly three types of governance structures, that is spot markets, long-term contracts (over 1 year), and ownership. Second, the number of players in the export process. We found there are three (commercial group, trader, foreign customer), two (commercial group and foreign customer) or one (foreign customer owns producer) firms involved. The third item measures the level of responsibility taken by the commercial group or trader to export its ethanol. The ICC defined the trade contract responsibilities and liabilities between buyer and seller export negotiations by three items; Ex works, where the buyer is responsible for both the loading at the seller's premises, and all costs and risks; FOB (Free On Board), with the seller arranging and paying for the delivery and loading of goods on board the vessel; and CIF (Cost, Insurance and Freight), with the seller arranging and paying the delivery of goods and cargo insurance to the named port of destination (discharge). The fourth measure considers the type of relation between the commercial unit or trader, and the customer abroad. Again we use the classification spot markets, long-term contracts, and ownership. The ownership of sugar cane fields has been excluded from consideration, because, within the Centre/South region of Brazil, the amount of land available for buying varies strongly. We gave the first measure a 1-10 scale, compared to a 1-5 scale for the other measures. The reason is that it requires much more efforts and investments to achieve the highest level of vertical integration compared with the other measures. Finally, when the score is between the grades for the three unique items, then practice holds a combination of the nearest items. The following table shows the results of the four measures for the chains from the sample.

Table 1: Results on vertical integration in governance structure

	Measure 1	Measure 2	Measure 3	Measure 4	Total
Chain A	6	2	4	2	14
Chain B	10	1	3	2	16
Chain C	6	3	3	2	14
Chain D	6	1	3	1	11
Chain E	5	1	3	1	10

When one recalls that the first measure (Measure 1) relates to the type of relationship between the mill and the commercial group, we find that chain B has the highest score. In Chain B the commercial group fully owns its supplying ethanol mills. At chain A, C and D the commercial group owns a minority share of the mills, or vice-versa, combined with preferred supplier relationships. Chain E uses merely contractual relationships between the mills and the commercial group.

The second measure (Measure 2) concerns the number of players in the export process. Chain C presents the score of 3 as the commercial group exports all its ethanol directly to the customer abroad. Chain A has an intermediary score between level 1 and 2. This score represents that Chain A has been exporting part of its ethanol directly and another part through trade companies. The other chains, B, C and D, export exclusively via trade companies.

The third item (Measure 3) measures the level of responsibility taken by the commercial group or trader to export its ethanol. Chain A is the only one that has some negotiations in the CIF (Cost, Insurance, and Frieght) form. However, it primarily sells the export via FOB (Free on Board), so they have an intermediary score between level 2 and 3. The rest of the chains, B, C, D and E, have a score of 3, which represents the predominance of FOB form. Field research learned that some other traders and commercial groups use ex works-deals.

The fourth measure (Measure 4) considers the relation between the commercial group or trader and the customer abroad. No foreign customer, within the sample, owns the ethanol production in Brazil. Chain A, B and C present a score of 2, meaning that these chains use both long-term and spot contracts. Chain D and E have sold their ethanol just on spot markets.

Overall, we may conclude that chain B has the highest total score that is the highest level of vertical integration. Chain A and chain C follow. However, with the spread of total scores between 10 and 16, we may conclude that none of the 5 chains is close to full vertical integration (25 pts) amongst its stakeholders. The determinant measure for the differentiation among these three chains is the overweighed measure 1. If we do not overweigh measure 1, then the total score of these three chains will look like the same. Interestingly, we find a poor correlation between (the home country oriented) measure 1 and (the internationally oriented) measure 2. This calls for further detailing. Nevertheless, it is clear that chain D and chain E are the least vertically integrated chains.

5.2 Strategic Alliances

In an endeavor to further our understanding on governance structures, we studied the strategic alliances, i.e. coalitions occurring among parent firms. Figure 3 presents the degree of vertical integration for the different types of strategic alliances. Recall that merger & acquisition has a higher degree of vertical integration than joint venture, next than formal cooperative, and so on. During the interviews it was found out that each of the five ethanol chain presents a different type of alliance with its mills. The results on strategic alliance are presented at the bottom of Figure 3.

Figure 3: Strategic Alliances among mills from the same commercial group

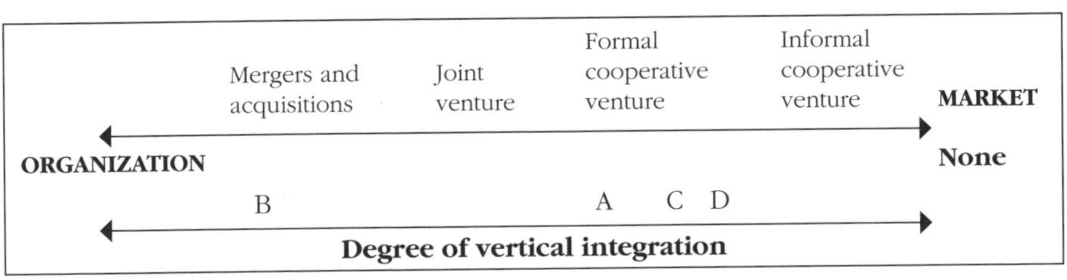

We will now discuss the results. In Chain B the mills are strategically united by acquisition. The commercial group fully owns all the mills from this chain. Next, the mills from Chain A cooperate with each other by means of a formal cooperative. They jointly sell their ethanol and the cooperative invest in the development of new technologies and other assets. The mills from Chain C and D are linked by a joint ownership of the commercial group. The main difference between these two chains is that the commercial group from chain D sporadically trade with other parties. Finally in chain E, which is located at the end of the continuum, we see that the mills are linked by long-term contracts with the commercial company. These mills do have an informal relationship. Moreover, the contracts are between mill and commercial group and not between mill and mill. The commercial unit in Chain E is totally independent. The company itself seeks for profit when the others are just representing the mills.

5.3 *Asset Specificity*

As stated another route to further our understanding on governance structures, is discussing asset specificity as the main feature of the internal organization of the supply chain (Farina and Zylbersztajn 1997). Asset specificity is the most predictable factor of transaction cost economics. In this section the asset specificity is analyzed among three different transactions; sugar cane production, ethanol production and ethanol sales. The sugar cane has high asset specificity regarding location, i.e. site specificity, as it is unfeasible to grow sugar cane more than 50 km away from the ethanol mill, due to the high transportation costs. Moreover, the sugar cane is a temporal specific asset, because the burnt cane needs to be quickly crushed at the expense to loose quality otherwise (Waack and Neves 1998). The ethanol mill itself is considered as a high physical specific asset. The ethanol mill is specially tailored to a particular transaction, produce ethanol, and it is impossible to switch its activity (Waack and Neves 1998). For trading ethanol the main specific assets are transportation, storage and time. Transport and storage of alcohol are physical assets, which are tailored specifically for the ethanol transaction. Both types of assets may be used for other purpose, for example as transportation and storage of chemicals, however this implies in high costs. Either ethanol may be contaminated by chemicals, or cleaning the truck and storage may bring high costs. The temporal specificity concerns the possible deterioration of the ethanol quality or corrosion problems in case the ethanol takes too long to be used.

The asset specificity is roughly similar for all chains, except for the ethanol trading. The specific assets involved in sugar cane production and ethanol production are quite similar for all the five chains from the sample. The site specificity characteristic of the sugar cane is a problem that concerns every one. At the same time, ethanol mills are huge investments specifically designed for producing ethanol. The only specific asset that varies among the chains refers to the ethanol trade. The majority of the chains use trucks as their transportation model. However, with a small percentage Chain A transports ethanol via trains. For doing so, this chain had to invest heavily in the development of this transportation system. It implies that this chain has specific assets in the transportation process. Moreover, the other chains do not have their own trucks for transport from the mill to the harbor. In these case the specific asset is in the hands of independent transportation companies. Two chains, chain B and chain C, invested heavily in storage capacity in the harbor. The other chains outsource these services from special storage companies.

To summarize, one may claim that chain B and chain C have the highest asset specificity in the sales transaction, while Chain A has middle asset specificity. Chain A has been investing in the train transportation system, but for a small amount of ethanol. Chain D and chain E have the lowest asset specificity, while sugar cane production and ethanol sales are quite similar for all the chains. Before summarizing the different indicators we look at the variable to be explained, that is the performance of the international ethanol supply chains.

5.4 Ethanol Supply Chain Performance

This paragraph explains the set of indicators for measuring ethanol chain performance, defines the indicators, applies them and compares the chains accordingly. The performance indicators should measure the supply chains according with to their strategy and goal (Beamon 1999). In the course of the research the primarily set of indicators had to be modified for reasons of (1) data availability and (2) consistency with the chain-strategies and goals. Because cost related data were too sensitive the actors in the ethanol chains were not willing to inform the researchers on it. Secondly, as the interviews and other field research progressed, the differences on strategies became more clear. The result was that some indicators were adapted.

After the deregulation and market liberalization of the ethanol markets the strategies from the sugarcane complex has realized substantial changes. First, new products have emerged, new market were developed for existing products and new production techniques were introduced. Secondly, vertical upstream integration has been promoted. For long, the sugar cane sector in Brazil knows vertical downstream integration exercised by the sugar/ethanol mills. Nowadays, for example, there are mills belonging to economic groups that have fabrics of soft drinks and other beverages. Third, the companies have been investing in product differentiation (e.g., crystal sugar and liquid sugar), production diversification (e.g., energy cogeneration), and the use of sugar cane byproducts (e.g., the use of vinasse as fertilizer). We may conclude that the chains in the sample present a wide variation of strategies. Consequently, the set of indicators to measure the chains performance should also be diversified.

Taking resources, output and flexibility, as the three types of measures (cf. Beamon, 1999), see literature overview, we arrived at the following set of 6 indicators; (1) transportation distance to the Port of Santos; (2) production efficiency, i.e. production per hectare; (3) customer reliability; (4) share of exported volume; (5) purity of anhydrous ethanol; and (6) flexibility in ethanol vs sugar production. The table below presents the rank ordering, following the calculation of the absolute values for the performance indicators. Indicators 1 and 2 are resource related; indicators 3-5 are output related, and indicator 6 is flexibility related.

Table 2: Ranking of the performance indicators (1 is worst performer; 5 is best performer).

Indic. \ Chains	Chain A	Chain B	Chain C	Chain D	Chain E
1	5	4	2	1	3
2	1	4	3	5	2
3	3	4	5	2	1
4	3	5	4	1	2
5	1	2	2	1	1
6	5	1	3	4	2
Total	**18**	**20**	**19**	**14**	**11**

Regarding Transportation distance to the port of Santos, indicator 1, we first had to calculate the distances of the mills to the city of Sao Paulo, and, next, added 85 kilometers, as this is the distance from Sao Paulo to Santos. Clearly the best performing chain is Chain A and the worst performing chain is Chain D. Production efficiency, indicator 2, is the result of the division of the sugar cane production (tones) by the size (hectares) of the sugar cane plantation, including own land, land leasing and land from suppliers. Surprisingly in contrast to indicator 1, the chain performing best for indicator 2 is Chain D and the chain performing worst is Chain A.

Customer reliability, indicator 3, is defined as the preference of the customer abroad by one specific chain. This preference could either be based on the commercial group's brand name or on trust of delivering the product within the conditions agreed upon (e.g. standards and due date). For designing this indicator four experts in the Brazilian sugar cane field were asked to make a ranking of the five chains from the sample concerning customer reliability. According to their expertise, the favorite chain for the customer is Chain C and the less favorite is Chain E. Actually, the differences were considered minimal. Indicator 4 shows the export orientation of the chains. For this indicator the total amount of ethanol exported in the year 2005 was divided by the total ethanol production, and checked for various years. The chain that exports more ethanol proportional to its production is Chain B and the chain that presented the lowest exports is Chain D. As there are various good dehydration processes, we scored only 1 or 2 for indicator 5, purity of anhydrous ethanol. Finally, with regard to production flexibility indicator 6 shows the capability to maximize the ethanol output compared to sugar. The final number is given by the division between production of ethanol in liters by production of sugar in bags (50 kilos). Chain A presents a higher inclination for producing ethanol than the other chains, while chain B was more inclined to produce sugar.

When we analyze these review it is clear that Chain B is the best performing chain, while Chain E is the worst performing international ethanol chain. On one hand, Chain B scored (rather) high for five out of the six performance indicators. The exception is the indicator for mix flexibility. However, we may comment that our operationalization of this indicator may not really measure the mix flexibility of the chains. In contrast to Chain 6 is Chain E, which presented at best one average ranking that is with indicator 1, transportation distance. However taking the total scores Chain E is not so oriented at the export market, so why are their mills located in the most expensive areas of land, near Sao Paulo and the Port of Santos? It may be explained by historical reasons, for in the beginning the mills were built near Sao Paulo. In that case Chain E would have primarily have the path-dependency of using older mills, instead of having chosen for new mills placed in an expensive located. Further research, may resolve this outlier. While the behavior presented for Indicator 1, 2 and 6 are not in accordance with the final results, Indicator 3, 4 and 5 showed a great similarity with the final results. The best scores are concentrated in Chain A, B and C, while Chain D and E represent the worst scores for these indicators. For that reason Indicator 3, 4 and 5 are considered to have a direct relation among each other and also with regard to the aggregate results.

5.5 Analysis

Finally, having studied the five international ethanol supply chains in relation to governance structure, strategic alliances, asset specificity and chain performance, it is now possible to answer the subquestion on the relation between organization and the performance of Brazilian ethanol chains. The table below shows the rank-ordered results for the four areas.

Table 3: Final results

	Performance	Gov. Structure	Strategic Alliances	Asset Specificity
Chain A	3	2	2	2
Chain B	1	1	1	1
Chain C	2	2	3	1
Chain D	4	3	4	3
Chain E	5	4	5	4

From this table is possible to conclude that Chain B, which presents the highest scores for governance structure as well as strategic alliances and the highest investments on specific assets, is the chain that performs best. Chain E represents the other extreme, the lowest levels of vertical integration, the lowest investments on specific assets and, at the same time, the worst performance. There is a clear contrast between Chain B and E on the explanation of the differences in performance of international ethanol supply chains, in the sample. It is possible to conclude that Chain B and E presented a positive relation between these four components. Also the scores for C and D are roughly in line. That leads us to the conclusion that governance structure, with its underlying items strategic alliances and asset specificity, and performance have a very tight relation with regards to international ethanol supply chains.

6. Conclusions

The aim of this chapter was defined in the introduction as to contribute the literature on managing international ethanol supply chains by analyzing and comparing the structure and performance of the international ethanol supply chains from Brazil to other countries. By our research we tried to answer the research question how international ethanol chains can be organized efficiently, so as to facilitate the further expansion of international ethanol supply chains. We analyzed five exporting Brazilian supply chains on their governance structure, strategic alliances asset specificity, to explain their chain performance, to arrive at conclusions on the type of organization that is driving the best performing chain. Amongst the participating Brazilian international ethanol supply chains it is shown that the higher levels of vertical integration go together with the better chain performance (Chain B). The contrary is also true as the chain that performed worst has the lowest degree of vertical integration (Chain E). Given the restrictions of our research, we can thus conclude that vertical integration increases the performance of international ethanol chains. The results are in line with other experts (Akkerman and Borgerd et al 1999; Klasse and Whybark 1994; Humphrey and Schmitz 2001; and Oppen 2002), indicating that new international ethanol supply chains should pay special attention to the integrated management of supply chains.

Considering the measurements in this research some statements can be made. For the research on governance structures (see par. 5.1.), i.e. The level of vertical integration, we selected four measures taking us along the international ethanol supply chain. The strongest predictive variable turned out to be Measure 1, which was on the relation between the mills and commercial groups. In an endeavor to further our understanding on governance structures, we studied the strategic alliances, i.e. coalitions occurring among parent firms. The degree of vertical integration was clearly discriminating between the 2 contrasting ethanol chains. In Chain B the mills are strategically united by acquisition, while in chain E, the mills are linked with the commercial company merely by long-term contracts. The other route analyzed to further our understanding on governance structures, is by analyzing the degree of asset specificity as feature of the internal organization of the supply chain. Chain B and chain C have the highest asset specificity in the sales transaction, which is especially due to investments in dedicated storage capacity in the harbor. Chain D and chain E have the lowest asset specificity. The set of indicators for measuring ethanol chain performance should grade the supply chains according to their strategy and goal. Interestingly 3 out of 6 indicators, i.e., indicators 3, 4 and 5, show a direct relation among each other and also with regard to the aggregate results. However, indicator 3 (i.e., customer reliability), turned out to be a very difficult to get discriminating scores on from respondents. The remaining useful indicators 4 and 5, respectively on share of exported volume, and purity of anhydrous ethanol are all output related. Here, the best scores are concentrated in Chain B and C, while Chain D and E represent the worst scores for these indicators. Finally, and interestingly, the analysis confirmed that the consolidated scores on governance structure, strategic alliances, asset specificity and chain performance showed a positive relation.

When we address the restrictions of this research we should, first, state that the international ethanol fuel trade is young new business, as is illustrated by the strong jump in exports by Brazil, from low levels around 2004. Young markets are uncertain, requiring major investments. However as the global demand for fuel ethanol has grown rapidly since 2004, due to policy interventions, one may expect a rapid growth of the total market, market entry and specialization. That may interfere with our results. Next, some indicators, e.g. mix flexibility, turned out to be ad odds with the overall results, not measuring the concept they were supposed to measure. Nevertheless, the result seems sufficiently robust. Furthermore, the data gathering took place in 2006. The research lacked longitudinal data, making the research vulnerable to the perceptions or interests of the interviewees. In a similar vein, it must be mentioned that this research was unable to gather detailed information on costs and benefits. The sensitivity of the data is a more general issue for research but that leaves it a partial analysis at best. Evidently, the researchers tried to enhance the internal validity of the research by careful triangulation of data, sources and method. The selection of chains and their aggregated market share should safeguard the external validity of the research. Finally, we investigated only international ethanol supply chains sourcing from Brazil. Together, the restrictions make it difficult to conclude definitively whether the conclusion shown by the sample is of general value or has merely restricted usefulness. Further research is necessary to find out. Future research may also develop and include additional indicators to measure chain performance, especially bringing in longitudinal data.

References

AKKERMANS, H., P. BOGERD, et al. (1999). Virtuous and vicious cycles on the road towards international supply chain management. *International Journal of Operations & Production Managemen* 19(5/6): 565-581.

ALVARADO, U. Y. and H. Kotzab (2001). Supply chain management: the integration of logistics. *Industrial Marketing Management* 31: 183-198.

AMARAL, T. M. d., M. F. Neves, et al. (2003). *Cadeia productiva de açúcar do Estado de São Paulo e da França:* comparação dos sistemas produtivos, organização e ambiente institucional. Agric. São Paulo, SP 50(2): 65-80. (in Portuguese)

ARAMYAN, L., C. Ondersteijn, et al. (2006). *Performance indicators in agri-food chains.* Not published yet.

BEAMON, B. M. (1999). Measuring Supply Chain Performance. *International Journal of Operations and Production Management* 19(3): 275-292.

BERG, C. (2004). World fuel ethanol analysis and outlook. Retrieved March, 2006, from http://www.distill.com/World-Fuel-Ethanol-A&O-2004.html.

BNDES. (2003). Ampliação da produção de etanol e co-geração de energia elétrica. from www.bndes.gov.br. (in Portuguese)

CAMPS, T. (2004). *Chains and Networks:* theory and Practice. The emerging world of chains and networks: bridging theory and practice. T. Camps, P. Diederen, G. J. Hofstede and B. Vos. 'sGravenhage, Reed Business Information.

CARVALHO, E. (2005). Industrial perspective on expansion of ethanol production capacity for export in Brazil. Retrieved January 2006, from www.unica.com.br.

CARVALHO, E. (2005b). Uma visão geral do programa Brasileiro de etanol Presented. *Experiência brasileira com etanol combustível.* São

Paulo, August. Retrieved January 2006, from www.unica.com.br (in Portuguese).

CARVALHO, E. (2004). The whereabouts of a fuel-ethanol world-market. Retrieved January 2006, from www.unica.com.br/i_pages/files/ethanolmarketnov04.doc.

COASE, R. H. (1937). The Nature of Firm. *Economica* 4: 386-405.

DOUMA, S. and H. Schreuder (1998). Economic Approaches to Organizations, Prentice Hall.

IEA (2004). Biofuels for Transport. An International Perspective. International Energy Agency.

FARINA, E. M. M. Q. and D. Zylbersztajn (1997). *Deregulation, chain differentiation and the role of government.* First Brazilian Workshop of Agri-Chain Management. The University of Sao Paulo, School of Economics and Business, Campus Ribeirao Preto.

FAULKNER, D. (1995). *International Strategic Alliances:* Co-operating to Compete. London, McGRAW-HILL.

HUMPHREY, J. and H. Schmitz (2001). Governance in global value chains. *IDS Bulletin* 32(3).

KLASSE, R. D. and D. C. Whybark (1994). Barriers to the management of international operations. *Journal of Operations Management* 11: 385-396.

LAZZARINI, S. G., F. R. Chaddad, et al. (2001). Integrating supply chain and network analyses: The study of netchains. *Chains and Network Science* 1(1): 7-22.

LEE, H. and C. Billington (1992). Managing Supply Chain Inventory: Pitfalls and Opportunities. *Sloan Management Review.*

LORANGE, P. and J. Roos (1992). *Strategic Alliances:* Formation, Implementation and Evolution, Blackwell Business.

MACEDO, I. C. (2002). *Energia da cana de áçucar no Brasil.* Centro de Tecnologia e Gestão Educacional, Sao Paulo, Brazil. From http:// http://libdigi.unicamp.br/document/?view=22. (in Portuguese)

MAZAFERRO, M. N. (2004). *Strategies and Policies for Ethanol-Biofuel-Blending Implementation into Latin American and Caribbean Countries University of Calgary.* Quito, Ecuador. Master

MÉNARD, C. (2004). The economics of hybrid organizations. *Journal of Institutional and Theoretical Economics* 160 345- 376.

MURRAY, D. (2005). *Ethanol's potential:* Looking Beyond Corn, Earth Policy Institute.

OMTA, S. W. F., J. Trienekens, et al. (2001). *Chain and network science:* a research framework. Chain and Networl Science 1(1): 1-6.

OPPEN, M. V. (2002). Germany Global chains and developing countries: Governance, legislation and trade barriers. The Challenge of Global chains: Integrating developing countries into international chains, a potential risk or an opportunity?

PAULIEN C. M., N. Verloop, et al (2002). Multi-method triangulation in a qualitative study on teachers' practical knowledge: an attempt to increase internal validity. *Quality and Quantity* 36: 145-167.

PERSSON, F.; OLHAGER, J. (2002). Performance simulation of supply chain designs. *International Journal of Production Economics* 77: 231-245.

PGG (Platform Biobased Raw Materials) (2006b). Duurzame productie en ontwikkeling van biomassa, zowel in Nederland als in het buitenland (in

PROCANA (2006). A febre dos carros flex. Jornalcana.

PROCANA (2006B). www.jornalcana.com.br

SHIKIDA, P. F. A.; ALVES, L. R. A. (2001). Panorama estrutural, dinâmica de crescimento e estratégias tecnológicas da agroindústria canavieira paranaense. *Nova Economia* 11(2): 123-150. (in Portuguese)

VERSCHUREN, P.; DOOREWAARD, H. (1999). Designing a Research Project. Utrecht, Lemma.

WAACK, R. S.; NEVES M. F. (1998). Competitividade do sitema agroindustrial da cana-de-áçucar. Competitividade no agribusiness brasileiro V. (in Portuguese)

WILLIAMSON, O. E. (1998). Transaction cost economics: how it works: where it is headed. *De Economist* 146(1): 23-58.

WILLIAMSON, O. E. (1999). Strategy research: governance and competence perspectives. *Strategic Management Journal* 20: 1087-1108.

Part 5

Chain Theory and Method

- Mathematical Modeling and Optimization of Quality and Logistics in Food Supply Chains, an Example
- *ChainPlan*: A Method for Demand Driven Strategic Planning and Management of Chains

Mathematical Modeling and Optimization of Quality and Logistics in Food Supply Chains, an Example

PAUL VAN BEEK

1. Introduction

In many cases there are two ways (and all relevant combinations) to keep quality of fresh food products in supply chains on desired levels:

- by spending effort on cooling the products during their stay in the supply chain
- by spending effort on speeding up the goods flow in the chain by choosing smaller production and transportation lots.

In the framework of research in food supply chains we developed a model that describes a very simple two-echelon situation of a perishable product (milk) that is stored in a warehouse and is forwarded, in batches, to the retail store periodically.

For this highly simplified situation we illustrate how to balance on the one side the cooling efforts in the chain (determination of temperatures in warehouse and retail store) and on the other the reduction of sojourn time in the chain by choosing smaller lot sizes in warehouse and/or in the retail store.

The only purpose of this contribution is to give impetus to research in simultaneous control of temperature and logistics in more realistic chains of perishable goods.

The contribution is structured as follows. First we discuss the isolated situation of the retailer. Second we discuss the two-echelon situation in which the warehouse and the retailer are considered together.

2. Determination of Lot Size and Temperature at the Retailer Store

Consider a very simple lot sizing situation (see Figure 1) with constant demand D and lot size Q.

In Figure 1 the development over time of the inventory is described. At points of time where inventory drops to zero a replenishment of Q takes place (see Silver et al., 1998).

Figure 1: Inventory at the retailer store

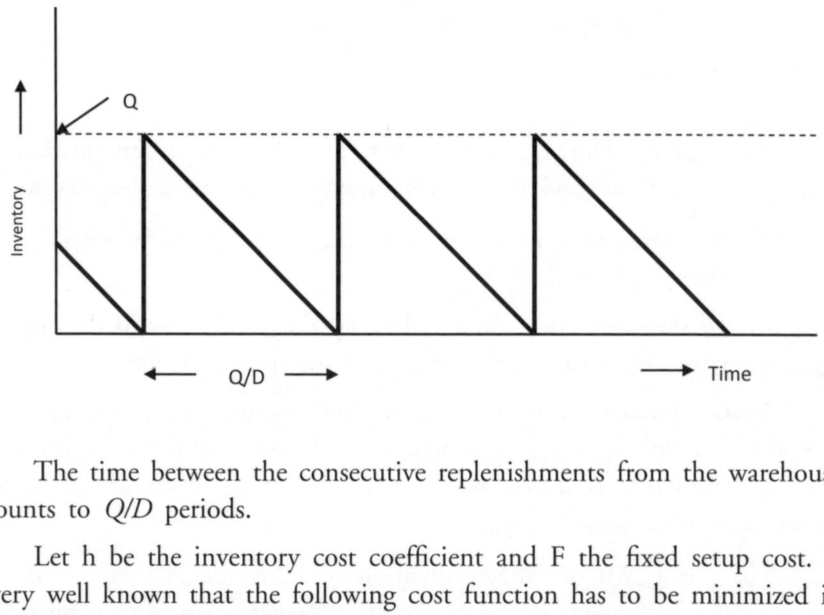

The time between the consecutive replenishments from the warehouse amounts to Q/D periods.

Let h be the inventory cost coefficient and F the fixed setup cost. It is very well known that the following cost function has to be minimized in order to obtain the best value for Q:

(1) $$C_{tot}(Q) = \frac{1}{2} hQ + \frac{FD}{Q}$$

By putting $C_{tot}'(Q) = 0$ the so-called Economic Order Quantity (EOQ) is obtained:

$$EOQ = \sqrt{\frac{2FD}{h}} \; .$$

Now assume that the underlying product is perishable (e.g. milk) and its decay depends on time and temperature.

In the case of milk the process of decay is induced by micro-organisms and their growth is assumed to obey (as an illustration) the following formula:

(2) $$N_{t+1} = N_t e^{\mu(T)W}$$

where: N_t : = # micro-organisms per ml (time t)

W : = sojourn time

$\mu(T)$: = growth coefficient of the micro-organisms

T : = temperature

Other perishables (e.g. meat) require alternative formulae.

Furthermore, let $G(T)$ be the cost per period for for keeping the product on T degrees. Now we can draw up the following optimization model:

(3) $$\min_{Q,T}\left\{\frac{1}{2}hQ+\frac{FD}{Q}+G(T)\right\}$$

subject to:

$$N_0\, e^{\,\mu(T)W} \leqq \text{MAX}$$

In our case we can substitute W = Q/D because Q/D is the maximum time an item can be in stock. MAX is a parameter to be determined in advance.

Problem (3) can easily be reduced to (4):

(4) $$\min_T\left\{\frac{1}{2}h\frac{D}{\mu(T)}\,\text{h}\,\left(\frac{\text{MAX}}{N_0}\right)+\frac{F\mu(T)}{\ln\left(\frac{\text{MAX}}{N_0}\right)}+G(T)\right\}$$

because (obviously) in the optimum the inequality in problem (3) will be equality.

It is interesting to compare the solution of the optimization problem (3) with $Q = EOQ$ with the solution of (4) because this provides insight into the difference of simultaneous control (in Q and T) and control based on $Q = EOQ$ and T.

3. Determination of Lot Sizes and Temperatures at Warehouse and Retail Store

Now consider a more complex situation with two echelons: the warehouse (W) and the retail store (R).

For the sake of simplicity we assume that we are faced with constant demand D at the retailer site.

Now let us describe the development over time of the inventory at the retail store. In fact the picture resembles Figure 1. For the sake of clarity we now use the notation QR instead of Q.

Figure 2: Inventory at the retailer store

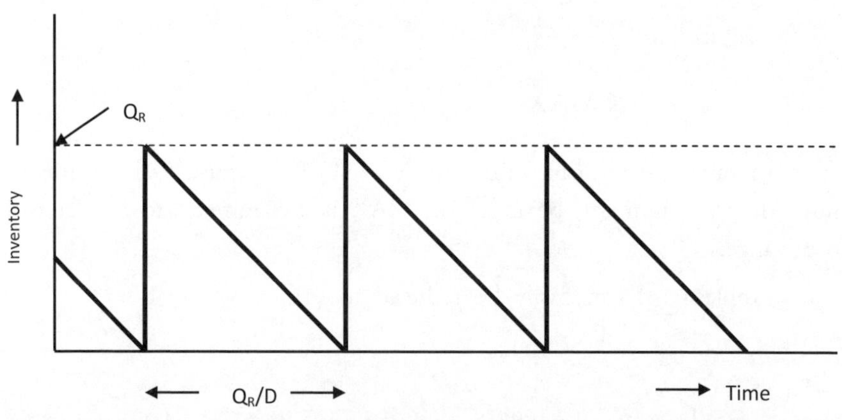

The retailer is supplied every QR/D periods, at times where inventory drops to zero, with replenishment quantity QR.These supply quantities imply a decrease of stock at the warehouse site of QR (see Figure 3) in which, for the sake of clarity, also Figure 2 has been incorporated. In Figure 3 we assume, as an illustration, that $QW = 3\ Q_{R.}$ The quantity Q_W is the replenishment quantity with which the warehouse is supplied. Figure 3 is a slightly modified version of Figure 12.5 (see Silver et al., Chapter 12).

Figure 3: Inventory at the retailer store and at the warehouse site

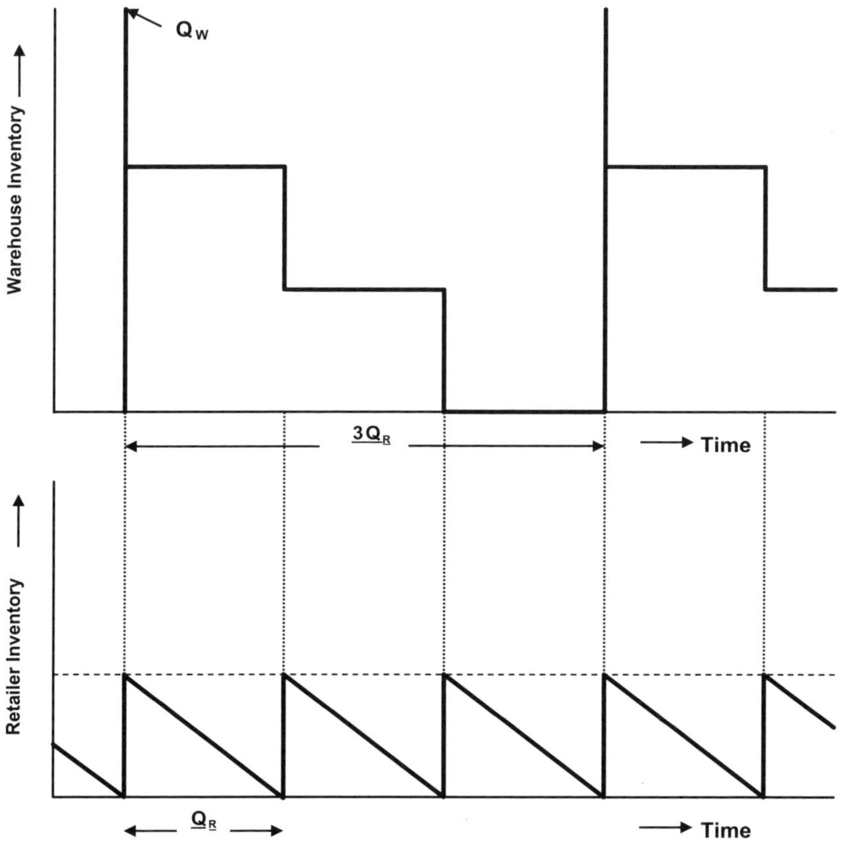

In Figure 3 we have illustrated the development over time of both inventories using the relation $QW = 3\ QR$. In the sequel we assume $QW = n\ QR$ with n = 1, 2, …

This is called the "Integrality Property", for obvious reasons. In our example we have $n = 3$.

From Figure 3 we can conclude that the maximum sojourn time for the product under consideration is:

- At the retailer site: Q_R/D periods
- At the warehouse site: $(n - 1)\ Q_R/D$ periods

If we assume that transportation time of the product from warehouse to retailer is negligible, the total sojourn time of the product in the chain amounts to:

$$\frac{Q_R}{D} + (n-1)\frac{Q_R}{D} = n\frac{Q_R}{D}$$

Furthermore, if we assume different cooling regimes at the warehouse and retailer site we need the two different sojourn times

$$\frac{Q_R}{D} \text{ and } (n-1)\frac{Q_R}{D}$$

because each of both sojourn times influences the growth of micro-organisms in dependence of the actual cooling regimes in each of the two echelons.

Now we formulate how to determine the optimal solution in the two-echelon case.

Let h_R, h_W be the inventory cost coefficients for Retailer and Warehouse, respectively and F_R, F_W the corresponding fixed setup costs.

Now we can draw up the two-echelon optimization model:

(5) $$\min\left\{\frac{1}{2}h_R Q_R + \frac{F_R D}{Q_R} + \frac{1}{2}h_W(n-1)Q_R + \frac{F_W D}{nQ_R}\right\}$$

This expression (5) depends on Q_R and n and can be minimized easily by choosing the procedure as described in Silver *et al.* (1998) (chapter 12.3).

As in the one-echelon situation we assume that the underlying product is perishable and its decay depends on time and temperature. Again we make use of formula (2) for calculating the growth of micro-organisms in each of the two echelons.

Applying this formula in each of the two echelons we arrive at the following optimization problem (now using G_R and G_W instead of G as different cost functions related to cooling):

(6) $$\min\left\{\frac{F_R D}{Q_R}+\frac{1}{2}h_R Q_R+G_R(T_R)+\frac{F_W D}{nQ_R}+\frac{1}{2}h_W(n-1)Q_R+G_W(T_W)\right\}$$

Subject to:

$$N_0 e^{\mu(T_W)Q_R(n-1)/D+\mu(T_R)Q_R/D}\leq \text{MAX}$$

Solving (6) is an optimization problem in the variables n, Q_R, T_R and T_W and can be solved easily by using standard software for non-linear programming problems.

This solution process can be simplified by concluding that in the optimal solution the restriction in (6) will be equality rather than inequality (compare formula (4)).

Solving the resulting equation gives the following expression for Q_R:

(7) $$Q_R=\frac{D}{(n-1)\mu(T_W)+\mu(T_R)}\,\text{h}\left(\frac{\text{MAX}}{N_0}\right)$$

If we substitute (7) into the object function of (6) an optimization problem in the variables n, T_W and T_R results which can be solved by minimizing the cost function (6) for different values of n.

References

SILVER, E.A., PYKE, D.F., PETERSON, R. Inventory management and production planning and scheduling, 3. ed. (1998). John Wiley & Sons, Inc.

ADVANCES IN SUPPLY CHAIN ANALYSIS IN AGRI-FOOD SYSTEMS

ChainPlan: A Method for Demand Driven Strategic Planning and Management of Chains

Marcos Fava Neves

1. Introduction

Several important changes are happening and even more intensively in agribusiness in the last five years. In one side, there is a new and huge food demand, coming from factors like growth in population, economic development of largely populated nations, income distribution and urbanization. At the other side, the booming demand of biofuels, in all parts of the world, is also pressuring the demand for grains, lands and other agricultural resources. These factors are bringing food prices inflation and even a fear of lack of some products in the near future. Several food and biofuels chains were not prepared for this growth.

Dutch researchers – for a long time - have already been focusing the construction of North-South chains and networks highway. They have for granted that more and more food will be produced in the South and consumed in the Northern hemisphere. It is the OMC role to speed up - or just to set back - the fact. Productive assets (plants) are being transferred from countries with high environmental pressures to countries with more space, more competitiveness and potential of growth. Although, the liberalization of exchanges must be done providing small producers the possibility for access the market. For income distribution and regional development it is necessary that the value also reach the thousands of producers, effectively putting into motion other sectors of the economy. This will demand coordination and even the creation of a third part (vertical organization) to verify the unbalance and to facilitate the value development with coherence, justice, objectives, strategies, and abilities. At the same time, everything must be done having in mind the attendance of the final consumer, more concerned with food safety, diversity, regular supply, socio-environmental responsibility, information and transparency.

To face all these changes in international business environment and growth opportunities for food and biofuels chains, strategic planning is essential. The construction and elaboration of a process of strategic planning and management of chains and its applications is the objective of this paper.

2. Relevant Theoretical Review

2.1 Considerations on Agribusiness Chains and Networks

Table I: Similarities of different network system approaches

<table>
<tr><th>Author/ Local</th><th>Thought</th><th>Common Points</th></tr>
<tr><td>Davis and Goldberg (1957); Goldberg (1968), EUA</td><td>Commodity System Approach (CSA)</td><td rowspan="2">-They focus on the productive process and have described its character;
- They share systemic analytical base and emphasize the technological variable;
- Interdependence amongst the strategies in the company and system plan, implying the possibility of development for systemic coordination mechanisms;
- Vertical integration is important to explain the systemic coordination mechanism, being the substitute for the concept of vertical integration and contract.</td></tr>
<tr><td>Morvan (1985), France</td><td>Agribusiness (Filière) System</td></tr>
</table>

Source: Elaborated by the author based on Zylbersztajn and Neves (2000); Batalha (2001)

According to Zylbersztajn and Neves (2000) and Batalha (2001), the agribusiness systems (chains) hold the following basic elements for its descriptive analysis: the agents, the relations between them, the sectors, the supporting organizations, and the institutional environment. It is more of a macro analysis of a product flow from the suppliers to the final consumers.

From then on, the theoretical model of the company network was defined as the process used to analyze a company and its suppliers and dealers, the existing relations between them and their relationship with the environment. Basically it is an interaction and relationship approach (NEVES, 2003; FORD, 1998). To draw the company network and to establish strategies, two very relevant theories, among others, are important for its coordination: the distribution channel, as defined by Stern *et al* (1996): "a set of involved interdependent organizations in the process to make the product or service of the available company for consumption or use" (STERN, 1996, P. 1) and the supply chain, or the involved organizations for that particular company to provide all the supplies needed to carry out and sell its production. Other important contributions come from Heide and John (1990), Corey et al (1989), Rosembloon (1999).

Lazzarini et al. (2001) integrates the concepts of networks and systems (chains) in a new approach of studies termed as *netchains*. According to these authors, the integration of these approaches allows us the consideration of the existence of organizational interdependences within the network as well as the different coordination mechanisms (business plan, process standardization and adjustments) and value sources (operations and production optimal, reduction of transaction costs, diversity and co-specialization of knowledge). Thus, the concepts of the *Supply Chain Management* (SCM), distribution channels, networks and the idea of netchains are the theoretical framework and empirical knowledge more applied to the development of agribusiness systems (chains). The theory regarding agribusiness systems and chains is used at step 2 of the *ChainPlan* Method.

2.2 Considerations on Collective Actions in Chains

Another relevant theory for the *Chain Plan* Method is regarding the cooperation and collective actions. The idea of cooperation can be extended to the elaboration and implementation of the collective actions. According to Nassar (2001), collective actions can be defined as social interactions that involve a group of individuals searching for common interests that require joint actions, which can be carried through collectively but not individually. Thus, collective action is based on the statement that individuals have common necessities that can only be met by means of joint action.

However, the first author to establish an economic explanation for the formation of the social groups was Olson (1999). His – "The Logic of Collective Actions" – thoughts brought some contributions, among them, that groups provide collective goods, that its existence is harmed by the presence of the free rider and that the action for groups can get worse instead of promoting the collective welfare. The creation of associations implies in two types of costs to its participants: maintenance costs of structure and association activities and transaction costs (its employees' and directors' monitoring costs; negotiation costs, communication, organization performance congestion and provision of collective goods costs). Each member evaluates if such costs are higher or lower than the probable benefits that the organization must generate.

Thus, the chain agents can create vertical organizations intended to develop collective actions. According to Saes (2000), there are three types of collective actions that can characterize distinct strategies for the organizations. They are: (i) Type I actions, which benefit all the participants (actors); (ii) Type II action, which benefits part of the group without prejudice of others (without objection); (iii) Type III action, which benefits part of the group in detriment of others (conflicts, compensation mechanisms).

Although type I and II actions must be the priority in a vertical organization, for minimizing the risk of dissatisfaction for one of the involved parts, in some cases, to implement type III action is inevitable for the improvement of the system. This is used at the step 3 of the *ChainPlan* Method.

2.3 Considerations on Strategic Management Models, Strategic Planning and Marketing Plans

Several definitions and concepts of strategy are found in literature, some with similar and complementary views and some with divergent ones. In spite of this, Besanko et al. (2000) comment that many use common phrases such as "long term goals" and "politics" that suggest that the strategy is related with decisions the company takes and the consequences of its success or failures. Several other important contributions in this field come from the works of Andrews (1987), Ansoff (1965), Chandler (1962), Digman (1990), Pearce and Robinson (1988), Henderson (1984), Mintzberg et al. (1988), Moore (1992) and others.

Throughout time several authors have proposed methods of strategic and marketing plans for organizations. For the proposed method, the review of nine different proposals of strategic planning were used by the researcher in order to make the steps of the *ChainPlan* more complete: (Lambin (2000), Westwood (2000), Wright et al. (2000), Las Casas (1999), Kotler (2000), Campomar (1982) Jain (2000) and Gilligan & Wilson (2000), Neves (2007). These methods proposed by theory were used in step 4 of the *ChainPlan* Method.

2.4 Considerations on Transaction Cost Economics (TCE) and the Role of Contracts

In his work Coase (1937) states that the company is a nexus of contracts. According to Williamson (1985), this nexus of contracts has some kind of governance (management) and the form by which it is done varies from markets to vertical integration. The rationality question is treated in the TCE referential, mainly regarding the individuals limitation in foreseeing all the future conditions in a relationship (contract) (WILLIAMSON, 1985; RINDFLEISCH and HEIDE, 1997). Williamson (1985, p. 234) defines the opportunism as "... the search of the auto-interest with eagerness...", that is, in many situations the companies will tend to explore situations for their own advantage. Uncertainty is treated in the transaction costs economy as the exogenous disturbances that affect the transactions (ZYLBERSZTAJN, 1996). According to Farina et al. (1997), the uncertainty has as its main role 'the magnifying of gaps that a contract cannot cover'.

Considering this view, contractual arrangements decide some coordination problems, but on the other hand they create others. By definition, the contracts are mechanisms that regulate the transactions, and are used to reduce risks and uncertainties in the exchange processes (MACNEIL, 1974; LUSCH and BROWN, 1996). However, the contracts are by its very nature incomplete and therefore they must be subject to adjustments and improvements. Finally, the role of the institutions must be kept in mind. They are not neutral; they affect the economic activity of the organization as well as the chains. All these subjects are strongly present in the food chains' relationships, and this theory is very relevant in almost all steps of the *ChainPlan* Method, particularly in step 5.

After this literature review, the next section shows the methodology used to propose the *ChainPlan* Method or Framework.

3. Methodology

The elaboration of the *ChainPlan* Method used several research methodologies. As pointed in Chapter 2, theory (literature review) was used to academically and theoretically build a preliminary framework with the purpose of doing a Strategic Planning and Management Process for a food chain. The starting point was a demand coming from the orange chain in Brazil for quantification and the planning process. This came from its exporters' association, named ABECITRUS. Further on, after this first empirical study was finished, other demands came from the different food chain actors.

New empirical work was done for the orange chain (2004), wheat chain (2005) and the milk chain (2007) in Brazil. In each of these applications, interventions were done in the *ChainPlan* method, since some parts did not work as in theory. So the method improved at each application. It was also applied for the wheat chain in Uruguay (2007) and milk chain in Argentina (2007). Further empirical work is proposed for 2008, mainly in sheep, soybean in Brazil and milk in Uruguay.

Each time the *ChainPlan* Method is applied, it improves, since new creative analysis emerges from a particular chain; and more support comes from theory being developed around the world and in new publications. The version that will be shown in section 4 considers the improvements done till the end of 2007.

4. Demand-Driven Strategic Planning and Management of Chains Method (*ChainPlan* Method)

Based on the literature review and empirical research, it is proposed, as a methodological contribution, a 5-step process aiming at the implementation of strategic planning and management in production chains. The method is summarized in Figure 1.

Figure 1: The *ChainPlan* Method Proposed for Strategic Planning and Management of Production Chains

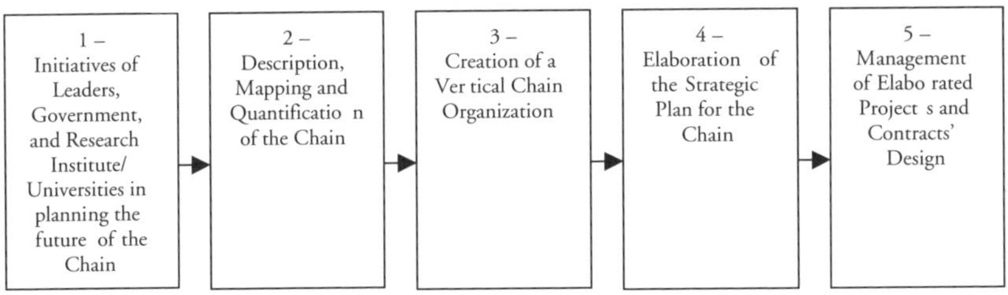

Source: Elaborated by the author.

4.1 *Initiatives of Leaders, Research Institutes and Universities to Plan the Future of a Chain*

The *ChainPlan* begins from an initiative. This can be some existing organization of the sector (normally sector organization), along with government, universities and research institutes, which attempt to organize a planning process and future vision for the particular chain. The initiative can also come from the Government, through "sectoral chambers". Also in this stage information is received from research organizations, government and private sector about related important topics to the chain.

4.2 *Description, Mapping and Quantification of the Chain*

The description, mapping and quantification phase can be summarized in six stages. A detailed explanation is provided in Table 2.

The four empirical applications of this chain quantification process showed some advantages of it: a) the application is relatively simple and direct, and the collection of information does not depend on public sources of data; b) the obtained description allows an easy visualization of positioning and relevance of the different existing sectors in the chain; c) the validation of results by means of workshop increases the research credibility; d) the formation of heterogeneous focal groups, to discuss generates commitment amongst the participants in the final workshop. Agribusiness systems and chains theory highlighted in Chapter 2 is very relevant here.

Table 2: Summary description of methodology phases for mapping and quantification.

Phases	Procedures
a. Agribusiness Chain Description (in focus)	Designing the chain by means of "boxes" representing the product flows from the input up to the final consumer (drawing of the chain).
b. Presentation for private sector professionals and other experts to make adjustments in the structure	With the first version of the description, some in-depth interviews with executives from operating companies in the sector and other specialists (researchers, sector leaders, among others) must be carried out to adjust the considered drawing.
c. Research in associations, institutions and publications for secondary data	Some private associations make sales data available to its members, and sometimes even via the Internet. A careful bibliographical revision also must be carried out, incorporating recent dissertation/thesis aside from articles in magazines/periodicals with large or academic readership.
d. Interview with professionals for primary data	This is the central point of this methodology. Interviews with managers to raise the financial sums sold by the companies in the studied sector. Interviews with purchase directors would also be conducted to estimate the market from the opposite side of a system link.
e. Quantification and Strategic Proposals	At this point, all the gathered data are processed and included in the system description below the industry name. The data for analysis are sent to companies that have collaborated. The companies send the data back with their commentaries and contributions. In this stage, a lot of material is already available to elaborate on the strategy suggestions to be presented in the final workshop.
f. Workshop to verify data	In the final phase, a workshop is conducted to present and discuss and the results.

Source: Neves et al, 2001.

4.3 Creation of a Vertical Chain Organization

Some chains are very disorganized; for instance, the beef chain of a particular country, and of sectoral associations (horizontal, such as farmers association, processing industry association, among others). It is very difficult to see a vertical organization (involving all the actors) established. The creation of a vertical organization can contribute to reach the following objectives: a) organization of existing and information exchanges, b) forum for strategy discussion, c) organization with flexibility to catch and use resources, d) to be responsible of chain communications and representation with institutions, lobbying and others e) to work a positive agenda to the chain, and, finally, to build and implement the *ChainPlan*. Collective actions theory highlighted in Chapter 2 is very relevant here.

For the structure of a vertical sector organization, the following sequence is proposed at this step of the *ChainPlan*:

Table 3: Sequence of steps to create a vertical organization in the chain

1 – **Propose the Idea of the Chain Vertical Organization:** The idea of organization must be presented to all the participants;

2 – **Formally Establish the Organization:** All the founders' agents of organization will be defined. At this stage, all bureaucratic questions must be solved (adherence to the legislation and statute preparation, among others);

3 – **Define the Financing Mechanism of Organization:** This stage delineates which contributions would be given to the private sector on the basis of their participation and the dependence of the production system, and which resources would come from financing public sources and how to charge it;

4 – **Create a Board and Define an Operational Structure:** The board must be formed considering the heterogeneity and the relevance of agents for the system. The necessary operational structure for the organization functioning will be financed by the participation tax demanded from the agents;

5 – **Increase the Number of Associates:** Initial actions must be focused on gaining new associates to increase the participants' level of involvement. In every case, a periodic participation tax will be charged;

6 – **Measurement of the Performance:** The results obtained have to be measured preferentially with quantitative criteria (increase of consumption, production, jobs, and profit range, among others) and widely communicated throughout the organization.

Source: Elaborated by the author

4.4 The Demand-Driven Strategic Plan for the Chain

Figure 2 shows the stages that could be used for the five-year strategic plan. Each stage will be elaborated in Table IV.

Figure 2: Summary of the *ChainPlan* plan (step 4)

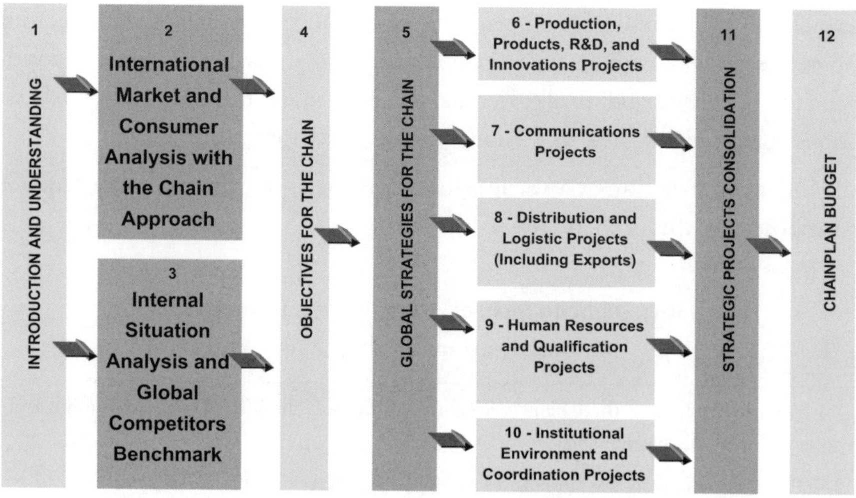

Source: Elaborated by the author

Table 4 – Demand-driven planning and strategic management for the production system – a detailed sequence for proposed steps

Stage	What has to be done
Phase 01 – Introductory	
1 – Introduction and Understanding	- To verify if the chain has other plans done and to study them; - To verify the planning method of the studied chain; - To verify which teams will take part in the process; - To study plans made for production chains in other countries, for benchmarking; - To identify a member of the team who could promote relationships with other chains; - Finally, in the case of chains with sophisticated planning processes it must be verified how this model can help the existing model, and how to adapt, gradually, the chain to this one.

2 – International Market and Consumer Analysis with Chain Approach	- To address threats and identify opportunities from the so-called uncontrollable variables (possible changes in the legal/political, economical and natural, sociocultural and technological environment) both in the domestic as well as in the international market; - To understand existing barriers (tariff and non-tariff) and check collective actions to reduce them; - To analyze the final and intermediate (dealers) consumer's behavior and their purchase decision process; - To analyze opportunities to fit environment, fair trade, sustainability and sustainable development goals; - To analyze opportunities to fit the national and international labor institutional environments; to set up an Information System to support informed decision-making; - To describe the main national and international competitors.
3 – Internal Situation Analysis and Global Competitors Benchmarking	- To identify all the strong and weak points of the chain; - To map contracts and existing forms of coordination; - To describe the existing structures of management and its transaction characteristics; - To make an analysis of main competitors; - To analyze the value creation, resources and abilities of the chain; - To analyze the critical success factors of the chain; - To select, amongst the chains (which may or may not be a competitor) where the benchmark (sources of good ideas) will be.
4 – Objectives for the chain	- To define and quanitify the major chain objectives in terms of production, exports, imports, sales to achieve sustainable growth and to develop solutions for the weak points;
5 – Strategies to reach proposed Objectives	- To list the major strategies (action) that will be used to reach the considered objectives in item 04 in terms of positioning, exports, value capture, and market segmentation;

Phase 02 – Plans of Strategic Vectors: Production, Communication, Distribution Channels, Qualification and Coordination (Institutional Adequacy)	
6 – Production, Products, R & D, and Innovations Projects	- To analyze productive potentials and production capacities; - To map and plan for production risks (sanitary and others); - To analyze products and product lines, as well as complementary product lines for expansion decisions; - To develop innovation opportunities in the chain, and in the launch of new products; - To identify opportunities to settle national and international innovation networks; - To foster university partnerships and with medical and health areas; - To detail all offerings and potential services; - To make decisions related to the joint construction of brands, and labels for the system use; - To analyze and implement the certification process for the chain; - To ensure product adequacy with respect to the rules and institutional environment; - To ensure environmental sustainability; - To make packaging-related decisions (labels, materials, design); - To calculate recurrent investments at this stage.
7 – Communication Projects	- To identify the target public for the communication (messages from the production chain); - To develop goals for this communication (product knowledge, product reminders, persuasion, among others) and try to define the unique positioning and message that will be generated by the chain; -To define the communication tools to be used; that is, define advertising or public relations strategies to boost sales, among others. -To make films and international materials that benchmark those already used in other production chains; - To review communication actions and determine the annual promotion budget involving all the network agents; - To indicate how communications results will be measured so that the chain learns more and more about the best tools to achieve revenue on investments.

8 – Logistic and Distribution Projects *(Including Exports)*	- To analyze the product distribution channels and to search for new ones; - To analyze the possibilities of value capture in the distribution channels; - To identify possible demands of international dealers and consumers to suit the existing services; - To define new ways to the penetrate the markets (through franchising, joint ventures and other contractual forms, or through vertical integration); - To determine annual budget for distribution; - To verify how distribution actions can be done together with other chains.
9 – Enabling Decisions in the Productive Chain/ Human Resources	- To conduct trainings in management for the chain participants; - To conduct trainings in control of costs and use of technologies - To conduct trainings in national and international sales; - To transmit information from technological centers/research; - To conduct trainings in food production; - To offer technical assistance to improve properties; - Others
10 *Institutional Environment Coordination and Adequacy Projects*	- To develop projects to finance the chain; - To develop basic infrastructure improvement projects; - To develop projects to increase consumption in government programs; - To develop programs for isolated productive areas; - To push for tax reduction in the production chain project; - To strengthen export activity through export promotion agencies; - To support laws that provide incentives for the use of technologies (fiscal incentive, etc); - To develop a product and product name standardization project; - To promote more transparency in legislation referring to products and processes projects; - To develop proposals for chain conflict solutions; - To ensure coordination in the development of contracts and proposals.

11 – Strategic Projects Consolidation	- All projects generated in steps 6 to 10 will be consolidated and priorities will be settled.
12 – ChainPlan Budget	- Budget of Every Project, which contains costs and total budget.

Source: Elaborated by the author.

Strategic Planning and Management theory highlighted in Chapter 2 is very relevant at step 4 of the *ChainPlan* Method.

4.5 Management of Elaborated Projects and Contracts' Design

Several projects have emerged at the plan (step 4). These projects must be developed on the basis of the traditional stages, analyzing and describing its objectives, action, implementation suggestions, performance indicators, related projects and plans, its inter-relations, teams, stated periods, budgets, and management forms. Chain contracts also can be designed here, following the contract design model proposed by Neves (2003).

5. Managerial Implications

This paper is brought as a contribution – as a method that is being used for Chain Strategic Planning and Management – with five empirical applications. Once the *ChainPlan* method approaches the strategic management of production chains (chains), the focus is: (I) in the general concern with the direction of the chain in a long term period, (II) in the development of a viable and sustainable structure in a long term period, (III) in the general orientation necessary to combine the chain organization and its development, and (IV) for the definition of objectives and collective strategies that will be evaluated in a general perspective. However, comparing it with the strategic management of companies, the *ChainPlan* brings some advantages and opportunities, and additional challenges and difficulties to the chain's agents who intend to organize themselves in order to develop and implement a process of chain strategic management. Table 5 summarizes these points.

Table 5: Summary of advantages and challenges on *ChainPlan* method

Advantages	Challenges
(i) describes a value chain and the chain leadership philosophy, which guides a common future vision for the chain;	(i) gives greater emphasis on planning, techniques and tools than the agents' involvement and the sharing of creative thoughts on the objectives, positioning and strategy of the chain;
(ii) allows the sharing of information and experiences among the agents about conditions and evolutions in the environment;	(ii) great demand for information and discussions and little emphasis on making decisions;
(iii) serves as a coordination tool between the several functions and agents of the chain, allowing bigger coherence between the chain objectives and, in case of conflicts and incompatibilities, favors arbitrations on the basis of objective criteria;	(iii) may foster naive management that does not raise basic questions about the chain capacity, objectives and markets;
(iv) stimulates a cooperative, integrated and enthusiastic approach to chain problems;	(iv) may interest groups to maintain the *status quo* and power, which can damage chain interests;
(v) increases the chain reaction flexibility in facing unexpected changes;	(v) conservative managers who refuse to substitute former proposals for new ideas, and who find it difficult to break other poor management habits;
(vi) allows a more rigorous and professional collective management based on norms, budgets, responsibilities sharing and timetables, not on improvisation;	(vi) unsuitable resources allocation, without proper definition of the priorities of the chain;
(vii) provides a better chain positioning – helping to evolve in the routes – through the committees formed by the leadership, which are considered more adequate;	(vii) focus on the planning itself, with little capacity and/or interest to implement what had been planned;
(viii) takes to results that are more interesting to the chain as a whole economically and socially	(viii) more focus on structuring actions related to agents' operational activities instead of a focus on activities for coordination and the final consumers

Source: Elaborated by the author

The *ChainPlan* method considered here was developed and improved in the recent years in an effective attempt to: (i) construct a vertical chain organization capable of executing the strategies, along with an organizational supporting structure with distinctive abilities and competences, and select people in key positions; (ii) establish a supporting budgetary strategy that is fair and coherent between the links and members of the system, ensuring the efficient use of these resources; (iii) settle administrative support systems, with the politics and procedures that support the critical capacities for strategy of the settled organization; (iv) define an incentive system related to the objectives and strategies, to motivate the chain agents and links to carry out planned actions, to induce the desired performance and to guide actions for the chain results; (v) model of an "associative" culture, with the establishment of shared values, ethical standards and an institutional environment that support the collective strategy of the chain; and (vi) establish and exercise a strategic leadership for the chain organization, with process-involved leaders to format values, shape the culture, to keep the vision innovative and responsive to market chances and to initiate corrective measures that can improve strategy execution for the chain.

6. Research Limitations and *ChainPlan* Proposed Method

The following limitations can be listed: a) in the considered method there is a simplification of the involved processes in the strategic management of organizations; b) in trying to deal with many aspects in a single work, there is a superficiality in the treatment of the subjects from the point of view of a whole body of theory c) in the same way, a synthesis of other authors' proposals was done, and all synthesis has a direct influence from the researcher, that may not have caught the essence in this process; d) the literature review may have missed to find other proposals and methods of chain strategic management; e) the subject treatment's simplicity and the researcher's applied vision is another limitation factor of this research; f) as it is still a theoretician's method, there must be some prudence in its application, and more empirical tests are recommended for its validation.

References

ANDREWS, K. R. *The concept of corporate strategy*. 3. ed. Irwin: Homewood IL, 1987.

ANSOFF, H. I. *Corporate strategy: an analytic approach to business police for growth and expansion*. New York: McGraw-Hill, 1965.

BATALHA, M. O. (Coord.). *Gestão agroindustrial*. 2. ed. São Paulo: Atlas, 2001.

BESANKO, D.; DRANOVE, D.; SHANLEY, M. *Economics of Strategy*. New York: John Wiley and Sons, 2000.

BONOMA, T. V. Case research in marketing: opportunities, problems and a process. *Journal of Marketing Research*, v. 22, p. 199-208, may 1985.

CAMPOMAR, M.C. *Contribuições ao estudo de planejamento e confecção de planos em marketing (uma aplicação em concessionárias de automóveis)*. Tese (Livre-docência em Administração) – Faculdade de Economia, Administração e Contabilidade. São Paulo: Universidade de São Paulo, 1982. 249 p.

CHANDLER, A. D. *Strategy and structure*. Cambridge, MA: MIT Press, 1962.

COASE, R H. The nature of the firm. *Economica*, New Series, v. 4, n. 16, p. 386-405, 1937.

DAVIS, J. H.; GOLDBERG, R. A. *A concept of agribusiness*. Boston: Division of Research, Graduate School of Business Administration, Harvard University, 1957. 136 p.

DIGMAN, L. A. *Strategic management:* concepts, decisions, cases. 2. ed. Boston: BPI Irwin, 1990.

FARINA, E. M. M. Q.; AZEVEDO P. F.; SAES, M.S.M.. *Competitividade: mercado, Estado e organizações*. São Paulo: Singular, 1997. 285p.

FORD, D. Two Decades of interaction, relationships and networks. In: NAUDÉ, P.; TURNBULL, P.W. *Network dynamics in international marketing*. Oxford: Pergamon, 1998. 321 p.

GOLDBERG, R. A. *Agribusiness coordination: a systems (chains) approach to the wheat, Soybean, and Florida orange economies*. Division of Research. Graduate School of Business and Administration. Harvard University, 1968. 256 p.

HEIDE, J. B. Inter-organizational governance in marketing channels. *Journal of Marketing*, v. 58, p. 71-85, Jan. 1994.

HEIDE, J. B.; JOHN, G. Alliances in industrial purchasing: the determinants of joint action in buyer-supplier relationships. *Journal of Marketing Research*, v. 27, p. 24-36, 1990.

HENDERSON, B. D. *The logic of business strategy*. Cambridge: Mass, 1984.

JAIN, S. C. *Marketing planning & strategy*, 6. ed. Cincinnati: Thomson Learning, 2000.

KOTLER, P. *Administração de marketing: análise, planejamento, implementação e controle*. São Paulo: Prentice Hall, 2000. 725 p.

LAMBIN, J. J. *Marketing estratégico*. 4. ed. Lisboa: McGraw-Hill, 2000. 756 p.

LAS CASAS, A.L. *Plano de marketing para micro e pequena empresa*. São Paulo: Atlas, 1999. 156 p.

LAZZARINI, S.G.; CHADDAD, F.R.; COOK, M. Integrating supply and network analysis: the study of netchains. *Journal on Chain and Network Science*, v. 1, n. 1, p. 7-22, 2001.

MAcNEIL, I. R. The Many futures of contracts. *Southern California Law Review*, v. 47, p. 691-816, may 1974.

MINTZBERG, H.; QUINN, J. B.; JAMES, R. M. *The strategy process: concepts, contexts and cases*. Englewood Cliffs, NJ: Prentice-Hall, 1988.

MOORE, J. L. *Writers on strategy and strategic management*. London: Penguin Books, 1992. 311 p.

NASSAR, A. M. *Eficiência das associações de interesse privado: uma análise do agronegócio brasileiro*. Dissertação (Mestrado em Administração) – Faculdade de Economia, Administração e Contrabilidade. São Paulo: Universidade de São Paulo, 2001.

NEVES, M. F. Marketing and Network Contracts (agreements). *Journal on Chain and Network Science,* v. 3, n. 1, May 2003.

______. Strategic marketing plans and collaborative actions. *Marketing Intelligence and Planning*, v. 25, n. 2, p. 175-192, 2007.

NEVES, M. F; VAL, A. M.; MARINO, M. K. The orange network in Brazil. *Fruit Processing, Schönborn, Germany*, v. 11, n. 12, p. 486-490, 2001.

NEVES, M. F.; ZUURBIER, P.; CAMPOMAR, M. C. A model for the distribution channels planning process. *Journal of Business & Industrial Marketing*, 2001; 16(6/7): 518-539.

OLSON, M. *The logic of collective action.* Cambridge: Harvard University Press, 1965. 232 p.

PEARCE, J. A., II; ROBINSON JR., R. B. *Strategic management: strategy formulation and implementation.* 3. ed. Homewood, IL: Richard D. Irwin, Inc., 1988. 988 p.

RINDFLEISCH, A.; HEIDE, J. B. Transaction cost analysis: past, present and future applications. *Journal of Marketing*, v. 61, p. 30-54, Oct. 1997.

ROSEMBLOON, B. *Marketing channels.* 6. ed. Chicago, IL: The Dryden Press, 1999. 688 p.

SAES, M. S. M. Organizações e instituições. In: ZYLBERSZTAJN, D.; NEVES, M. F. (Org.). *Economia e gestão dos negócios agroalimentares.* São Paulo: Pioneira, 2000.

STERN, L.; EL ANSARY, A.I.; COUGHLAN, A.T. *Marketing channels.* 5. ed. Prentice Hall, 1996. 576 p.

WESTWOOD, J. O. *Plano de marketing.* São Paulo: Makron Books, 1996.

WILLIAMSON, O. E. *The economic institutions of capitalism.* New York: Free Press, 1985.

WOOD, M. B. *Marketing planning: principles into practice.* Harlow: Prentice Hall, 2004. 379p.

WRIGHT, P.; KROLL, M. K.; PARNELL, J. *Administração estratégica: conceitos.* Trad. Celso A. Rimoli e Lenita R. Esteves. São Paulo: Atlas, 2000. 433p.

YIN, R. K. *Case study research: design and methods.* 6. ed. Newbury Park CA: Sage Publications, 1989.

ZYLBERSZTAJN, D.; NEVES, M. F. (Org.) *Economia e gestão dos negócios agroalimentares.* São Paulo: Pioneira, 2000.

Part 6

Innovation and Entrepreneurship

- Strategy and Organization in Agribusiness: the role of the Entrepreneur
- Dutchmen in Latin America: Some lessons about cross-cultural business
- Does the Developed World Still Have a Competitive Edge in Innovation? A comparative study of leading food processing companies in the Shanghai area and the Netherlands

Strategy and Organization in Agribusiness: the role of the entrepreneur

MARIA SYLVIA MACCHIONE SAES

FABIO MATUOKA MIZUMOTO

Abstract

This chapter introduces the analysis of the entrepreneur to a more comprehensive understanding of strategies and organizations in Agribusiness. Current theories on Economic literature explain strategy adoption according to forces of the competitive environment (Porter 1985), organization arrangements and coordination among agents by the characteristics of the transactions (Williamson 1985) but provide limited explanations about what firms innovate and induce heterogeneity of strategies and organizational forms. Indeed, firms seek alternatives to the equilibrium to create and appropriate value, for instance, in Agribusiness; farmers switch to a differentiation strategy or organize themselves in collective action to obtain a distinctive performance above the average of the industry. In this sense, the literature on Entrepreneurship complements the explanations from Porter's Strategic Positioning Framework and Transaction Cost Economics. Entrepreneurship provides an alternative understanding of competitive environment by introducing the creative destruction (Schumpeter 1926) and makes possible the investigation of the entrepreneur that has been neglected by the Economic literature. The entrepreneurs differ on their judgment capacity (Knight 1964), alertness to identify opportunities (Kirzner 1973) and entrepreneurial ability related to human capital (Shultz 1975) that are theoretically explored and empirically illustrated by case studies in this chapter.

1. Introduction

The role of the entrepreneur has been neglected on the Economic literature to explain strategy and organization of firms. In this traditional literature, price is the main coordination mechanism that determines performance of the firms and, consequently, explains the strategic and organizational decisions given the consumer's preference, technological possibilities and resource endowment. This leaves no role for the classical entrepreneurial task of coordinating, arbitrating, innovating and dealing with uncertainty (Bhidé 2000).

Moreover, assuming homogeneous entrepreneurial ability of the firms, the Economic literature provides answers that are incomplete at best. What explains different patterns of strategies adopted by firms in the same competitive environment? Why do some firms innovate on organizational arrangements or establish alternative mechanisms of coordination? What firms innovate and induce variability of strategy and organization in the industry?

All questions are relevant in the Agribusiness context. In order to have alternatives to the equilibrium, firms create and appropriate value by switching to a differentiation strategy or by organizing themselves in collective action to obtain a distinctive performance above the average of the industry. Thus, we observe firms that induce changes on the traditional Agribusiness System (Zylbersztjan 1996) by means of innovation on goods, services and coordination arrangements.

"Entrepreneurship is about the new – new goods and services, but more generally new economic knowledge – and about how the new enters the economic system. To put it in another way, entrepreneurship is about change" (Langlois 2005:2). Entrepreneurship provides an alternative understanding of competitive environment by introducing the creative destruction (Schumpeter 1912, 1934) and makes possible the investigation of the entrepreneur that has been neglected by the Economic literature. The entrepreneurs differ on their judgment capacity (Knight 1964), alertness to identify opportunities (Kirzner 1973) and entrepreneurial ability related to human capital (Shultz 1961).

This chapter discusses the role of the entrepreneur as the inductor of innovation (Foss & Klein 2004; Witt 1998; Casson 2005) and the source of variability on strategies and organizations of firms. To fulfill this objective, this chapter is organized in four parts. The first part presents the classic literature on Entrepreneurship by discussing the arguments of Schumpeter (1926), Kirzner (1973), Knight (1964) and Schultz (1961). The second part develops connections between the Entrepreneurship literature and value creation in Agribusiness. Connections between Entrepreneurship literature and Governance in Agribusiness are addressed in the third part. Finally, we illustrate the concepts discussed in this chapter with case studies and empirical research.

2. Who is the Entrepreneur?

Richard Cantillon was the first author to consider the entrepreneur as an important agent in the economic environment in his seminal work "An essay about the nature of the overall trade", dated 1755. However, Schumpeter is one of the best known pioneers to discuss the entrepreneurial role in the economic theory through his work "The theory of economic development"[1] dated 1912. The Schumpeterian entrepreneur is not a common businessman, but an innovator motivated by the opportunity of profit. This entrepreneur plays a key role in creating new businesses through a process of "destructive creation".

Essentially, the entrepreneur does things not done in the ordinary course of business routine. The entrepreneur is, therefore, the first mover that can be present both in a small activity and in large corporations, as a single physical person or a group. The effect of innovation is to unbalance and alter the structure of the market until the exhaustion of this process occurs and the beginning of a new innovation wave appears. This process comprises five cases: (1) The introduction of a new good – i.e., one with which consumers are not yet familiar – or a new quality of a good; (2) The introduction of a new method of production, i.e., one not yet tested by experience in the branch of manufacture concerned, which needs by no means be founded upon a discovery scientifically new, and can also exist in a new way of handling a commodity commercially; (3) The opening of a new market that is a market into which the particular branch of manufacture of the country in question has not previously entered, whether or not this market has existed before; (4) The conquest of a new source of supply of

1 In a later work, published in 1926, "Capitalism, socialism and democracy", Schumpeter (1942) was concerned with the general process of concentration in the markets started in the early 20th century and the role of large corporations in the performance of capitalism. The author argues that innovations in the large companies prevailing in the world scenario as of this period routinely appeared in their research centers. For this reason, many authors interpret that there are, in effect, two Schumpeters, the one that wrote "The theory of economic development" in 1912, and this later one, who denies the former (Langlois 2002).

raw material or half-manufactured goods, again irrespective of whether this source already exists or whether it has first to be created; (5) The carrying out of the new organization of any industry, like the creation of a monopoly position (for example through trustification) or the breaking up of a monopoly position (Schumpeter 1926:66).

In Kirzner's framework, the entrepreneur is interpreted as the arbitrageur who discovers the profit opportunity rooted in the discrepancy among present prices. The knowledge of where to discover this market data and how to open up the possibilities for profit opportunities is what he calls entrepreneurship as "alertness". However, alertness per se cannot characterize the entrepreneur. In this sense, the Schumpeterian approach emphasizes that the entrepreneur requires "intuition and the leap of logic", suggesting an action outside the familiar routine in the process of innovation (Langlois 2002:18).[2] However, the question turns to how to understand the cognitive heuristic of the entrepreneur. Although not directly identifiable, Knight (1964) and Schultz (1975) provide a productive framework towards the understanding of the entrepreneurs' decisions. The former highlights the entrepreneurs' behavior in conditions of uncertainty and the latter investigates the entrepreneurial ability by means of education and experience.

Uncertainty is an important factor, since business decisions made in a "world that is full of uninsurable risks ('uncertainty') will in general produce results that diverge more or less widely from the expected ones and thus sometimes lead to surplus gains and sometimes to losses. It is thus a common experience that presses upon us very strongly. This idea may be true, but needs not be added to the element of business ability and is of course, still more obviously, not quite the same as the element of risk: but we need not stress these relations" (Schumpeter 1934:67-68). Knight (1964) in his 1921 work "Risk, uncertainty and profit" explains the importance of the evaluation or judgment of an entrepreneur in decision-making under uncertain conditions. Those who venture have expectations (and not scientific knowledge) of a result to be achieved, within limits that can be more or less

2 It is worth bearing in mind that contemporary authors, like Sarasvathy (2001), address the issue decision-making based on a cognitive approach. This psychological theoretical perspective seeks to understand the inherent logic of the decision-making by adopting as methodology experimental research, drawing on works by Kahneman & Tversky (1979).

narrow. The inclination to invest is thus guided by the opinion or belief in the real possibility of future gains (Knight 1964:237). "Judgment primarily refers to the process of businessmen forming estimates of future events in situations in which there is no agreement or idea at all on probabilities of occurrence" (Foss & Klein 2004:8).

At the bottom of the uncertainty problem in economics is the forward-looking character of the economic process itself. The entrepreneur faces two elements of uncertainty, which correspond to two types of foresight that must be exercised with regard to the production of goods aimed to meet consumers' desires. The first element regards the need to estimate the end of productive operations from the beginning. It is impossible to tell accurately what their results will be in physical terms (quantities and / or qualities of goods) before the resources are entered in the production process. Second, the wants that the goods are presumed to satisfy are also in the future to the same extent, and their prediction involves uncertainty in the same way. Producers, then, must estimate (1) the future demand they are striving to satisfy and (2) the future results of their operations in attempting to satisfy that demand. The author also uses the terms 'objective' and 'subjective' probability to designate risk and uncertainty, respectively. For him, the best example of uncertainty is in connection with the exercise of judgment or the formation of those opinions as to the future course of events, in which opinions (and not scientific knowledge) actually guide most of our conduct (Knight 1964:233).

Schultz (1975) affirms that entrepreneurship is the ability to adjust in response to changing circumstances. This is consistent with the uncertainty conditions assumed by Knight (1964), but Schultz emphasizes that adjustments to disequilibrium are costly and time consuming. Moreover, entrepreneurship is the ability to respond to disequilibrium increases through education, training and experience. "Schultz conceives entrepreneurial ability as a form of human capital (...) emphasizing the temporal aspect of entrepreneurial adjustment, particularly important for agricultural production in which temporal specificities loom large" (Klein & Cook 2005).

Finally, Knight and Schultz have complementary approaches to entrepreneurship. With uncertainty regarding the future, the firm is able to make positive profits although it belongs to a long-term competitive equilibrium framework (term that only exists in theory). Indeed, to capture the value created on disequilibrium, the entrepreneur relies on his judgment about the uncertain condition (Knight, 1964) and on his previous experience, education and training (Schultz 1975). Those arguments have a relevant and revealing implication for the Economic Theory and the field of strategy.

3. The Entrepreneur in Agribusiness and Value Creation

Previous studies of entrepreneurship in agribusiness are related to generation of economic activity in rural areas (Gladwin et al 1989) and to regional development (Reid 1987). "These studies were mainly descriptive of the firms located in rural areas, probably were useful to policy makers, but provided few insights into the impacts of entrepreneurs on the economy" (Gladwin et al 1989). Thus, we take the analytical lenses of Knight and Schultz to provide a comprehensive understanding of the entrepreneur on firms' strategy and organization that will ultimately impact its performance and will impact the industry.

Agribusiness provides many sources of uncertainty, from the weather conditions to the way the resources are allocated. In addition, this industry is characterized by constant changes on the input and output price ratio and by great impact on government policies. All are sources of disequilibria where the entrepreneur emerges to create and appropriate value in Knight's sense. From the perspective of Schultz, the adaptation to changing conditions is greatly improved by the knowledge that the farmer accumulates by previous decisions. Moreover, the farmer accumulates a type of experience that is relevant to strategic decisions because it is firm-specific and resource-specific (Kor, Mahoney and Michael 2007). Indeed, codified knowledge such as manuals or recommendations cannot replace the knowledge about how the resources will respond to a change or a treatment defined by the entrepreneur.

The entrepreneur is "someone who specializes in taking judgmental decisions about the co-ordination of scarce resources" (Casson 1982:23). In his view, the concept of entrepreneurial judgment is of paramount importance; judgment is not based on the simple application of marginal rules regarding resource allocation, but, rather, it is based on individuals, their perceptions and the information that they have available (or choose to acquire). Central to this concept is the recognition that different individuals will make different decisions that will produce different outcomes because information is necessarily imperfect and costly to acquire.

Thus, the heterogeneity of judgment may be a source of value creation. This makes sense when we observe that entrepreneurs do not share their judgment with their peers (Witt 2000). Hence, individuals differ in their ability to process information. Even though information may originate in the same source, they interpret their expected gains in different ways (Casson 2005). That explains the heterogeneity in the configuration of firms even within the same industrial sector. No firm is like any other, because each has its own printed logo: the judgment of its entrepreneur.

4. The Entrepreneur in Agribusiness and Governance

Considering the complexity of activities involved in the Agribusiness System (Zylbersztajn 1996), entrepreneurial activities are expected to be observed in integrated governance structures rather than in market relationship to avoid moral risk and adverse selection.

A person creating or discovering new attributes is motivated to use them directly because it is costly to transfer knowledge that is not easily measurable. There are costs to discover what the relevant price is, costs for negotiating, for measuring unknown attributes and for formatting contracts. Therefore, entrepreneurs usually avoid negotiation costs in order to prevent value dissipation. They cannot become idea "sellers", since knowledge is susceptible to problems of moral risk and adverse selection.[3] However when contingencies can be properly specified or when the parts' decision to cooperate does not affect one another, contracts are possible and integration is unnecessary.

In essence, the transaction cost is, therefore, for Langlois (1992), a short-term phenomenon that loses importance in the long term. For him, long term is defined as a period of time long enough for learning to occur so that adjustments can be small and appear only in response to exogenous

3 Once information is known, it is worthless; before it is known, it is not possible to assess it properly. It is not known whether it is a good idea. Besides, we could add two other problems: (a) In general, an innovative idea is only considered as such after its success; (b) Often, a creative idea is not properly conceived, is not easily communicated to the markets and depends upon a process of adaptation / experimentation that requires mainly the "mind" of the strategy creator.

changes. For that reason, the boundaries of the firm cannot be considered without also taking into account the learning process both within firms and in the markets. This viewpoint associates competitive advantages with dynamic transaction costs (Langlois 1992, 2002).

5. Empirical Research on Entrepreneurship and Agribusiness

To provide illustrations about the role of the entrepreneur on firms' strategy and organization, we organized two case studies and a model for strategy choice for the Agribusiness System of Coffee in Brazil. The lenses to capture the entrepreneur phenomena are the ones developed in the previous sections, especially Knight's and Shultz's frameworks.

5.1 Case Illycaffè

The Italian company illycaffè is well known by its high quality blend of coffee. Dr. Ernesto Illy had to overcome many challenges to establish his company, from the development of "in house" machines and equipment for a specific pattern of coffee roast, to the establishment of a supply chain that guarantees high quality raw material for the illycaffe blend. This illustration sheds light on the latter solution and the role of the entrepreneur to achieve it.

The challenge: how to create incentives for coffee producers to invest in equipment, machines and agronomic practices in order to supply high quality coffee to illycaffè? Brazil supplies 65 to 70 percent of illycaffe's raw material every year. Brazil is the largest coffee producer in the world and one of the few countries that apply sun-dry-processed coffee beans, an essential method in the composition of the *espresso.* This process promotes a higher content of sugar that migrates from the fruit to the coffee beans and gives more aroma and body to the blend (Zylbersztajn & Neves 1997). The illycaffè company has bought Brazilian coffee since 1933, but until the early 1990s the volumes and quality of coffee for the international market was regulated by the IBC (Brazilian Coffee Institute), so there was not much room for private strategies. By the time of regulation, all exported coffee was mixed with different qualities from different Brazilian regions, making hard for illycaffè to obtain the desired standard. For instance, only one sample in ten that was sent to Trieste would be approved for purchase by illycaffè at this time. Moreover, because this practice of commercialization carried out in Brazil did not value the product that had a higher quality, producers ceased to invest in quality. After the regulation was over in the mid 1990s, illycaffè faced a challenge to create incentives for farmers to invest in high quality coffee. Dr. Illy saw that the main problem was the coordination of harvesting, drying, processing and trading activities. Problems occurred because the agents involved were not receiving adequate incentives to produce the quality he needed. The solution would not lie in acquiring properties because coffee quality is influenced by weather conditions, which cause large variations in its quality from region to region in a given crop.

Entrepreneur's human capital and judgment. There were two key drivers in Dr. Illy's choice of strategy: his experience in the company and his academic background. Francesco Illy, Ernesto Illy's father, founded illycaffè in 1933 in Trieste, Italy. Before taking over as co-owner and C.E.O. of the company in 1956,[4] Dr. Illy had worked in several economic sectors, but it was through his experience with clients that he realized the extent to which consumers valued the consistency, the aroma and the flavor of the beverage. In addition to that, his education in Chemical Engineering fostered in him a high regard for laboratory analyses of the drivers of the quality in the coffee beverage, which had been previously carried out based on the subjectivity of specialists. The alliance of these two types of knowledge enabled Dr. Illy to visualize the potential of the high-quality coffee business. Moreover, to solve the supply challenge, Dr. Illy was based on his experience and the observation of the Italian fashion designer Ermenegildo Zegna. Faced with difficulties in buying quality cashmere, Zegna's company had created a quality contest offering financial incentives to communities that supplied the best fabric (Saes & Ishikawa 2007). Replicating this strategy, illycaffè started to promote an annual contest in 1991, the *Brazil Coffee Quality Prize for Espresso,* aimed at identifying the superior quality coffee produced in a given year. The company awards a prize premium that is 20 to 30 percent above international prices of good quality coffee beans, and purchases the coffee beans that are thus classified. The incentive structure enabled by the contest

4 Dr. Illy remained in the position until 2000, when his son Andrea Illy took over as illycaffè's C.E.O.

allows illycaffè to identify the parties present in the transaction, a relevant aspect in the product's final result. In this case, since the spot market became inadequate to coordinate the transactions, the hierarchy structure could be replaced through an innovative solution (Zylbersztajn 1996).

Heterogeneity of Strategy and Governance. Considering the Coffee Agribusiness System, illycaffè introduces the contest as a mechanism to incentive high quality of coffee production. The supply is a fundamental base to illycaffè strategy of differentiated blends. In 2006, illycaffè had some 40 thousand sales points around the globe, where over 5 million cups of *espresso* were served daily, with its unique and always constant blend of nine origins of Arabica (Saes & Ishikawa 2007). Illycaffè supplies 12 countries, benefiting from differences found in climate and altitude conditions, among other aspects. From June to October it purchases coffee from Brazil and from January to May from Central American countries, India and Ethiopia (Neves, Saes & Rezende 2003). The company acquired about 200 thousand coffee bags from Brazil in the 2006-2007 crop year, which is considered a large quantity in terms of high quality coffee. The illycaffè quality contest brought a change in the pattern of competition in the coffee market. The number of candidates to supply coffee to illycaffè increases every year. Through a multiplying effect, similar contests were adopted and regions that traditionally produced low quality beans have sought new technologies to improve their production processes. That happened, for instance, in Minas Gerais' Zona da Mata (in Portuguese, "forest zone"), whose coffee beans had been given a low score in the classification (Rio Zona).[5] After implementing a new technology for processing the beans, local producers started to be classified in quality contests[6] (Saes 2008). Consumers identify the illycaffè brand with the quality of their espresso coffee. The brand reputation ensures the attributes that consumers desire; they know that the company has selected the best suppliers, no matter who they are. For this reason, the company does

5 Coffee classification, according to the drink, in decreasing order of quality is the following: Strictly soft, Soft, Softish, Riada, Rio and Rio Zona. The classification per type admits seven categories (types 2 through 8, with decreasing quality), according to the number of defects verified in a 300-gram sample.

6 The technology used is called hulled cherry. Through a huller, green and dry beans (floats) are separated from ripe beans (cherries) and washed. After the skin is removed the beans go to the patio. In the drying process, the mucilage adheres to the beans providing unique characteristics like body, acidity and sweetness.

not need to format contracts or establish a formal relation with producers. The incentive to produce quality is dictated by the market signals that a price premium exists in comparison with the commodity price. Therefore, the relation established between illycaffè and producers is characterized by a relation that depends solely upon quality. Both the structure of the contest and the premium have led to the creation of an elastic supply of quality product, thereby bringing about an extremely efficient situation for the supply chain. The competition in the market of factors produces the participants' maximum effort (those who do not strive are expelled from the market). In addition to the price premium signaled by the market, information systems were created, thus providing producers with technology to enable them to increase the supply of high quality beans.

5.2 *Case Cooxupé*

Cooxupé is the largest farmer-owned cooperative in coffee production in the world. By the time of the cooperative foundation, the main motivtion was to obtain economies of scale and alternatives to add value to coffee. Cooxupé profited from both Brazil's economic boom and the incentives of the agricultural policy during the so-called "economic miracle", in the 60s and 70s. It expanded its infrastructure and the number of members, while advancing to other Brazilian regions.[7] It acquired storage facilities, coffee processing equipment, warehouses and regional offices, creating better conditions to benefit from the externalities of the network, both in the purchase of inputs and in the negotiation of the green coffee. One of the first actions of the cooperative in this period was in March 1965, when it acquired a warehouse with a capacity for 200 thousand bags of coffee, financed by

7 The cooperative operates in over 100 municipalities in the Alto Paraíva River and Southern Minas regions (Minas' Cerrado) and in the Pardo River Valley (state of São Paulo). It has 16 regional centers located in the following municipalities: Guaxupé – headquarter and center (MG), Monte Santo de Minas (MG), Cabo Verde (MG), Caconde (SP); Guaranésia (MG); Nova Resende (MG); São Pedro da União (MG); Alfenas (MG); Carmo do Rio Claro (MG), São José do Rio Pardo (SP), Monte Carmelo (MG); Alpinópolis (MG); Campestre (MG); Coromandel (MG); Paranaíba River (MG); Serra do Salitre (MG); 5 advanced units: Botelhos (MG); Campos Gerais (MG); Campos Gerais (MG); Monte Belo (MG); Muzambinho (MG) and an exporting office in the city of Santos (see Cooperative's website: www.cooxupé.com.br).

the Brazilian Coffee Institute (IBC) (Chaddad, 2007). Able to stock coffee, producers could choose the best moment to sell it, thereby increasing their negotiation power with buyers. In 2008, Cooxupé had 18 warehouses and a storage capacity of 1.9 million 60-kg bags with a capacity to receive over 3 million bags per year. Another advantage of the storage system regards input acquisition. By acquiring inputs at large volumes and being able to stock them in the periods between crop seasons, the cooperative could resell them to its members at a lower price than the market price. However, as the cooperative grew, additional challenges emerged. This illustration focuses the challenges that Cooxupé overtake to achieve the international market directly.

The challenge. Having stepped into the role of Cooxupé's C.E.O. at the age of 46, Isaac Ferreira Leite, known as Dr. Isaac, was driven by the objective of finding possibilities to add value to coffee, whereby Brazilian growers' remuneration could be enhanced (Saes 2008). One alternative was to achieve the international market directly. However, this implied investments to be done in a higher uncertainty environment. Dr. Isaac certainly had asked: Why do Brazilian cooperatives have to rely on exporters? Why not export directly? Why not standardize coffee quality to add value to it instead of leaving this task to buyers?

Entrepreneur's human capital and judgment. Dr. Isaac had brought to Cooxupé his observations of the dynamics of large firms, which included, for instance, gains in economies of scale and scope in textile manufacturing, as well as a professional work ethic in the workplace and in negotiations with clients. This happened at a time when Brazilian cooperatives placed almost no emphasis on professional management, and, even less, on internationalization strategies.

Heterogeneity of Strategy and Governance. What distinguishes Cooxupé from other coffee cooperatives is Dr. Isaac's strategic proposal concerning the means to commercialize the product directly to international markets. Anticipating the world market trend of segmentation by quality, Cooxupé built tools and processes aimed at classifying the coffee being traded in the 1950s, and hence brought consistency to the standardization of its product. This system was adopted at a time when the priority of the governmental policy was the volume of coffee exports, detrimentally affecting the quality of the product. This pioneering initiative allowed Cooxupé to develop unique resources to trade coffee directly with international buyers in the 1980s. Thus product standardization was the first step toward changing the rules of the game that established how the coop's coffee was exported. It was important because, over time, buyers adapted to this system even when purchasing the product through third parties. Dr. Isaac believed that the success in direct exports would be achieved through the creation of a long-term relationship based on trust and reputation and, of course, the quality of the product.[8] In 1984, the cooperative opened an office in the city of Santos, the world's main coffee exporting port. In 1990, export director Joaquim Libânio took over with the responsibility of developing that relationship, a task facilitated by his previous experience as the IBC's Brazilian representative at the International Coffee Organization (ICO). In the same year, Cooxupé made direct exports of 200 thousand bags of coffee. In 2005, the largest part of the 3 million bags traded by Cooxupé, i.e., 1.4 million bags, was directly exported (to 30 countries and 150 clients); 988 thousand bags were indirectly commercialized and 630 thousand bags were traded in the domestic market.[9] Allied to the "conscious and responsible consumption" movement, the increased demand for specialty coffees of the early 2000s offered the opportunity to trade high-quality coffees produced in a sustainable manner, with price premiums in comparison with the commodity market. In parallel to that, several quality contests appeared in Brazil as a means to foster the production of quality coffees.[10] Cooxupé's initial strategy, i.e., eliminating intermediaries in the commercialization process and negotiating with a stronger bargaining power, enabled it to obtain gains that resulted in higher incomes for producers. Each producer within a group gives an autonomous and well-defined contribution, and the relations among producers are scarce, generally without the need for strong social ties. That represents a type of relationship of low complexity. Prices reflect the totality of incentives required. Once the coffee is classified by the cooperative, its price is determined by the market. The standardization adopted by Cooxupé was highly instrumental in solving problems of information asymmetry. Producers'

8 In 1992, the Cooperative joined the specialty coffee market by becoming a member of the Specialty Coffee Association of America (SCAA).

9 See Cooperative's website: www.cooxupe.com.br

10 A number of quality contests were implemented in Brazil in the 1990s: the first was sponsored by illycaffè, the next promoted by BSCA (*Brazilian Specialty Coffee Association*)—*Cup of Excellence*—and several other state contests followed in São Paulo, Minas Gerais and Espírito Santo, among others.

largest gains are related to the scale and scope in coffee commercialization, the joint purchase of inputs and the creation of knowledge and management resources that, through the cooperative, enabled them to build partnerships with other companies that buy quality product.

5.3 *What explains which Brazilian coffee producers adopt differentiation strategies?*

With the growth of firms like Starbucks and Seattle's Best, the market for this differentiated Arabica coffee has been increasing fast over the past two decades representing by 2004, about 8% of the world coffee production and 35% of the USA coffee market (Chaddad & Boland, 2007). As this market grew some Brazilian farmers switched some or all of their production capacity to Arabic while some farmers remained focused on commodity production. What explains which Brazilian coffee producers adopted differentiation strategies? What contributes to the entrepreneurial ability of farmers to adopt a differentiation strategy?

To explore who adopts a differentiation strategy, this research turns to human capital theory (Becker & Tomes 1986) as a key element to the understanding of strategy choice. Considering that farmers possess equivalent physical assets and identical information about production and the market, differences in decisions then must be attributed to the way in which they process information, their mental models and cognitive structures. While these models and structures cannot be observed directly, human capital theory can provide a window into these structures by exploring how the relationship between formal education[11] and the experience of the decision maker influence the firms' positioning in the market. Indeed, Shultz argued long ago that it is the stock of skills and knowledge (Schultz 1961) that determine the individuals' entrepreneurial ability (Schultz 1982) to respond to changes in economic environment.

The empirical study is possible because we collected data by interviewing 409 farmers by phone, following a structured questionnaire from July to November of 2007. The sample of farmers was provided by coffee processing industries and cooperatives. The data base covers all relevant

[11] Becker & Tomes (1986) consider formal education as an investment that an individual can make to increase his human capital.

production areas in Brazil with relatively the same proportion of volume of coffee harvested.

In this study, the dependent variable is the probability of strategic choice that takes value of 1 for differentiation strategy or 0 for commodity strategy. Considering a binary dependent variable, the logit analysis is the appropriate method to estimate the coefficients in the model:

$$\Pi i = ezi / (1+ezi) \text{ or } zi = \log (\Pi i / (1 - \Pi i))$$

Where:

Πi is the probability of ith case experiences the event of interest

zi is the value of the unobserved continuous variable for the ith case

The arguments from human capital and transaction cost to explain strategy choice are introduced in our model. Considering the former, we introduced Formal Education, Experience from diversification, Experience from previous family generations and Family influence proxies to explain Strategy choice. The latter test if the adoption of contractual arrangements rather than spot market relationship between coffee farmer and coffee buyer explains strategy choice. Control variables include Region, Owner's Age and Size. The model is:

$$Zi = \beta_0 + \beta_1 \text{Region} + \beta_2 \text{Owner's Age} + \beta_3 \text{Size} + \beta_4 \text{Contract} + \beta_5 \text{Education} + \beta_6 \text{ Diversification} + \beta_7 \text{Generation} + \beta_8 \text{Family Influence}$$

"Education" is a categorical variable for 8 levels of education, from 1 "elementary incomplete" to 8 "College degree". "Diversification" is a measure for other activities that owners experience that, in extreme; vary from 0 if owners are focused on coffee business to almost 100, if owners are much diversified. "Generation" takes value of 1 for owners that are founders' child or grandchild or value of 0 if the owner is the business founder. "Family Influence" variable was created by factor analysis of the F-PEC based questions, in which high values indicate strong family influence. Eingenvalue indicates that 1 factor is appropriate to represent the 4 questions, standardized by z-scores. "Contract" assumes value 1 for contract arrangement or value 0 for market relationship. "Region" is a categorical variable to control for differences on 8 Federal States, "Owner's Age" is measured in years and "Size" is measured in hectares (unit of area).

The logit analysis maximize the "likelihood" that an event will occur. Considering that the farmer has equal chance to choose one of the two possible strategies, in column (A) is indicated 0.500 of probability for differentiation strategy and 0.500 for commodity strategy. The introduction of explanatory variables changes the probabilities as discussed below.

	Sig.	Exp(B)	(A)	(B)	(C)
Use of Contract Arrangement	0.001	3.766	0.500	0.790	0.290
EducationLevel *	0.026	1.494	0.500	0.599	0.099
Experience from diversification	0.023	1.008	0.500	0.501	0.002
Experience from generation	0.023	1.786	0.500	0.641	0.141
Family influence	0.012	0.725	0.500	0.420	-0.079

We found support to the hypothesis that contractual arrangements improve the probability to adopt a differentiation strategy (sig < 0.01). The odds ratio (Exp(B)) to differentiation strategy choice is 3.766 times greater for an owner that set contractual arrangements with coffee buyers rather than the odds ratio to differentiation strategy choice of someone that keeps market relationship with coffee buyers, all other factors being equal. Considering equal odds ratio to differentiation and commodity strategy (column A), the probability to choose a differentiation strategy increases to 0.790 (column B) if owner has contractual arrangements to coffee buyers, an increase of 0.29 percent points (column C).

We found support to the hypothesis that formal education improves the probability to adopt a differentiation strategy (sig < 0.05). Although a categorical variable, we run another logistic regression considering formal education as a continuous variable to capture the incremental effects; all other variables had no significant changes from original model 3. The increase in one level of formal education increases the probability to invest in differentiation strategy from 0.500 (column A) to 0.599 (column B).

Although we found support to the hypothesis that experience from diversification improves the probability to adopt a differentiation strategy (sig < 0.05), there is almost the same probability to adopt a commodity strategy as our assumption (column A).

We found support to the hypothesis that experience from owners' previous generations in the same business improves the probability to adopt a differentiation strategy (sig < 0.05). The odds ratio to differentiation strategy choice is 1.786 times greater for an owner with previous generations in the same business rather than the odds ratio to differentiation strategy choice of someone that started the business, all other factors being equal. Considering equal odds ratio to differentiation and commodity strategy (column A), the probability to choose a differentiation strategy increases to 0.641 (column B) if the owner has previous generations in the same business, an increase of 0.141 percent points (column C).

We found support to the hypothesis that family influence changes the probability to adopt a differentiation strategy (sig < 0.05). Moreover, we found that family influence reduces the probability to adopt a differentiation strategy. Here the interpretation of effects on levels of family influence to strategic decision is not straightforward because of treatments for original scales (z-scores and data reduction by factor analysis). Still, the results are consistent with the contradictory findings of family influence in the literature, as indicated by Murphy et al (2008), the family may also represent a source of costs to the business as result of nepotism, agency costs and conflict.

Finally, we recognize limitations in this effort to integrate the human capital analysis to SPF and TCE into an empirical study. First, a financial capital constrain may impose a bias towards a commodity strategy and the influence of human capital may be underestimated. Second, results may be biased by endogeneity problems that require further analysis. Third, we are sure that other competing or complementary explanations from, for instance, entrepreneurship and family business literature may provide new hypotheses to be tested or may condition some of our findings. Still, we expect that human capital, proposed by T. Schultz, amplifies the explanations of SPF strategic choices.

6. Final Remarks

This chapter discusses the role of the entrepreneur as an inductor of innovation (Foss & Klein 2004; Witt 1998; Casson 2005) and the source of variability in strategies and organizations of firms. To fulfill this objective, we provided an analytical framework based on arguments by Schumpeter (1926), Kirzner (1973), Knight (1964) and Schultz (1961).

We illustrated the importance of the entrepreneur in two case studies. Dr. Ernesto Ily's previous experience with the Italian fashion designer Ermenegildo Zegna and his academic background were fundamental to the establishment of an innovation both for strategy and for governance in the

Coffee Agribusiness System in Brazil. The establishment of a supply based on differentiated coffee was an innovation introduced by illycaffe in Brazil, a country that used to be a traditional commodity supplier. Regarding governance, we considered the adoption of a contest an innovation that clearly signaled a price premium for quality and created incentives for many producers to invest towards quality improvements. The second case study illustrated how Dr. Isaac's observation of management in large firms contributed to decisions at Cooxupé, particularly those regarding scale, professional management and internationalization strategies. The great innovation devised by Dr. Isaac was the establishment of direct exports from Cooxupé, which turned out to be the first cooperative to fulfill the requirements of standards and scale to reach the international markets.

Moreover, we collected data from 409 coffee producers to run a logit model. Our results support that formal education is the most important element among all of the coffee producer's attributes for adopting differentiation strategies. This corroborates Shultz's argument that education contributes to more entrepreneurial activity. Indeed, formal education is one of the differentiated attributes found in Dr. Illy and Dr. Isaac.

Shultz conceived entrepreneurial ability as a form of human capital (Klein & Cook 2006) that is an important aspect for adjustments. This is the case on which we shed light whilst focusing our investigation on the Brazilian Coffee Agribusiness System, which faced an institutional change in the late 80s. In response to this change, some coffee producers entered the differentiated coffee system, to supply illycaffè and other coffee importers, while other producers maintained their focus on commodity production. Through Knight's lenses, the entrepreneur producer is the one who has evaluation and judgment capacity under uncertain conditions. Here, we argue, Knight's and Schultz's frameworks are compatible and complementary because the more entrepreneurial ability someone accumulates (one aspect of human capital), the more judgment capacity he will have to face uncertainty and to deal with adjustments.

References

BECKER, Gary S.; TOMES, Nigel. 1986. Human Capital and the Rise and Fall of Families. *Journal of Labor Economics*, v. 4(3), p. S1-39, University of Chicago Press, July.

BHIDÉ, A. V. 2000. *The origin and evolution of new business.* New York: Oxford.

CASSOL, Mark. 2005. An entrepreneurial theory of the firm. In: *Competence, governance, and entrepreneurship.* Advance in economic strategy research. Edited by Nicolai Foss and Volker Mahnke. Oxford University Press.

CHADDAD, Fabio R. 2007. Cooxupé and the world coffee industry: strategies to increase producer income. *XXXI Encontro Nacional da ANPAD,* Rio de Janeiro.

FOSS, Nicolai; KLEIN, Peter, G. 2004. Entrepreneurship and the economic theory of the firm: any gains from trade? *Danish Researdh Unit Industrial Dynamics.* DRUID Working Paper, n. 04-12, July.

GLADWIN, Ch.; LONG, B. F.; BABB, E. M.; BEAULIEU, L. J.; MOSELEY, A.; MULKEY, D.; ZIMET, D. J. (1989). Rural entrepreneurship: one key to rural revitalization. *American Journal of Agricultural Economics,* v. 71, n. 5, p. 1305-1314.

KAHNEMAN, D.; TVERSKY, A. 1979. Prospect theory: an analysis of decision making under risk. *Econometrica,* XLVII, p. 263-291.

KIRZNER, I. M. 1973. *Competition and entrepreneurship.* Chicago: University of Chicago Press.

KLEIN, Peter G.; COOK, Michael L. 2006. T. W. Schultz and the Human-Capital Approach to Entrepreneurship. *Review of Agricultural Economics,* v. 28, n. 3, Fall 2006, p. 344-350(7).

KNIGHT, Frank H. 1964. *Risk, uncertainty and profit. Reprint of economic.* Classics. Augustus M. Kelley. New York: Bookseller.

KOR, Yasemin, Y.; MAHONEY, Joseph T.; MICHAEL, Steven C. 2007. Resources, capabilities and entrepreneurial perceptions. *Journal of Management Studies,* v. 44, n. 7, November, 1187-1212p.

LANGLOIS, Richard N. 1992. Transaction-cost economics in real time. *Industrial and Corporate Change,* v. 1, n. 1.

______. 2005. The entrepreneurial theory of the firm and the theory of the entrepreneurial firm. *Working Papers* 2005-27, University of Connecticut, Department of Economics, revised Oct 2005.

______. 2002. Schumpeter and the obsolescence of the entrepreneur. *Working Paper* 2002-19, University of Connecticut, Department of Economics.

NEVES, Marcos Fava; SAES, Maria Sylvia Macchione; REZENDE, Christiane Leles. 2003. Estudo de caso: illycaffè e os desafios do crescimento no Brasil. In: GIORDANO, Samuel Ribeiro; LELES, Christiane (Eds.). *Cadernos da universidade illy do café.* São Paulo: Universidade Illy do Café. v. 1, p. 69 -121.

PORTER, Michael E. 1985. *Competitive advantage:* creating and sustaining superior performance. New York: The Free Press.

REID, J. N. 1987. Entrepreneurship as a community development strategy for the rural south. *The rural south in crisis:* challenges for the future. Boulder CO: Westview Press, Ed. L. J. Beaulieu. p. 325-43.

SAES, Maria Sylvia Macchione. 2008. *Strategies for differentiation and quasi-rent appropriation in agriculture: the small-scale production.* <http://www.pensa.org.br/Biblioteca.aspx>.

SAES, Maria Sylvia Macchione; ISHIKAWA, Ibuki. 2007. Entrepreneurship and competitive advantage: examining the case of illycafè. *17 Th Annual IAMA World Food and Agribusiness Symposium*, Parma- Italy, June.

SARASVATHY, S. D. 2001. Causation and effectuation: toward a theoretical shift from economic inevitability to entrepreneurial contingency. Academy of Management. *The Academy of Management Review* 26(2), p. 243.

SCHUMPETER, Joseph A. 1942. *Capitalism, socialism, and democracy*. New York: Harper & Row.

______. 1926. *The theory of economic development.* Cambridge: Harvard University Press. (New York: Oxford University Press, 1961). Translation based on Schumpeter, 1934.

SCHULTZ, Theodore W. 1961. Investment in human capital'. *American Economic Review*, v. 51.

______. 1982. Investment in entrepreneurial ability. *Scandinavian J. Econ* 82, n. 4, p. 437-48.

______. 1975 The value of the ability to deal with disequilibria. *Journal of Economic Literature*, 13, n. 3, Sept, p. 827-46.

ZYLBERSZTAJN, Decio. 1996. Governance Structures and Agribusiness Coordination: a transaction cost economics based approach. Research. *Domestic and international agribusiness management.* Harvard University, Ray Goldberg Ed. v. 12, p. 245-310.

ZYLBERSZTAJN, Decio; NEVES, Marcos Fava. 1997. Illycaffè: coordenação em busca da qualidade. In: FARINA, Elizabeth Maria Mercier Querido (Coord.). *Estudos de caso em Agribusiness.* São Paulo: Pioneira/Pensa.

WILLIAMSON, Oliver E. 1985. *The economic institutions of capitalism.* New York: The Free Press.

WITT, Ulrich. 2000. Changing cognitive frames: changing organizational forms: an entrepreneurial theory of organizational development. *Industrial and Corporate Change*, v. 9, n. 4.

______. 1998. Imagination and leadership: the neglected dimension of an evolutionary theory of the firm. *Journal of Economic Behavior & Organization*, v. 35, p. 161-177.

Dutchmen in Latin America: some lessons about cross-cultural business

Gert Jan Hofstede

Jan Omvlee

1. Introduction

Cooperation between Brazil and the Netherlands has a long history. Even in these 15 years of collaboration between WU and Pensa, other joint initiatives between the Netherlands and Latin America have taken shape. Rijk Zwaan (www.rijkzwaan.com) is a company of Dutch origin that breeds and sells vegetable seeds. They operate internationally, with currently around 1200 employees who work in offices in over twenty countries on all continents. This is the story of Rijk Zwaan's entry into Latin America, and of some of the surprises the Dutch encountered. From it, lessons can be drawn for North-West Europeans and Latin Americans who wish to do business with people from one another's countries.

2. Entering Latin America

The Portuguese discovered what is now Brazil in 1500, and started a colony. But when sugar cane turned out a profitable trade, other European nations made incursions. From 1630-1654, at the height of Dutch power, a colony Nieuw Holland existed at the North-Eastern tip of Brazil. This colony flourished under the statesmanlike leadership of the young Johan Maurits van Nassau between 1637 and 1644. Johan Maurits renamed Recife to Mauritsstad and set out to make big reforms. He furthered scientific discovery, religious tolerance, and social housing. Local Portuguese settlers thrived under his rule. But when the directors of the Dutch West Indian company forbade him to continue his grand schemes, he chose to leave rather than to obey. The Dutch colony went into decline after that, and was ousted by the Portuguese ten years later.

Today, the Dutch are again active in Latin America. This chapter is about one such venture by the Dutch company RijkZwaan. Once more, the collaboration aims to profit both parties. In 1994, Rijk Zwaan decided to do a marketing study in Latin America. The aim was to find out what market potential there was for our vegetable seeds, whether it would be of sufficient interest to start activities and, if so, to develop a marketing strategy. This is the first-hand story, told by 'Jan', the export director.

2.1 The First Trip

"We did not know much about these countries. Of course we knew that they differed from the ones we were familiar with, but we had no idea how these differences would impact doing business with them. The issue of whom to choose for doing the Latin American marketing study was vital to us. Rijk Zwaan is named after its Dutch founder, but by 1994 it had internationalized into a company with subsidiaries in several European countries, including Spain. Responsibility for sales in countries outside of Europe rested with the Export department, headed by myself in the function of director of export. I led a team of export area managers. Nobody at the department of export had any experience with Latin America. That is why we decided to create a team for the marketing study that consisted of the director of export, together with the head of our Spanish subsidiary, whom we shall name Paco. This enabled us to combine my Dutch export knowledge with Paco's knowledge of the Spanish language. We also expected Paco to understand the cultures of Latin America better than I would.

Through business contacts in Spain and the Netherlands, and also through embassies, we tried to obtain interesting addresses to visit. Our first trip was to Brazil, Uruguay and Chile. Our first mistake was trying to visit too many addresses in one trip. In the 14 days of this trip we slept in 13 different hotels. Only once did we stay in the same hotel for two nights. During the day we flew from one area to another. Additionally we covered a total of 2000 kilometres in rented cars. We had severely underestimated the vastness of distances in this gigantic continent. In Europe, if you travel 200 kilometres, chances are that you are in a different country and people speak a different language. Not so in Latin America. This was a demanding trip, also physically.

Paco drove our rented cars. I served as a co-pilot and navigator, not always successfully. I noticed that it could be very dangerous to actually drive on at a green traffic light, or to stop at a red one! But we soon got used to Latin American driving habits and found our way to many potential clients and interesting relations in the various regions of the countries we visited.

One big advantage of our business is that we spend most of our time in the countryside. Melons, tomatoes and cucumbers are not grown in cities but on the vast fields of the countryside of Sinaloa, Salta, Mossoro and La Plata. We were struck by the huge differences between rich and poor. The many seasonal labourers work and live in primitive conditions. Their working days are long and monotonous, they have little time off, and they live in small, poor dwellings, often in large families. For us Europeans, this came as a shock. We have gotten used to 40-hour work weeks and good housing for everyone.

2.2 Time Management

At Rijk Zwaan Netherlands, there is a tight agenda culture: meetings start and end at previously agreed times, to allow for efficient working days. In Latin America there is more time. Everyone has or makes time to discuss matters. An appointment does not necessarily start at the appointed time. It could easily start a few hours later! The closing time is not fixed either. If it is pleasant and interesting, a meeting could lead to a shared lunch or dinner. We found that it was not helpful to start reminding our hosts that we had another meeting to go to, and we learned to let events take their natural course.

Still there were surprises. One day, when our first host of the day proposes to us to go and visit a melon field 200 kilometres away in San Fernando, we agree willingly, even if it means many hours of road, which will make us late for our afternoon meeting. But out relation's car turns out to take us not to the melons, but to a small airport near Santiago, where we board his one-motor Cessna airplane. A short time afterwards, we are admiring the melons, and back in Santiago it turns out that we are still in time for our afternoon meeting.

And so we learnt, through many errors, that que será será, whatever will be, will be, and we Dutchmen should not get worked up about changes in agendas. That would be spending our energy on the wrong things. It is better to spend our energies on building good relationships with our future business partners. Paco taught me some of this. Being Spanish he was able to bridge the gap between my usual Rijk Zwaan habits and the Latin American way of life. As I became more aware of differences in perception of time, distance and relationships, I became better able to anticipate and to avoid mistakes.

2.3 Honesty

But on one point we did not make any concessions. This is one of the central issues in our company charter, and it is about honesty in business. In selecting our partners, this was a rock-hard criterion. We looked for partners who would stay away from black money, bribery, issuing false invoices, and similar things. By luck it turned out not difficult to find such partners who shared our business values.

After the first trip, our operations in Latin America thrived and grew. Some years ago we decided to open a full subsidiary in Argentina. In Buenos Aires we were expertly advised by legalists and fiscal specialists from the Argentinean branches of internationally renowned consultancy companies. At this point there were few differences with other countries. Likewise our hiring criteria in Argentina were the same ones that we use in our other offices. During job interviews we require that candidates explicitly endorse our company charter.

2.4 Hospitality

One of the important themes in Latin America, and one that gives us great pleasure, is the hospitality of Latin Americans. In order to get a good impression of how our varieties are doing in the field, and what our growers think of them, we regularly visit the main areas of cultivation. After having visited a great number of greenhouses in the morning we are routinely invited for a big lunch party in one of the growers' stables. Many other growers and family members join in for a copious lunch with a lot of meat, many vegetables and of course generous amounts of excellent wine. In the afternoon, when we resume our greenhouse visits, the cucumbers look even more beautiful!"

3. National Culture

The chapter now takes the academic perspective once more. Can we use theory to interpret the experiences of Jan and Paco, and to predict what

Latinos might experience in the Netherlands? Yes, we can. In particular, we shall use Geert Hofstede's framework of dimensions of national culture.

3.1 Unexpected Differences

In the seventies, Geert Hofstede conducted a large-scale study of employee job satisfaction at IBM, at that time one of the world's biggest multinational companies, thought to have its own very distinctive corporate culture. He collected over a hundred thousand questionnaires from employees of all ranks and from over fifty countries. These results showed similarities when one compared across job types or gender, but large and consistent differences across countries. Apparently, despite the common corporate environment, the country where a respondent was born had an influence about his or her opinions about the importance of salary, career opportunities, opportunities for family life, relations with colleagues and with bosses, and so on.

Geert took the challenge. After years of study, he wrote the book Culture's Consequences (1980). A less academic version of his theory appeared later: Cultures and Organizations (1991). Still later Geert reworked the former of these books (Hofstede, 2001) and together with his son Gert Jan he also reworked the latter (G. Hofstede & G.J. Hofstede, 2005). These second editions include an enormous number of culture studies that have appeared since the publication of Geert's first study.

As one would expect with a widely used theory in the social sciences, there are limitations, rough edges, and controversies around Hofstede's model. For an overview of these see Kirkman et al. (2006). New and promising extensions based on data from other sources can be found in Minkov (2007). Despite its limitations the model is widely applied due to its obvious applicability for understanding our social world.

3.2 Five Dimensions of Values

At the core of this work are the five big issues of social life that are called dimensions of culture. These are the orientations that a society has taken towards basic social issues. All people have the same basic needs for belonging and for esteem, but each society has found different ways of dividing these social resources. One could call this the unwritten rules of the social game. They prescribe how to be a good boy, girl, man, boss, woman, mother, father. They are transmitted from parents and peers to children from a very tender age. These different ways of dealing with the same basic issues can be expressed in Hofstede's five dimensions. Each of them spans a continuum between two extremes. Here are the five issues and the names of the extremes:

- the social cohesion of society (individualism versus collectivism),
- relationship of subordinates to authority (large versus small power distance),
- emotional roles of men and women (masculinity versus femininity),
- attitude towards the unknown (uncertainty avoidance versus uncertainty tolerance),
- gratification of needs (short-term versus long-term orientation).

It is worthwhile understanding these dimensions, because societies do not change easily. Many readers will wonder how these cultural differences occurred in the first place. The answers to this question are usually largely hidden in historical events, some of which occurred thousands of years ago. In the case of Latin America, there is a clear influence of both the cultures of immigrants and the cultures of Indian peoples.

Cultures can change, subject to evolutionary pressures, but they only do so very slowly. Practices change all the time, but the underlying value systems resist change. Even though new technologies are invented each year and Coca-cola is sold all over the world, all citizens of the world are still not equal, and there is no evidence that they are converging. Knowledge about cultural differences today will still be valuable in fifty years. They held centuries ago; for instance, the policies initiated by Johan Maurits van Nassau in 'Nieuw Holland' in 1637 that aimed at religious tolerance and social housing are exactly the sort of things that modern Dutch governments are doing or have done in the recent past. For an account of the cultural significance of the history of the Dutch East Indies Company in the 17th century, and another argument for cultural continuity since that time, see Hofstede (2008).

Cultural differences between the Netherlands and Latin America

Table 1 shows country scores on the five dimensions for the Netherlands, the USA, Spain, and several Latin American countries. The scores are expressed as a figure that runs approximately from 0 to 100. Zero means "people in this country have a tendency to behave according to values at the minimum end of this spectrum". So for instance, the USA have a very individualistic culture, Argentina and Spain are intermediate on this dimension, while Venezuela has an extremely collectivist culture.

Table 1: culture dimension scores for selected countries

Country	Individualism	Power distance	Masculinity	Uncertainty avoidance	Long-term orientation
USA	91	40	62	46	29
Netherlands	80	38	14	53	44
Spain	51	57	42	86	19
Argentina	46	49	56	86	-
Brazil	38	69	49	76	65
Chile	23	63	28	86	-
Mexico	30	81	69	82	-
Venezuela	12	81	73	76	-

From Hofstede & Hofstede, Cultures and Organizations, 2nd edition 2005

Table 1 shows that on the dimension of individualism and also on the dimension of uncertainty avoidance, all the Latin American countries are more similar to one another and to Spain than they are to the Netherlands and to the USA. For power distance, there are big differences among the Latin countries, but they all score higher than the Netherlands and the USA. Only for masculinity, the picture is different. The Netherlands are the exception, but there is enormous variation among all the other countries with Chile being feminine, many countries being average, and Mexico and Venezuela being quite masculine. As far as long-term orientation goes, data are lacking for many countries. Brazil is likely to be an outlier here.

Countries can be quite heterogeneous internally. For Brazil this has recently been studied (G. Hofstede, Garibaldi de Hilal, Malvezzi, Tanure de Barros, & Vinken, forthcoming). Based on empirical research, the article finds four major subcultures in Brazil; yet the differences are small compared to differences with neighbouring countries. Even for a gigantic country such as Brazil, it seems that there is such a thing as a national culture.

3.3 How Culture Works

Culture is not in your brain but in your heart. Consider individualism and uncertainty avoidance. People from collectivist cultures have much more interdependent relationships, and conceive of themselves as elements of a larger structure, rather than as independent, free-moving individuals. From a collectivist perspective, time is not a resource for individuals. Time is just there. People from uncertainty avoiding cultures are more emotional in their daily life. They react with what a Dutchman would call 'emotional outbursts' to any event, whether threatening or joyful. Because North-West Europe and Latin America differ systematically on these two dimensions, there is a clear pattern for Europeans to find Latin Americans very warm and hospitable but excitable and always wasting time on socializing, and unreliable. On the other hand, Latin Americans typically find North-West Europeans reserved, unsociable, and blunt – but very efficient and hard-working. In fact almost all people from both groups are just trying to be good members of society – but according to different rules.

3.4 Explaining RijkZwaan's Experiences

Can these figures help us explain the adventures of Rijk Zwaan's export director and his Spanish friend? Yes, they can. The biggest differences are in individualism. In individualistic cultures such as the Netherlands, people are supposed to be independent and to lead their own life, do their own thing, choose their friends and partners. They spend time actively finding their own way. In collectivistic cultures, people see themselves as part of a larger whole: they have stable, long-term relationships and they spend a lot of time maintaining these relationships. So we would expect Dutch businesspeople to try and find new opportunities and casual acquaintances, and to want to be boss of their own agenda, as did Jan and Paco with their elaborate trip planning. We would expect the Spanish and the Latin Americans to spend much more time socializing and turning acquaintances into friends, and not worrying about time. This is exactly what happened to our Rijk Zwaan pioneers. They were met with more hospitality and less punctuality than they had expected, and the relationship was more important than time. Fortunately, Jan had anticipated cultural differences and taken Paco with him on the trip, and both quickly adapted. In fact they behaved as good traders, in Dutch tradition.

The high status of the Dutch also played a part. The Rijk Zwaan visitors came from a country with a smaller power distance. In the Latin countries, respect for people of high position is more important than they were used to. Jan and Paco were VIPs in the eyes of local growers. Jan probably did not quite realize just how much respect their Latin hosts paid to him. Some of the copious meals Jan mentions may have cost their hosts a small fortune –relatively more than Dutch hosts would have spent on two foreign guests.

3.5 Corruption

What about corruption and bribery? Fortunately, RijkZwaan was able to stay clear of it; but not all who do business in Latin America are so fortunate. Corruption is of course related to wealth; in a rich country such as the Netherlands, there is no economic need to engage in corrupt practices. But unfortunately, there is some corruption in every society (See the world corruption perception index at www.transparency.org). It turns out that the cultural dynamics of corruption differ according to a country's wealth (Hofstede & Hofstede, 2005). Among poorer countries, collectivistic and masculine countries are more plagued by corruption than individualistic and feminine ones. For masculinity, the logic is simple: poor countries have not got well-functioning institutions for protecting property rights. In a masculine culture people are prone to fighting instead of talking and will use the right of the strong if they can, in the absence of strong policing institutions. For individualism, the logic is that rights and rules should be the same for all, whereas in a collectivist mindset it makes all the difference whether somebody is a member of one's own group or not, and one will be more tempted to take advantage of outsiders. So the Netherlands, both very individualistic and very feminine, is one of the least corrupt countries on the world corruption perception index. A Dutch businessman might be upset about a falsified invoice when a businessman from a collectivistic culture called it 'helping out my friends'.

In countries that are at bottom EU level or higher, the relation changes, and it is uncertainty avoidance and power distance that correlate with corruption perception. Her, the logic is that uncertainty avoidance correlates with institutional distrust. One expects institutions to be untrustworthy, and so one defrauds them – this is of course a two-sided dynamic. For power distance, the logic is that in an environment of large power distance, corrupt leaders are less likely to be checked by their subordinates.

Together this picture is not very optimistic for Latin America. Sustained efforts by citizens, and excellent leaders, will be required to keep a check on corruption. But that huge topic is beyond the scope of this chapter.

4. Conclusion

This chapter has told the story of one Dutch firm's entry into the Latin American market as perceived by the first settler. It has demonstrated how traits of national cultures, i.c. Hofstede's dimensions of national culture, can be used to explain the experiences of the Dutch. By extrapolation, anybody else who bridges the Atlantic between North-West Europe and Latin America can use this knowledge to be prepared for the kind of experiences that they might have.

References

HOFSTEDE, G. 1980. *Culture's consequences, international differences in work-related values*. Beverly Hills, Ca: Sage.

______. 1991. *Cultures and organizations*. New York: McGraw Hill.

______. 2001. *Culture's consequences, comparing values, behaviors, institutions, and organizations across nations* (2nd ed.). Thousand Oaks: Sage.

HOFSTEDE, G., GARIBALDI DE HILAL, A. V., MALVEZZI, S., TANURE DE BARROS, B., & Vinken, H. (forthcoming). Comparing regional cultures within a country: lessons from Brazil. *Journal of Cross-cultural Psychology*.

HOFSTEDE, G.; HOFSTEDE, G. J. 2005. *Cultures and Organizations*. New York: Mc Graw-Hill.

HOFSTEDE, G. J. 2008. *Governance in the east indian company*. Paper presented at the System Dynamics and Innovation in Food Networks.

KIRKMAN, B. L.; LOWE, K. B.; GIBSON, C. B. 2006. A quarter century of *Culture's consequences*: a review of empirical research incorporating Hofstede's cultural values framework. *Journal of International Business Studies* 37, 285-320.

MINKOV, M. 2007. *What makes us different and similar: a new interpretation of the World Values Survey and other cross-cultural data*. Sofia: Klasika i Stil.

Does the Developed World Still Have a Competitive Edge in Innovation? A comparative study of leading food processing companies in the Shanghai area and the Netherlands

Frances T.J.M. Fortuin

S.W.F. (Onno) Omta

This chapter aims at comparing the innovativeness and competitiveness of leading food processing companies in emerging and developed economies. We asked ourselves how the clearly differing economic and social conditions of two areas that are only comparable in terms of their number of inhabitants (about 16 to 18 million), namely a fast growing emerging economy (the Shanghai area in China) and a developed economy (The Netherlands) affect competitiveness and innovation of their leading prospector companies. Our study population consisted of 31 respondents (CEOs, CTOs and R&D directors) from 18 leading prospector companies in the food processing industry: nine in the Netherlands and nine in Shanghai. We focus on how the combination of external forces exerted by actors in the network (competitors, suppliers and buyers) and internal forces (especially innovation capabilities) affect competitiveness and innovation performance of these companies. A 52-item research questionnaire, based on industrial organization theory and the Resource-Based-View, was designed for this study, including quantitative questions on innovative input and output and business performance, and qualitative questions about competitive pressure and the quality of the innovation process.

Interesting findings are that both innovative as well as business performance are predominantly related to the companies' internal (innovation) capabilities. As expected, clear differences between Chinese and Dutch companies were found regarding the external forces as well as in the internal capabilities they deploy to survive The pressure from the external environment, especially the power of buyers and the threat of new entrants is clearly felt more strongly by the Dutch companies than by their Chinese counterparts.

The Chinese companies report to significantly use more KPI's to monitor the R&D process, whereas the Dutch companies are significantly more active in stimulating an innovative culture. Interestingly, however, neither of these differences leads to significant differences in business or innovation performance between the two groups in our study.

In the introduction we asked the question whether agri-food companies in developed economies still have a competitive edge compared to those in emerging economies, such as China. The answer that emerges from the data collected so far points in the direction of the disappearance of the traditional advantage of the companies from developed economies: no significant differences could be found neither in innovation performance, nor in business performance among the companies from the Netherlands and the Shanghai region in China.

1. Introduction

According to the Economist (2007-11-15) the world is experiencing one of the biggest revolutions in history, as economic power shifts from the developed world to China, Brazil and other emerging economies. Fueled by relative low income levels and economic liberalization (Hoskisson et al., 2000) these emerging economies are growing much faster than the developed ones, there is a widening gap between their growth rate and that of the developed world (see Figure 1). The reader should realize, however, that current growth figures will be (much) lower, both for the developed as well as for the emerging economies, because of the recent economic crises. Emerging economies account for approximately one-third of the world's GDP and about half of global GDP-growth at market exchange rates. Their exports are about 45% of the world total; they consume over half of the world's energy and have accounted for four-fifths of the growth in oil demand in the past five years.

Cheap labor, availability of raw materials, geographical location combined with the possibility of opening new markets were the traditional reasons for multinational companies to invest in production sites in developing economies. However, international investments were accompanied by knowledge and technology transfer to the receiving economies. As multinational companies were involved in direct business contacts with local enterprises (e.g. as suppliers and buyers) their activities contributed to upgrading local business, as domestic companies were forced to innovate in order to survive. Often, domestic companies copied innovations and management instruments of the multinational companies. As a consequence, also the innovation capabilities and the international competitiveness of these economies increased (Hendriks-Gusc 2007).

Figure 1: Percentage increase of GDP compared to previous year

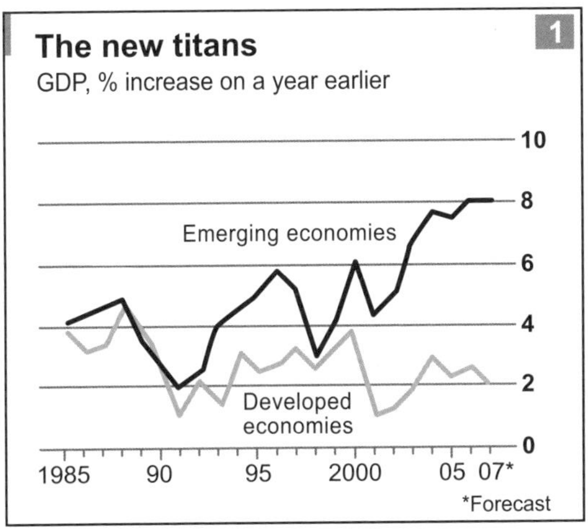

Source: IMF

It is increasingly recognized that innovation has become essential for food processing companies to maintain competitive in the fast globalizing world [e.g. Traill and Meulenberg, 2002, Fortuin et al 2007]. Traditionally, innovation activities were conducted in the central R&D labs of the large multinational agri-food companies in the developed world. However, nowadays:

- multinational companies increasingly shift parts of there R&D to countries with emerging economies;
- companies in emerging economies develop there own innovative capabilities and increasingly compete on national and global markets with the established multinationals.

We asked ourselves whether agri-food companies in developed economies still have an competitive edge compared to those in emerging economies, such as China. To investigate this, we conducted a comparative study including nine leading food processing companies in the Netherlands and nine located in the Shanghai region in China. Both locations have approximately the same number of inhabitants (about 16.5 million in The Netherlands and 18 million in the Shanghai region), are both characterized by a strong international focus, with large international airports and the largest (Shanghai) and the second largest (Rotterdam) sea harbor in the world, while the agri-food sector in The Netherlands is generally acknowledged as one of the strongest in the world. Similarly, China is seeing a rapid growth in demand for high-quality food and beverage products as national income increases [Boel 2007].

We have structured this chapter as follows. Section 2 describes the theoretical foundation of the study. Section 3 presents the conceptual model, its operationalization into the research questionnaire, and the methods of data collection. Section 4 introduces the food processing industry and the study sample in the Netherlands and in Shanghai and a summary of the main results of the study is presented. Finally, in Section 5 the conclusions are drawn, and we elaborate on how they can be used for future collaboration.

2. Theoretical Background

In this chapter innovation is defined in the broad sense, as proposed by Schumpeter (1934):

> ... any doing things differently in the realm of economic life.... He elaborates this by stating: The introduction of a new good -that is one with which consumers are not yet familiar- or of a new quality of a good. 2) The introduction of a new method of production, which need by no means be founded upon a discovery scientifically new, and can also exist in a new way of handling a commodity commercially. 3) The opening of a new market that is a market into which the particular branch of manufacture of the country in question has not previously entered, whether or not this market has existed before. 4) The conquest of a new source of supply of raw materials or half-manufactured goods, again irrespective of whether this source already exists or whether it has first to be created. 5) The carrying out of the new organization of any industry, like the creation of a monopoly position (for example through trustification) or the breaking up of a monopoly position.'

Essentially, according to Schumpeter, innovation is about change; changes in the products and/or services of a company and in the way the company produces them, but also changes in business models, management techniques, and organizational structures [Hamel and Prahalad, 1994]. There are degrees of change; from only minor incremental improvements, adaptations or refinements of existing products and processes to very radical changes leading to totally new products or new production processes [Tidd *et al.* 1997].

The innovation process is not a simple linear sequence of functional activities. In the '*Fifth Generation*' model, Rothwell [1992] considers the innovation process as an interactive and co-operative phenomenon in which actors from inside and outside the firm participate. Competitive advantage depends on the firm's ability to integrate, build and reconfigure internal and external resources to address rapidly changing environments.

It is important to note that innovation is not the same as invention. In general, an invention refers to the result of research activities (e.g. a patent), while an innovation is a commercial product, process or service. Martin (1985) describes it as follows: *An invention may be viewed as a new idea or concept, but this invention only becomes an innovation when it is transformed into a socially usable product.* In the present study we assess the company's innovativeness in the broad sense of Schumpeter, including innovativeness in marketing, product design, product quality etc. The in-depth analyses, however, concentrate on product innovation, because this came out as the major field of innovation in the investigated companies.

To gain an understanding of the role of innovation in the food-processing industry we turn to the two main theoretical perspectives that acknowledge the important role of innovation for creating competitive advantage: the Industrial Organization Theory and the Resource Based View. Industrial organization theorists [e.g., Milgrom and Robberts, 1990] emphasize the importance of industry forces that provide opportunities for competitive advantage, defined as a positional advantage derived by a firm, which, compared to competition, provides its customers with lower costs or perceived uniqueness. The industry environment can be characterized by its degree of turbulence, complexity, dynamics and (un-)predictability [Lawrence and Lorsch, 1967]. The main forces affecting companies in an industry are summarised by Porter's [1985] 'five-major-forces' framework: (1) rivalry among existing firms, (2) threat of new entrants, (3) threat of substitute products or services,

(4) bargaining power of suppliers, and (5) bargaining power of buyers. The interplay of these five forces is thought to determine the boundaries of a firm's competitive strategy. The competitive forces model can help a firm to position itself in an industry so that it can best defend itself or influence the forces at play in its favor.

In contrast to the Industrial Organization perspective, the Resource-Based View (RBV) takes the firm's own resources (including the firm's financial, physical, and organizational assets), competencies (skills and knowledge), and capabilities (management systems) as the starting point for gaining competitive advantage [e.g., Barney, 1991]. This perspective focuses on a firm's internal resources and how these are acquired from factor markets, e.g., the labor and financial markets. In contrast to the industrial perspective that views resources as immediately accessible, the RBV stresses the inherent immobility or stickiness of valuable factors of production and the time and costs required to accumulate those resources [Peteraf, 1993]. This causes firms to be idiosyncratic because throughout their history they accumulate different physical assets and, often more importantly, acquire different intangible organizational assets of tacit learning and dynamic routines [Dosi, 1988]. Competitive imitation of these assets is only possible through the same time-consuming process of irreversible investment or learning that the firm itself underwent [Dierickx and Cool, 1989].

A number of factors have been identified in literature as drivers, cq, barriers, to innovation success. Fortuin [2007] points at the importance of strategic alignment between innovation and business. Strategic alignment is finding the right balance between the relevant contingencies in the business environment and the firm's internal resources, competencies, and capabilities. Innovation can only fulfill its role as a strategic tool when the innovation process is closely linked to the internal competencies and capabilities of the firm and when innovation projects are well aligned with the market needs and technological opportunities. For an effective internal innovation process, its structuring, using stage gates, and key performance indicators (KPIs), is a first priority [Cooper, 1999]. Many studies have pointed at the importance of cross-functional communication for innovation success [e.g., Little, 1991; Griffin, 1997]. From a study of the American Management Association (AMA) including 1,396 executives of large multinational companies in North America and Europe it was concluded that customer centricity, teamwork, and cooperation, together with the appropriate resources (time and money) and organizational communication are the most important drivers of innovation [Jamrog, 2006]. The ability to select the right ideas and freedom to innovate are other factors that play an important role.

Successful innovating companies, however, do not have to rely on internal competencies alone when it comes to innovation. According to Chesbrough [2003], innovative companies increasingly realize that the 'closed' model of innovation, in which the internal R&D department exclusively provides for new products and processes to foster the company's growth, does not work any more in the current highly dynamic business environment. Indeed, as proven empirically by Caloghirou et al. [2004], interacting with external partners enables a firm to access a variety of new knowledge that increases its innovation performance. Under the paradigm of open innovation, R&D results that otherwise would have gone unutilized are transferred across the firm's boundary, for example, by out licensing to another company or in a joint venture, or by spinning out and launching a new venture that uses the technology. Similarly, a firm may license in technologies created by other firms that are useful to its own core business. e.g., by forming alliances with start-up firms or building own internal venturing groups of senior managers scouting for new ideas, products and processes to fill the R&D pipeline. Huston and Sakkab [2006] refer to this new paradigm of open innovation as 'Connect and Develop', instead of 'Research and Develop'.

3. Innovation in the Food Processing Industry

In the present study we focus on the food processing industry. In this industry, companies increasingly have to compete on the basis of new and more advanced products. Studies show that new food products are more successful in the market than line extensions and me-too products, that generally deliver only short term, low-margin benefits (Knox et al. 2001; Van Trijp and Meulenberg 1996; Hoban 1998; ECR Europe 1999). In the past, food processing companies tended to focus on minimizing production costs with little attention for customer benefits [Lienhard, 2004]. Recently, a change in focus can be observed within the industry, which makes it more directed at creating products that match consumer demands. This phenomenon is known as 'chain reversal', a change from a supply-based approach to a demand-based approach. In this process of creating products that align with consumer demands innovation clearly plays a key role.

It is important to realize that most insights in the key success and failure factors of innovation are based on research in high-tech industries, such as the computer, biotech, or pharmaceutical industry, where other industries, for instance, supplier dominated industries such as the food processing industry, remained largely unexplored. Recently, some empirical work has emerged on innovation in the food processing industry. Batterink et al. [2006] have indicated that successful innovating food processing companies have a strong market orientation, while economic considerations and insufficient innovation competencies are the main barriers to innovation in this industry, which was also found by Garcia Martinez & Briz [2000]. Costa and Jongen [2006] list as major barriers to food innovation a lack of concrete guidelines for the effective implementation of consumer oriented food development, a sequential approach of the innovation process and a lack of intra- and inter-organizational coordination or integration of R&D and Marketing activities and know-how. Customer orientation was also identified as one of the main critical success factors for innovation in a comparative study of over 80 innovation projects in 12 multinational agrifood prospector companies in the Netherlands and France [Fortuin et al., 2007]. Although there is limited evidence on the use of open innovation in the agrifood sector to date, its potential for the sector with its many chain and network ties should not be underestimated.

3.1 Comparing Food Processing in the Netherlands and the Shanghai area in China

The Dutch food processing industry plays an important role in the Dutch economy. According to the CIAA (2006) report, it comprises about 4500 firms, employing 135,400 people. In 2003, about 66% of the people working in the sector was employed in the 245 largest companies (LEI, 2006). Its contribution to the total Dutch industry in percentage of net turnover in that year was about 27%, and its contribution to the Dutch manufacturing employment amounted to 20% with 95,000 employees. In 2004 the Dutch food processing industry had a turnover of 39 € billion, and a gross value added of € 11.3 billion. The Netherlands is very export-oriented, 46% of net turnover is based on export income. It is the third largest food-ingredients exporter in the world, just after the US and France. Many important multinational companies have their headquarters in the Netherlands, and several international companies have strong operations in the country. This makes it one of the biggest players in the EU. In 2005 six Dutch companies belonged to the Top-25 of European food processing companies. Unilever is by far the largest Dutch food processor, with an annual turnover of nearly 40 € billion, of which 1.2 billion is earned in the Netherlands. Its total number of employees worldwide is 206,000. Other large firms are Heineken, VION, and Campina-Friesland Foods. Also in terms of innovation the Dutch food processing industry is performing very well, as seven Dutch companies belong to the Top-20 EU companies according to their R&D-investments (CIAA 2006).

In China, the food processing industry is one of the most important industries. In 2002, the food processing industry accounted for € 95.7 billion, being 9.7% of China's total GDP [Walsh and Li, 2004]. From 2000 to 2005, the total gross value, the total industrial added value and the revenues maintained an annual growth rate of around 18%. In some main sectors such as grain, oil, processed meat, and dairy sectors, the growth rates of industrial added values and revenues exceeded 20 % annually (10th five year plan of the Chinese food processing industry). However, the sales and added value of the food processing industry show large regional disparities, the coastal region around Shanghai being one of the best performing ones in China [Walsh and Li, 2004]. This region has a high population density and comparably high income life level in the coast region guarantees a strong market pull for the food processing industry [Walsh and Li, 2004]. Especially after China entered the WTO, the Shanghai region was given priority to form a mature economic market in China. It is said *Shanghai covers less than 0.1 percent of China's land mass and nonetheless provides 5.2 percent of the country's GDP and 9.8 percent of the export value* [Asia Times, 2003]. Looking at the analysis of the life expenditures in Shanghai, it can be seen that food purchases represent the largest expenditure of consumer expenditure. Urban households currently spend 39% of their annual living expenditure on food purchases.

4. Study Design

4.1 Conceptual Model

In Section 2 we argued, that two theoretical perspectives are relevant to gain an understanding of the role of innovation in the food-processing industry: the Industrial Organization Theory and the Resource Based View. From these theories the concepts relevant for the present study were derived and brought together in the conceptual model, depicted in Figure 2. This model is discussed below.

Figure 2: Conceptual model

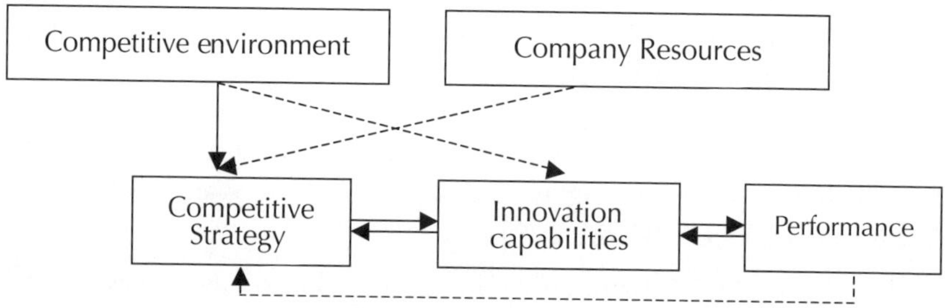

From Industrial Organization Theory it is expected, that the company's business performance will be dependent on the opportunities and constraints of its competitive environment. When opportunities become scarcer, and constraints higher, a company will try to find or even create a new environment by developing an innovation strategy. This however, we assume will not automatically lead to new business success. We assume that a company's innovation performance (and ultimately its business performance) is dependent on the way in which it is able to put its innovation strategy into action. Based on the Resource-based View, we expect that this will be dependent on the following factors: the resources it makes available for innovation, whether it is able to make the right choices regarding on which R&D projects these resources will be spent (strategic alignment), and its capability to effectively manage the innovation process. If this is all done well, it will lead to a higher innovation performance, which will in turn raise the overall business performance, and may ultimately change the competitive environment of the company. By selecting leading prospector companies we aim at getting a homogeneous study population of companies that intentionally pursue an active innovation strategy.

The concept of strategy in the present study is investigated using the research variables of prospector strategy, strategic focus and open innovation. Prospector strategy refers to one of the four generic strategy types as identified by Miles and Snow (1978) namely the one in which companies want to be at the forefront of innovation, in order to be able to reap the initially high profits associated with customer acceptance of a new or greatly improved product. This variable is operationalized as the extent to which the company is striving for market leadership and the importance it attaches to innovation as a tool for achieving and maintaining this goal. We use the research variable of strategic focus to assess how the strategy is operationalized in concrete choices regarding price, quality, speed to market, customers, technology, or product uniqueness. The research variable of open innovation (Chesbrough, 2003) is added to assess in how far a company uses external sources to make full use of its innovation potential. This research variable is operationalized as the percentage of the total R&D budget that is allocated for external research (in universities or research institutes, or in other specialized companies), and the extend to which a company is engaged in strategic alliances and joint ventures

To investigate the *competitive environment* of the company, the research variables of stability, opportunities and constraints are used. Stability refers to the safety of the business environment, as provided by the institutional environment, the predictability of consumer trends and desires and the predictability of competitors (Lawrence and Lorsch, 1967). Opportunities are assessed in terms of market and investment opportunities, and constraints, in terms of the power of suppliers, of buyers, the influence of available substitutes, the threat of new entrants and the number of competitors, as reflected in Porter's five forces framework (Porter, 1985).

The concept of *innovation resources* comprises the tangible and intangible resources that form the inputs for the innovation process. The research variable of tangible resources is assessed by collecting data on the R&D expenditures of the companies as percentage of total sales. The research variable of intangible resources is operationalized as the respondent's subjective assessment of protection that the products and processes of the company receive, and the educational level of the emplyees, both as compared to the competition.

Strategic alignment, defined as finding the right balance between the relevant contingencies in the business environment and the firm's internal resources, competencies, and capabilities (Fortuin, 2007) Is investigated through the research variable of external alignment (operationalized as monitoring of customer needs), and the variable of internal alignment (operationalized as the extend to which corporate and business unit managers are involved in the selection of R&D projects).

Once the resources are available, and the choices for R&D projects are made, the extend to which the company is able to effectively manage the innovation process, in this study termed innovation capabilities, becomes essential. To investigate the *innovation capabilities* we use the research variables of innovation process management, internal and external R&D communication, and human resource management. The variable of innovation process management is operationalized as the respondent's subjective assessment of overall quality of the R&D process, the use of Key Performance Indicators (KPI's) to monitor the process and the extend to which at the end of each innovation project the lessons learned are recorded. Internal R&D communication is operationalized as the extend to which there is a cross-functional screening process for market and technology opportunities, the extend to which market information is passed on to R&D, and the quality of the communication between R&D and marketing, manufacturing, and purchasing. External R&D communication is operationalized as the quality of the communication of R&D with the main suppliers and buyers. The variable of *innovative culture* is operationalized as the presence of efficient reward systems and motivation drivers for innovation, and the extend to which the company tries to lower the burden of administrative regulations and restrictions.

The concept of *innovation performance* is investigated using the research variables of innovativeness, time to market and R&D performance. The variable of innovativeness is operationalized as the respondent's subjective assessment on the level of innovativeness of their company in marketing, product design, product quality, distribution and manufacturing. The variable of time to market is operationalized as the respondent's assessment of their company's flexibility of market response, and the extent to which the new products of their company reach the market before those of competitors. R&D performance is operationalized as how satisfactory the return on R&D investment is according to the respondents.

The concept of *business performance* is investigated using qualitative subjective assessments of the respondents on the research variables of sales volume, financial performance and overall performance. The variable of sales volume is operationalized as the current sales volume relative to competitors and the expected sales growth in the coming three years; financial performance is operationalized as the company's financial position relative to competitors, the profitability relative to competitors and the company's growth rate relative to competitors. Overall performance is operationalized by asking the respondent's judgement on their company's general position as compared to competitors and its reputation in the market.

The research questionnaire, based on these concepts, contains a first section of 10 questions where respondents are asked to provide factual information about their organizations (i.e., total revenues, operating profit margin, R&D spending, number of (R&D) employees). The remainder of the questionnaire contains 43 questions, asking for judgements of the respondents, using seven-point Likert scales, ranging from strongly disagree (1) to strongly agree (7). Structured interviews with at least one respondent per company were used to cross-check the information as well as to gain deeper insight into the innovation management issues covered by the research questionnaire.

4.2 Data Collection

The data were collected in spring 2007. Thirty of the most innovative food processing companies (fifteen In the Netherlands and fifteen in Shanghai) received an invitation letter to participate in the study and a copy of the research questionnaire. For the Chinese companies all questions in the questionnaire appeared in English as well as in Chinese. As an incentive to participate an individualized report was offered to each company, in which their results would be compared to the findings of the entire sample. All companies were then approached by phone in order to confirm their participation. Nine Dutch and nine Chinese companies accepted the invitation to participate in the research. The resulting study population consisted of 31 respondents (CEO's, CTO's and R&D directors), one to three per company. Data were collected not only based on the answers to the questionnaires, but also during on-site interviews with the CTO and/or R&D director of each company.

5. Results

5.1 Base Line Description

Table 1 presents the baseline description of the participating companies. The participating companies from the Shanghai region are smaller than those from the Netherlands, but are leading in their region. They also report a higher operating profit margin. The R&D staff varies from 0.3% to 11%, with most companies having an R&D staff of about 1% of the total number of employees.

Table 1: Baseline description of the participating companies (range)

Companies	Shanghai	The Netherlands
Sales Volume	20 € Million – 0.7 € Billion	0.1 – 39 €Billion
Operating profit margin	10 – 30%	5 – 13%
Number of employees	80 – 10,000	300 – 200,000
R&D employees	4 – 200	10 – 8,000

Of the nine participating companies in the Shanghai area two produce dairy products, two confectionary, two ingredients and flavor, one company produces canned food, one processed meat and the last produces frozen food. Five companies are publicly-listed, three are privately owned and one is (still) owned by the government. Five companies are headquartered in China, two in the EU and two in Japan and Taiwan. All companies primarily focus on the regional and national market with on average 6 to 7 subsidiaries in other areas in China.

Of the nine companies participating from the Netherlands seven are large multinational food processing companies with a Dutch (five) or USA headquarters (two). The latter two have major operations in the Netherlands. Their annual sales volume (far) exceeds 1 € Billion. The other two are smaller Dutch prospector companies with minor multinational operations. The biggest two companies are diversified food producers, two are ingredient suppliers, the other five are specialized in meat processing, bakery, soups, salads, and dairy.

5.2 Correlations in the Research Model

First the total study sample was used to test in how far the correlations reflect the expectations as laid out in the conceptual model (see Figure 1). To this end two linear regression analyses were performed: one with innovation performance and one with business performance as the dependent variable.

A linear regression analysis over the total study sample using time to market as the dependent variable and predictability of the task environment, external strategic alignment, and internal R&D communication as the independent variables showed that 68% of the total variance of the extend to which these companies are able to have their new products enter the market faster than competitors can be explained by the extend to which consumer trends and desires are easy to forecast; the importance attached to monitoring in how far their products align to their customers' needs, and the quality of the communication between R&D and marketing (see Table 2).

Table 2: Stepwise linear regression concerning innovation performance ($R^{2\ adjusted}$: 68%)

Dependent variable:
- Our new products enter the market faster compared to our main competitors' products

Independent variables:
- Predictability of the task environment (consumer trends and desires are easy to forecast).
- External strategic alignment (we monitor on a regular basis the extent to which our products and processes align to our customers' needs).
- R&D – marketing communication (there is an excellent communication between R&D and marketing)

A lineair regression analysis over the total study sample using the financial position of the company relative to its competitors as the dependent variable and the importance the company attaches to innovation, the systems it has in place to stimulate an innovative climate, and the quality of the communication of corporate R&D with their internal business unit customers and with the external buyers as the independent variables, showed that 58% of the total variance of the dependent variable can be explained by the three independent variables of innovation strategy, innovative culture and communication (see Table 3).

Table 3: Stepwise linear regression concerning business performance ($R^{2\ adjusted}$: 58%)

Dependent variable:
– Our company distinguishes itself positively compared to our main competitors by a strong financial position.
Independent variables:
– Innovation is important in our company in maintaining competitiveness.
– Our company has efficient reward procedures and motivation drivers to stimulate innovation.
– The progress of all R&D projects is communicated regularly to the business units clients.
– There is an excellent communication between R&D and our main buyers.

These findings give strong support for the proposed relations in the conceptual model.

5.3 Comparison of the Chinese and Dutch Companies

The comparison of the respondents' assessment of the task environment (Table 5) shows two interesting results. The Shanghai as well as the Dutch respondents assess the predictability of the competitive environment as relatively high, they think that actions of competitors are not very hard to predict. The mean value of both groups amounts to exactly the same 4.4 on the 7 point Likert scale. In the constraints posed by the competitive environment, however, we see a clear difference: the Dutch respondents assess the bargaining power of buyers as significantly higher and number of substitutes for their products as very significantly higher than their Shanghai colleagues.

Table 4: Comparison of the respondents' assessment of the predictability and constraints of the competitive environment (means, 7 point Likert scales)

Question	Shanghai	NL	t-test
Actions of competitors are easy to predict	4.2	4.4	
The bargaining power of our business buyers has a strong influence on the business results of our company	4.9	5.9	**
The number of substitutes for our products is very low (1) to very high (7)	3.5	4.8	**

Tables 4 through 7: * $p < 0.1$; ** $p < 0.05$; *** $p < 0.01$

No significant differences were found in the research variables of prospector strategy and strategic focus (Table 5). There was a strong consensus among all participating companies about the strategic importance of innovation. The answer to the question 'innovation is important to our company in maintaining competitiveness' showed the highest mean of all Likert seven-point scale questions (6.3 for the Shanghai companies and 6.0 for the Dutch ones). The importance of innovation in maintaining competitiveness was also confirmed by the contents of the interviews, with most respondents stating that innovation is essential for the survival of their products and brands. Both groups of companies also attach high importance to the aim of achieving market leadership (an average of 5.0 for the Shanghai and of 5.1 for the Dutch companies). This strategic choice is reflected in the strategic focus of the participating companies: all participants stated that design and launch of new products was the top priority of their R&D investments. Process development was mentioned as the second most important priority, increasing the efficiency of the existing processes as third.

The fact that no significant differences were found in the type of strategy or the strategic focus of the companies under study, indicates that they all fulfill the inclusion criteria, as formulated in Section 3.2.

The variable of open innovation Showed a mixed result. no significant difference was found in the percentage of the total R&D budget being used for external research (around 10% in both groups). The answer to the question ‘ Our company uses joint ventures and alliances to make full use of our R&D capabilities’ however, shows a significant difference, with the shanghai companies indicating this was more important (an average of 4.79 on the 7 point Likert scale) than the Duch ones (3.27). When comparing the dutch sample with Shanghai participants from companies headquartered in china however, the difference becomes smaller and is no longer significant. Probably the higher score for open innovation through alliances and joint ventures for these companies must be explained as mainly an exchange with the foreign parent company.

Table 5: Comparison of the strategy of the participating companies (means, 7 point Likert scales).

Question	Shanghai	NL	t-test
Innovation is important in our company in maintaining competitiveness	6.3	6.0	
Our firm fights the competition and is directed towards market dominance	5.0	5.1	
Our company uses joint ventures and alliances to make full use of our R&D capabilities	4.9	3.3	***

Table 6 shows that the tangible resources available for the innovation process, namely the R&D budget as percentage of total sales is relatively high in all investigated companies: 2.1 % for the Shanghai companies and 1.8% for the Dutch ones. This is substantially higher than the European average of 0.24% and the USA average of 0.35% (CIAA, 2005). The high level of resources available for innovation also supports the general characteristic of the sampled companies as prospector companies.

Overall the innovation resources are found to be somewhat higher in the Shanghai companies than in the Dutch ones. Only in one item, namely patent protection, this difference was found to be significant. When splitting the shanghai sample into China based companies and foreign based companies the china based ones are found to report the highest protection (4.3 vs 3.7 on a 7 point Likert scale). Perhaps this should be interpreted as a higher dependency on licences in the Chinese companies.

Table 6: Innovation resources (means, 7 point Likert scales)

Question	Shanghai	NL	t-test
Our company distinguishes itself positively compared to our main competitors by the protection that our products and processes receive by patents, licensees etc.	4.0	2.6	***
Our company distinguishes itself positively compared to our main competitors by the educational level of our employees	4.5	3.8	*

In how far a company is able to make the right choices regarding on which R&D projects the investments in innovation resources will be spent depends heavily on the availability of relevant information from the internal as well as the external environment. As can be seen in Table 7, the Shanghai companies seem to put more effort in collecting this information, although the differences found are not significant.

Table 7: Comparison of the respondents' assessment of efforts made to secure strategic alignment (means, 7 point Likert scales)

Question	Shanghai	NL	t-test
We monitor on a regular basis the extent to which our products and processes align to our customers' needs	5.9	4.8	**
Corporate managers and BU managers actively participate in the selection of R&D projects	5.3	4.9	

The results on innovative capabilities presented in Table 8, show that the Shanghai respondents consistently assess the indicators for the variable of innovation process management and for the variable of the level of internal R&D communication higher than their Dutch colleagues. They assess the effectiveness of the overall R&D process significantly, and the use of KPI's and learning from previous innovation projects very significantly higher than the respondents from the Netherlands. The internal R&D communication with marketing is assessed somewhat, but not significantly, higher, the communication with manufacturing is assessed significantly and that with purchasing very significantly higher by the Shanghai respondents than by the Dutch ones. No significant differences were found in the variable of external R&D communication with suppliers and business buyers. The Dutch respondents however clearly rate the level of measures taken to stimulate an innovative culture higher than the Shanghai respondents. This is interesting, because in an international comparative study performed ten years ago, the effectiveness of reward systems in Dutch companies was still assessed lower, and the level of restrictions posed on R&D higher than in other countries (Fortuin, 2007).

Table 8: Comparison of the respondents' assessment of their company's innovative capabilities (means, 7 point Likert scales)

Question	Shanghai	NL	t-test
Our company distinguishes itself positively compared to our main competitors by an effective R&D process	5.1	4.0	**
KPIs are used to monitor the innovation processes	5.1	3.4	***
We consistently codify the lessons learnt at the end of innovation projects	4.7	3.3	**
There is an excellent communication between R&D and marketing	4.9	4.0	
There is an excellent communication between R&D and manufacturing	5.5	4.6	**
There is an excellent communication between R&D and purchasing	5.0	3.9	**
Our company has efficient reward procedures and motivation drivers to stimulate innovation	4.9	3.7	**
Few restrictions are imposed on R&D by administrative regulations (e.g. regarding travel, budget, etc.)	3.7	4.6	

The research variable of innovation performance showed little differences between the assessments of Shanghai and the Dutch respondents. The innovativeness of their company relative to that of competitors in marketing was assessed somewhat higher by the respondents from Dutch companies,

(3.5 Shanghai respondents vs 4.3 Dutch respondents), the innovativeness in product design, distribution and manufacturing somewhat higher by the respondents from the companies in Shanghai. They also assessed the flexibility of market response of their companies higher than did the Dutch respondents, although this difference was not significant (4.8 vs 4.3). The research variable of return to R&D investment showed no difference between the two groups.

Also for the research variable of business performance no significant differences could be found between the Dutch and the Chinese companies, which is surprising when one keeps in mind the differences found in the external forces as well as in the internal capabilities deployed between the two groups of companies. We will discuss this finding more in detail in Section 5.

6. Discussion and Conclusions

Interesting findings are that both innovative as well as business performance are predominantly related to the companies' internal (innovation) capabilities. Linear regression shows that innovation performance in terms of faster market entrance of new products is positive related to better alignment of new products to customers' needs, combined with the ability to forecast consumer trends and the quality of R&D-marketing communication. Business performance in terms of the companies' strong financial position is related to the importance the firm attaches to innovation, the systems they have to stimulate an innovative climate, and the quality of the communication of corporate R&D with their business unit customers and their external buyers.

As expected, clear differences between Chinese and Dutch companies were found regarding the external forces as well as in the internal capabilities they deploy to survive The pressure from the external environment, especially the power of buyers and the threat of new entrants is clearly felt more strongly by the Dutch companies than by their Chinese counterparts. Chinese companies make significantly more use of joint ventures and license agreements with international partners, and report (as a consequence) that their products receive better protection by patents and licenses. In terms of internal innovation capabilities the Chinese companies report to have a significantly more effective R&D process as compared to their competitors. They also report to significantly use more KPI's to monitor the R&D process and make more consistent use of lessons learned at the end of each project. The Dutch companies are significantly more active in stimulating an innovative culture by reward systems and motivation drivers. Interestingly, however, neither of these differences leads to significant differences in business or innovation performance between the two groups in our study.

In the introduction we asked the question whether agri-food companies in developed economies still have a competitive edge compared to those in emerging economies, such as China. The answer that emerges from the data collected so far points in the direction of the disappearance of the traditional advantage of the companies from developed economies: no significant differences could be found neither in innovation performance, nor in business performance among the companies from the Netherlands and the Shanghai region in China. When looking at the internal capabilities, it can even be expected, that in the near future the Shanghai companies might gain an advantage over the Dutch ones, because of their higher scores on a number of internal factors proven in this same study to correlate so strongly with innovation performance.

References

BARNEY, J. (1991), Firm resources and sustained competitive advantage, *Journal of Management*, 17, 99-120.

BATTERINK, M.H., E.F.M. Wubben, and S.W.F. Omta (2006). Factors related to innovative output in the Dutch agrifood industry. *Journal on Chain and Network Science*, 6(1): 31-45.

CALOGHIROU, Y., Kastelli and A. Tsakanikas (2004). Internal Capabilities and External Knowledge Sources: Complements or Substitutes for Innovative Performance? *Technovation*, 24, 29-39.

CHESBROUGH, H.W. (2003). *Open Innovation: The New Imperative for Creating and Profiting from Technology*, , Cambridge, Mass: Harvard Business School Press.

China Statistical Yearbook on Science and Technology, 2007. China Statistics Press, Beijing.

CIAA, (2006). *Data and Trends of the European Food Industry,* CIAA, Brussels

COOPER, R. (1999). The Invisible Success Factors in Product Innovation. *Journal of Product Innovation Management*, 16, 115-133.

COSTA, A.I.A. and W.M.F. Jongen (2006). New insights into consumer-led food product development. *Trends in Food Science & Technology*, 17(8): 457.

CUI, S. 2008, Feeding frenzy. China's budding food industry faces global scutinity, Business Forum China, Special issue: A Culinary Evolution. *China's Changing Consumption Habits*, 4, July-August, 10-15.

DIERICKX, I. and K. Cool (1989). Asset Stock Accumulation and Sustainability of Competitive Advantage. *Management Science*, 35(12), 1504-1511.

DOSI, G., 1988. Sources, Procedures and Microeconomic Effects of Innovation. *J. Econ. Lit.*, 26, 1120-1171.

ECR Europe (1999) Efficient product introductions: the development of value-creating relationships, *Report of the findings of the Efficient Consumer Response Europe initiative*, by Ernst & Young and AC Nielsen.

FORTUIN, F.T.J.M. (2007), *Strategic Alignment of Innovation to Business. Balancing exploration and exploitation in short and long life cycle industries.* Wageningen, The Netherlands: Wageningen Academic Publishers.

FORTUIN, F.T.J.M., M. Batterink and S.W.F. Omta (2007). Key success factors of innovation in multinational agrifood prospector companies, *International Food & Agribusiness Management Review*, 10(4), 1-24.

GARCIA MARTINEZ, M. and J. Briz (2000). Innovation in the Spanish food & drink industry. *The International Food and Agribusiness Management Review*, 3(2): 155

GRIFFIN, A. (1997). PDMA Research on new Product Development Practices: Updating Trends and Benchmarking Best Practices. *Journal of Product Innovation Management*, 14, 429-458

HAMEL, G. and Prahalad, C.K. (1994). *Competing for the Future.* Harvard Business School Press, Boston, Mass.

HENDRIKS-GUSC, J.S. (2007). *Headquarters-subsidiary relationship governance in emerging markets of Central Eastern Europe. A study in Poland.*

International chains and networks series – Vol 2. Wageningen, The Netherlands: Wageningen Academic Publishers.

HOBAN, T.J. (1998) Improving the success of new product development, *Food Technology*, 52, 46-49.

HOSKISSON, R. E., Eden, L., Lau, C. M., & Wright, M. (2000). Strategy in emerging economies. *Academy of Management Journal*, 43, 249-267.

HUSTON, L. and Sakab, N. (2006). Connect and Develop: Inside Procter & Gamble's New Model for Innovation. *Harvard Business Review*, March, 60-72

JAMROG, J.J. (2006). *The Quest for Innovation: A Global Study of Innovation Management 2005-2016*, Human Resource Institute, Tampa, FL: University of Tampa.

KNOX, B., H. Parr and B. Bunting (2001) Model of 'best practice' for the food industry. In *Proceedings of the British Nutrition Society*, 60, 169a.

LAWRENCE, P.R. and J.W. Lorsch (1967). *Organization and Environment: Managing Differentiation and Integration.* Boston, Mass.: Harvard University Press.

LIENHARDT (2004). *The Food Industry in Europe, Statistics in Focus – Industry, trade and services*, 39/2004, Eurostat, European Communities.

LITTLE, Arthur D. (1991). *The Arthur D. Little Survey on the Product Innovation Process*, Cambridge, Mass.: Arthur D. Little.

MARTIN, M.J.C. (1985). *Managing Technological Innovation and Entrepreneurship.* Reston, Virginia: Reston Publishing Company,.

MILES, R.E. and C.C. Snow (1978). *Organizational Strategy, Structure, and Process. Technical excellence; or customers.* New York: McGraw-Hill.

MILGROM, P. and J. Robberts (1990). The Economics of Modern Manufacturing: Technology, Strategy, and Organization. *American Economic Review*, 80(3), 511-528.

PETERAF, M. (1993). The Cornerstones of Competitive Advantage: A Resource-Based View. *Strategic Management Journal*, 14(3), 179-191.

PORTER, M.E. (1985). Technology and Competitive Advantage. In: *Competitive Advantage: Creating and Sustaining Superior Performance.* M.E. Porter (ed.), pp. 164-200. New York: The Free Press.

ROTHWELL, R. (1993). The Fifth Generation Innovation Process. In: *Privates und Staatliches Innovationsmanagement*. Oppenländer, K.H. (ed.), München, Germany.

SCHUMPETER, J.A. (1934). *Theory of Economic Development*, Cambridge, Mass.: Harvard University Press.

TIDD, J., J. Bessant and K. Pavitt (2005). *Managing Innovation: Integrating Technological, Market, and Organizational Change*. New York: John Wiley & Sons.

TRAILL, W.B., M.T.G. Meulenberg (2002). Innovation in the Food Industry. *Agribusiness*, 18(1) 1-21

VAN TRIJP, H.C.M. and M.T.G. Meulenberg (1996) Marketing and consumer behaviour with respect to foods. In: *Food Choice, Acceptance and Consumption*, H.L. Meiselman and H.J.H. McFie (eds.), London: Blackie Academic & Professional.

WALSH, G and Li. D. (2004). The food industry and provincial economies, *Asia Pacific Journal of Clinical Nutrition*, 13(2) 166-170.

Este livro foi composto
na fonte Adobe Garamound, corpo 11